Smart Learning Objects for Smart Education in Computer Science

Vytautas Štuikys

Smart Learning Objects for Smart Education in Computer Science

Theory, Methodology and Robot-Based Implementation

 Springer

Vytautas Štuikys
Department of Software Engineering
Kaunas University of Technology
Kaunas, Lithuania

ISBN 978-3-319-38663-8   ISBN 978-3-319-16913-2   (eBook)
DOI 10.1007/978-3-319-16913-2

Springer Cham Heidelberg New York Dordrecht London
© Springer International Publishing Switzerland 2015
Softcover reprint of the hardcover 1st edition 2015

Printed on acid-free paper

Springer International Publishing AG Switzerland is part of Springer Science+Business Media (www.springer.com)

Preface

The technology revolution has resulted in that already today we are living and working in a digital world surrounded by the modern technology infrastructure – the multiple devices (computers, mobile phones, cameras and robots) being integrated within networks are a commodity of our lives now. In the near future, however, not only humans and computers but also everyday life items will be interconnected to create the new computing infrastructure – *the Internet of Things* (IoT). This move from the 'interconnected computers' to the 'interconnected things' is a great challenge for the ICT workers, computer scientists and society on the whole. It is most likely that there will be the need for changes in computer science (CS) curricula to provide the adequate knowledge to support the development of new applications and services.

On the other hand, today there is also an evident shift in learning paradigms. The e-learning community commonly agrees on the need of moving from the *teacher-centred learning* towards the *student-centred learning*. What are the signs of this paradigm change in teaching CS topics? First, there is the ever-increasing number of publications and discussions at all levels. Second, there is the clear understanding of ever-growing challenges to teach CS in the twenty-first century at all levels: primary, high school and university. Those challenges are widening and sharpening continuously under the technological advances, social demand and market pressure. Third, there is an extremely high interest in the interdisciplinary teaching based on the STEM (Science, Technology, Engineering and Mathematics) concepts. Fourth, the MOOC concept (Massive Open Online Courses) is also at the door of CS lecture rooms. Finally, there are signs of the student mind-sets changing. Now, the students want to be more independent in teaching and learning. They want to win more with less in planning and carrying out activities to support the future careers.

What should be done to respond to those challenges? The first thing is clear understanding at all levels what is happening in the field and around the related areas now. Having in mind the recent initiatives in Europe and worldwide on advanced teaching and learning in CS, it is possible to state that this understanding already exists, perhaps not yet at all levels. Next, the real breakthrough in advanced CS learning and teaching is hardly possible without new concepts, innovative methodologies and better understanding of both the pedagogical and technological issues. I agree with those researchers who argue that the currently existing capabilities of technology are not yet exploited in e-learning as fully as that could be. There is still a big gap between technological capabilities and pedagogical approaches. The seamless integration of both technology and pedagogy should be seen as the primary concern with advancing CS education. Therefore, a great deal of research effort is still needed to close the gap. Our research on the meta-programming-based generative learning objects (GLOs) and the use of educational robots in teaching CS topics aims at integrating different technologies with the known pedagogical approaches.

This book is a monograph representing the current state of our research on this topic. The word 'smart' in the title should be understood (1) as our efforts to extend generative and adaptive (i.e. context-aware) capabilities of the GLOs using meta-programming, (2) as our efforts to add more and more functions to educational robots in solving CS teaching tasks and (3) as our efforts to integrate the applied technologies and pedagogical approaches as seamlessly as possible.

What are the most distinguishing attributes of the book? To my best knowledge, the CS education modelling at the higher level of abstraction using feature-based modelling approaches (borrowed from Software Engineering) is applied and presented for the first time here. Next, the meta-programming-based GLOs with advanced features (such as preprogrammed context-aware and multistage representation for the content adaptation) have been proposed by the author (again, to my best knowledge for the first time). Therefore, it was possible to recall the previously researched GLOs and here treat them as smart LOs by providing extended research on those advanced features. This book also provides the more extensive study on the feature model transformations as compared to the book 'Meta-Programming and Model-Driven Meta-Program Development' (V. Štuikys and R. Damaševičius, Springer, 2013). Finally, the proposed methodology is not just an innovative proposal. The methodology, as a case study, has been already approved, tested and evaluated in the real setting to teach programming fundamentals.

How has the book been written? It was written as a result of reconsidering, generalizing, extending and integrating the concepts that can be found in our published papers during the years 2007–2014. During that period, our research group was involved, among other themes, in researching the methodology based on using meta-programming for the e-learning domain. The accumulated experience, the continuous discussions with my Ph.D. students and the research group members had also been for me the source of new ideas that are reflected in the book.

What is the content of the book? I have divided the content into two parts. Part I first deals with the challenges of CS education in the twenty-first century, motivates the needs for innovations and then outlines the reuse-based context of the book topics and introduces CS e-learning modelling concept on which basis it was possible to specify, to create and to test the so-called smart LOs. Part I also presents a background of smart LOs from the teacher's perspective. Part II deals with the theoretical background of smart LOs (SLOs) from the designer's perspective in order it would be possible to create the authoring tools for designing and transforming SLOs to support adaptation in learning. Part II also presents a methodology of creating smart educational environments using robots and SLOs and the use of the methodology in real setting to teach CS (programming).

Part I includes (1) A Vision of Smart Teaching in CS (Chap. 1); (2) Understanding of LO Domain Through Its Taxonomies (Chap. 2); (3) Reuse Framework of the LO Domain (Chap. 3); (4) Modelling of CS Teaching and Learning in Large (Chap. 4); (5) Model-Driven Specification in Designing Smart LOs (Chap. 5); (6) Smart LOs Design: Higher-Level Coding and Testing Aspects (Chap. 6); (7) Enhanced Features of SLOs: Focus on Specialization (Chap. 7); and (8) Context-Aware Adaptation of Smart LOs (Chap. 8). Part II includes (1) Background to Design Smart LOs and Supporting Tools (Chap. 9); (2) Authoring Tools to Design Smart LOs (Chap. 10); (3) Authoring Tools to Specialize and Adapt Smart LOs (Chap. 11); (4) Robot-Based Smart Educational Environments to Teach CS: A Case Study (Chap. 12; co-author Renata Burbaitė); and (5) Smart Education in CS: A Case Study (Chap. 13; co-author Renata Burbaitė); Term Index; What Is on the Horizon?

Who could be the potential reader of the book? The book is dedicated in the first place to the CS researchers; researchers in CS education, especially to those who are interested in using robots in learning and teaching; course designers; educational software; and tools developers. The CS teachers should also be highly interested not only in reading but in studying the adequate chapters as their advanced teaching material. I hope that the content of the book will be understandable to anybody who has enough skill in programming. Therefore, students studying CS-related courses, especially master-level and Ph.D. students, are also seen as potential readers. As the book includes the wider context (e.g. reusability aspects of e-learning, the whole LO research activities), the other e-learning community members might be interested in the reading of the book as well (especially the modelling of CS education and the integrative aspects of technology and pedagogy).

How should the book be read?

There is no specific algorithm in selecting and prioritizing the chapters to be read. Nevertheless, this depends on the reader's status, previous knowledge and his or her intention. The book is composed using the sequence that it is possible to select easily the chapter or chapters of interest from the title. But I recommend using the following scheme. The senior researchers and policymakers should first read Chap. 1 and, perhaps, all introductions in each chapter and then to move to the ending sections in each chapter. After that the readers will have the possibility to make the relevant choice for the in-depth studies of what is presented within the chapters. Experts and knowledgeable researchers first could read the introduction and concluding parts of each chapter or some selected chapters depending on the reader's flavour. If they will find interesting ideas, they could be involved in more intensive studies within a particular chapter or even go through the referenced sources. The readers who will select some material as own research topic should also go through the research and exercise questions given at the end of each chapter before the list of references.

What is about the CS teachers and students? For those readers, the book's content should be used differently. Chapters 12 and 13 are mainly dedicated to the secondary (high) school teachers and students. For example, Sect. 12.5 presents *the full scenarios* on how to use smart LOs and educational robot-based environments to teach and learn CS topics at the school level. The university-level educators and students should use the book content with regard to their teaching/ learning topics. For example, Chap. 4 is relevant to teach and learn the feature-based modelling methodology; Chaps. 5, 6, 7, 8, 9, 10 and 11 better fit for teaching and learning the model transformation topics. The educators of CS teachers should use the book entirely.

I hope that the book will be a beneficial methodological instrument (through the use of multiple illustrative examples and case studies) for those educators who are ready to provide the innovative models and methods in CS education.

Kaunas, Lithuania   Vytautas Štuikys

Acknowledgements

This monograph would be hardly written without the collaborative work and numerous discussions with my Ph.D. students and research group members. First of all, I would like to thank Prof. Robertas Damaševičius for our very fruitful and long-term collaboration in research on meta-programming (about ten years after his doctoral studies). This collaboration has resulted in writing together the book on meta-programming (published by Springer in 2013). Some ideas on generative learning objects, the basics on multistage meta-programming already have been reflected in that book. The discussions with him on the topics of this monograph at the stage of its planning were also very useful and have contributed to the extension of my own ideas.

The value of this monograph would remain as a pure theoretical work without the experimental and methodological contribution of Renata Burbaitė, Ph.D. holder and CS teacher (both at the gymnasium and university levels). She has constructed and tested the robot-based educational environments to approve the ideas of smart CS education in the real teaching setting. Therefore, she has made the main contribution as a co-author in writing Chaps. 12 and 13. Here, in fact, my role was to provide the editorial work only.

I would like also to thank Kristina Bespalova, the Ph.D. student, for the development of two authoring tools to support the creation and context-aware adaptation of smart learning objects. The experimental investigation and approval of the basic concepts of the monograph would be hardly possible without using the tools. Many thanks are also for her technical support in designing a great deal of graphical illustrations for the book.

Acknowledgements

Contents

Part I
SLOs Advent Context and Basics of Their Model-Driven Development

The aim of Part I is twofold: (1) to outline the context of the main topics to be discussed in the book and (2) to define and deal with the creation of smart learning objects (SLOs) from the CS teachers' and researchers' perspective. Here, by the context, I mean the following issues: (a) consideration of the challenges in CS education for the twenty-first century; (b) motivation of the need to introduce the new approach based on the smart LOs (SLOs) and robot-based smart education environment; (c) analysis of CS e-learning and LO research in order to provide links with the topics of the book; and (d) analysis of reuse in e-learning as well in SW engineering (SWE); both are seen as a source of the proven decisions to provide the further innovations toward the creation of SLOs and smart education. The first three chapters are about the context. Knowing the context is beneficial for all flavours of the potential book readers.

Chapter 4 introduces the feature-based modelling approach taken from SWE but adapted for using in CS education. The feature-based models serve as a means (1) to represent the whole CS teaching domain abstractly and (2) to specify CS learning variability to define SLOs at the early stage of their design. Therefore, this chapter is about the model-driven approach that should fit better to those researchers who aim at researching reuse-based SWE approaches and applying them to the CS education. However, the CS teachers who intend to accept the SLOs as the tool for representing CS teaching resources will also find the useful information here.

The remaining chapters of Part I are devoted (1) to the development of the SLO specifications, (2) to coding the specifications using meta-programming techniques and (3) to adapting the executable SLO specification to the context of their use. All these require a series of transformations. Those are the topics of Chaps 5, 6, 7 and 8. The topics include (a) abstract of the CS feature models' transformation into the concrete feature models to define the CS learning variability; (b) SLO design by transforming (mapping) the variability onto the models that define meta-programming; and (c) specializing the initial SLO specification for adaptation. All together, they are treated as a model-driven design of SLOs on the basis of properties and rules described for both the problem domain (i.e. CS learning variability) and the solution domain (i.e. meta-programming).

Chapter 1
A Vision of Smart Teaching in CS

1.1 Introduction

The aim of this chapter is twofold. The first aim is to describe the context to ease the understanding of the subsequent topics. Here, by the context, I mean the analysis of research trends in the e-learning and *learning object* domains (the latter is treated as a very significant branch of e-learning) so that the reader could be able first to understand the essence of the domain and then be aware of the intention of our approach which focuses on two novel concepts, *smart learning object* and *smart educational* environment, to teach computer science. The second aim is to present the primary knowledge on those *smart items* to be considered in detail later throughout the book.

Therefore, I address two interrelated tasks in this chapter as follows: (1) understanding the LO research evolution from the original learning object concept, its maturity and consolidation (through standardization initiatives, digital library creation, research expansion, etc.) and the introduction of the *generative* learning concept to meta-programming-based learning objects and, finally, to smart learning objects and (2) understanding the educational environment evolution in the context of technology advances and the expansion of learning object research and e-learning in the whole.

At the very beginning, one should accept the following abbreviations of the terms widely used in the literature: CS, computer science; LO or LOs, learning object(s); and GLO or GLOs, generative LO (LOs). I start our discussion by addressing some challenges in CS teaching in the information age as follows.

© Springer International Publishing Switzerland 2015
V. Štuikys, *Smart Learning Objects for Smart Education in Computer Science*,
DOI 10.1007/978-3-319-16913-2_1

1.2   Challenges to Teaching CS in the Twenty-First Century

To understand the challenges, we need first to resolve some terminological issues and then to clarify the content of the subject as follows. There are two closely interrelated terms, *informatics* and *computer science*, interchangeably used in the literature to deal with topics on various aspects of computing, including educational computing. The first term is more popular in Europe, while the second in the USA. However, despite of some terminological issues and differences in the topic's scope and content the terms intend to describe, the two are often regarded as synonymous. I do the same and use the abbreviation CS to denote the second term throughout the book. As there is no precise and unified definition of the subject CS (due to the historical, methodological, technological and other reasons), I present some of them below.

The *Dictionary.com*, for example, defines CS as 'the science that deals with the theory and methods of processing information in digital computers, the design of computer hardware and software, and the applications of computers'.

The *Linux Information Project* defines CS as 'the study of the storage, transformation and transfer of information'. The source continues: 'the field encompasses both the theoretical study of algorithms (including their design, efficiency and application) and the practical problems involved in implementing them in terms of computer software and hardware'.

The *Free Encyclopaedia* provides the following definition: CS is 'the systematic study of the feasibility, structure, expression, and mechanization of the methodical processes (or algorithms) that underlie the acquisition, representation, processing, storage, communication of, and access to information, whether such information is encoded in bits and bytes in a computer memory or transcribed engines and protein structures in a human cell'.

The *ACM Model Curriculum for K-12 Computer Science* [TMD+06] provides a highly useful definition for high school educators. This model emphasizes that CS is neither programming nor computer literacy. Rather, it is 'the study of computers and algorithmic processes, including their principles, their hardware and software design, their applications, and their impact on society'. In the context of CS teacher certification, the report [CSTA08] identifies 14 areas CS includes (programming, hardware design, networks, graphics, databases and information retrieval, computer security, software design, programming languages, logic, programming paradigms, translation between levels of abstraction, artificial intelligence, the limits of computations, applications in IT and IS and social issues). If we look at the ACM Computing Classification System [ACM12], we find even a much wider spectrum of topics' subcategories within each area ranging from hardware, networks, software, some robotics aspects, etc., to human-machine interaction, information security, privacy and education.

Thus, CS spans the theory and practice of computer hardware and software as well as computer-based systems practised in all aspects of their design and use. Therefore, CS requires computational thinking both in abstract terms and in concrete terms. Nowadays, the practical side of computing can be seen everywhere because practically everyone is a computer user and many professions require a programming skill to support their activities.

CS can be also seen on a higher level, as a *science that supports and links to other sciences* for *problem* solving in *quite different domains*, where the main focus are modelling, decision making, design and development methodologies. CS has a long history and evolves extremely rapidly. Its evolution curve follows the technology advances over more than 60 years. As a result, technology advances have stimulated the growth of CS by filling the field with new problems and challenges.

The technology revolution has resulted in that we already now live and work in a digital world surrounded by the modern technology infrastructure – the multiple devices integrated within networks (computers, mobile phones, cameras and robots) are a commodity of our lives now. In the near future, however, not only humans and computers but also everyday life items will be interconnected to create the new computing infrastructure – *The Internet of Things* (IoT). This move from 'interconnected computers' to 'interconnected things' is a great challenge for the ICT workers, computer scientists and society in the whole [AIM10]. It is most likely that there will be the need for changes in CS curricula to provide the adequate knowledge to support the development of new applications and services.

Yet another aspect should be highlighted in the context of CS role in the information society. As a result of the technological revolution, there are evident signs of the extremely rapid growth of the application system *diversity*, system *complexity* and *software content* within systems, especially in the context of the embedded system sector. As a consequence, the demand of CS workplaces, perhaps, will grow adequately. According to estimates [MSD13], the field of computer and mathematical sciences is expected to grow dramatically through 2018. The Bureau of Labor Statistics in the USA, for example, projects that there will be a 25.6 % increase in demand in this field.

Therefore, changes of the social context, which are due to technology expanses, the nature of the CS content and its role to further enhancing computing opportunities in the digital world have enabled us to formulate some challenges directly or indirectly related to teaching CS as follows:

- Understanding the impact of ICT technology in general and CS as its fundamental part in particular to the society today and in the near future.
- Understanding that (i) CS brings fundamental knowledge and computational thinking [FL09, BC11] for many separate fields such as software engineering, hardware engineering, game industry and educational technology to name a few (ii) and understanding the interplay among those technologies and education. On this account, for example, Drake [Dra13] notices that 'many – perhaps most – computer scientists grew up sharpening their brains on games. Computer science has returned the favour, providing the foundations for an extremely robust electronic game industry'.
- Understanding the history and trends of technology-enhanced learning that 'reflects an evolution from individual toward community learning, from

content-driven learning toward process-driven approaches, from isolated media toward integrated use, from presentation media toward interactive media, from learning settings dependent on place and time toward ubiquitous learning, and from fixed tools toward handheld devices' [Low14]. This understating and realization of that in practice, even partially in some concrete setting, could be understood as a contribution to smart learning.

- In the context of ICT advances, understanding the e-learning paradigm shift from traditional e-learning to m-learning and u-learning (meaning ubiquitous learning) [LH10, VMO+12].
- Understanding the specific role of CS [BEP+09, BC11] because the discipline stands for the fundamental piece of knowledge and can be aligned along with natural sciences such mathematics, physics or chemistry. On the other hand, CS is a cross-disciplinary subject.
- CS-related courses are provided at different levels at both schools and universities; there is a need of broad spectrum knowledge, skill and competencies bringing additional challenges.
- The wideness of CS topics, which tends to be continuously enlarged, results in the need of cross-disciplinary views and approaches. The audience to be educated is extremely large and diverse that includes (i) technology-literate citizens for the twenty-first century, (ii) cross-disciplinary engineers and scientists working in the variety of fields and (iii) CS professionals responsible for the further enlargement of the IT sector.
- CS content of the topics is abstract in nature; thus it requires various forms of transformations (social, pedagogical, technological) to acquire knowledge in the field.
- The rapid technology advances stimulate the need to continuously reconsider, renew and reevaluate the content, teaching approaches and methodology [FL09]. As a result, there are the challenges of integrating technologies for learning [ECE+10].
- There is the need for changes in attitudes to accept innovations in CS teaching (inspired by the ICT and educational theories) at all levels: government politics, administrative (institutional), teachers and students.
- There is a gap between educational theories and teaching methodologies and ever-increasing capabilities of technologies.
- There is a contradiction between the tendency of the enrolment decrease to study CS and the demand increase of CS-oriented specialties [CSTA08].
- There is the need for more extensive research in CS and more effective learning and teaching methods due to the stated challenges and the ever-growing market pressure.

Finally, I summarize the previously formulated challenges by the need of transformations in learning as they are formulated by the title of the book [THE09] and by the call of the first International Congress for Advanced Research in Education (ICARE'2014): *Reshaping Learning: Transforming Education through the Fusion of Learning and Technology.*

Though CS teaching, with respect to the help of technology innovations and educational theories aside, is a separate field, there are many aspects common to the very broad and extensively explored domain known as e-learning. In the next section, the aim is to outline those common features.

1.3   E-Learning Domain in Large: A Framework to Understand It

In the literature on education, there is a long list of kindred terms used to describe technology-driven educational activities. Examples are technology-enhanced learning, Internet-based training, multimedia learning, online education and virtual education to name a few. However, *e-learning* stands for the more general term which refers to the use of any kind of electronic media and any kind of information and communications technology (ICT) in education. There are also specific forms of e-learning such as distance learning, m-learning (meaning mobile learning), blended learning, long-life learning, etc. The variety of terms indicates on the obvious fact – the importance and the extremely wide stream of research in the domain. How should this intensively explored domain be understood in the context of the topics we consider in this book?

Though there are a variety of approaches to analyse the domain from various perspectives [McG04, RJR+05, Had09, HLR11], the *process-based view* seems to be the most relevant to understand the domain in the whole and in our context in particular. Figure 1.1 outlines a structural framework, revised from [ŠBD13] for this purpose. At the very abstract level, we can identify a set of components inherent

Fig. 1.1 A framework to understand e-learning in large

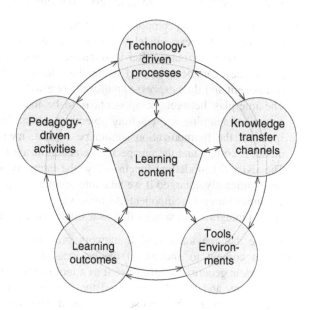

to the field as follows: *pedagogy-driven activities, technology-driven processes, knowledge transfer channels with actors* involved, a set of *tools* used (they can also be identified as a technology and, when implemented in a concrete setting, it is also known as the *educational environment*), *teaching/learning content* and the *pedagogical/learning outcome*.

The introduced framework reflects at least two important attributes of e-learning: (i) high heterogeneity of the domain and (ii) and extremely diverse interplay between the components or their constituents. Indeed pedagogy-driven activities indicate on the interplay among e-learning, pedagogy and educational theories. Technology-driven processes describe how the information induced by other components is transformed and processed using educational tools to achieve the prescribed learning objectives. The tools serve as a means to ensure the functionality and efficiency of the whole system. The knowledge transfer channels with two actors (student and teacher) at different ends of the channels are the core of the education process as a pure social activity.

The teaching/learning *content* plays a specific role in e-learning. First, content is neutral with respect to the technological and social aspects of the domain. Second, from the pure functionality viewpoint, content stands for *data basis* to fuel other components with the *information* to start the processes, to initiate and to support the functioning of the components and the whole system. As a result of the two, content can be seen as an intermediate link to connect and integrate the different nature domains – social and technological. Finally, the pedagogical (teaching/learning) outcome can be seen as a measure (in a social sense) to reason on how the component interaction was relevant to prespecified objectives, what bottlenecks might or could be identified within components and what improvements might or could be introduced in the future.

In this context, there are some observations important to state as follows:

1. The interplay among components specifies the functionality of a learning/teaching process. We can model this functionality through component attributes. Though those attributes differ in semantics, when specified for modelling purposes, they can be evaluated using the adequate measures specific to each component and then *expressed uniformly* (we will show that later).
2. The interplay between components is to be harmonized with respect to the prescribed learning and teaching objectives. From the pure technological perspective, the harmonization should be correct, meaning that the interaction model is correct and the prespecified constraints are taken into account.
3. The *space* for modelling functionality (the interplay between components) can be significantly enlarged if we take into account the possible values of different attributes for each component. As these values are expressed uniformly, we are able to integrate and specify that as a single content-based specification.

I hope that the introduced framework provides the reader with a good and sufficient context to understand the essence of e-learning. I believe that this framework is generic enough. I use it as a tool to understand the essence of CS e-learning here, and later I will extend the framework accordingly to the aims of subsequent chapters. The next section is about the *teaching content*.

1.4   The LO Concept and Its Evolution

In the scientific literature on e-learning, there is another term, *learning object* (LO), which stands for specifying teaching/learning content. Research on LOs is a very wide and rapidly evolving subdomain of e-learning now. This term is accepted and widely used in CS research and education as well [see, e.g. GA03, JB07, MHC12]. With regard to analysis and general understating of the subdomain (further domain), I present a few important observations below.

1. There was a *well-founded intent* or idea of introducing the term (due to W. Hodgins in 1994) – to resolve the problems related to *systematization, interoperability and reuse of the learning resources.*
2. Fuelled by this event, now research topics on LOs are very broad, ranging from design, evaluation and use of instructional theories, standardization initiatives and the evolution of e-learning per se ([McG04, Nor07, ECE+10]).
3. There is *the abundance of the kindred terms* to characterize the domain now. Indeed, one can meet terms in the literature as follows:

   - *Knowledge object* [Mer98].
   - *Reusable learning object* [Boy03, Pol03].
   - *Generic learning object* [KH07, AM10].
   - *Generative learning object* [MLB05, Old08].
   - *Testable, reusable unit of cognition* or TRUC [Mey06].
   - *Online resource* [Nas05].
   - *Mobile learning object* [AC08].
   - *Customized learning object* [GA03].
   - *Learning object generator* [For04].
   - *Interactive LO* [LLR06].
   - *The ontology of instructional objects* (OIO) [Ull08].
   - *Others are asset, unit of learning, media object, component, learning resources,* etc. (see, e.g. [Fri04]).

   Though each term has some specific meaning and a concrete context of use (e.g. OIO [Ull08] stands for the item to characterize the courseware generation of Web-based learning), all those can be treated as derivatives from the basic term 'learning object'.
4. There is *no unique definition* of the term LO. Though the role of the concept is well understood in the e-learning community, the understanding of what is meant by LO in essence, however, is still poor with various definitions proposed. For example, IEEE provides the most general definition stating that LO is 'any entity, digital or non-digital, which can be used, re-used or referenced during technology supported learning' [IEEE00]. Another definition identifies LO as the 'aggregation of one or more digital assets, incorporating metadata, which represent an educationally meaningful stand-alone unit' [Dal02]. For other definitions, see [McG04, RJR+05, Wil00, Pol03, SH04]. Note that the list of references is far from being exhaustive.

5. There are *a variety of taxonomies* [KP05, LP04, Red03, SMS08, TLW+08] *and standards* [RJR+05, McG04, IEEE00, SCORM04] related to the LO domain to name a few.
6. There might be identified the *latest evolutionary* periods or significant events (meaning the appearance of novel approaches) within the domain *as follows*:

  • Introduction of the term by W. Hodgins in e-learning in 1994 (though the origin of the term *learning object* can be tracked to the seventeenth century as Zuckerman indicates in his report [Zuc06]).
  • Consolidation of the concept/standardization of LO and introduction to LO instructional design theories [Wil00] (2000–...); here dots mean a continuation of research.
  • Adding generative aspects – the introduction of generative LOs (GLOs) due to the contribution of Boyle, Morales and their colleagues (2003–...).
  • Introduction of the concept *learning through generation* [Ker04] (2004–...).
  • Introduction of *ontology instructional objects* (OIO) [Ull04], agent-based LOs [SGV06] and knowledge-based GLOs [ŠD07] to move the domain toward a higher level of intelligence (2004–...).
  • Introduction of meta-programming-based GLOs [ŠD08, DŠ08] and parameterizable LOs [HK09] (2008–...).
  • Evolution of GLOs by connecting generative aspects [ŠDB+08] with product line engineering (PLE), the well-known concept in SWE [CN02] (2008–...).
  • Adding interactive features to LO generation [Kra09] (2009–...).
  • Further evolution of GLOs by introducing the context model and multistage architecture [ŠB12] (2012–...).

It is possible to identify the beginning of the periods exactly (e.g. according to the first publication date), whereas the ending boundary of the period does not exist at all due to the research continuation. Nevertheless, the aforementioned scheme is useful and serves us as a framework to analyse the related work as follows here and also in other chapters.

1.5   Related Work

As there is an extremely large stream of research topics, here I present a *roadmap to reviewing the related work* relevant to the CS education only. I will extend the proposed scheme by more intensive studies later in the adequate chapters. The aim of the presented scheme is to extract the most important facts to motivate the tasks we consider in this chapter. I have excluded three large categories of the topics as follows: challenges in teaching CS (Sect. 1.5.1), learning models (Sect. 1.5.2) and educational environments for teaching in CS (Sect. 1.5.3).

1.5.1 Challenges to Teach CS Topics

In Sect. 1.3, I have discussed overall challenges as they are related to technology expanses, social demand and impact on society in a long perspective. Here, I focus on *local challenges* to teaching in CS. A great deal of research papers focuses on problems and difficulties to teach programming for novices. In this aspect, it is possible to formulate the following interrelated groups of problems:

- *Pedagogical problems* (e.g. the used learning models do not correspond to the learner's needs [SSH+09, LY11]); often it is difficult to personalize learning [GM07, SGM10]; problems of selecting the relevant teaching context [Fig06, KS08, CC10]; learner's motivation problems [KPN08, JCS09, CTT10, GGL +12, AG13, SHL13])
- *Cognitive problems* (e.g. the use of high-level abstractions [GM07, Chu07, CMF +09, CTT10]; the need to keep trade-offs between the theoretical knowledge and practice [RRR03, GM07, PSM+07, CMF+09, SSH+09, LY11, SPJ+11]; differences in programming paradigms such as structural and object-oriented ones [Sch02, MR02, RRR03, SH06, CMF+09, CTT10]; syntax of programming languages is oriented to the professional use [GM07, CMF+09, CTT10]; the need for creativity enhancement [KR08])
- *Learning content problems* (e.g. often static materials are used, though programming is a highly dynamic course [GM07, PSM+07, NS09, VBH13]; difficulties in a content adaptation to the learner's context [AG03, GA03, LYW05, AHH12]; content visualization problems [Chu07, MV07, KPN08, RöΒ10, AHH11, MT12])
- *Technical problems* (e.g. a lack of tools to provide adaptation and generalization [AG03, PSM+07, CMF+09]; traditional learning management systems (LMS) do not cover all contexts needed for teaching in programming [CMF+09, ADP +11]; interactive learning in programming has many obstacles due to pedagogical and cognitive problems and lack of technical support [BBC04, GC06, MV07, GM07, CMF+09, BB09, LLY10, APH+11, CAL12, DAB12])

1.5.2 Learning Models

Motivation models, among many others, stand for the most essential and complicated arguments to describe human behaviour aspects of teaching. On the other hand, there is a common understanding in the domain that the models are also the most influential factors to achieving learning performance and efficiency. Here, I consider only those models that, in my view, to the largest extent correspond to the aims of this chapter. They are as follows:

- *Pedagogical frameworks* combining the theory and practice of teaching in CS [Sch02]
- *Game-based learning models* [JCS09, SHL13]

- *Program behaviour visualization models* [Chu07, Pea10]
- *Pair-programming models* [DSS+08, SMG11]
- *Robot use-based models* [CAC12, HS12, Tou12]

1.5.3   Educational Environments for Teaching in CS

First, one needs to know the main characteristics that define an effective educational environment. According to [GM07], they are as follows: (1) identification of the learner's knowledge level and also identification of dominating learning style to make learning more personalized, (2) the use of models to construct the program, (3) the use of elements of gaming to enforce capabilities in problem solving and (4) the use of tools within an environment that are dedicated to constructing algorithms.

Kelleher's and Pausch's taxonomy [KP05] categorizes programming and language environments into two groups: (1) *teaching systems* and (2) *empowering systems*. The first aims at taking the support for learning programming per se; usually those systems contain programming kits that highlight the essential aspects of the programming process. Teaching systems have many common or similar features with *general-purpose languages* and relate to *mechanics of programming* (such as a simplification of programming language, automatic repair of syntactic errors, presenting of alternatives for coding, learning support, networked interaction, etc.).

There are also mobile environments to support m-learning. Researchers, however, take the exclusive role of the robot-based educational environments in teaching CS and other related topics. The main reasons for that are as follows:

- Possibility to transform the abstract items (such as a data structure, algorithm, program) into physically visible processes, enabling to better understand the essence of programming and its practical benefits.
- The paradigm introduces the way for interdisciplinary teaching.
- There is the support of real (physical) visualization through robots' moves and actions.
- Educational robots can be also treated as gaming tools to significantly enforcing the learner's motivation to learn and the engagement in the process.
- There is a wide room for the experimentation and exploratory learning.
- All these can be easily connected with learning styles and models.

I assume that the presented statements provide enough arguments to start a discussion in Sect. 1.8. In the next section, I continue our discussion on LOs.

1.6 Specificity of CS LOs

Here, I try to draw a distinguishing line between e-learning in general and e-learning in CS (with respect to LO research only) to identify what is common and what is different for both. We first look at the existing discrepancies in terminology as related to the teaching content in e-learning, and then, we discuss how well-known initiatives in e-learning such as standardization are accepted, interpreted or enhanced by the CS research community.

Metadata is a principal attribute that is independent upon the subject to prespecify the field of LOs. In general, metadata is structured data that describe characteristics of information-bearing entities to aid in the identification, classification, discovery, assessment and management of those entities. Since their introduction in the 1970s, metadata has been the object of systematic research in such areas as data warehouse managing and WWW. Often, metadata is shortly defined as descriptions of data [Sol99].

In the context of e-learning, the information-bearing entities are learning resources, i.e. LOs. Metadata provides attributes to describe LOs. The approved standard [IEEE00] defines the overall structure – syntax and semantics – of the metadata schema for LOs.

What are the main attributes to define LOs and processes pertained to them? As there is a variety of attributes (they are defined by the standard), we enlist only a few ones: granularity, compositionality and semantic density. One can learn more on that from the indicated or other standards.

The paper [Mat06] highlights benefits of using LOs in CS teaching. On the other hand, the CS content and its delivery as LOs are specific with respect to many attributes as follows:

1. The large body of teaching content in CS are programs (algorithms) or their parts such as data structures.
2. Program as an LO is abstract. The essence of the topic to be learned is hidden and the cognition process requires a good understanding of other topics such as the computer architecture, operating system (OS) and Internet. Therefore, students, especially novices, have difficulties in comprehending the essence to be taught.
3. In contrast to the other type of LOs, program is an executable specification with the well-formed internal structure. The program can produce not only data as a result of calculation but also the other program as a new LO.
4. The program is a soft thing. There are practically unlimited opportunities for its change, modification and adaptation or even for visualization of the algorithm behaviour. Transferring to the different e-learning environments is easy.
5. For the learning purposes, programs can be incorporated into other things (such as educational toys, robots, etc.) to enable them to perform the real-life processes (such as the physical items moving, carrying or finding by robot, etc.).

6. Teaching in CS (e.g. programming) can be seen as problem solving (as it takes place, e.g. in mathematics) to enable the creation of a flexible means to the testing and self-testing of the acquired knowledge.
7. LOs to teaching in CS can be also viewed as a tool to provide researching with the nearly unlimited possibility for experimentation in various domains such as design, automation, gamification and many more.

As the topic overlaps with the challenges formulated in Sect. 1.2, there are no reasons to continue the discussion. Rather, it is more important to convince the reader of knowing two findings. The first is that there are many attributes *hindering* the learning and teaching in CS topics. The second is that there are also many attributes *facilitating* the process, if those attributes are correctly understood and properly applied. I leave the room as *a research task* for the reader to extend the list of the hindering and facilitating attributes.

I summarize this short discussion with the following statements:

1. No matter of the existing efforts and a variety of contributions to improve and to enhance teaching in CS (see Sect. 1.5), there is still enough room for the further innovations in this field.
2. The formulated specificity (both hindering and facilitating attributes, presented explicitly or left undisclosed) might be seen as a driving force to discover the new solutions, the new innovations and the new technologies.

In the next section, I try to describe that conceptually.

1.7 What Is Smart LO?

The term 'smart' is used in different contexts. There are *smart people* who, in comparison to others, are able to perform a prescribed activity as well and effectively as possible. There are *smartphones* that possess extra characteristics not inherent to the traditional phones. Now are emerging *smart things* – items of the Internet of Things (IoT), which are interconnected and able to communicate among themselves or to send messages to humans [AIM10]. Therefore, the term 'smartness' reflects the evolutionary aspects (in the context of technological capability and market demand expanses) of items to which it pertains. Indeed, if we look at the functional characteristics of smartphones or objects of the IoT more carefully and will compare those characteristics with traditional ones, we can observe the augmentation of their features, functionality and capabilities.

Here, for the initial understanding of the smart LOs, I apply this principle along with a descriptive framework. The framework includes:

1. A *context* that has contributed to the emergence of this new concept
2. *Predecessor* of the concept (or what is a start position to deal with the concept)
3. *The extended definition* by features of the smart LOs (SLOs) as they are seen in practice already now
4. How *SLO* might look in *the nearest future*

1.7.1 Reusability: The Context to Understand SLO

In fact, we have already started the discussion with the reader on this topic in Sect. 1.5, where it was shown that reusability was the primary objective of the introduction of the LO concept and also the context for the concept further evolution. Here, our aim is to extend the discussion by highlighting new reuse aspects that are directly relevant to the context of SLO.

For a long time in e-learning (and this time is not over yet), reusability and usability of teaching resources were understood as a 'library concept'. The latter can be described from a user perspective in the simplified form as four activities as follows:

- *To find* the resource (meaning within a library or repository)
- *To understand* the resource
- *To modify* the resource (if needed)
- *To apply* the resource in a new teaching context

The concept is so powerful that it is widely exploited and further evolves not only in e-learning. The library concept, due to its methodological soundness, is widely applied in practice in two different ways: either as an *internal library* of a variety of tools (such as compilers, design tools, etc.) or as an *external repository* to store and share information asset in a variety of domains for wide-scale reuse (e.g. software reuse libraries [Big94], digital libraries for teaching and learning [TMV04], design reuse repositories [Mar04], databases) to name a few.

Now we look at the reuse concept as it is understood in SW engineering (SWE). I do that due to two reasons: (1) systematic reuse research provided in SWE for more than three decades has contributed to the creation of powerful design methodologies such as object oriented, product line, etc., and (2) the e-learning domain has borrowed and adopted many ideas from SWE in the past and this process is continuing till now.

There are two general aspects to deal with and understand reuse in the field: *managerial* (social) and *technological*. The first encompasses a long list of human-based and organizational-oriented activities ranging from the strategy formulation and planning to standards and legal issues [Lim98]. The second includes two technological approaches: *component-based reuse* and *generative reuse*.

In general, it is possible to characterize the component-based reuse by two different models: black-box model (meaning the use of components in the mode use-as-is) and white-box model (meaning the use with adaptation). Both support the library concept mentioned before. In this approach, the item for reuse is usually represented as an instance ready for use without intent for the explicit automation. Generative reuse, in contrast to the first approach, focuses on either *producing components* automatically or *integrating components* into a system also automatically. Thus, generative reuse deals with the automatic generation of instances. This approach requires developing the specification from which instances are to be derived. The tool such as a language processor that uses the specification as the input to produce instances on demand is called component or program generator. The program generator, if it is designed correctly and is used properly, among other possibilities, ensures a higher productivity and quality. The program generator can be viewed as a component too, if we look at its structure using the black-box model (without the interest of the internal implementation and functional possibilities). In such a case, the program generator may reside in a digital library as a component with a specific mode of use.

Now we are able to make a *conceptual juxtaposition* of two systems: repositories of SW components and LO repositories. Conceptually, both are similar systems, though they are built for quite different purposes and may be with the different internal organization. If we take into account the fact that the same items such as data structures or sorting programs could be found in both repositories, the similarity would be even more evident. We are also able to extend such a juxtaposition of reusability aspects widely exploited in two different domains (SW design and e-learning). This enables us to raise the following question: (1) Are reusability aspects understood to the same extent in CS learning (or in e-learning in general) as they are understood in SWE? Or in other words, are the reuse maturity levels roughly the same in the two domains? The answer is that the maturity of reuse is much higher in SWE due to many reasons such as historical, industry support, etc. Knowing the fact (and not only that), it becomes clear why the e-learning community (where computer scientists are important actors) seeks to adopt the suitable approaches from SWE. There is a plethora of examples to motivate that (see, e.g. [CNC12, DDA12] to name a few).

In this context, another question can be raised as follows: what were the critical problems already met in SW reuse that might also emerge for LO reuse? Take for example the SW reuse library *scaling problem* that already was raised by Biggerstaff in 1994 [Big94]. The essence of the problem is that there is a great amount of *similar component instances* to be stored in the library. In this case, the procedures of classifying, storing, searching and recognizing what instance is actually needed are becoming indeed difficult. The space limits are also evident. This problem was partially solved using generative reuse instead of applying the pure component instance reuse. The solution is due to applying of program generators as library entities as much as possible.

Though in the LO domain we are still needed to live up this level of maturity, the introduction of GLOs, and especially the meta-programming-based GLOs, gives a good direction for dealing with and solving a variety of *content reuse-related problems* in teaching and learning as it will be shown throughout the book.

In summary, I argue that the capabilities of generative reuse are a main objective (if not to say more – the tool) to define the context for the emerging of the new kind of LO which I call smart LO (SLO).

1.7.2 SLO Predecessors

As it is stated in the previous section, conceptually, an SLO predecessor might be regarded the GLO concept proposed by Boyle and his colleagues. They nominated this innovation as a 'next-generation' learning object [BLC04]. By introducing such a concept, they have sent an evident sign to the e-learning community to move from the *component-based reuse model* to the *generative reuse model* in the field. The Boyle's GLO and the authoring tool [www.glomaker.org] is an example of how to apply generative reuse for e-learning. As it was also noticed in Sect. 1.7.1, there might be a variety of technologies (preprocessing, templates, various kinds of meta-programming) to implement the generative approach. The template-based approach is the basic technology on which the authoring tool was built.

To our best knowledge, we were first who suggested to applying meta-programming as a generative technology to specify GLO [ŠD08]. Therefore, from the technology-based perspective, it is possible to regard the paper [DŠ08], where the feature diagrams were used to specify GLO at a higher-level of abstraction and meta-programming was applied to implement the specification, as a predecessor of SLO. It is also needed to state that there were a lot of proposals very close to our approach as I have disclosed partially in Sect. 1.5.

Now it is possible to summarize the discussion presented in this and previous sections as follows: generative reuse brings the *generification* idea as a basic attribute to start defining SLO. As generative reuse has many dimensions, the generification of GLO can be developed and extended in a variety of ways as it will be shown firstly in the next subsection and be enforced later.

1.7.3 SLO: An Extended Generification of GLO

So far I have introduced two generative approaches: Boyle et al.'s GLO model along with their authoring tool [Boy03, BLC04, www.glomaker.org] and meta-programming-based GLOs [ŠD08, DŠ08]. The background of the two lies in the model describing the interaction among the technology and content. The difference in the interaction model enables to view a principal distinction between those approaches. In the first approach, the model takes the priority to technology and tool to proposing a template for the users to construct the content by themselves. The tool, such as the GLOMaker, gives the guidance and the GLO structure to be filled in by the user-provided content. Thus, it is the only tool that introduces *generative aspects* automatically.

In the second approach, the *generative aspects are preprogrammed* within the content in advance, while the supporting tool is standard, i.e. a processor (compiler) of the language using which the generative aspects are specified. This approach requires the introduction of two essential innovations. The first concerns with changes in the GLO model. Two explicit structural units appear in this GLO model: *internal metadata* and *meta-body*. In fact, the internal metadata is the *interface* containing high-level parameters to specify the generative aspects. Metadata is seen as new capabilities for *annotation learning artefacts*.

The meta-body specifies the implementation of the generative aspects. The second innovation refers to the introduction of a prespecified *learning variability* [ŠBD13]. The latter means not only the content variants but also the *learning context variants* (social, pedagogical, etc.). The learning variability has to be identified in advance (e.g. through the domain modelling similarly as it is done in SW engineering using some domain analysis methods [CHW98]). When meta-programming is used as a generative technology, we are able to represent the learning variability uniformly and express it explicitly through parameters within the GLO specification. This specification is, in fact, a meta-program to be interpreted by the meta-language processor to produce a content variant or variants on demand automatically.

In summary, the underlying concept of our approach is the primary focus on the learning content and context variability and implementation of the variability within the preprogrammed specification using meta-programming techniques. Now we are able to define the meta-programming-based (MPGB) GLO as follows. The GLO is a higher-level specification from which the lower-level LOs are generated. What features of such GLOs are treated as smart to define SLOs?

The technology we use to implement the GLO is meta-programming. Though there are many slightly different approaches which might be treated as meta-programming, we use heterogeneous meta-programming in the structured programming mode [ŠD13]. This technology is smart in the following aspects:

- It is a generative technology.
- It is independent upon the type of the target language and meta-language used.
- It supports well the conceptual (structural) model which is flexible and extensible to constructing the different MPGB GLO architectures for adaptation, maintenance and evolution.
- It enables to express the different types of *learning variability* (pedagogical variability, social variability, content variability, technology variability and interaction among the variability constituents) *through parameters uniformly* [ŠBD13].
- It ensures *a flexible management of learning variability* first through selecting the adequate parameter values and then through the generation process which is supported by the meta-language processor.

This is possible due to the uniform *representation* of the different *variability constituents*. The latter we specify in advance first through modelling. Then, using meta-programming techniques, we are able to express them through parameters uniformly [ŠD08, ŠDB+08].

At the use time, by selecting the adequate parameter values, the user is able to generate the learning content (i.e. LO) on demand automatically.

At this point, some questions can be raised as follows:

1. To which extent are we able to define and extract the learning variability?
2. Is the enlargement of the variability space (meaning the augmentation of the number of parameters and their values within the specification) induces 'smartness' of GLO?

From the pure technological perspective, there are no limitations to use analysis methods, for example, borrowed from SWE to extract variability [CHW98]. The limitations may appear with regard to our restricted ability and lack of knowledge to understand the e-learning domain due to its heterogeneity and complexity. The course designer or a group of designers should possess enough competence to cover the complexity issues in modelling. All limitations along with other requirements to design SLOs should be stated in the requirement document.

The answer to the second question is positive because the space prespecifies the functionality (we are able first to represent and then to generate more slightly different variants for choice in teaching); however, there are also some limitations related to the implementation. By enlarging the variability space, when implemented, the SLO specification may become too much abstract and too much complicated to understand, due to the so-called overgeneralization problem [Sam97]. It is especially true in the case when some changes are to be introduced. As the enlargement of the variability space also means the increase of the generalization level, a balance should be kept between the need of generalizing (to ensure generative features) and overgeneralization. The designer should solve this problem, because the SLO users (teachers and students) usually apply the SLO specification as a black-box entity.

Thus, so far, I have defined the SLO as a MPGB GLO with extended generative features. Is it possible to extend this generation-based model with some other important features? In the paper [ŠBB14], we have proposed the approach which concerns with (semi)automatic adaptation of the generated LO to the context of use. The approach extends the former GLO model with the context model to support adaptation. We describe the context model by parameter priorities (such as high, intermediate, low) as a part of the enhanced GLO model. To implement the automatic adaptation, there is the need to introduce some essential changes in the structural model described above. In the paper [ŠB12], we have presented the two-stage GLO model and later we have generalized this model as the multistage GLO model. Using the developed refactoring tool [BBŠ14] and some predefined adaptation rules incorporated within the tool, it is possible to connect stages with the priority-based context and automatically generate the adapted lower-level GLOs or LO instances.

The short description of the introduced innovations indeed is smart as compared to the previous MPGB GLOs.

Now it is possible to define the concept SLO as it stands at the current level of the development and understanding.

Smart LO (SLO) is such the MPGB GLO structure that:

(i) *Enables to implement* generative aspects through the explicit representation of *learning variability*

(ii) *Allows the use of* the *priority-based context model* [ŠBB14] as an extension of the learning variability *model*

(iii) *Allows the use* of the multistage model [ŠB12] for adaptation purposes of specifying the models as multistage meta-programs to support automatic adaptation (through the use of the refactoring tool [BBŠ14])

(iv) *Does* not contain restrictions for using different teaching environments (e.g. stand-alone PC, Internet-PC setting, PC-robot, etc.)

The implementation of the smart features is hidden from the user (teacher, student); the user communicates with the environment containing the smart LO through the user-friendly interface; the latter presents metadata to select the parameter values.

Note that the presented concepts are not only theoretically possible solutions, but they were realized in the real CS teaching setting as it was described by case studies in our published papers [ŠBD13, ŠB12, BBD+14], though there are many research problems we need yet to resolve in this monograph. No matter what technology we use, GLO is a starting position to define SLO in this context. Thus, the generative attribute is at the core of our approach. But first the principal question should be dealt with before applying the generative approach: either we will focus on the tool that brings generative technology or we need to focus on the internal structure of the content and change it so that it would be possible to apply generative reuse. Also, the following questions might be raised as follows: *what* are the dimensions of generative attributes and *why* are they important? I postpone a more thorough discussion on the *what* and *why* aspects. I do not consider the *how* aspects at all here. This is a matter of subsequent chapters.

As a summarizing result, I present the following two statements:

1. *Smart LO (SLO) is a generative LO with the enhanced generative reuse capabilities. The latter is incorporated within the pedagogically sound SLO specification to support flexibility, adaptability, reusability and interoperability in CS education.*

2. *I argue that SLO could be seen as an engine to drive advanced CS education in the twenty-first century.*

How does the *SLO* look already now and might look in *the near future?* That is the topic to be considered in the monograph.

1.8   A Primary Understanding: What Is Smart Environment to Teach CS?

As it has been shown by the review of the related work, there are a variety of tools to construct e-learning environments; however, the educational robot-based environments prevail in CS teaching due to the reasons indicated in Sect. 1.5. On the other hand, we argue that the potential of using educational robots in teaching is not yet exploited as fully as possible so far (neither in CS teaching, nor in other disciplines). Therefore, we accept that educational robots such as Lego Mindstorms NXT [Ben12] or Arduino-based ones [Rob10] should be at the core, e.g. as a primary concept, to construct the *smart environments.* The presence of a robot within education environments (due to the capability of it to perform a variety of tasks) predefines the possibility to construct and investigate various constructivist-based teaching models. There are some important features of educational robots to support *smartness* of the concept as follows.

First, most educational robots (such as NXT) are constructed on the Lego principles; their architecture is simple and reconfigurable. Such reconfiguration can be easily done by teachers, depending on the context of use and teaching objectives. Students may also be involved in that activity as apprentices due to the attractiveness of the activity, its nearness to gaming and the extremely high level of self-motivation. When students are constructing environments for themselves on the basis of self-motivation, such *a process* should be treated as *smart* (the social and pedagogical perspectives).

Second, the robot's functionality can also be extended by adding extra *external* components such as *cameras* to send graphical views for monitoring what is going on in the robot's surrounding within the classroom or outside. The use of cameras enlarges the functionality of the robot-based environments significantly. In this case, it is possible not only to make the learning process more attractive and more effective. It is possible also to introduce elements of new forms of teaching such as *distance teaching* (e.g. in the case of disability or illness).

In most cases, it is enough to use a *single educational robot* in the smart environment to demonstrate a relatively simple task solving [BSM12]. In this case, the robot stands for a stand-alone teaching facility, but with the external support of the Internet and PC. Both ensure the preparation of control programs and then transfer them to the robot's environment.

Third, the robot's functionality can be extremely enlarged in creating smart environments, if we make essential architectural changes moving from the use of a single robot to the cooperating robots [BSD13]. For more complicated tasks, where the physical processes are concerned with simultaneous activities, the need of using *ensembles of robots* may arise. For example, the teaching of parallel programming concepts may be just the case. The move from the single robot use to the robot ensembles in creating teaching environments is indeed the challenging (smart) problem in both technological and methodological aspects.

So far, with regard to the concept of the smart environment, I have outlined three possibilities to improve the functionality of the robot-based CS teaching on the basis of the structural changes. At this level, those changes should be interpreted as purely hardware oriented. Further, I should outline the software-oriented capabilities to define the smartness of such environments.

The *flexibility* in using robots by changing their control programs, thus enforcing robots to perform different tasks, opens new ways for innovations and improvements. Indeed, the preprogrammed control is a great potential to support maintenance and evolution of environments aiming at their adaptation to various teaching objectives. It is possible, for example, to flexibly change the functionality of the environment only by means of changing the robot control programs. Furthermore, the robot itself is able to accept information through sensors out of the operating environment and, in this way, to change own behaviour. Of course, such a possibility should be preprogrammed in advance. Nevertheless, this possibility largely contributes to the flexibility in managing functionality of the environment in the whole.

With regard to flexibility aspects, it should be remembered the role and potential of using SLOs. From the pure technological perspective, SLOs are control program *generators*. A particular generator, for example, enables to produce an *instant* of the control program on demand automatically. As computational resources of robots are limited, the generator usually resides in a remote server. Nevertheless, one is able to gain a great deal of flexibility through the fast regenerating and reloading of a new instance to control the task. Here, the SLO-generating tool, the tool for adapting SLO to the context of use, should be viewed as components of the smart environments, though I omit considering such features here.

In summary, the flexible features of a single educational robot, the integrative features of a single robot with other external components to enhance the functionality of the environment, the integrative features in the context of using SLOs and their supporting tools and, finally, the integrative features of robots' ensembles with the rest part of the e-learning environment are *indicative features* to define *a smart e-learning environment*. In other words, putting together specific features of robots in some well-established way with other tools, even if those features and tools are not so much smart in separation, we are able to construct a *smart e-learning environment*. This statement is not a pure theoretic prediction. The statement has already been approved in practice, though in the only one real teaching setting with the restricted extent of experience and testing (see Chaps. 12 and 13). The first results, both theoretical and practical, enable us to formulate the concept of smart e-learning environments here. In PART II of the book, the concept will be extended through the thorough investigation.

1.9   Driving and Hindering Forces to Advancing Learning in CS

The reader should accept this short section as a summary of some (in my view is the most important) statements which were discussed previously. Here, however, I look at those statements from the other perspective, trying to draw a relationship between driving and hindering forces. In my vision, there are no *pure driving* and *pure hindering forces* to advancing learning in CS. Both are highly underpinned. Nevertheless, for methodological purposes, I consider them separately.

As it was stated, now ICT is the main driver of progress in the modern society. As a consequence, ICT underpins innovation and competitiveness across a broad range of private and public markets. ICT is also the main enabler of scientific progress in all disciplines. In this context, learning is seen as the most important social activity now. As CS brings fundamental knowledge about computing – the conceptual framework – needed to understand ICT, the latter can be seen as a main driver to advancing learning in CS too. Therefore, I present some list of factors (it is by no means full) that might be regarded as driving forces to advancing in this field as follows:

1. *Advances in ICT* and social understanding of the CS role to further progress of ICT per se are regarded as the most important factors.
2. *The ever-growing requirements* for more effective and more advanced learning as a social order and demand in general and in CS in particular (perhaps requirements are growing, or they should be growing, at the similar rate as ICT advances do).
3. The extremely *broad front of research in CS education* (that might be measured, e.g. by the number of conferences, scientific journals and publications) is also an important factor in advancing CS learning.
4. The *great deal of* the formulated *challenges* such as the interdisciplinary character of CS adds new stimulus for the improvements and innovations.
5. *Migration* of more mature ideas, models and solutions from other fields makes a positive impact on advancing e-learning in general and on education in CS in particular (e.g. adaptation of software reuse-based models, such as GLO, white-box LO, glass-box LO to e-learning domain and many more).
6. There is a long list of *organizational activities* that aim at enforcing and stimulating the engagement of young generation in computational sciences. Examples are organized worldwide Olympiads in programming, the International Contest on Informatics and Computer Literacy, local Olympiads and other forums within separate countries and 'Hour of Code' to name a few. The latter was provided by ACM (from December 9 to 15, 2013) as a part of *the Computer Science Education Week* that 'aims to introduce more than 10 million students of all ages to the basics of coding and to underscore the critical role of computing in all careers'.
7. I believe and hope that the *smart LOs* and *smart educational robot-based environments,* to be discussed throughout the book in the context of CS education, should also be a significant contribution in this field.

Below I present some hindering factors as related to CS education. Again, this list is by no means comprehensive. Many of those items could also be regarded either as challenges or at the same time as stimulating factors. This depends upon the fact from what perspective one is dealing with the problem.

In my understanding, the hindering factors are as follows:

1. There is no precise definition of CS and informatics.
2. There are no clear distinguishing lines between CS topics and related teaching topics such as IT, SW engineering and informatics. On this account, Syslo and Kwiatkowska [SK08] wrote: 'Today, many people, among them policy makers

(even some in education), teachers, academics and parents do not consider computer science as an independent science and, therefore, as a separate school subject. The fundamental problem is that they do not distinguish between using computer and network technology and studying the *general principles of computing'*.

3. Though the interdisciplinary character of CS topics extends the scope of knowledge in positive sense, it is also affecting negatively teachers to concentrate their focus on fundamentals of computing.
4. Specificity of CS may be seen to some extent as a hindering factor.
5. In most cases, the level of teacher preparation to teach CS is far from being relevant to challenges that currently exist in the field [CSTA08, BC11].

1.10   The Topics This Book Addresses

This book is about the novel approach to teach CS. The book is, in fact, a monograph, in which I have summarized and generalized our research on the meta-programming-based generative learning objects as well as the research of my former Ph. D. students. One of them, Renata Burbaitė, has made a significant contribution to the book. Therefore, she is a coauthor of Chaps. 12 and 13.

What is the content of the book? I have divided the content of the book into two parts. PART I first deals with the challenges of CS education in the twenty-first century, motivates the needs for innovations and then outlines the context of the book topics and introduces CS e-learning modelling concept on which basis we are able to specify, create and test the so-called smart LOs (SLOs). PART I also presents a background of SLOs from the teacher's perspective. PART II deals with the theoretical background of SLOs from the designer's perspective in order that it would be possible to create the authoring tools for designing and transforming SLOs to support adaptation in learning. PART II also presents a methodology of creating smart educational environments using robots and SLOs and the use of the methodology in real setting to teach CS (programming).

PART I includes (1) A Vision of Smart Teaching in CS (this chapter), (2) Understanding of LO Domain Through Its Taxonomies (Chap. 2), (3) Reuse Framework of the LO Domain (Chap. 3), (4) Modelling of CS Teaching and Learning in Large (Chap. 4), (5) Model-Driven Specification in Designing Smart LOs (Chap. 5), (6) Smart LOs Design: Higher-Level Coding and Testing Aspects (Chap. 6), (7) Enhanced Features of SLOs: Focus on Specialization (Chap. 7) and (8) Context-Aware Adaptation of Smart LOs (Chap. 8).

PART II includes (1) Background to Design Smart LOs and Supporting Tools (Chap. 9), (2) Authoring Tools to Design Smart LOs (Chap. 10), (3) Authoring Tools to Specialize and Adapt Smart LOs (Chap. 11), (4) Robot-Based Smart Educational Environments to Teach CS: A Case Study (Chap. 12) and (5) Smart Education in CS: A Case Study (Chap. 13); What Is on the Horizon?

1.11   Summary and Concluding Remarks

At this point, it is possible to summarize our discussion as follows. Though reusability aspects in e-learning research dominate at least a decade or so, in my view, the reuse potential in e-learning, no matter in which subject and no matter from what perspective, is not yet exploited as it might be. Though the notion of reuse was introduced (initially implicitly, i.e. without the use of the word) almost from the emergence of computer science (CS), it still has to live up to its promises: higher productivity and quality through the *library concept and automation*. A major stumbling block to achieving the promised benefits in e-learning is the *understanding and learning* the reuse-based approaches. One reason may be that we do not yet thoroughly understand the fundamental concepts that define reusability. The other reason may be the lack of understanding of how the concepts should migrate across different fields such CS, software, hardware and education. The difficulties with reuse-based approaches relate to the following stages: (1) understanding, (2) adoption and (3) application. For example, meta-programming – the powerful technology or methodology to support generative reuse we use in different domains [ŠD13] – does not allow achieving its promises at once. Rather, it demands a thorough domain analysis, investment into the creation of meta-programming tools such as meta-language processors, refactoring/transformation tools, development of generic component libraries and code generators, etc. The payoff will come only after some time, and designers will have to accept that. Adoption of generative reuse also requires some shift of attitudes and mindset of educational software developers as well as CS educators.

Currently, a majority of programmers and designers are accustomed to producing specific solutions and applications for a particular domain such as e-learning. They like to *reuse* the existing software artefacts (meta-programming-based GLO and SLO are really domain-specific programs, i.e. valuable assets or artefacts), but not much is done and invested into designing *for reuse*. If the *design with reuse* in e-learning is understood well enough, the *design for reuse* is still in its infancy in the domain.

In this introduction, I have motivated the benefits of two novel concepts – *smart LO* and *smart educational environment* – to teach CS. The aim is to achieve at least two objectives. The first is the enhancement and widening of generative reuse through focusing on *design for reuse* and exploiting its potential for advancing CS learning and teaching. The second is to respond to *some existing challenges* and *bottlenecks* in teaching CS (such as *semi-automatic adaptability, personalization, visualization of reality, exploratory learning*). I believe and hope that those concepts will attract attention within the educational research community. Our vision is to combine the two concepts as seamlessly as possible and open the way for *smart learning* in CS. To present this vision as thoroughly as possible to the reader, it is the main task to be considered throughout the book.

1.12   Research and Exercise Questions

1.1. Draw a distinguishing line among disciplines CS, SWE and informatics. What aspects are in common?

1.2. Draw a distinguishing line among disciplines CS, educational technology and gaming technology. What aspects are in common?

1.3. Define CS from two perspectives: (1) as it is understood at the school level and (2) at the university level.

1.4. What are the consequences of challenges formulated in Sect. 1.2?

1.5. Invent new challenges to CS teaching as regarded to the appearance of the Internet of Things – the new paradigm in computing.

1.6. Develop a framework to analyse and evaluate the reuse paradigm in e-learning.

1.7. Outline the basic trends in CS education research.

1.8. Why are there so many definitions of the term LO? What is the definition most relevant to your research?

1.9. What is generative LO (GLO)? Compare two models: Boyle et al.'s and meta-programming-based GLO.

1.10. What is meta-programming? Why is it needed? Study the basics (definitions and taxonomy) of the paradigm more thoroughly from [ŠD13].

1.11. What is smart LO? Why it is possible to 'transform' the meta-programming-based GLO into smart LO through the augmentation of generative aspects (parameters) and by adding a new functionality?

1.12. What is the smart educational environment? What are the components of the environment? Why might educational robots be regarded as central components?

1.13. Outline the driving and hindering forces to advancing learning in CS in your concrete context.

1.14. Outline your view: how might *SLOs* look in *the nearest future*?

References

[AC08]   Ayala G, Castillo S (2008) Towards computational models for mobile learning objects. In: 5th IEEE international conference on wireless, mobile, and ubiquitous technology in education, Beijing, 23–26 Mar 2008

[ACM12]   Computing Classification System (2012) Association for Computing Machinery. www.acm.org

[ADP+11] Antonis K, Daradoumis T, Papadakis S, Simos C (2011) Evaluation of the effectiveness of a web-based learning design for adult computer science courses. IEEE Trans Educ 54(3):374–380

[AG03]   Adamchik V, Gunawardena A (2003) A learning objects approach to teaching programming. In: Proceedings of the international conference on information technology: computers and communications, IEEE Computer Society, Las Vegas, pp 96–100

[AG13] Anderson N, Gegg-Harrison T (2013) Learning computer science in the comfort zone of proximal development. In: Proceedings of the 44th ACM technical symposium on computer science education, ACM, New York, pp 495–500

[AHH11] Alharbi A, Henskens F, Hannaford M (2011) Computer science learning objects. In: IEEE international conference on e-education, entertainment and e-management, Jakarta, pp 326–328

[AHH12] Alharbi A, Henskens F, Hannaford M (2012) Student-centered learning objects to support the self-regulated learning of computer science. Creat Educ 3:773–783

[AIM10] Atzori L, Iera A, Morabito G (2010) The internet of things: a survey. Comput Netw 54:2787–2805

[AM10] Allen CA, Mugisa EK (2010) Improving learning object reuse through OOD: a theory of learning objects. J Object Technol 9:1–22

[APH+11] Alharbi A, Paul D, Henskens F, Hannaford M (2011) An investigation into the learning styles and self-regulated learning strategies for computer science students. In: Proceedings ascilite 2011 Hobart, pp 37–46

[BB09] Bygholm A, Buus L (2009) Managing the gap between curriculum based and problem based learning: deployment of multiple learning strategies in design and delivery of online courses in computer science. Int J Educ Dev ICT 5(1)

[BBC04] Boyle T, Bradley C, Chalk P (2004) Improving the teaching of programming using a VLE enhanced with learning objects. In: Proceedings of the 2nd international conference on information technology research and education ITRE 2004, 28 Jun 2004, London Metropolitan University, London, pp 74–78

[BBD+14] Burbaitė R, Bespalova K, Damaševičius R, Štuikys V (2014) Context-aware generative learning objects for teaching computer science. Int J Eng Educ 30(4):929–936

[BBŠ14] Bespalova K, Burbaitė R, Štuikys V (2014) MePAG tools. http://proin.ktu.lt/metaprogram/MePAG/

[BC11] Barr V, Stephenson C (2011) Bringing computational thinking to K-12: what is involved and what is the role of the computer science education community? ACM Inroads 2(1):48–54

[BSD13] Burbaite R, Stuikys V, Damasevicius R (2013) Educational robots as collaborative learning objects for teaching computer science. In: IEEE international conference on system science and engineering (ICSSE 2013), pp 211–216

[Ben12] Benitti FBV (2012) Exploring the educational potential of robotics in schools: a systematic review. Comput Educ 58(3):978–988

[BEP+09] Berglund A, Eckerdal A, Pears A, East P, Kinnunen P, Malmi L, Thomas L (2009) Learning computer science: perceptions, actions and roles. Eur J Eng Educ 34 (4):327–338

[Big94] Biggerstaff T (1994) The library scaling problem and the limits of concrete component reuse. In: International conference on software reuse, Rio de Janeiro, 1–4 Nov 1994, pp 102–110

[BLC04] Boyle T, Leeder D, Chase H (2004) To boldly GLO: towards the next generation of learning objects. World conference on eLearning in corporate, government, healthcare and higher education. Washington, November 2004

[Boy03] Boyle T (2003) Design principles for authoring dynamic, reusable learning objects. Aust J Educ Technol 19:46–58

[BSM12] Burbaite R, Stuikys V, Marcinkevicius R (2012) The LEGO NXT robot-based e-learning environment to teach computer science topics. Electron Elect Eng 18(9)

[CAC12] Costa CJ, Aparicio M, Cordeiro C (2012) A solution to support student learning of programming. In: Proceedings of the workshop on open source and design of communication, pp 25–29

[CAL12] Campos AM, Alvarez-Gonzalez LA, Livingstone DE (12) Analyzing effectiveness of pedagogical scenarios for learning programming. A learning path data model. In: First international workshop on open technology transfer and learning solutions for programming education, pp 51–60

[CC10]   Cooper S, Cunningham S (2010) Teaching computer science in context. ACM
           Inroads 1(1):5–8

[Chu07]   Chudá D (2007) Visualization in education of theoretical computer science. In:
           CompSysTech'07, pp IV.15-1–IV.15-6

[CHW98]   Coplien J, Hoffman D, Weiss D (1998) Commonality and variability in software
           engineering. IEEE software, November/December 1998, pp 37–45

[CMF+09]   Castillo JF, Montes de Oca C, Flores ES, Elizondo PV (2009) Toward an approach
           to programming education to produce qualified software developers. In: IEEE 22nd
           conference on software engineering education and training, pp 101–104

[CN02]   Clements P, Northrop L (2002) Software product lines: practices and patterns.
           Addison-Wesley, Boston, MA

[CNC12]   Castro J, Nazar JM, Campos F (2012) EasyT: Apoiando a Construção de Objetos
           de Aprendizagem para uma Linha de Produtos de Software. Conferencias LACLO
           3(1)

[CSTA08]   Ensuring exemplary teaching in an essential discipline: addressing the crisis in
           computer science teacher certification. Final report of the CSTA Teacher Certifi-
           cation Task Force, September 2008

[CTT10]   Corney M, Teague D, Thomas RN (2010) Engaging students in programming. In:
           Proceedings of 12th Australasian computing education conference (ACE 2010),
           Brisbane, pp 63–72

[DAB12]   Dillon E, Anderson M, Brown M (2012) Comparing feature assistance between
           programming environments and their "effect" on novice programmers. JCSC 27
           (5):69–77

[Dal02]   Dalziel J (2002) Reflections on the COLIS (Collaborative Online Learning and
           Information Systems) demonstrator project and the "Learning Object Lifecycle"
           WebMCQ Pty Ltd & Inst. for Teaching and Learning Univ. of Sydney. http://www.
           ascilite.org.au/conferences/auckland02/proceedings/papers/207.pdf

[DDA12]   Díez D, Díaz P, Aedo I (2012) The ComBLA method: the application of domain
           analysis to the development of e-learning systems. J Res Pract Inform Technol 44
           (3)

[Dra13]   Drake P (2013) Games, Computer Science, and Education (Editorial). Computer
           Science Education 23(2):85–86

[DŠ08]   Damaševičius R, Štuikys V (2008) On the technological aspects of generative
           learning object development. In: Informatics education-supporting computational
           thinking: third international conference on informatics in secondary schools-evo-
           lution and perspectives, ISSEP 2008 Torun, Poland, 1–4 Jul 2008 Proceedings, Vol
           5090. Springer, pp 337–348

[DSS+08]   Dorairaj SK, Singh J, Shanmugam M, Shamini S (2008) Experimenting with
           industry's pair-programming model in teaching and learning programming. In:
           Proceedings of the 4th international conference on information technology and
           multimedia at UNITEN (ICIMU' 2008), Malaysia

[ECE+10]   Eshet-Alkalai Y, Caspi A, Eden S, Geri N, Tal-Elhasid E, Yair Y (2010) Challenges
           of integrating technologies for learning: introduction to the IJELLO special series
           of Chais conference 2010 best papers. Interdiscip J E-Learn Learn Objects 6:240–
           244

[Fig06]   de Figereiro AD (2006) From content to context in technology supported computer
           science education. In: E-learning conference computer science education

[FL09]   Fletcher GHL, Lu JJ (2009) Human computing skills: rethinking the K–12 experi-
           ence. Commun ACM 52(2):23–25

[For04]   Ford L (2004) A learning object generator for programming. SIGCSE Bull 36:268–
           268

[Fri04]   Friesen N (2004) Three objections to learning objects and e-learning standards. In: McGreal R (ed) Online education using learning objects. Routledge, London, pp 59–70

[GA03]   Gunawardena A, Adamchik V (2003) A customized learning objects approach to teaching programming. ACM SIGCSE Bull 35(3):264

[GC06]   Gulatee Y, Combes B (2006) Identifying the challenges in teaching computer science topics online. In: Proceedings of the EDU-COM 2006 international conference. Engagement and empowerment: new opportunities for growth in higher education, Edith Cowan University, Perth Western Australia

[GGL+12]   Goldberg DS, Grunwald D, Lewis C, Feld JA, Hug S (2012) Engaging computer science in traditional education: the ECSITE project. In: Proceedings of the 17th ACM annual conference on innovation and technology in computer science education, pp 351–356

[GM07]   Gomes A, Mendes AJ (2007) An environment to improve programming education. In: CompSysTech'07:-IV.19-1–IV.19-6

[Had09]   Hadjerrouit S (2009) Teaching and learning school informatics: a concept-based pedagogical approach. Inform Educ 8(2):227–250

[HK09]   Han P, Kramer BJ (2009) Generating interactive learning objects from configurable samples. In: Mobile, hybrid, and on-line learning, ELML'09, IEEE, pp 1–6

[HLR11]   Hazzan O, Lapidot T, Ragonis N (2011) Guide to teaching computer science: an activity-based approach. Springer, New York

[HS12]   Hamada M, Sato S (2012) A learning system for a computational science related topic. Proc Comput Sci 9:1763–1772

[IEEE00]   IEEE (2000) IEEE Learning Standards Committee, WG 12: learning object metadata. Available: http://ltsc.ieee.org/wg12. Last accessed 20 Nov 2013

[JB07]   Jones R, Boyle T (2007) Learning object patterns for programming. Interdiscip J Knowledge Learn Objects 3(1):19–28

[JCS09]   Jiau HC, Chen JC, Ssu KF (2009) Enhancing self-motivation in learning programming using game-Based simulation and metrics. IEEE Trans Educ 52(4):555–562

[Ker04]   Kerren A (2004) Learning by generation in computer science education. In: ITiCSE '04 proceedings of the 9th annual SIGCSE conference on innovation and technology in computer science education, ACM, pp 77–81

[KH07]   Koohang A, Harman K (2007) Learning objects and instructional design. Institute Informing Science, Santa Rosa

[KP05]   Kelleher C, Pausch R (2005) Lowering the barriers to programming: a taxonomy of programming environments and languages for novice programmers. ACM Comput Surv 37(2):83–137

[KPN08]   Kasurinen J, Purmonen M, Nikula U (2008) A study of visualization in introductory programming. Lancaster, PPIG

[KR08]   Knobelsdorf M, Romeike R (2008) Creativity as a pathway to computer science. In: ITiCSE'08, 30 June – 2 July 2008, Madrid

[Kra09]   Kramer BJ (2009) Generating interactive learning objects from configurable samples. In: International conference on mobile, hybrid, and on-line learning (ELML'09), Cancun, pp 1–6

[KS08]   Knobelsdorf M, Schulte C (2008) Computer science in context – pathways to computer science. In: Seventh Baltic sea conference on computing education research (Koli Calling 2007), Koli National Park, Finland, 15–18 Nov 2008

[LH10]   Liu GZ, Hwang GJ (2010) A key step to understanding paradigm shifts in e-learning: towards context-aware ubiquitous learning. Br J Educ Technol 41(2): E1–E9

[Lim98]   Lim WC (1998) Managing software reuse: a comprehensive guide to strategically reengineering the organization for reuse components. Prentice Hall PRT, Upper Saddle River

[LLR06]   Lim CP, Lee SL, Richards C (2006) Developing interactive learning objects for a computing mathematics models. Int J E-Learn 5(2):221–244

[LLY10] Kris MY, Law KMY, Lee VCS, Yu YT (2010) Learning motivation in e-learning facilitated computer programming courses. Comput Educ 55:218–228

[Low14] Lowyck J (2014) Bridging learning theories and technology-enhanced environments: a critical appraisal of its history. In: Michael Spector J, David Merrill M, Jan E, Bishop MJ (eds) Handbook of research on educational communications and technology. Springer, New York

[LP04]   Lejeune A, Pernin JP (2004) A taxonomy for scenario-based engineering. In: Cognition and exploratory learning in digital age (CELDA 2004) proceedings, pp 249–256

[LY11]   Lau WWF, Yuen AHK (2011) Modelling programming performance: beyond the influence of learner characteristics. Comput Educ 57(1):1202–1213

[LYW05] Lee MC, Ding Yen Ye DY, Wang TI (2005) Java learning object ontology. In: Proceedings of the fifth IEEE international conference on advanced learning technologies (ICALT'05)

[Mar04] Martin G (2004) IP reuse and integration in MPSoC: highly configurable processors. Tensilica Inc. Presentation at MPSoC'2004, H.tellerie du Couvent Royal, Saint-Maximin la Sainte Baume, France

[Mat06] Matthiasdottir A (2006) Usefulness of learning objects in computer science learning. The Codewitz project. In: Proceedings of the Codewitz open conference methods, materials and tools for programming education, Tampere

[McG04] McGreal R (ed) (2004) Online education using learning objects. RoutledgeFalmer, London

[Mer98] Merrill MD (1998) Knowledge objects. *CBT Solutions*, March/April issue, pp 6–11

[Mey06] Meyer B (2006) Testable, reusable units of cognition. Computer 39:20–24

[MHC12] Matthews R, Hin HS, Choo KA (2012) Merits and pitfalls of programming learning objects: a pilot study. In: Proceedings of the 10th international conference on advances in mobile computing & multimedia, pp 293–296

[MLB05] Morales R, Leeder D, Boyle T (2005) A case in the design of generative learning objects (GLOs): applied statistical methods. In: Proceedings of world conference on educational multimedia, hypermedia and telecommunications. AACE, Chesapeake

[MR02]   Milne I, Rowe G (2002) Difficulties in learning and teaching programming – views of students and tutors. Educ Inf Technol 7(1):55–66

[MSD13] McGill MM, Settle A, Decker A (2013) Demographics of undergraduates studying games in the United States: a comparison of computer science students and the general population. Comput Sci Educ 23(2):158–185

[MT12]   Mtebe JS, Twaakyondo HM (2012) Are animations effective tools for teaching computer science courses in developing countries? Int J Digit Inf Wirel Commun 2 (2):202–207

[MV07]   Mierlus-Mazilu I, Vaduva MA (2007) Learning objects for programming. In: ICTA'07, 12–14 Apr, Hammamet, Tunisia, pp 167–172

[Nas05] Nash S (2005) Learning objects, learning object repositories, and learning theory: preliminary best practices for online courses. Int J Knowl Learn Objects 1:217–228

[Nor07] Northrup PT (2007) Learning objects for instruction: design and evaluation. Information Science Publishing, Hershey

[NS09]   Narasimhamurthy U, Shawkani KA (2009) Teaching of programming languages: an introduction to dynamic learning objects. In: International workshop on technology for education (T4E), 4–6 Aug 2009, Bangalore, pp 114–115

[Old08] Oldfield J D (2008) An implementation of the generative learning object model in accounting. In: Proceedings of ASCILITE, Melbourne

[Pea10] Pears AN (2010) Enhancing student engagement in an introductory programming course. In: 40th ASEE/IEEE frontiers in education conference, 27–30 Oct, Washington, DC

[Pol03]   Polsani PR (2003) Use and abuse of reusable learning objects. J Digit Inf 3. Available: http://journals.tdl.org/jodi/article/view/89/88. Last accessed 2 Jan 2012

[PSM+07] Pears A, Seidman S, Malmi L, Mannila L, Adams E, Bennedsen J, Devlin M, Paterson J (2007) A survey of literature on the teaching of introductory programming. ACM SIGCSE Bull 39(4):204–223

[Red03]   Redeker GH (2003) An educational taxonomy for learning objects. In: Proceedings of the 3rd IEEE international conference on advanced learning technologies, 2003, Athens, pp 250–251

[RJR+05] Rossano V, Joy MS, Roselli T, Sutinen E (2005) A taxonomy for definitions and applications of LOs: a metaanalysis of ICALT papers. Educ Technol Soc 8(4):148–160

[Rößl10] Rößling G (2010) A family of tools for supporting the learning of programming. Algorithms 3(2):168–182

[Rob10]   McRoberts M (2010) Beginning Arduino. Apress, New York

[RRR03]   Robins A, Rountree J, Rountree N (2003) Learning and teaching programming: a review and discussion. Comput Sci Educ 13(2):137–172

[Sam97]   Sametinger J (1997) Software reuse with reusable components. Springer, Berlin

[ŠB12]   Stuikys V, Burbaite R (2012) Two-stage generative learning objects. In: Information and software technologies. Springer, Berlin/Heidelberg, pp 332–347

[ŠBB14]   Štuikys V, Bespalova K, Burbaitė R (2014) Refactoring of heterogeneous meta-program into k-stage meta-program. Inf Technol Control 43(1):14–27

[ŠBD13]   Štuikys V, Burbaitė R, Damaševičius R (2013) Teaching of computer science topics using meta-programming-based GLOs and LEGO robots. Inf Educ 12(1):125–142

[Sch02]   Schulte C (2002) Towards a pedagogical framework for teaching programming and object-oriented modelling in secondary education. In: Proceedings of SECIII 2002

[SCORM04] SCORM (2004) Sharable courseware object reference model. The SCORM overview advanced distributed learning (ADL) initiative. SCORM 2004 3rd ed

[ŠD07]   Štuikys V, Damaševičius R (2007) Towards knowledge-based generative learning objects. Inf Technol Control 36(2):202–212

[ŠD08]   Stuikys V, Damaševičius R (2008) Development of generative learning objects using feature diagrams and generative techniques. Inf Educ Int J 7_2:277–288

[ŠD13]   Stuikys V, Damaševičius R (2013) Meta-programming and model-driven meta-program development: principles, processes and techniques, vol 5. Springer, London, pp 174–178

[ŠDB+08] Štuikys V, Damaševičius R, Brauklytė I Limanauskienė V (2008) Exploration of learning object ontologies using feature diagrams. In: Proceeding of world conference on educational multimedia, hypermedia and telecommunications (Ed-MEDIA 2008), 30 June–4 July, Chesapeake: AACE, Vienna, pp 2144–2154

[SGM10]   Santos Á, Gomes A, Mendes AJ (2010) Integrating new technologies and existing tools to promote programming learning. Algorithms 3:183–196

[SGV06]   Silveira RA, Gomes ER, Vicari R (2006) Intelligent learning objects: an agent approach to create interoperable learning objects. http://sedici.unlp.edu.ar/bitstream/handle/10915/24370/Documento_completo.pdf?sequence=1. Accessed 18 Nov 2013

[SH04]   Sosteric M, Hesemeier S (2004) A first step towards a theory of learning objects. In: McGreal R (ed) Online education using learning objects. Routledge, London

[SH06]   Sajaniemi J, Hu C (2006) Teaching programming: going beyond "objects first". In: Romero P, Good J, Acosta Chaparro E, Bryant S (eds) Proceeding PPIG 18, pp 255–265

[SHL13]   Schäfer A, Holz J, Leonhardt T, Schroeder U, Brauner P, Ziefle M (2013) From boring to scoring–a collaborative serious game for learning and practicing mathematical logic for computer science education. Computer science education, (ahead-of-print), pp 1–25

[SK08]   Syslo MM, Kwiatkowska AB (2008) The challenging face of informatics education
           in Poland. In: Mittermeir RT, Syslo MM (eds) ISSEP 2008. LNCS, vol. 5090.
           Springer, Heidelberg, pp 1–18
[SMG11]   Salleh N, Mendes E, Grundy JC (2011) Empirical studies of pair programming for
           CS/SE teaching in higher education: a systematic literature review. IEEE Trans
           Softw Eng 37(4):509–525
[SMS08]   Starr CW, Manaris B, Stalvey RH (2008) Bloom's taxonomy revisited: specifying
           assessable learning objectives in computer science. ACM SIGCSE Bull 40(1):261–
           265
[Sol99]   Soltes D (1999) Metadata and metainformation – old concepts and new challenges.
           IASSIST Q 23:12–14
[SPJ+11]   Saeli M, Perrenet J, Jochems WMG, Zwaneveld B (2011) Teaching programming
           in secondary school: a pedagogical content knowledge perspective. Inf Educ
           10(1):73–88
[SSH+09]   Sheard J, Simon S, Hamilton M, Lönnberg J (2009) Analysis of research into the
           teaching and learning of programming. In: ICER'09, 10–11 Aug 2009, Berkeley, pp
           93–104
[THE09]   Mayes T, Morrison D, Mellar H, Bullen P, Oliver M (eds) Transforming higher
           education through technology-enhanced learning (2009) www.heacademy.ac.uk/
           assets/. Accessed 20 Nov 2013
[TLW+08]   Thompson E, Luxton-Reilly A, Whalley JL, Hu M, Robbins P (2008) Bloom's
           taxonomy for CS assessment. In: Proceeding 10th Australasian computing educa-
           tion conference (ACE2008), Wollongong, pp 155–161
[TMD+06]   Tucker A, McCowan D, Deek E, Stephenson C, Jones J, Verno A (2006) A model
           curriculum for K-12 computer science: report of ACM K-12 task force computer
           science curriculum committee, 2nd edn. Association for Computing Machinery,
           New York
[TMV04]   Tzikopoulos A, Manouselis N, Vourikari R (2004) An overview of learning object
           repositories. In: Northrup PT (ed) Learning objects for instruction: design and
           evaluation. Information Science Publishing, Hershey, pp 29–55
[Tou12]   Touretzky DS (2012) Seven big ideas in robotics, and how to teach them. In:
           Proceedings of the 43rd ACM technical symposium on computer science education,
           pp 39–44
[Ull04]   Ullrich C (2004) Description of an instructional ontology and its application in web
           service for education. In: Proceedings of workshop on applications of semantic web
           technologies for E-learning, SW-EL'04, Hiroshima, 17–23 Nov 2004
[Ull08]   Ullrich C (2008) Pedagogically founded courseware generation for web-based
           learning. Springer-Verlag, Berlin/Heidelberg
[VBH13]   Vincenti G, Braman J, Hilberg JS (2013) Teaching introductory programming
           through reusable learning objects: a pilot study. J Comput Sci Coll 28(3):38–45
[VMO+12]   Verbert K, Manouselis N, Ochoa X, Wolpers M, Drachsler H, Bosnic I, Duval E
           (2012) Context-aware recommender systems for learning: a survey and future
           challenges. IEEE Trans Learn Technol 5(4):318–335
[Wil00]   Wiley DA (2000) Learning object design and sequencing theory. Ph.D. thesis,
           Department of Instructional Psychology and Technology, Brigham Young Univer-
           sity. Available: http://opencontent.org/docs/dissertation.pdf. Last accessed 2 Jan
           2012
[Zuc06]   Zuckerman O (2006) Historical overview and classification of traditional and
           digital learning objects, MIT Media Laboratory. http://llk.media.mit.edu/courses/
           readings/classification-learning-objects.pdf

Chapter 2
Understanding of LO Domain Through Its Taxonomies

2.1 Introduction

The aim of this chapter is to introduce and discuss a taxonomy-based framework to understand the CS LO domain in large. I motivate the need of such a framework by the following reasons: (1) LO domain is commonly recognized as the heart of e-learning in general; (2) the LO concept is accepted and its role well understood for teaching CS as well; (3) the LO domain is continuously evolving in horizontal (meaning in general) and vertical dimensions (meaning in CS); and (4) a taxonomy-based approach is fundamental in many aspects (knowledge and artefacts systemizing, standardizing, sharing, gaining and teaching). Here, within the introduced framework, we highlight and consider (to some extent only) the following tasks: (1) concept-based modelling and experimentation using a restricted database of literature sources (about 500) and (2) creation of ontology-based models among those concepts that are most likely relevant to our approach.

All these are supported by facts extracted through an extensive literature review. We (I mean also readers) start the discussion with definitions, role and the general principles along with the introduced taxonomies as Sect. 2.2 states.

2.2 What Is Taxonomy and What Is Its Role?

Taxonomy is the science of classification according to a predetermined system. The Webster Online Dictionary defines taxonomy more precisely as follows:

> A systematic arrangement of objects or concepts showing the relations between them, especially one including a hierarchical arrangement of types in which categories of objects are classified as subtypes of more abstract categories, starting from one or a small number of top categories, and descending to more specific types through an arbitrary number of levels.

© Springer International Publishing Switzerland 2015
V. Štuikys, *Smart Learning Objects for Smart Education in Computer Science*,
DOI 10.1007/978-3-319-16913-2_2

Taxonomy plays a significant role in the cognition of any domain, any discipline or even any process and artefacts because 'there is nothing more basic than categorization to our thought, perception, action and speech' [Lak87, Dav97].

Now look more carefully at the aforementioned definition. Two important aspects are highlighted there, though not directly. The first is 'A systematic arrangement of objects or concepts' also implies their definition. The second is the statement of basic principle – the *use of a hierarchy and abstraction levels* – on which the categorization is to be formed. The e-learning community actors know well the following fact – there is the abundance of definitions of the term LO (see also Sect. 2.4).

In this regard, one may ask: (1) What are the aspects the definitions cover? (2) What are the relationships among those definitions? (It will be clarified in Sect. 2.4.) The next question arises: (3) what are the course designers and planners doing in designing LOs? The course plan, roughly speaking, is taxonomy. Many other examples might be provided to motivate the role of taxonomy. Knowing that and also knowing principles on which taxonomy is formed, the following framework is helpful for analysing and better understanding the LO domain.

2.3 A Framework to Outline LO Domain

As the LO domain is very dynamic and extremely large (e-learning might be considered as a super domain of the first), the knowledge systemization in the field is of great importance. The importance can be seen at least from two perspectives: theoretical (e.g. educational research, instructional design) and practical (e.g. the development of educational environments and the use of LOs within teaching settings). As, in many aspects, CS has a tight relationship (including teaching) with software engineering (SWE), where the term domain is widely used, we need first to define the term *domain* itself (meaning independently upon LOs). Note that there are many efforts to introduce SWE concepts and design principles into the LO domain (see, e.g. [Boy03]).

In SWE, the domain is treated as a really existing space of data, and knowledge for extracting artefacts is needed to develop a SW system. SWE investigates domains systematically. Though there is no unified definition, the following definitions might be relevant in our context. *Domain* is an 'area of activity or knowledge containing applications that share common capabilities and data' [Sam97]. *Domain* is 'a set of objects or entities bearing a common terminology'. *Domain* is 'an area of knowledge or activity characterized by a set of concepts and terminology understood by practitioners in that area' [BCD+99]. What is a general framework to deal with and understand domains? In our view, such a framework could be described by three interrelated attributes: *domain scope identified by its boundary, domain context* (what is outside of the boundary?) and *subdomains within a domain* (what are entities within the boundary?). This view is known since 1990 when the SWE Institute of Carnegie Mellon University (USA) has introduced the FODA (Feature-Oriented Domain Analysis) method [KCH+90].

I apply this SWE-based approach in our case as follows. I consider e-learning as a context of the whole LO domain (in other words, e-learning is a super domain, while the LO domain is a subdomain of the first). It is possible to exclude within the LO domain three *subdomains* (we do that implicitly). The first subdomain is the *known definitions* and *types* of LOs extracted from the literature. We present it as an evolutionary-based taxonomy. The second subdomain is the *models* to characterize LOs. As there are a variety of proposals to deal with LO models, we also analyse their taxonomies. The third subdomain is the *relationship* among main concepts that characterize the LO domain itself. They are structural units defined as *category classes*, *their properties* and *processes* pertained with those classes. I define such a relationship as *ontology* of the domain under consideration. Finally, I consider *the scope* of the domain we analyse in this chapter as overall aspects to which the aforementioned three subdomains pertain. Figure 2.1 summarizes the introduced framework.

The top layer is characterized by the following attributes: e-learning domain, learning objects (LOs), LO repositories and courseware designs. Each bottom division (having the form of trapezium in Fig. 2.1) is to be understood as a subdomain of the upper division. The topics we are concern in the book cover the middle and bottom layers. The topic of this chapter is marked by the darkened trapezium.

Now we need to characterize the top layer as the *super domain* (or, in terms of domain analysis [KCH+90], as a *context* and the *boundary*) to *our domain* of interest. Here, I focus on the paper [Str06], which presents the generic multidimensional reference model (MRM) for e-learning standards as the main outcome. First, the paper states the tasks of interoperability as well as quality development and their relationship. In e-learning their connection and interdependence are evident: interoperability is one basic requirement for quality development. It is shown how standards and specifications are supporting these crucial issues. Then the MRM is evaluated according to e-learning standardization committees and initiatives (ISO/IEC JTC1 SC36, IEEE LTSC, IMS and ADL) and their published standards and specifications. As a conclusion, the paper outlines the challenges and potentials for e-learning standardization for the future. Three types of e-learning standards are differentiated:

- *Implementation standards* for ensuring the interoperability within all domains of e-learning
- *Conceptual standards* offering generic and theoretical solutions to compare and harmonize the entities and objects corresponding to the standard
- *Level standards* to define the quality level that should be reached by the application of the e-learning

These three types of e-learning standards can be attributed to the two main purposes and functions of e-learning standardization, i.e. interoperability and quality development. The differentiation of the implementation standards (and their

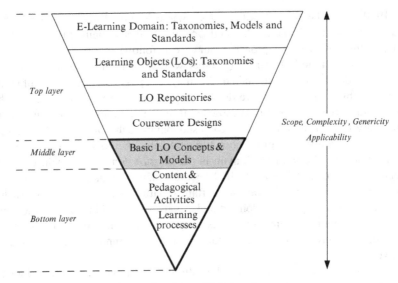

Fig. 2.1 A framework to analyse and understand LO domain

corresponding conceptual standards) is not so easy. Depending on their focus, many different types of implementation standards can be identified: metadata standards, architecture standards, infrastructure standards, interface standards, etc.

There are six main domains of e-learning with relevance to standards:

- *Meaning* (that focuses on the general understanding and deals with the disciplines semiotics, pragmatics and semantics)
- *Quality* (that covers all aspects of the development, assurance and management of quality and deals with results, processes and potentials)
- *Didactics* (that deals with all pedagogical questions and issues concerning methods, learners and environments)
- *Learning technology* (that includes all technological solution especially developed for learning objectives and purposes and deals with data exchange, interfaces, accessibility questions, etc.)
- *Learning content* (that covers all aspects that are necessary for e-learning objects and deals with the resources, their aggregation, their packaging, etc.)
- *Context* (that combines all other disciplines and information with regard to e-learning and its given context and deals with, e.g. rights, laws and experiences)

The e-learning domain taxonomies include different aspects such as *learning styles* [BCS+05], *collaborative learning* [Sal06], *learning activities* [Con07], etc. The e-learning models and frameworks are discussed in [MF04, SVC12, Nat12]. One can read and learn more on LO taxonomies from the following sources: (1) Wiley LO [Wil00], (2) Redeker's LO [Red03], (3) Finlay LO [Fin04] and (4) Churchill LO [Chu07].

The LO standards and repositories are directed to higher level of reusability and interoperability. The latter is related with the quality of metadata. The *National Information Standards Organization* (NISO) defines metadata as structural information that describes, explains, fixes or otherwise facilitates the search, use and management of the learning resources [BC10]. Roy et al. [RSG10] carried out a comparative analysis of LO metadata models and showed that the IEEE LOM, Dublin Core and CanCore standards are used most frequently.

One can learn more on courseware designs from [Goo14, DPW11, RM13]. Now we return to our topic of interest.

2.4 Taxonomy of LO Definitions

Here, we discuss the first subdomain of the LO domain as it was identified in Sect. 2.3. There was a great deal of efforts to introduce taxonomies to identify various aspects of LOs through analysis of LO properties, structure, type and other attributes such as similarities and differences given by different sources. As the LO domain is highly heterogeneous, different taxonomies present different aspects. For example, the Bloom's taxonomies (there is a long list of the extensions of the base taxonomy [Blo56] (see, e.g. [Kra02])) mainly focus on learning objective and processes. Wiley's taxonomy [Wil00] focuses on LO types and characteristics. Redeker's taxonomy [Red03] aims *to conceptualize a didactical taxonomy* of LOs and provides a didactic metadata approach for the facilitation of reusable instructional navigation patterns. More specifically, he presents an educational taxonomy for LOs for the facilitation of generic sequencing strategies. The OSEL taxonomy [CAM+06] represents the joint product of Redeker's and Wiley's taxonomies. Rossano et al. [RJR+05] provide a meta-analysis and present a taxonomy for definitions and applications of LO as they were presented in the ICALT'05 papers.

Our taxonomy comprises a more durable period of time and is oriented to extract not only definitions per se but also processes and activities applied to LOs (see Table 2.1).

The presented summary provides readers with the following information. As I have presented the definitions and main concepts in a strict chronological order, it is possible to see the evolution of the LO concept definitions during about two decades here. Sometimes authors try not to present a precise definition but rather to emphasize a specific property the suggested LO has. On the basis of the proposed scheme (it can be also treated as our taxonomy), it is possible to exclude three main streams of works to determine the evolution trends.

The first stream defines LOs as the *first-generation* entities (the term was coined by Boyle). According to this trend, LOs are seen *as instances* having a variety of discriminating properties. Among those properties, the following ones prevail in most cases: structure, behaviour, reusability, composition, adaptation and context. In general, we can characterize the first-generation LOs either by the pure black-

Table 2.1 LO taxonomy defined by the conceptual evolution since 1997 till 2014

Year, author: main focus	Definitions
1997, L'Allier: *compositional and structural view combined with pedagogical attributes*	Learning object (LO) is a 'structural component, which is defined as the smallest independent instructional experience that contains an objective, a learning activity and an assessment' [All97]
1998, Merrill 1. *LO as knowledge object* 2. *Structural and process-based view*	A knowledge object is 'a way to organize a data base (knowledge base) of content resources (text, audio, video, and graphics) so that a given instructional algorithm (predesigned instructional strategy) can be used to teach a variety of different contents' [Mer98]
2000, Wiley 1. *Structural and process-based view* 2. *Relationship to OO*	Learning objects 'are elements of a new type of computer-based instruction grounded in the object-oriented (OO) paradigm of computer science' [Wil00]
2000, Merrill: *LO as knowledge object with extended structural, process-based and property-based views*	The components of a knowledge object 'are a set of defined containers for information', including an *entity* or its part, property, action triggered by the process, conditions and consequences of executing the processes [Mer00]
2001: Ip et al.: *pure structural view*	A learning object is a structure that 'must have at least 4 subcomponents: content, functions, learning objectives and 'look and feel'' [IMC01]
2001, IEEE std.: *technology and reuse*	*Any entity, digital or non-digital, which can be used, re-used or referenced during technology supported learning* [LTSC01]
2002, Sosteric and Hesemeier: *structure, pedagogy and context*	A learning object is a 'digital file (image, movie, etc.) intended to be used for pedagogical purposes, which includes, either internally or via association, suggestions on the appropriate context within which to utilize the object' [SH02]
2002, Orrill: *structure of the process, interaction and feedback*	'The learning object presents the information, provides the student with an infinite amount of practice, and provides a test that allows the computer to provide feedback' [Orr02]
2003, Polsani: *independency, reuse and context*	A learning object is 'an independent and self-standing unit of learning content that is predisposed to reuse in multiple instructional contexts' [Pol03]
2003, Gunawardena and Adamchik: *customization, integration*	A customized learning object (CLO) is defined as 'an integrated module containing the core text, code examples, review questions, and other supplemental material' [GA03]

(continued)

Table 2.1   (continued)

Year, author: main focus	Definitions
2003, Mohan and Greer: *structure, process and reuse*	LO is 'an item of content, a learning resource, or an entity of learning capable of being reused from one course to another' [MG03]
2003, Paris: *the learning and design perspectives, with the latter being stemmed from the object-oriented paradigm in CS*	LOs are considered from (1) '*the learning perspective*, with a focus on learning objectives, content, and assessment in order to derive small instructional components from existing resources; (2) *the object perspective*, with a focus on the development of small, reusable components, which are characterized in terms of accessibility, reusability, and interoperability' [Par03]
2003, Redeker: *LO as the knowledge reduction in its essential unit*	A learning object, at its most basic level, "is made up of several knowledge units (KUs) which may consist of texts, audio and video presentations, or animation. At this point the problem of granularity of learning objects arises" [Red03]
2003, Boyle: *design, composition and repurposing aspects, introduction of SWE principles to design LO*	'A compound object consists of two or more independent learning objects that are linked to create the compound, to provide pedagogical richness and a significant basis for re-purposing' [Boy03]
2004, Leeder et al.: *composition, interactivity and assessment*	'A reusable learning object (RLO) is based on a single learning objective, comprising a stand-alone collection of three components: (1) *Content*: a description of the concept, fact, process, principle or procedure to be understood by the learner in order to support the learning objective; (2) *Interaction*: something the learner must do to engage with the content in order to better understand it; (3) *Assessment*: a way in which the learner can apply their understanding and test their mastery of the content' [LDH04]
2004, McGreal: *reuse and composition*	'Any reusable digital resource that is encapsulated in a lesson or an assemblage of lessons grouped in units, modules, courses, and even programs' [McG04]
2004, Sicilia et al.: *as digital information on the Web*	The authors consider learning objects to be digital entities – the resources in the Web – which represents 'information bearing things that contain digitally coded information readable by a computer' [SGS+04]
2004, Silveira et al.: *focus on interaction among LOs and LOs and other agents aiming at improving adaptability through intelligence*	Intelligent learning objects (or pedagogical agents) are those to 'improve adaptability and interactivity of complex learning environments built with this kind of components by the interaction between the learning objects

(continued)

Table 2.1 (continued)

Year, author: main focus	Definitions
	and between learning objects and other agents in a more robust conception of communication than a single method invocation as the object oriented paradigm used to be' [SGP+04]
2004, García-Valdez et al.: *structure, context, process and adaptability*	An adaptive learning object (ALO) is the one that 'inherits from the Learning Object type and is associated with the following adaptive components: Knowledge Domain Model (KDM), User Model (UM), Session (S), Context Model' [GRC+04]
2005, Stamey and Saunders: *customization through intelligence*	Intelligent learning objects are those enabling to 'extend the idea of Learning Objects (LOs) whereby the learner receives customized training like that found in Intelligent Learning Environments' [SS05]
2005, Morales et al.: *based on concept separation with the focus on quality and productivity*	The concept of generative learning objects (GLOs) is based on separating the learning design from the surface instantiation of a learning object. This gives a number of advantages: (i) *focuses attention on the quality of the learning design that is at the heart of the GLO;* (ii) *provides a basis for a marked improvement in productivity* [MLB05]
2005, Oliver et al.: *LOs are able to support specific outcomes (rules, facts, etc.)*	In such cases, when the developers set very firm guidelines for size, form, assessment and pedagogy, 'learning objects in these instances take the form of discrete elements able to support very targeted learning outcomes, e.g. rules, facts, procedures' [OWW+05]
2006, Chitwood: *structural, knowledge units causing learning*	A **Wisc-Online learning object** is (i) 'A different way of thinking about learning content; (ii) Small, independent chunks of knowledge or interactions stored in a database; (iii) Based on a clear instructional strategy – intended to cause learning through internal processing and/or action; (iv) Self-contained – each learning object can be taken independently' [Chi06]
2006, Mierlus-Mazilu: *focus on visualizing, aiming at understanding programming structure more easily*	**The Codewitz learning objects** 'are interactive visualizations of program code examples or programming tasks... can cover any specific programming problem in any programming language. The problem-solving logic at the algorithmic level. A learning object focuses on one specific learning goal. Each learning object has to be independent, without links to other objects or resources' [Mie06]

(continued)

Table 2.1 (continued)

Year, author: main focus	Definitions
2006, Boyle: *structure and design principles to develop GLO. The basic idea is the separation of concerns (surface form from the content) and template-based approach*	Boyle (one of the pioneers of GLOs) describes the GLOs design process as follows
	'The first step in developing generative learning objects is the separation of surface form from content. Unlike the first generation approach, the primary focus here is to make forms reusable rather than the content (although the content may be reusable as well) – an approach hinted at by Wiley. At its most basic level, this leads to a 'template-based' approach. This separates the surface structure from the specific content and captures this as a template. Tutors can load content into these reusable RLO forms. This could be particularly useful in areas such as statistics, where there is a common statistical pattern, but users want content adapted to their specific subject area. The next stage in articulating a conceptual structure for generative learning objects is to elucidate the underlying hierarchical structure of learning objects' [Boy06]
2007, Štuikys and Damaševičius: *GLO as learning variability mapping on generative technology (meta-programming)*	The authors extend the known concept of GLOs by connecting commonality-variability analysis in the domain with heterogeneous meta-programming techniques for generating LO instances on demand from the generic LO specification [ŠD07]
2008, Khierbek et al.: *explicit metadata, reusability and composition*	The authors define 'RLOs as the basic building blocks of a learning content that are well-defined by metadata and can be easily combined to be reused in different learning contexts' [KST08]
2008, Štuikys and Damaševičius: *further discussion on meta-programming- based GLOs, GLO as a mini library*	'A GLO is a specification describing a family of the related LO instances. It has the user manageable metadata for deriving instances on demand. A particular GLO can be seen as a mini repository of LOs providing the possibility to automatically generate from the repository a concrete LO instance on demand depending on the metadata values that the user identifies. A GLO may be a member of a conventional LOs repository too, but each LO instance of GLO must be first generated before using' [ŠD08]
2009, Han and Krämer: *interactivity and parameterization*	The authors use Bloom's taxonomy to qualify and relate learning tasks and activities and combine them with different instances of content. They call this 'pedagogical parameterization of information objects' [HK09]

(continued)

Table 2.1 (continued)

Year, author: main focus	Definitions
2009 Villalobos et al.: *interactivity and generation of programming skill*	The authors present interactive learning objects (ILOs) as one of the components that reinforce their 'pedagogical model, by supporting the generation of high-level programming skills' [VCJ09]
2009, Boyle: *further discussion on GLO design using GLO-maker tools*	'The idea of capturing successful learning designs and making these the basis for reuse, rather than content, is at the core of the concept of generative learning objects (GLOs). The authoring and adaptation of generative learning objects is achieved through a specially developed authoring tool called GLOMaker. Crucially, tutors can also use the tool to adapt existing GLO based learning objects to suit the local needs of their students' [Boy09]
2010, Men and Jin: *focus on dynamic context. The concept 'smart LO' has been met for the first time*	The authors take the learning object 'as a chunk of information with the description of its context. This means the learning object is passive, but with a description about context information which is dynamic. This is different from the *smart learning object*, which targets to 'perform many of the tasks typically associated with the LCMS" [MJ10]
2012, Vlachos: *LO is characterized as a bundle of various media elements (text, image, video, multimedia, podcast, animation, glossary, assessment, etc.) of related state and behaviour*	'The 'wrapper' around this digital learning material describes the structure of the LO and includes the descriptive metadata; the ways that a LO can be managed, linked and searched. This encapsulation is liable for the increase in efficiency of a LO each time it is adapted and reused in a learning activity. In accordance to a programming object, a LO should be small – less contextual – and perform few tasks in order to be applied easier. LOs are typically small content components. Despite that fact, for measuring the granularity, or aggregation level, of a LO we consider the approach based on the nature of its' content as important as the media-centric one, which is based on the size of its media' [Vla12]
2012, Alharbi et al.: *focus on student-centred learning through the context, adaptation and learning styles*	The main objective of the research presented in this paper was to design learning objects to support students in their self-regulated learning of programming language concepts based on the theory of learning styles [AHH12]
2012, Štuikys and Burbaitė: *focus on refactoring of GLO to produce two-stage GLOs to support adaptation*	Structural and functional models of one-stage and two-stage GLO to support the following issues: (i) complexity management and (ii) reuse and adaptability [ŠB12]

(continued)

Table 2.1   (continued)

Year, author: main focus	Definitions
2013, Burbaitė et al.: *focus on the use of robots as physical LOs in CS education*	Robots as physical learning objects (PLO) are considered; that extends the notion of a traditional LO beyond the virtual domain (e-content, web page) to a physical domain (robot hardware and physical processes that are demonstrated by the hardware). A PLO is a smart thing (e.g. a mobile robot) that has sensors and/or actuators to interact with its environment and content (a control program) to control its behaviour [BDŠ13]
2014, Burbaitė et al. focus on a new type context-aware GLOs; the use of refactoring tool to transform and adapt multistage GLOs	Context-aware generative learning objects (GLOs) aim at supporting wide-scale reusability and automatic adaptability through refactoring-based transformations to produce adapted LO to teach computer science (CS) topics within the educational Arduino-based environment [BBD+14]

box model (meaning the use of LOs *as is*, i.e. without adaptation) or a 'weak' white-box model (meaning the use with manual adaptation).

The second stream defines the so-called generative LOs (GLOs). Boyle treats them as the 'next-generation' LOs. The main intention of introducing this kind of LOs was to enhance the previously mentioned properties of the first-generation LOs through the new property such as the ability to *generate the content*. This new property requires focusing more in-depth on two aspects: *design processes* and *technology* to support the design and use of this kind of LOs through the generation process. Here, the technology plays a significant role because it predefines the capabilities of designing and generating processes. Boyle and his colleagues use the *template-based approach* to construct their GLOs by means of the tools called GLO Maker [Boy10]. One can track the evolution of this approach using the given extracts taken from their papers published in between 2003 and 2012. In general, we can characterize the second stream by generative reuse model, i.e. a more advanced white-box model which focuses on semi-automatic generation.

The third stream of research on LOs concerns with the new kind of GLOs, namely, meta-programming-based GLOs. Meta-programming is a powerful generative technology, enabling to automatically transform and generate the content from the preprogrammed specifications called meta-programs [ŠD13]. Meta-programs is seen as a programs generator (along with a meta-language processor). Therefore, the technology enables semi-automatic or even automatic adaptation if the initial preprogrammed specification has additional information such as context for adaptation (we will discuss that in detail later).

2.5   Taxonomy of LO Models

Since there are a variety of the slightly different definitions of LOs, so is with their models. However, I have selected only a few models treating them as most representative ones to our context. CISCO Systems [CISCO03] propose a structural LO model to support reuse. This model consists of five components (objective, metadata, content, practice and assessment; see Fig. 2.2). Content may be static and interactive and may contain practice as a separate component.

The model aims at achieving one learning objective. The quality of the LO model is measured by evaluating whether or not the objective was achieved. The interior of the content is created from the text, audio, video, animation fragments and Java code applets. The model is described using metadata for storing and searching to support reuse.

Verbert and Duval [VD04] first present the overview of Learning Object Content Models and then suggest their own model (see Fig. 2.3). The overview includes the Learnativity Content Model of Duval and Hodgins, 2003, SCORM Content Aggregation Model, CISCO RLO/RIO Model and NETg Learning Object Model (L'Allier 1997).

In this model, the authors distinguish between the content fragments, content objects and learning objects as follows. Content fragments are learning content elements in their most basic form, such as text, audio and video. They represent individual resources not combined with any other. A further specialization of this level will need to take into account the different characteristics of time-based media (audio, video and animation) and static media (photo, text, etc.). Content objects are sets of content fragments. They aggregate content fragments and add navigation. Content fragments are instances, whereas content objects are abstract types. The authors argue that it is possible to extend content fragments with activities and people and analogously content objects with activity types and roles.

Meyer [Mey06] proposes the TRUC model as *testable, reusable unit of cognition*, which consists of concepts, skill and assessment. The following attributes characterize the model:

Fig. 2.2 LO structural model (According to [CISCO03])

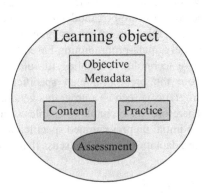

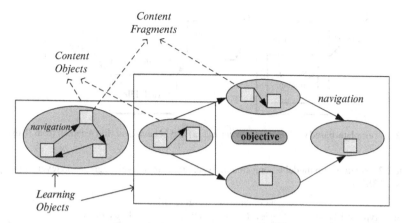

Fig. 2.3 General learning object content model (Adapted from [VD04])

1. TRUC components are created on the clearly defined concept.
2. TRUC components are clearly defined and oriented to multiple uses.
3. TRUC has one or more assessment criteria.
4. The scope of the TRUC use covers a few lessons.
5. TRUC is grouped into a hierarchical structure.

The Boyle's GLO structural model (Fig. 2.4a) contains the *deep structure* and *surface structure* [Boy06]. The behavioural model of the GLO consists of *authoring tool*, XML *file* and player *program* (see Fig. 2.4b). As the main merit of the model, Boyle emphasizes the opportunity to change the XML file, flexibly, using the authoring tool in order to create instances from the template-based GLO.

LO models are to be considered at the different representation levels. In this regard, the aggregation of the content parts, along with learning objectives, stands as a primary concern [SAA+07]. Furthermore, the relationships between the resource type, granularity levels and reusability aspects play a significant role [BMO08]. On this basis, we have summarized the relationships as it is outlined in Table 2.2.

The presented LO model taxonomy is by no means exhaustive. We do that consciously, having in mind the following: (a) here we have presented those models that are either general enough or, to some extent, relate to our models to be presented later and (b) the reader is asked to provide research on LO model taxonomy in Sect. 2.8.

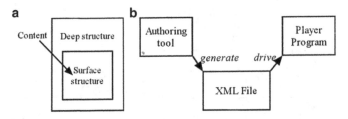

Fig. 2.4 Template-based GLO models: structural (**a**) and behavioural (**b**) (Adapted from [Boy06])

Table 2.2 Relationship model among content type, granularity level, aggregation level and scope of reuse [BS11]

Element type of LO	Granularity level	Aggregation level	Reusability
Raw media: images, audio-video files, text snippets	Very fine	Low	Reused on the 'use-as-is' basis
Anything that focuses on a single piece of information	Fine	Low	Reused as self-contained units. Can be disassembled in order to reuse their content assets
A collection of information objects that are assembled to teach a single learning objective	Medium	Medium	Reused as self-contained units. Can be disassembled in order to reuse their information objects or content assets
Lessons, courses and general learning resources composed by multiple LOs with multiple learning objectives	Coarse	Medium	Entirely reused, but coarse granularity reduces reuse potential
Learning environment – combination of content and technology with which a learner interacts	Very coarse	High	Reused depending on the coupling they maintain among them

2.6   Keyword-Based Description of CS Education Research

Here, the aim is clarifying two issues: (1) What are the basic concepts used in the scientific literature to characterize research in CS education? (2) What are relationships among those concepts? In order to receive an answer, we have provided the following research experiment. First, we have created the initial database for our research. It included about 500 scientific papers on e-learning and CS education. The papers were published in journals, books and proceedings of worldwide conferences, symposiums or workshops during the years 1998–2013. Next, we have selected 126 papers that were regarded as *strongly* related to the CS education research. By the word *strongly*, we mean the following here: there was mentioned in the title and/or keywords of the papers either the term *CS education* (and synonymous, such as *learning, teaching*) or programming teaching-related terms

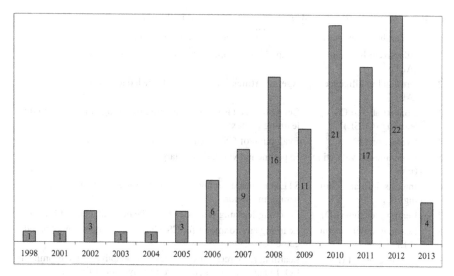

Fig. 2.5 The number of the selected papers strongly related to CS education being published in 1998–2013

(such as *algorithms, computer languages, programming,* etc.). The great deal of selected papers was published in recent years (see Fig. 2.5).

After that, on the basis of intuition and experience, we have created a list of generalized keywords and have identified the scope of their meaning by presenting either synonyms or those words that were very close in meaning. In Table 2.3, we summarize those keywords and the scope of their meaning (here, by 'we' I mean the help of Renata Burbaitė). Finally, we have calculated the frequency of those keywords in each paper of the list. In Fig. 2.6, we present the results of the calculation ordered by the value (in percent).

What can one learn from this diagram? Though the experiment was not exhaustive, nevertheless, the trend is clear: there are terms that define the field best, i.e. most frequently used (e.g. pedagogical features, evaluation, visualization, learning environment, LO and contextualized learning). There are also terms that define the field exceptionally rarely (e.g. LO sequencing, interdisciplinary learning, adaptive e-learning, experimental validation).

It should not be thought that those research areas by no means are less important. On the contrary, it might be thought that the areas are more complicated and researchers should pay more attention to that. But on the other hand, we need to take into account the strong correlation between the different generalized keywords. Having this in mind, the results of the interdependency of the keywords are more informative (see Table 2.4).

Table 2.3 Generalized keywords and their synonym used in the experiment

#	Generalized keywords	Scope of their meaning and synonyms
1.	Adaptive e-learning (AEL)	Adaptability, adaptive course, adaptive e-learning
2.	Artificial intelligence (AI)	Agents, artificial intelligence, knowledge based
3.	Contextualized CS learning (CCSL)	Contextualized learning, contextualized programming learning, learning context, etc.
4.	Evaluation (E)	Evaluation of CS education in large, assessment
5.	Experimental validation (EV)	Experimental validation in large
6.	Interdisciplinary learning (IL)	STEM (science, technology, engineering, mathematics) paradigm support
7.	Learning design (LD)	Teaching-learning processes that take place in a unit of learning
8.	Learning environment (LE)	Learning environments for CS education: adaptive, robot based, game based, etc.
9.	Learning object (LO)	Learning resources for CS education: adaptive LO, customized LO, LO as patterns, generative LO, dynamic LO, etc.
10.	Learning object sequencing (LOS)	Connecting LO to LD and LE
11.	Metadata and LO repositories (MR)	Available LO metadata and repositories
12.	Modelling (M)	Pedagogical, technological and content models of CS science education domain
13.	Pedagogical features (PF)	Learning objectives, motivation, learning theories, learner's preferences, pedagogical assessment aspects, learning activities, scenarios, etc.
14.	Reusability (RS)	Creation and using reusable learning objects for CS education
15.	Robotics (R)	Robot-based environments for CS education, robots programming, etc.
16.	Simulation (S)	Interactive algorithm, data structure, program visualization
17.	Software engineering (SE)	Software engineering methods and principles for modelling CS education domain, LO specification
18.	Visualization (V)	Algorithm, data structure, program visualization (interactive +real)

2.7   Summary and Concluding Remarks

In this chapter, I have analysed the LO research domain in general and in CS education in particular. As this domain, indeed, is very dynamic and extremely large, the knowledge systemization in the field is of great importance. The LO domain and discussed topics here should be treated as the essential part of the context of our main topic – smart LOs. To provide the analysis systematically, first I have introduced a framework. To describe the framework, I have used concepts borrowed from SW engineering (i.e. a domain understanding through its modelling). Next, I have introduced LO taxonomy by providing basically the original

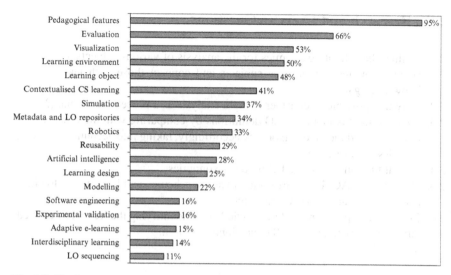

Fig. 2.6 The frequency of using the generalized terms in the selected sources

Table 2.4 Interdependencies between generalized keywords

	LO	LE	R	RS	LD	AEL	E	MR	PF	V	IL	SE	CCSL	S	AI	EV	LOS	M
LO	100%	68%	16%	43%	34%	25%	77%	32%	98%	63%	16%	16%	43%	46%	30%	29%	20%	29%
LE	68%	100%	29%	34%	38%	24%	76%	34%	98%	72%	10%	21%	45%	53%	26%	19%	16%	29%
R	16%	29%	100%	13%	21%	5%	61%	37%	87%	53%	16%	16%	37%	47%	45%	11%	11%	8%
RS	43%	34%	13%	100%	44%	29%	74%	41%	94%	59%	12%	15%	41%	44%	24%	26%	24%	32%
LD	34%	38%	21%	44%	100%	28%	76%	21%	100%	62%	17%	21%	52%	48%	31%	21%	21%	28%
AEL	25%	24%	5%	29%	28%	100%	76%	41%	88%	65%	24%	12%	12%	47%	29%	29%	29%	41%
E	77%	76%	61%	74%	76%	76%	100%	33%	99%	55%	17%	14%	42%	41%	30%	20%	14%	30%
MR	32%	34%	37%	41%	21%	41%	33%	100%	88%	63%	18%	23%	43%	45%	35%	23%	10%	30%
PF	98%	98%	87%	94%	100%	88%	99%	88%	100%	54%	15%	16%	43%	37%	27%	17%	12%	24%
V	63%	72%	53%	59%	62%	65%	55%	63%	54%	100%	11%	19%	50%	53%	31%	19%	18%	23%
IL	16%	10%	16%	12%	17%	24%	17%	18%	15%	11%	100%	31%	44%	31%	44%	19%	6%	25%
SE	16%	21%	16%	15%	21%	12%	14%	23%	16%	19%	31%	100%	56%	61%	56%	17%	6%	39%
CCSL	43%	45%	37%	41%	52%	12%	42%	43%	43%	50%	44%	56%	100%	44%	25%	19%	8%	19%
S	46%	53%	47%	44%	48%	47%	41%	45%	37%	53%	31%	61%	44%	100%	42%	16%	19%	19%
AI	30%	26%	45%	24%	31%	29%	30%	35%	27%	31%	44%	56%	25%	42%	100%	16%	16%	31%
EV	29%	19%	11%	26%	21%	29%	20%	23%	17%	19%	19%	17%	19%	16%	16%	100%	21%	42%
LOS	20%	16%	11%	24%	21%	29%	14%	10%	12%	18%	6%	6%	8%	19%	16%	21%	100%	31%
M	29%	29%	8%	32%	28%	41%	30%	30%	24%	23%	25%	39%	19%	19%	31%	42%	31%	100%

definitions, their main focus, in the perspective of conceptual evolution of the term. Additionally, I have discussed taxonomy of LO models. Finally, I have presented the keyword-based description of CS research aiming at identifying what terms are most frequently used to characterize this research field.

All extracted facts are treated as the boundary and the context to the main topics to be introduced in the subsequent chapters.

2.8   Research and Exercise Questions

2.1. Outline the role of taxonomies for the analysis of various subjects and understanding of items within the subjects and connect those with learning and knowledge gaining.
2.2. Why it is possible to consider domain analysis as a process of learning?
2.3. Evaluate the taxonomy of LO definitions by comparing with the other taxonomies. Extend the given taxonomy accordingly, taking into account the newest (or missed) references.
2.4. Repeat the same with the LO model taxonomies.
2.5. Consider the ACM and IEEE classification schemes and basic terms to characterize the educational CS research.
2.6. Repeat the experiment we have carried out in identifying the frequency of used terms to characterize the CS educational research.

References

[All97]   L'Allier JJ (1997) Frame of reference: NETg's map to the products, their structure and core beliefs. NetG. http://www.netg.com/research/whitepapers/frameref.asp

[AHH12]   Alharbi A, Henskens F, Hannaford M (2012) Student-centered learning objects to support the self-regulated learning of computer science. Creat Educ 3:773–783

[BBD+14] Burbaite R, Bespalova K, Damaševičius R, Štuikys V Context-aware generative learning objects for teaching computer science

[BC10]   Barker P, Campbell LM (2010) Metadata for learning materials: an overview of existing standards and current developments. Technol Instr Cogn Learn 7(3–4):225–243

[BCD+99] Boss L, Clements P, McGregor J, Northrop L (1999) Fourth product line practice workshop report. SWE Institute, November

[BCS+05] Brown E, Cristea A, Stewart C, Brailsford T (2005) Patterns in authoring of adaptive educational hypermedia: a taxonomy of learning styles. Educ Technol Soc 8(3):77–90

[BDŠ13]   Burbaitė R, Damaševičius R, Štuikys V (2013) Using robots as learning objects for teaching computer science. In: X world conference on computers in education (WCCE'13), Torun, Poland, pp. 103–111

[Blo56]   Bloom BS (1956) Taxonomy of educational objectives. Vol 1: cognitive domain. McKay, New York

[BMO08]   Balatsoukas P, Morris A, O'Brien A (2008) Learning objects update: review and critical approach to content aggregation. Educ Technol Soc 11(2):119–130

[Boy03]   Boyle T (2003) Design principles for authoring dynamic, reusable learning objects. Aust J Educ Technol 19:46–58

[Boy06]   Boyle T (2006) The design and development of second generation learning objects. In: World conference on educational multimedia, hypermedia and telecommunications, Orlando, vol 1, pp 2–12

[Boy09]   Boyle T (2009) Generative learning objects (GLOs): design as the basis for reuse and repurposing. In: First international conference on e-learning and distance learning, Riyadh

[Boy10]   Boyle T (2010) Layered learning design: towards an integration of learning design and learning object perspectives. Comput Educ 54(3):661–668

[BS11]   Burbaite R, Stuikys V (2011) Analysis of learning object research using feature-based models. Information technologies' 2011: proceedings of the 17th international conference on information and software technologies, IT 2011, Kaunas, 27–29 Apr 2011, pp 201–208

[CAM+06]   Convertini V, Albanese D, Marengo A, Marengo V, Scalera M (2006) The OSEL taxonomy for the classification of learning objects. Interdiscip J E-Learn Learn Objects 2(1):125–138

[Chi06]   Chitwood K (2006) 6th annual MERLOT international conference, 8–11 Aug 2006. http://conference.merlot.org/2006/MICO6/MIC06Wednesday/ChitwoodWorkshop. ppt

[Chu07]   Churchill D (2007) Towards a useful classification of learning objects. Educ Technol Res Dev 55(5):479–497

[CISCO03]   Reusable learning object strategy: designing and developing learning objects for multiple learning approaches. http://www.e-novalia.com/materiales/RLOW__07_03.pdf

[Con07]   Conole G (2007) Describing learning activities. Rethinking pedagogy for a digital age: designing and delivering e-learning. RoutledgeFalmer, Oxford, pp 81–91

[Dav97]   Davenport T-H (1997) Information ecology. Oxford University Press, New York

[DPW11]   Dang Q, Pan P, Wang T (2011) A practical approach to design and delivery of courseware for VLE-based learning. Innov Teach Learn Inf Comput Sci 10(3):4–15

[Fin04]   Finlay J (2004) Context-neutral e-learning objects: a tale of two projects. In: The 7th HCI educators workshop: effective teaching and training in HCI, Preston, UK

[GA03]   Gunawardena A, Adamchik V (2003) A customized learning objects approach to teaching programming. ACM SIGCSE Bull 35(3):264

[Goo14]   Goodyear P (2014) Instructional design. Instructional design: international perspectives II: vol I: theory, research, and models: vol II: solving instructional design problems. Routledge, London, p 83

[GRC+04]   García-Valdez JM, Rodriguez-Díaz A, Castañón-Puga M, Cristóbal-Salas A (2004) Adaptive learning objects. In: International conference on artificial intelligence, IC-AI, Las Vegas, USA, vol 4, pp 21–24

[HK09]   Han P, Kramer BJ (2009) Generating interactive learning objects from configurable samples. In: Mobile, hybrid, and on-line learning, ELML'09, IEEE, pp 1–6

[IMC01]   Ip A, Morrison I, Currie M (2001) What is a learning object, technically? In: WebNet, pp 580–586. http://users.tpg.com.au/adslfrcf/lo/learningObject (WebNet2001).pdf

[KCH+90]   Kang K, Cohen S, Hess J, Novak W, Peterson S (1990) Feature-oriented domain analysis (FODA) feasibility study. TR CMU/SEI-90-TR-21, Software Engineering Institute, Carnegie Mellon University

[Kra02]   Krathwohl DR (2002) A revision of Bloom's taxonomy: an overview. Theory Pract 41(4):212–218

[KST08]   Khierbek A, Salloum S, Tannous A (2008) An inference network model for retrieving reusable learning objects. In: 3rd international conference on information and communication technologies: from theory to applications, ICTTA 2008, IEEE, pp 1–5

[Lak87]   Lakoff G (1987) Women, fire, and dangerous things: what categories reveal about the mind. University of Chicago Press, Chicago

[LDH04]   Leeder D, Davies T, Hall A (2004) Reusable learning objects for medical education: evolving a multi-institutional collaboration. http://repub.eur.nl/pub/1230

[LTSC01]   Learning Technology Standards Committee (2001) Draft standard for learning object metadata. IEEE standard 1484.12.1. Institute of Electrical and Electronics Engineers, New York

[McG04]   McGreal R (2004) Learning objects: a practical definition. Int J Inst Technol Distance Learn 9(1):21–32

[Mer00]   Merrill MD (2000) Knowledge objects and mental models. In: IWALT 2000, Palmerston North, pp 244–246

[Mer98]   Merrill MD (1998) Knowledge objects. CBT Solut 2:1–11

[Mey06]   Meyer B (2006) Testable, reusable units of cognition. Computer 39:20–24

[MF04]   Mayes T, de Freitas S (2004) Review of E-learning theories, frameworks and models, JISC E-learning models study report, Joint Information Systems Committee. www.jisc.ac.uk/elp_outcomes.html

[MG03]   Mohan P, Greer J (2003) Reusable learning objects: current status and future directions. In: World conference on educational multimedia, hypermedia and telecommunications, vol 1, pp 257–264

[Mie06]   Mierlus-Mazilu I (2006) Types of learning objects. Int J Comput Internet Manag 14 (SP1):15.1–15.6, Special Issue

[MJ10]   Man H, Jin Q (2010) Putting adaptive granularity and rich context into learning objects. In: 9th international conference on information technology based higher education and training (ITHET), 2010, pp 140–145

[MLB05]   Morales R, Leeder D, Boyle T (2005) A case in the design of generative learning objects (GLOs): applied statistical methods. In: World conference on educational multimedia, hypermedia and telecommunications, Montreal, Canada, vol 1, pp 2091–2097

[Nat12]   Nath J (2012) E-learning methodologies and its trends in modern information technology. J Glob Res Comput Sci 3(4):48–52

[Orr02]   Orrill CH (2002) Learning objects to support inquiry-based, online learning. Instructional use of learning objects. In: Association for Educational Communications and Technology, Bloomington

[OWW+05] Oliver R, Wirski R, Wait L, Blanksby V (2005) Learning designs and learning objects: where pedagogy meets technology. In: Towards sustainable and scalable educational innovations informed by the learning sciences. IOS Press, Amsterdam, pp 330–337

[Par03]   Paris M (2003) Reuse in practice: learning objects and software development. In: Interact, integrate, impact: proceedings of the 20th annual conference of the Australasian Society for Computers in Learning in Tertiary Education (ASCILITE), Adelaide, Australia

[Pol03]   Polsani PR (2003) Use and abuse of reusable learning objects. J Digit inf 3(4). Retrieved from https://journals.tdl.org/jodi/index.php/jodi/article/view/89/88

[Red03]   Redeker GH (2003) An educational taxonomy for learning objects. In: Proceedings of the 3rd IEEE international conference on advanced learning technologies, 2003, Athens, Greece, pp 250–251

[RJR+05] Rossano V, Joy MS, Roselli T, Sutinen E (2005) A taxonomy for definitions and applications of LOs: a metaanalysis of ICALT papers. Educ Technol Soc 8 (4):148–160

[RM13]   Rao AS, Manuja M (2013) DDQ framework for courseware design and development. In: Innovation and technology in education (MITE), 2013 I.E. international conference in MOOC, IEEE, pp 67–70

[RSG10]   Roy D, Sarkar S, Ghose S (2010) A comparative study of learning object metadata, learning material repositories, metadata annotation & an automatic metadata annotation tool. Adv Semant Comput 2:103–126

[SAA+07] Silveira IF, Araújo CF, Amaral LH, Alcântara de Oliveira IC, Schimiguel J, Ledôn MF-P, Ferreira MAGV (2007) Granularity and reusability of learning objects. In: Koohang A, Harman K (eds) Learning objects and instructional design. Informing Science Press, Santa Rosa, pp 139–170

[Sal06]   Salmons JE (2006) Taxonomy of collaborative e-learning. Union Institute & University, Cincinnati

[Sam97]   Sametinger J (1997) Software engineering with reusable components. Springer, Berlin

[ŠB12]   Štuikys V, Burbaite R (2012) Two-stage generative learning objects. In: Information and software technologies, Springer, Berlin/Heidelberg, pp 332–347

[ŠD07]   Štuikys V, Damaševičius R (2007) Towards knowledge-based generative learning objects. Inf Technol Control 36(2):202–212

[ŠD08]   Štuikys V, Damaševičius R (2008) Development of generative learning objects using feature diagrams and generative techniques. Inform Educ 7(2):277–288

[ŠD13]   Štuikys V, Damaševičius R (2013) Meta-programming and model-driven meta-program development: principles, processes and techniques. Springer, London

[SGP+04] Silveira RA, Gomes ER, Pinto VH, Vicari RM (2004) Intelligent learning objects: an agent based approach of learning objects. In: Intelligent tutoring systems. Springer, Berlin/Heidelberg, pp 886–888

[SGS+04] Sicilia MÁ, García E, Sánchez S, Rodríguez E (2004) Describing learning object types in ontological structures: towards specialized pedagogical selection. In: World conference on educational multimedia, hypermedia and telecommunications, vol 1, pp 2093–2097

[SH02]   Sosteric M, Hesemeier S (2002) When is a learning object not an object: a first step towards a theory of learning objects. Int Rev Res Open Distributed Learn 3(2), http://www.irrodl.org/index.php/irrodl/article/view/106/557/

[SS05]   Stamey Jr JW, Saunders BT (2005) Designing intelligent learning objects. In: Fifth IEEE international conference on advanced learning technologies, ICALT 2005, IEEE, pp 323–325

[Str06]   Stracke CM (2006) Interoperability and quality development in e-learning. Overview and reference model for e-learning standards. In: Proceedings of the Asia-Europe e-learning Colloquy, e-ASEM, Seoul

[SVC12]   Sangrà A, Vlachopoulos D, Cabrera N (2012) Building an inclusive definition of e-learning: an approach to the conceptual framework. Int Rev Res Open Distance Learn 13(2):145–159

[VCJ09]   Villalobos JA, Calderon NA, Jiménez CH (2009) Developing programming skills by using interactive learning objects. ACM SIGCSE Bull 41(3):151–155

[VD04]   Verbert K, Duval E (2004) Towards a global architecture for learning objects: a comparative analysis of learning object content models. In: World conference on educational multimedia, hypermedia and telecommunications, vol 1, pp 202–208

[Vla12]   Vlachos E (2012) The spiral-in method for designing and connecting learning objects. In: 4th international conference on intelligent networking and collaborative systems (INCoS), 2012, IEEE, pp 677–681

[Wil00]   Wiley DA (2000) Learning object design and sequencing theory. Ph.D. dissertation, Brigham Young University

Chapter 3
Reuse Framework of the LO Domain

3.1 Introduction

The aim of this chapter is to discuss the LO reusability aspects to the much broader extent that it was done so far. There are many reasons for that. Let us remind some of them. *First*, reuse principles are universal and general to be applicable in many fields. Reuse experience taken from the other domains with a higher maturity level (e.g. hardware, software) can be easily transferred and adapted to e-learning. *Second*, reuse is a very promising approach because of well-defined objectives to design software-oriented educational systems (higher productivity, better quality, shorter time to market). *Third*, reuse might be seen as a very simple and attractive subject if it is considered at the individual level (say a teacher or learner) as the following paradigms: *copy-paste* and *use-as-is*. *Fourth*, reuse is a very complicated area if it is considered at the organization or cross-organizational levels because there should be taken into account both the technical and non-technical (social, pedagogical, economical, organizational, etc.) reuse aspects. These aspects are extremely broad and complex, indicating on managerial, social, technical and other issues.

Finally, it is worth to mention yet another important fact. As a consequence of the aforementioned facts, till now, reuse stands for the area of the extremely intensive study and research in software engineering (see, e.g. the content of tracks in ICSEA 2014 or related events). The latter field might be seen as a source of approved approaches to be applied in e-learning. Therefore, the reuse-based ideas, principles and approaches are also at the focus of CS and educational research communities. If reuse is so important, now the essential question can be raised as follows: how should *reuse be first understood* in a wider scale to enable then *more systematic* studies in CS *e-learning reuse*? Here, I argue again that, for this purpose, there is the need of some framework as a guideline. The next section provides such a framework. I also use the framework in analysis of the related work.

© Springer International Publishing Switzerland 2015
V. Štuikys, *Smart Learning Objects for Smart Education in Computer Science*,
DOI 10.1007/978-3-319-16913-2_3

3.2   A Framework to Better Understanding of Reuse Issues in E-Learning

What is reuse in e-learning? What are the dimensions and scope of reuse in CS education? What are the items we seek to make reusable: models, processes, LOs or a combination of all? When do we need to start taking into account the reuse aspects: *before* LO design, *during* instructional design or at *the use time* only? How can we measure reusability and then, on this basis, be able to enhance it? Despite of intuitiveness of the term itself, the answers to these questions are not as simple as might be seen from the first glance. Therefore, I first analyse *the known reuse definitions* in the field and then introduce the reuse framework and discuss some issues outlined by the framework. After that, using the framework, I analyse the related work trying to reveal the current state of the field and to identify those topics that are needed for further research with LO reusability in mind as it is stated by the formulated questions.

In this context, we need to extract knowledge to understand the current level of reuse maturity models in three dimensions (strategic, methodological and techno-logical). Such a vision is helpful because (1) LO domain is commonly recognized as the heart of e-learning in general, (2) the LO concept is accepted and its role well understood for CS teaching too, (3) the LO domain is continuously evolving in horizontal (meaning in general) and vertical dimensions (meaning in CS) and (4) a framework can be seen as a taxonomy-based approach; therefore, it is fundamental in many aspects (knowledge and artefacts systemizing, standardizing, sharing, gaining and teaching).

3.2.1   Definition of the Terms

Though reusability is gaining ever-increasing focus in different disciplines to develop systems or provide training (software engineering, system engineering [WVF10], knowledge engineering [SBF98], e-learning engineering [MH05], etc.), however, the concept reuse is often poorly understood, and the practice has not been as effective as expected. Thus, we need to look at the concept itself more thoroughly. One can meet in the literature the use of three related words with the same prefix and root as follows: *reuse*, *reusable* and *reusability*. The first is the general term having two forms: as verb 'use again or more than once' and as a noun 'the action of using something again' (English Oxford Dictionary). The word 'reusable' usually pertains to an artefact or asset (object, component, model, process, framework, etc.). The word 'reusability' defines the property as related to a reusable artefact.

Prieto-Diaz [Pri89], one of the software reuse guru, defines *reuse* as 'the use of previously acquired concepts or objects in a new situation, it involves encoding development information at different levels of abstraction, storing this representation for future reference, matching of new and old situations, duplication of already developed objects and actions, and their adaptation to suit new requirements'. In other words, *software reuse* is the process of incorporating into a new product any of the previously developed assets: tested code, developed requirements specifications, test plans, data and procedures. This process can be summarized as follows: recognition, decomposition/abstraction, classification, selection/retrieval, specialization/adaptation and composition/deployment [Hem93]. Reuse engineering can be described as the application of a disciplined, systematic, quantifiable approach to the development, operation and maintenance of software where reuse is a primary consideration.

I have consciously started defining reusability terms on the software ground. The main reason is as follows. In e-learning, there is a great belief that reusable LOs will bring to education and instructional design the same improvements (in terms of quality and productivity) as object-oriented programming did in software development [Dou01]. Even more, Jones has observed yet in 2005 the shift of the e-learning community toward creating an LO economy [Jon05]. In the sense of this shift, highly reusable LOs stand for the ground to create the truly LO economy through the development of a worldwide market. As a consequence, the reusability concepts are extremely popular and widely discussed in e-learning. However, to give precise definitions of the used terms is not an easy task, though a great deal of efforts and trials were taken by many respective authors.

Below I present a scheme that suggests not so much achieving precision in definitions; rather it focuses more on *attributes* of the terms (reuse, reusability, reusable) to which the terms pertain. In our view, we need to focus on general attributes such as *what-why-how* (of course, to some degree). Depending on the concrete context of reusability understanding, we need to ask *what* is an item to be reusable: *LO itself, the process* where an LO is to be used and reused or both? *Why do* we need reuse or what is the purpose of reuse: only the search and then *use-as-is* of the retrieved items or the use *through adaptation and modification? How* can we achieve reuse objectives having in mind a set of influential attributes: LO models, structural characteristics (granularity level), context, pedagogy, environments and reuse scope (individual or organizational level)? *How* can *reuse* truly ensure the great promises of productivity and quality?

We have developed the scheme first on the basis of our experience in teaching and researching reuse-based approaches in CS [ŠD13]. Furthermore, we have also found an approval of this vision (though implicitly) in the plethora of e-learning papers. Here, I have selected only the two as the most representative papers to support our vision.

The first considers LO reuse as a *four-tier model* using the triad of terms: *use-reuse-repurpose* [HP05]. Huddlestone and Pike give the following definitions of the terms [HP05]:

- Use – *the application or employment of a learning object within a learning event, for the purpose it was originally designed*

- Reuse – *the use of an existing object in a new learning event without any modification to its instructional treatment, context or content*
- Repurpose – *the use of an existing object in a new learning event with little to no modification to its instructional treatment, context or content.*

We will discuss their model in another context later.

Pitkänen and Silander (authors of the second selected paper [PS04]) present a slightly different vision as compared to the first paper. They discuss criteria for *pedagogical reusability* of LOs enabling the adaptation and individualized learning process. They do not make the distinction between reuse and repurpose treating the modification or adaptation similarly as the reuse activity in software (see definitions above). Their understanding of the LOs reusability model focuses on the multidimensional vision: content, context, pedagogical context, technical context and learning situation. On this basis, by introducing 3 levels for each constituent, the authors have formulated and approved 9 criteria to define pedagogical reusability of LOs.

Now, having a multidimensional vision to LO reusability, we are able to move in more details of the reuse framework.

3.2.2 Three-Layered Reuse Framework

The first observation is that in e-learning there is no unified view to the reusability issues. Therefore, systematization (e.g. through introducing some frameworks) is important. In our view, such a framework should specify at least two extremes: holistic perspective and individualistic perspective. Figure 3.1 outlines the three-layered model to define the holistic perspective. Here, reuse is seen as a strategy at the highest level, as a methodology at the middle level and as a technology at the lowest level. The highest level aims at describing and evaluating not only the current state and trends in the field, but it also provides a road map of how the

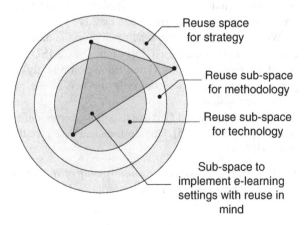

Fig. 3.1 Three-layered framework to deal with reuse in e-learning

Reuse space for strategy

Reuse sub-space for methodology

Reuse sub-space for technology

Sub-space to implement e-learning settings with reuse in mind e-learning and LO domains should evolve in the long-term period by considering and evaluating as many aspects as possible. The holistic vision, among other things, includes the already known initiatives with many bodies and organizations involved worldwide. The vision is about a systematic reuse in the way to creating the truly LO economy for the social activity such as learning and teaching.

The intermediate level of the introduced model should be considered in a broader sense, that is, with software engineering in mind. There are a variety of methodologies that can be called as *reuse driven*. Here, I name only the two as more popular ones: model-driven engineering [Sch06] and product line engineering (PLE) [Bos00] (also known as software product families). The basis of the first methodology is the OMG approach [OMG03]. It uses the *object* as a primary concept and focuses more on high-level modelling and model transformations, whereas the second typically operates with features (i.e. externally visible charac-teristics of programs that can be recombined in different ways to achieve different versions of program functionality), uses the *feature* concept and feature-based models and focuses more on architectural aspects of software products as systems of systems [AK09].

The PLE methodology focuses on maximizing reuse in software product lines (i.e. families of programs that share common assets). First, the architecture of the product family is created based on product commonalities and planned variabilities. Then, different product variants are derived from this architecture by reusing components and structures as much as possible and using a variety of component-based and generative reuse techniques [BBC+01].

Though both methodologies are not mutually exclusive with many common features, they are treated as separate approaches in the literature. To achieve *the benefits* of *systematic reuse* in creating new systems, the approaches (especially the second one) appeal to the *thorough understanding of domains* to be implemented through analysis and modelling. The latter is seen as a systematic activity to extract artefacts and knowledge needed for creating new systems. Sometimes domain analysis is treated as a *continuous process of learning* to gain and transfer knowl-edge. In this social aspect, learning in schools or universities is just the same as acquiring knowledge about a domain by an engineer or analyst. Of course, in each case, there are different goals, different actors and different products.

Thus, why not try to use ideas and features (models, methods) from the software domain that are common or might be treated as common, for example, after some adaptation for e-learning? The aim is to enrich and enforce the e-learning domain with well-proven models taken from the related fields, which are relevant to e-learning. Though this process has been started far ago and is continuously expanding, in our view, till now such potential is not yet exploited as fully as it might be. Therefore, this is also a reason why we are speaking about the reuse framework here.

The LO domain is relatively new. It is highly heterogeneous. There is no consensus on some important methodological issues such as the definition of the LO, taxonomies on the LO reuse attributes and inconsistency of LO repositories. There are also a variety of learning theories to be taken into account with LO use and reuse. There are a huge number of proposals of LO models to enforce reusability. There is a diversity of LO types and instructional design approaches used. The community working on those issues is extremely wide. In the large, the intermediate layer can be seen as the source to provide reuse-based knowledge for the rest of the layers as it will be shown in more details in Sect. 3.6.2.

Now we approach to the third component of our framework model. Here, by reuse as a technology, I mean the educational technology-driven processes that are supported by adequate tools. As the e-learning domain is indeed heterogeneous and the learning services hold the unquestable priority in the various societies world-wide, there is a huge field of educational tools. Often we refer to a kit of educational tools used in e-learning as an educational environment. The educational processes and tools are highly reusable items. When educational tools are being mastered by teachers and learners, the tools can be used and reused in multiple ways in multiple contexts to support learning. They are so reusable and to such a high reusability extent that we usually stop talking about them as reusable items. We do that because we use tools as *black boxes* taking into account the external view, that is, we focus on input-output data only with the full ignorance of what is within the boxes. This level, when first being adequately mastered and then properly applied, is the *truly matured reuse level*.

Finally, we return to the individualistic reuse perspective. In contrast to holistic reuse, by introducing the term *individualistic reuse,* we aim at narrowing the reuse scope to the level of individual or small groups of individuals. We do that knowing the following facts. Let us ask any individual (course designer, teacher or even a *studious* learner) how many times he/she was *changing*, *adapting*, *simplifying* or *extending – simply speaking, improving –* his/her previous or new teaching materials (coursework for students) over some period of time? For teachers, for example, this period might be measured in a dozen of years and by many trials to repeat the process seeking for improvements. Therefore, one should clearly understand that those activities are *reuse activities*. The individuals are involved in doing so through intuition, and thus they accept reuse in an ad hoc *manner*, even without any primary knowledge of the reuse potential. Another question is how much efforts were needed for an actor to achieve some prescribed objectives of the activities?

I hope that this vision will be helpful to community researchers (basically to those who are not so much reuse-based littered) to gaining a more systematic interest in studying and researching his/her field with reuse perspective in mind. We will continue our discussion on the introduced model more extensively in the three subsequent subsections.

3.3   Reuse as a Strategy

We refer to this reuse understanding level as a wide-scale or *horizontal reuse*. As it covers the whole e-learning domain and all activities performed by the huge communities, it is reasonable to narrow the topic by introducing the term *vertical reuse* (also borrowed from software reuse [Sam97]). Here, by vertical reuse, we mean reusability aspects within a *concrete organization* providing educational activities such as CS learning and teaching, educational research in CS or LOs. Note that vertical reuse is more relevant to the intermediate layer of the introduced framework as it will be detailed later. Note also that there is an *evident interaction* between horizontal and vertical reuse (e.g. many artefacts are equally spreading in both horizontal and vertical dimensions through conferences and other forums; there are also many CS LOs that reside within the general-purpose repositories; we treat the latter as a product of *the horizontal reuse processes* here).

Now we are able to formulate the aim of this analysis. It is not our intention to consider horizontal reuse in detail. Rather, our aim is (1) to summarize main activities and their products as they are seen and referenced in the literature on e-learning and (2) to outline *general issues to characterize the LO* domain from the reuse perspective as compared to reuse understanding in SWE. We do that because, at the very abstract conceptual level, we see *some analogy* between LOs and software products (later this vision will be supported by references). The book [Lim98], for example, presents software reuse as two large sub-domains: non-technical and technical (it will be discussed later). The first sub-domain includes a long list of fields contributing to reuse as follows: *adoption, economics, strategy, personnel, organization, metrics, marketing, legal* and *manufacturing*. Though all these are referred to as activities at an organizational level, many of them can be moved to a higher level, that is, cross-organizational, and considered as a topic of horizontal reuse.

Now let us return to the e-learning domain. As our literature review shows (see Sect. 3.6), currently many small to medium educational and research organizations do not declare on having *explicit reuse plans* as a strategy to implement their e-learning initiatives. Therefore, their reuse maturity model could be regarded as restricted by ad hoc reuse only. Only large worldwide organizations such as IEEE Learning Technologies Standard Committee, IMS Global E-Learning Consortium, Cisco Systems and Advanced Distributed Learning (ADL) initiative by the US Department of Defense (to name a few) are capable of providing activities for creating a truly LO economy as envisioned by Downes [Dow02] and have achieved the reuse maturity level that might be treated, perhaps to some extent only, as *systematic reuse* as we could reason from our restricted analysis.

In general, systematic reuse can be seen as a strategic goal for both organizations and cross-organizational levels. To achieve this goal in e-learning, the previously stated list of SWE activities might be helpful. However, trying to adapt these activities for e-learning, we first need to take into account not only similarities, but also differences of the two domains. Social aspects, such as extremely wide learner profiles, and a variety of psychology-driven pedagogic theories used in e-learning are two most important factors that enable to make a clear distinction of e-learning from other (e.g. software) domains.

The most evident activities at the strategical level are initiatives to creating and maintaining LO-related standards, researching to resolve some inconsistency among different standards, creating LO repositories to support wide-scale reuse, researching interoperability issues and many others. Various organizations along with numerous volunteers are involved in those activities. In large, this level being independent upon a concrete context governs the whole e-learning domain (see Sect. 3.6.1, for more details).

3.4   Reuse as a Methodology

Researchers and other actors within the community show an increasingly high effort and attention to the role of reusability aspects. However, again, there is no consensus on different reuse aspects. The main reason of the situation is that we so far, perhaps, do not thoroughly understand the reuse potential.

As in case of software, the methodological support should cover *all processes* to which LOs reusability pertains. Roughly, these reuse-based processes can be categorized into two large groups: content oriented and social oriented (they are also seen at the strategical level). In order to gain the actual benefits of reuse at the methodological level, both activities should be harmonized adequately. On this account, Sloep wrote [Slo04]: 'If we manage to embed *reusable resource* into *reusable scenarios*, then we've made a significant step toward creating a flourishing LO economy'. By reusable scenario the author means the creation of *a pedagogical meta-language* to describe such categories as 'activities', 'environments', 'roles', 'properties' and 'plays'.

To emphasize the role and complexity of LO reuse at a wider methodological level, the same author concludes: 'This is a first step. It will certainly not suffice to guarantee success. It takes actual people, instructional designers, developers and teachers, to get out and travel on the reuse road. People need incentives and rewards to get moving. They need to overcome their fears and anxieties. Organizations need to adapt. We've only just started to survey these social, economical, psychological and organization issues, let alone solve them. There still is a long way to go'.

Indeed, the understanding of overall LO reusability aspects is a great challenge for all players (strategy makers, instructional designers and teachers). However, this understanding may come through well-planned activities such as analysis and modelling of the LO domain, specification of LO *for reuse* and *with reuse* in mind (meaning creation and use of LO repositories, local libraries), instructional *design for reuse* and instructional *design with reuse*, development of the paradigms with quality and reusability measurements and assessments, deployment of the paradigms and evaluation of the impact of reusable LO on teaching and learning processes in the whole. This support, in fact, comes from two main sources: from the related domains such as software and from the internal activities within the e-learning community (individual and organized research, conferences, journal publications, forums on methodological issues at different levels, etc.). The first source has been already outlined to some extent. It should be clearly understood that the real value of the applied methodology comes only if it is implemented in the tools, and those tools are used in real teaching and learning settings.

3.5   Reuse as a Technology

By the term *reuse as a technology*, we mean tools that support *effective reusability* in searching, designing, generating, adapting and using LOs. As the LO domain is highly heterogeneous, the technological support is even more diverse. Due to this diversity, it is very difficult or even impossible to overview the aspects of educational tools that might be considered as effective instruments to support reusability. Therefore, I restrict myself only with those tools that, to the largest extent, relate to our approach. The concept we discuss throughout the book relates to generative reuse (this kind of reuse forms the technological basis of smart LOs as it was stated in Chap. 1). My vision is based on two strategic reuse goals:

1. *To write manually a new code as less as possible*
2. *To use the existing code and tools as much as possible*

Here, I use the term *code* as an LO to teach CS topics. What are the basic tools that support this strategic vision? In other words, what are basic tools that support generative reuse? I restrict the dealing with only those tools that are directly related and used to support the smart LO (SLO) concept. I categorize them into two large groups: (A) code-manipulating tools and (B) model-manipulating or transformation tools. This categorization, in fact, is relative because models are or should be expressed by some descriptive code in order to be executable (otherwise, the value of models would be highly restricted). Nevertheless, there is a clear, discriminating line between those categories. Typically category A represents tools that operate with objects which are represented at the lower level of abstraction, while tools of category B operate with objects represented at the higher level of abstraction. This categorization reflects the general trend of computational technologies: the evident shift to the higher level of abstraction in representing systems due to their continuous complexity growth. Category A includes *parsers, analysers, compilers, code generators* and *program partial evaluation tools* (specializers) to name a few. Category B includes *compiler-compilers, various modelling* and *transformation tools*. The latter class of tools is highly dependent upon the model types, transformation goals, specification languages used, etc.

The key to study these approaches is first to look at the program transformation taxonomy [Win04] and model transformation taxonomy [MCG06]. This is left as a separate research topic.

3.6   Literature Review: How the Introduced Reuse Framework Is Supported?

3.6.1   Context and Reuse

To be reusable the item first should be usable. Thus, reusability can be thought of as a property that extends the scope of usability. The extension of usability depends on multiple factors. Perhaps *context* stands for one of the most influential factors in this process. Context can be seen as a mediator or the source of additional information that is important for a larger usability and reuse. Intuitively, we can think about and deal with any item (object, process, component, etc.) as if it is the structure containing two parts: the *base part* and the *context part*.

Due to the importance of the context in e-learning and also due to the wideness of applications, where context is at the focus, there is no common understanding what is the essence of the term with multiple definitions proposed so far. Also, there is an observable trend to define context either independently upon the application domain [Dey01] or, on the contrary, introducing some context aspects that are relevant to a particular application. As stated in [VMO+12], one of the most cited definitions of context is the definition of Dey et al. [Dey01]. The definition treats context as 'any information that can be used to characterize the situation of an entity. An entity is a person, place or object that is considered relevant to the interaction between a user and an application, including the user and applications themselves'.

This definition is referenced extensively within various application domains, including researchers in technology-enhanced learning (TEL) [Sch07, VMO+12]. Dourish, for example, indicates that context has a dual origin: (1) technical and (2) social science based [Dou04]. From a social perspective, Dourish argues that context is not something that describes a setting or situation, but rather a feature of interaction. Researchers in TEL argue that this user-centred emphasis on factors affecting an activity is precisely what makes this notion of context meaningful for learning. From a technical perspective, there is a need to define context in a more specific way as an *operational term* [Win01]. To operationalize context, there are attempts [SAW94, DAS01] to define context by enumerating categories as follows: *computing context* (such as network connectivity, communication costs, communication bandwidth, etc.), *user context* (such as the user's profile, location, social situation, etc.), *physical context* (such as noise level, traffic condition, etc.), *time-related context* and *task-related context* [VMO+12]. The Zimmermann et al. [ZLO07] operational view to the context lists the following fundamental context categories: *individuality*, *activity*, *location*, *time* and *relations*. Individuality is subdivided into four elements: *natural entity*, *human entity*, *artificial entity* and *group entity*. This definition is perhaps one of the most comprehensive context definitions to date.

In TEL, such enumerations have also been proposed as an attempt to define the context of the learner or teacher as an operational term. Many enumerations are defined for mobile learning applications. For example, Berri et al. [BBA06] distinguish between technical and learner context elements. The first category deals with the technical aspects of mobile devices, their operational environment and constraints. The second category defines the learner context elements (e.g. aims and objectives of the learner, prerequisites, background, current level of understanding and subject domain). It is also essential to capture *interactions* between the *environment*, the *user*, their *tasks* and other *users*. The environment constitutes computing, time and physical context characteristics.

3.6.2   Context, Reuse Models and Processes

Desmoulins and Azouaou [DA06] aim at defining a context ontology of the teacher's personal annotation, in order to use it in a context-aware annotation tool 'MemoNote'. They define the uses of active and passive contexts in the tool (annotation ontologies selection, annotation memorization and pattern definition and selection) to develop the complete teacher's context annotation ontology using the classical method specified for Protégé.

The *content granularity* and *context information* are related. Both are important factors to the efficiency and reusability of learning objects (LOs). The context information, for example, is necessary to facilitate the discovery and reuse of LOs stored in global repositories or local libraries. Typically, LOs are incorporated into repositories without the context information. Users have to do some extension of the LO descriptions to fit their special use. Therefore, Man and Jin [MJ10] introduce a context-rich paradigm, the related service-driven tagging strategy and a context model of LOs. Their context model realizes the adaptive granularity of the content object to support the evolution from resource objects to LOs.

Huddlestone and Pike introduce a four-tier reusability model for making reuse happen in practice within organizations [HP05]. They argue that the factors affecting the viability of object reuse are the properties of the object itself (such as structural reuse and contextual reuse) and the organization's preparedness to undertake LO reuse (operational reuse and strategic reuse). They define *structural reusability* as a function of how the object has been engineered. *Contextual reusability* is determined by the applicability of the object to new learning events that are influential on the potential audience size. *Operational reusability* has dependencies on organizational culture, personnel, procedures and technology. *Strategic reusability* is defined as a function of organizational strategy that may favor systematic or opportunistic reuse of objects. In fact, the four-tier reuse model covers all layers of our framework; however, do it differently as follows: strategic layer, partially; methodological layer, fully (with some extensions such as contextual reusability); and technological level, implicitly.

Jones and Boyle [JB07] introduce the concept of LO patterns borrowed from design patterns, the well-known design technique in SWE. They show how existing LOs, that have previously proved to be successful, can be used to derive patterns that could be reused in the design of new LOs to master of computer programming by learners who had had no previous experience in the subject. Thus, the reuse of successful LO design has the potential for real pedagogical benefits. In a similar way to their use in object-oriented software design, patterns for the design of LOs can be derived from successful existing learning resources; these patterns can then be reused in the design of the new ones. This paper describes the LOs that were designed to aid new computer programmers and how patterns were extracted from those LOs. This results in a small LO pattern catalogue that has the potential for reuse in the construction of new LOs.

In another paper, Jones [Jon05] argues that in order for the process of constructing courses from LOs to be feasible, first they are to be designed for reuse. He also states that there is little done in designing LOs for reuse. Aspects of cohesion, coupling and freedom from specific contexts can be used in designs to help ensuring that LOs are reusable, and these aspects can be captured as *the design patterns* that may be employed to produce reusable designs for LOs. On the other hand, the requirements for reuse may be in conflict with those for effective learning. Therefore, the patterns used must ensure that the LOs constructed are *adaptable* to different contexts and remain pedagogically sound within those contexts. The paper shows how patterns can be used to create learning resources that are both *reusable* and *adaptable*.

Merriënboer and Boot formulate two kinds of obstacles that limit the reuse potential: the relatively *small obstacles* for reuse and relatively *large obstacles* for reuse [MB05]. The first group relates to the metadata problem, the arrangement problem and the exchange problem. The second relates to the context problem, the pedagogical function problem and the correspondence problem. As a possible solution to overcome both small and large obstacles to reuse, the authors propose an integrative approach that highlights (i) *re-editing instead of reuse*, (ii) *intermediate instead of final products*, (iii) *templates instead of instantiations* and (iv) *technical automation of what can be automated*. Finally, they suggest reconciling the fields of learning technologies and instructional design.

Mierlus-Mazilu [Mie06] analyses the Codewitz LOs as reusable items to help students to understand programming structures more easily. A Codewitz LO can cover any specific programming problem in any programming language as well as the problem-solving logic at the algorithmic level. Any LO focuses on one specific learning goal. Each LO has to be independent, without links to other objects or resources to ensure the real reusability of the LO.

The exploratory study [AHH11] aims at getting the insights into the characteristics of CS LOs and to study different factors related to them. These factors include growth over time, user ratings and personal collections. The initial source for the study is the MERLOT (Multimedia Educational Resource for Learning and Online Teaching) repository which contains many LOs under different disciplines. The study concludes with recommendations on the need for improving the quality of CS LOs.

Allen and Mugisa [AM10] focus on challenges related to the learning resource reusability and interoperability. In regard to the challenges, they present a theory of

LOs, including the Object-Oriented Generic Learning Object Model – OOGLOM. Also, they propose the UML-based models to illustrate OOGLOM as well as to illustrate how it provides interoperability.

The paper [BS11] analyses LOs from the reusability perspective, aiming to better understand the reuse dimension in e-learning and how to handle some reuse issues of LOs more effectively. The paper introduces feature-based modelling concepts borrowed from SWE for analysis, which outlines dominating factors (features) and the way they affect reusability of LOs. The content/context forming factors, such as content granularity, context independence, multiple content/context mappings and accumulative and flexible content updating and changing, are also at the focus. Based on knowledge extracted from the analysis, authors reconsider feature-based context and content models to analyse and to understand LOs research.

Cardinaels [Car07] introduces a reuse-based *dynamic learning object life cycle* for the courseware development, in which the dynamic character of the metadata is the key issue. Those metadata help to enhance the LO reusability because the metadata can contain much richer information. The paper also proposes a frame-work of automatic metadata generation for LOs to overcome the problems with manual indexing. Within this framework, metadata is generated automatically taking into account different sources of information that are available in the different phases of the life cycle. Examples are the LOs themselves, user feedback, relationships with other LOs and so on. At the core of this framework is a formal model of LO metadata. This model defines how metadata can be associated with LOs and how the metadata from different sources can be combined to overcome conflicts between sources. The formal model includes the notion of context aware-ness of LO metadata.

To be effective, a learning process must be adapted to the student's context. The latter should be described at least from the pedagogical, technological and learning perspectives. In this regard, Abarca et al. [AAB+06] state that the current e-learning approaches either fail to provide learning experiences within rich contexts, thus hampering the learning process, or provide extremely contextualized content that is highly coupled with context information, barring their reuse in some other context. Therefore, they discuss the context *decoupling* from the content as much as possible so that the latter can be reused and adapted to the context changes. This approach extends the LOM standard by enriching the content context, thereby allowing e-learning platforms to dynamically compose, reuse and adapt the content provided by third parties (i.e. providers of LOs). The paper also presents three context models along with a multi-agent-based e-learning platform that composes and adapts extended LOs according to learner's context changes.

To be possible to reuse LO, it is necessary to know its context of use and what learning outcomes can be achieved with it. Otherwise, LO reuse will be limited to the LO developers who know how to successfully apply it. To avoid that limitation, Azevedo et al. [ACC08] present a framework that describes the LO in relation to one or more learning scenarios that incorporate it. Teachers can then choose the most suitable scenario for a particular learning situation.

3.6.3 Reuse and Quality

Though the meaning of LO reuse can be captured easily, it is not so with the reuse definition and measurement. The paradigm of LO aims at facilitating the managements of the massive amount of educational resources available. Enabling users relying on this paradigm to use high-quality pieces of knowledge within different contexts represents a key challenge. Therefore, when designing LOs, reusability and quality must be a key consideration. Also, metrics to help measuring the quality and reusability represent a major issue. In this regard, Cuadrado and Sicilia [CS05] discuss the applicability of metrics borrowed from the field of SWE, providing analogies for several metrics that can be given an interpretation in terms of LOs. The other paper [CLF+09] expects the appearance of specific metrics for LOs that should be probably based on extended and improved metadata. In the meantime, authors attempt to bridge this gap by analysing and developing adapted metrics for LOs, based on existing metrics used in SWE.

The major bottleneck for end users is finding an appropriate LO in terms of content quality and usage. Chawla et al. [CGS12] state that the existing various approaches for evaluating LOs in the form of evaluation tools and metrics are either qualitative, i.e. based on human review, or are not supported by the empirical evidence. Therefore, they study the impact of current evaluation tools and metrics on quality of LOs and propose a new quantitative system LOQES that automatically evaluates the LO in terms of defined parameters so as to give assurance regarding quality and value.

Another paper [ANK10] considers a framework to evaluate the information quality of e-learning systems to support the needs of the systems designers, providers and users. The framework includes (i) 14 information quality attributes that are grouped in three quality dimensions, intrinsic, contextual representation and accessibility, (ii) original questionnaire data and (iii) factor analysis to support conclusions.

3.6.4 Generative LO Reuse vs. Component-Based LO Reuse

As it was stated, in SWE two general reuse approaches, namely, generative reuse and component-based reuse, are widely discussed and researched. Before the appearance of works of Boyle, Morales and their colleagues, there was the only one reuse vision (i.e. component-based reuse) in e-learning domain. Since the years 2003–2004, due to the mentioned contribution, we can speak explicitly about generative reuse in the e-learning domain too. The generative LOs is not something exclusive and denying component-based LOs, rather they extend the component-based reuse with new technological capabilities in creating the content semi-automatically or even automatically. We do not continue the discussion on this topic here, because (1) this topic was already was discussed in Sect. 3.2.2 and (2) it will be discussed in the subsequent chapters in the other contexts.

3.6.5   Systematic Reuse vs. Ad Hoc Reuse

In the paper [DLP+12], Drira et al. introduce a model-driven approach (MDA) to construct the technology-enhanced learning (TEL) systems. They argue that the approach addresses the limits of Learning Technology Standards (LTS), such as SCORM and IMS-LD. Although these standards ensure the interoperability of TEL systems across different learning management systems (LMS), they are generic and lack expressiveness. In addition, the use of LTS limits designers to using a compliant LMS. MDA addresses these limits by allowing *pedagogic modelling based on specific modelling languages* and by ensuring interoperability across LMS *based on model transformations*. Authors propose the system, named ACoMoD, to help designers to bridge the gap between pedagogic modelling and LMS specifications based on graphic and interactive model transformations. Their approach, implemented with a tool called Gen-COM, enables designers to choose more effective LMS tools, based on a contextual recommendation of the best practice for the LMS tool use.

Fernandes et al. [FLD+12] consider how to improve students' performances on the basis of detection and adjustment of students' learning styles. They present an innovative approach for student modelling through probabilistic learning style combination. Their approach gradually and constantly adjusts the student model, taking into account students' performances, obtaining a fine-tuned student model.

The next two representative papers reflect the common trend in e-learning to use *advanced software engineering techniques*. For example, Dalmon et al. [DBB+12] propose the system to create Interactive Learning Modules (iLM) which provide key functionalities to facilitate the teacher's work. To build the system, the domain engineering approach (DEA) in the form of *the software family* is applied. Furthermore, this paper presents the core features of existing systems and describes the method used to produce an application framework and how to instantiate it. Restructuration of existing iLM using the proposed DEA is reported with initial high gains in productivity and system quality.

Diez et al. [DDA12] consider reusability as one of the most important qualities of e-learning systems. The paper recognizes that 'reusability refers to prospective and future usage scenarios', resulting in difficulties to manage and achieve reuse without the use of a systematic approach. Therefore, their approach focuses on the *Domain Analysis* (DA) paradigm. DA relies on the definition of an information model that compiles knowledge from different information sources in order to address the analysis of a new system in the domain. The application of DA to a specific context, such as e-learning systems, requires explicit design artefacts that lead the domain-modelling process. This paper presents an approach, based on *feature modelling*, specially conceived to apply the DA paradigm to the e-learning context.

3.7   Summary, Evaluation and Conclusion

Reuse is a buzzword in the literature. It can be met in a variety of disciplines such as software and computer engineering. It gained a huge popularity in e-learning too, almost since the introduction and use of the learning object concept. Though the meaning of the term *reuse* can be conceived intuitively, the understanding of its actual weight and role is not a simple and easy task as it might be seen from the first glance. The evidence of that comes, for example, if one tries to look at (or to study with some specific focus) a huge amount of papers and books on reuse. Therefore, the first question (after the initial intuitive understanding of the term itself) that could be asked by anyone who starts the journey in this field is as follows: What is the main reuse goal and objectives? The answer perhaps is the same for any discipline in which reuse is at the focus. We present the answer taken from the software domain: reuse aims at *better quality*, *higher productivity* and *shorter time to market* of products created using the reuse-based approaches. In pursuing the goal and trying to describe reuse in large, we have proposed a framework to understand the reuse issues. We have presented this reuse vision as the 3R paradigm: *reuse as a strategy*, *reuse as a methodology* and *reuse as a technology*.

Reuse as a strategy refers to the vision that defines the known cross-organizational worldwide activities such as standardization and systematization toward creating the truly LO economy. Reuse as a Methodology comprises activities at the intermediate level, i.e. those activities that are carried out within large organizations providing systematic researching and teaching activities in e-learning with reuse in mind. Finally, Reuse as a Technology is understood as the use of adequate tools that support a variety of reuse-oriented processes related to e-learning and teaching. In fact, all parts of the framework are dependent in the following sense: Strategy also includes Methodology and the latter also includes Technology. In other words, the framework describes two-way information streams: from the highest level to the lowest one and vice versa.

Though the analysis was restricted, I hope that (1) it gave some evidence for the reader on the correctness and usefulness of the introduced framework; (2) the analysis also has shown the direction toward which e-learning community is moving now and how it interprets reusability. This road leads to the systematic reuse (i.e. planned, predetermined, pursuing strategic goals, involving not only a solitary actor, but the related groups of actors and perhaps different organizations and bodies). Researchers within the e-learning community already recognize the role and the need of applying *the domain analysis and domain modelling* approaches. There is no other way to implement a *systematic reuse* as using these approaches. The e-learning domain analysis and modelling is not only the technological activity, but to the larger extent, the social activity. It can be also seen as a continuous learning process carried out on the basis of *extracting, approving, representing, applying* and *sharing new knowledge* through analysis.

With respect to the aim of the book, the topic of this chapter completes the motivation of our approach, because it is highly reuse driven. Therefore, I start the next stage of Part One with the analysis and modelling of the CS teaching domain.

3.8 Research and Exercise Questions

3.1. Explain the meaning of the terms: reuse, reusability and reusable.
3.2. Analyse the following items as candidates for reuse: LOs, LO models, learning scenarios and processes. What is the tool reusability about?
3.3. Learn what is the role of LO granularity in reuse.
3.4. Explain the meaning of the terms: design for reuse and design with reuse as they are understood in software engineering, for example, using the literature [Sem98] or any other available.
3.5. Discuss and research the applicability of terms *design-for-reuse* and *design-with-reuse* terms in e-learning domain to teach CS.
3.6. Once again analyse the introduced framework. Extract more information to support each part of the framework: reuse as strategy, reuse as methodology and reuse as technology.
3.7. Research modelling paradigms in CS learning and teaching.
3.8. Research analysis paradigms in CS learning and teaching.
3.9. What is the scope of reuse in e-learning and in CS teaching and learning?
3.10. What is the essence of component-based reuse in e-learning?
3.11. What is the essence of generative reuse in e-learning?
3.12. Explain why more and more software-based approaches migrate and are adapted to e-learning domain.

References

[AAB+06] Abarca MG, Alarcon RA, Barria R, Fuller D (2006) Context-based e-learning composition and adaptation. In: On the move to meaningful internet systems 2006: OTM 2006 workshops. Springer, Berlin/Heidelberg, pp 1976–1985
[ACC08] Azevedo I, Carrapatoso E, Carvalho CV (2008) A framework to scaffold the reuse of learning objects. In: Advanced learning technologies, 2008. ICALT'08. 8th IEEE international conference on advanced learning. Santander, Cantabria, pp 39–40
[AHH11] Alharbi A, Henskens F, Hannaford M (2011) Computer science learning objects. In: IEEE international conference on e-education, entertainment and e-management. Jakarta, pp 326–328
[AK09] Apel S, Kästner C (2009) An overview of feature-oriented software development. J Object Technol 8(5):49–84
[AM10] Allen CA, Mugisa EK (2010) Improving learning object reuse through OOD: a theory of learning objects. J Object Technol 9(6):51–75
[ANK10] Alkhattabi M, Neagu D, Cullen A (2010) Information quality framework for e-learning systems. Knowl Manag E-Learning Int J 2(4):340–362

[BBA06]   Berri J, Benlamri R, Atif Y. Ontology-based framework for context-aware mobile learning. Proceedings of the international conference on wireless communication and mobile computing. Vancouver, Canada, pp 1307–1310

[BBC+01]   Butler G, Batory DS, Czarnecki K, Eisenecker UW (2001) Generative techniques for product lines, In: ICSE'01: Proceedings of the 23rd international conference on software engineering, IEEE Computer Society, 2001, Toronto, Canada

[Bos00]   Bosch J (2000) Design and use of software architectures: adopting and evolving a product-line approach. Pearson Education, Reading

[BS11]   Burbaite R, Stuikys V (2011) Analysis of learning object research using feature-based models. In: Information technologies' 2011, proceedings of the 17th international conference on information and software technologies, Lithuania, pp 201–208

[Car07]   Cardinaels K (2007) A dynamic learning object life cycle and its implications for automatic metadata generation

[CGS12]   Chawla S, Gupta N, Singla RK (2012) LOQES: model for evaluation of learning object. Int J 3:73–79

[CLF+09]   Cervera JF, López-López MG, Fernández C, Sánchez-Alonso S (2009) Quality metrics in learning objects. In: Sicilia M-A, Lytras MD (eds) Metadata and semantics. Springer, pp 135–141

[CS05]   Cuadrado JJ, Sicilia MA (2005) Learning object reusability metrics: some ideas from software engineering. In: Proceedings of the international conference on internet technologies and applications. North East Wales Institute, Wreham

[DA06]   Desmoulins C, Azouaou F (2006) Using and modeling context with ontology in e-learning: the case of teacher's personal annotation. In: Proceedings of international workshop on applications of semantic web technologies for e-learning in adaptive hypermedia and adaptive web-based systems, Dublin, Ireland

[DAS01]   Dey A, Abowd G, Salber D (2001) A conceptual framework and a toolkit for supporting the rapid prototyping of context-aware applications. Hum Comput Interact 16:97–166

[DBB+12]   Dalmon DL, Brandão LO, Brandão AA, Isotani S (2012) A domain engineering for interactive learning modules. J Res Pract Inf Technol 44(3)

[DDA12]   Díez D, Díaz P, Aedo I (2012) The ComBLA method: the application of domain analysis to the development of e-learning systems. J Res Pract Inf Technol 44 (3):331–345

[Dey01]   Dey AK (2001) Understanding and using context. Pers Ubiquit Comput 5(1):4–7

[DLP+12]   Drira R, Laroussi M, la Pallec X, Warin B (2012) Contextualizing learning scenarios according to different learning management systems. In: IEEE transactions on learning technologies, TEL pp 213–225

[Dou01]   Douglas I (2001) Instructional design based on reusable learning objects: applying lessons of object-oriented software engineering to learning systems design. In: Frontiers in education conference, 2001. 31st Annual (Vol 3, pp F4E-1), IEEE, Reno, NV

[Dou04]   Dourish P (2004) What we talk about when we talk about context. Pers Ubiquit Comput 8:19–30

[Dow02]   Downes S (2002) The learning object economy. Presentation at NAWeb 2002 [Online] http://naweb.unb.ca/02/Downes.ppt

[FLD+12]   Fernandes MA, Lopes CR, Dorca FA, Lima LV (2012) A stochastic approach for automatic and dynamic modeling of Students' learning styles in adaptive educational systems. Inform Educ Int J 11(2):191–212

[Hem93]   Hemmann T (1993) Reuse approaches in software engineering and knowledge engineering: a comparison. In: Position paper collection of the 2nd International workshop on software reusability (No 93–69), Lucca, Italy

[HP05]   Huddlestone J, Pike J (2005) Learning object reuse-a four tier model. In: IEE and MOD HFI DTC symposium on People and systems-who are we designing for (Ref. No. 2005/11078), IET. London, UK, pp 25–31

[JB07]   Jones R, Boyle T (2007) Learning object patterns for programming. Interdisciplinary J Knowl Learn Objects 3(1):19–28

[Jon05]   Jones R (2005) Designing adaptable learning resources with learning object patterns. J Digit Inf 6(1)

[Lim98]   Lim WC (1998) Managing software reuse. Prentice-Hall, Englewood Cliffs

[MB05]   van Merriënboer JJ, Boot E (2005) A holistic pedagogical view of learning objects: future directions for reuse. In: Innovations in instructional technology, pp 43–64

[MCG06]   Mens T, Czarnecki K, Van Gorp P (2006) A taxonomy of model transformations. Electron Notes Theor Comput Sci 152:125–142

[MH05]   Meissonier R, Houze E (2005) The importance of institutional challenges in e-learning performance. PACIS 2005 proceedings, p 82. http://aisel.aisnet.org/cgi/viewcontent.cgi?article=1194&context=pacis2005

[Mie06]   Mierlus-Mazilu I (2006) Types of learning objects. Special issue of the International Journal of the Computer, the Internet and Management 14(SP1):15.1–15.6

[MJ10]   Man H, Jin Q (2010) Putting adaptive granularity and rich context into learning objects. In: 9th international conference on information technology based higher education and training (ITHET). Cappadocia, pp 140–145

[OMG03]   OMG. MDA guide version 1.0.1, 2003. Version 1.0.1, OMG document omg/03-06-01

[Pri89]   Prieto-Diaz R (1989) Classification of reusable modules. In: Ted JB, Alan JP (eds) Software reusability: concepts and models, vol 1. Addison-Wesley Pub. Co, New York, pp 99–123

[PS04]   Pitkanen SH, Silander P (2004) Criteria for pedagogical reusability of learning objects enabling adaptation and individualised learning processes. In: Proceedings of IEEE international conference advanced learning technologies. Joensuu, pp 246–250

[Sam97]   Sametinger J (1997) Software engineering with reusable components. Springer, Berlin

[SAW94]   Schilit B, Adams N, Want R (1994) Context-aware computing applications. Proceedings of the 1st workshop mobile computing systems and applications (WMCSA'94), pp 85–90

[SBF98]   Studer R, Benjamins VR, Fensel D (1998) Knowledge engineering: principles and methods. Data Knowl Eng 25(1):161–197

[Sch06]   Schmidt DC (2006) Model-driven engineering. IEEE Comput 39(2):25–31

[Sch07]   Schmidt A (2007) Impact of context-awareness on the architecture of e-learning solutions. In: Pahl C (ed) Architecture solutions for e-learning systems, Ch 16. Idea Group Publishing, Hershey, PA, pp 306–319

[ŠD13]   Štuikys V, Damaševičius R (2013) Meta-programming and model-driven meta-program development. Springer, London

[Slo04]   Sloep PB (2004) Reuse, portability and interoperability of learning content. Online education using learning objects, p 115

[VMO+12]   Verbert K, Manouselis N, Ochoa X, Wolpers M, Drachsler H, Bosnic I, Duval E (2012) Context-aware recommender systems for learning: a survey and future challenges. IEEE Trans Learn Techn 5(4):318–335

[Win01]   Winograd T (2001) Architectures for context. Hum Comput Interact 16(2):401–419

[Win04]   Winter VL (2004) Program transformation: what, how and why. In: Wah BW (ed)

[WVF10]   Wang G, Valerdi R, Fortune J (2010) Reuse in systems engineering. Syst J IEEE 4 (3):376–384

[ZLO07]   Zimmermann A, Lorenz A, Oppermann R (2007) An operational definition of context. In: Modeling and using context. Springer, Berlin/Heidelberg, pp 558–571

Chapter 4
Modelling of CS Teaching and Learning in Large

4.1 Introduction

In previous chapters (see Chaps. 1 and 2), I have outlined the most general issues of e-learning and CS teaching on the basis of the LO concept. The main focus was given to understanding of the issues through conceptual analysis of the domain literature at the level of LO concepts and their taxonomies. In Chap. 3, I have analysed all these with the emphasis on pedagogical reusability using the software reuse approaches. In this chapter, I provide more in-deep analysis of modelling CS learning and teaching using a systematic approach which is a synthetic product of some domain analysis methods well known in SWE as well as in e-learning domains. In general, the aim of modelling, as it is conceived in the large, for example, in software engineering, is to extract and represent artefacts and knowledge needed to build a software system. As a rule, the extracted artefacts from the domain to be modelled should be represented at a higher level of abstraction. Often we refer to those artefacts as a domain model. Modelling is a primary stage in developing systems.

The aim of this chapter is similar, i.e. to devise a set of models for the CS e-learning domain to be applied to meet our ultimate objectives – to present a systematic approach to build, analyse, evaluate and use the smart LOs. As it is impossible to achieve the ultimate objectives at once, this chapter should be considered as a bridge to connect the previous chapters with the remaining ones of the book. The reader should also accept the topics of this chapter as a part of the theoretical background of the approach we deal with in the book. Note that we perform modelling not so much at the CS content level, but to the larger extent on the whole domain level. Here, by the domain I mean CS learning and teaching processes as they were identified in Fig. 1.1 in Chap. 1. I start from the literature review to motivate our approach to be introduced later on.

© Springer International Publishing Switzerland 2015
V. Štuikys, *Smart Learning Objects for Smart Education in Computer Science*,
DOI 10.1007/978-3-319-16913-2_4

4.2 Literature Review

First, I introduce two categories of the relevant works, and then I analyse them separately in each category. The first stream represents the model-driven approach as they are known and understood in software engineering. A great deal of selected papers considers the *feature* concept as the basis for a feature-oriented modelling. The reason is that the intensive research and developments around formal semantics, reasoning techniques and tool support make feature models a de facto standard to model and manage variability now [BSC10, CW07, SHT+07, TBK09]. Furthermore, the OMG standard for variability modelling, the Common Variability Language, is also based on feature models [CVL14].

The second stream focuses on those works from the e-learning research domain, which already recognize the importance and relevancy of using feature modelling concepts. Unfortunately, this recognition is not yet widely spread. This stream also includes works on e-learning modelling developed within that domain as well as those references that are able to bring us pedagogy-driven artefacts and knowledge to synthesize our approach considered in this chapter. Note that to make the reading independable upon the previous chapters, it is need to repeat some sources that have been already analysed previously.

1. The development of modern complex software systems or their components is practically impossible without the representation of the domain concepts at multiple levels of abstraction, wide-range reuse and automatic program generation. Thus, in recent years two competing software development methodologies have been widely researched and used for this purpose. The first is Model-Driven Engineering (MDE) [Sch06], and the second is product line engineering (PLE) [Bos00]. It is also known as program families, or the development system of systems. The second methodology focuses on maximizing reuse in software product lines (i.e. families of programs that share common assets) and mainly operates with features (i.e. externally visible characteristics of programs that can be recombined in different ways to achieve different versions of program functionality). First, the architecture of the product family is created based on product commonalities and planned variabilities. Then, different product variants are derived from this architecture by reusing components and structures as much as possible and using a variety of component-based and generative reuse techniques [BBC+01].

The MDE methodology, on the other hand, advocates for the use of domain models (i.e. abstractions of domain concepts), which are independent upon the characteristics of technological platforms, as the key artefacts in all phases of the development process. Such models can be introduced at the multiple levels of abstraction, i.e. also above other models, thus leading to the multilevel modelling hierarchies. Models are created using concepts defined in a meta-model that represents domain concepts, relationships and semantics. Domain models are then transformed into the platform-specific models using transformation rules, which are defined by meta-model concepts: a rule (rules) transforms (transform) source model elements, which conform to a source meta-model, into target model elements, which conform to a target meta-model [OMG03].

In this context, one aspect should be highlighted separately – the importance of the term *separation of concepts*. The term has its roots in early works of Parnas [Par72] and Dijkstra and relates to information hiding. For example, Dijkstra applied the information hiding and separation of concepts to describe structural programming [Dij72]. We have widely discussed its role to formulate the basics of meta-programming [ŠD13]. The concept refers to the establishment of logical boundaries to define and delineate purpose typically expressed through concepts (in our case, they could be treated as features). The concept is fundamental and we fully agree with the statement of Greer that separation of concepts is both '*a principle* and a *process*' [Gre08]. According to Greer, the principle of separation of concepts might be stated as the premise that entities (e.g. in our case, concepts related to LOs such as models) should contain the essential attributes and behaviours inherent to their nature, but should be void of attributes and behaviours not inherent to their nature.

Over the decades of software evolution, the separation of concepts has played a significant role in devising new ideas, methods, approaches and methodologies (e.g. FODA (feature-oriented domain analysis) [KCH+90], SCV (scope-commonality-variability) analysis [CHW98], generative programming [CE00], to name a few). The e-learning community also recognizes the role [CBS+11], though in most cases implicitly uses other terms close in meaning such as classification. We use separation of concepts to motivate our approach to be discussed later in this chapter. The reader should be aware the fact that this term can be met in the literature under different names: *orthogonalization of concepts* (e.g. in hardware domain), *divide and conquer* and *separation of concerns* [CL13].

Now we return to the previously mentioned methodologies (MDE and PLE). What is common to both approaches is that they focus on using models, model-driven processes and variability modelling. What is different is the difference of using different concepts and therefore different model types. The background of the first approach is the *object* as a main concept and object-oriented modelling. The background of the second approach is the *feature* as a main concept and feature-based modelling. Note that there is a separate research stream aiming at combining two approaches (PLE and MDE) (see http://featuremapper.org/).

Variability modelling is the heart in the development software systems using both approaches. Further, however, I provide more extensive analysis of feature-based modelling. Note also that here I introduce some new terms which can be understood literally. Later on, I present their definitions in a separate section. In general, feature modelling is a family of notations and an approach for modelling commonality and variability in product families [KCH+90]. In the early stages of the system family development, feature models provide the basis for scoping the system family by recording and assessing information such as which features are important to enter a new market or remain in an existing market, which features incur a technological risk, what is the projected development cost of each feature, etc. [BS99]. Later, feature models play a central role in the development of a system family architecture, which has to realize the variation points specified in the feature models [Bos00, CE01]. In application engineering, which is the process of building individual systems based on assets supplied by the system family development, feature models can drive requirement elicitation and analysis as well as model transformations [LC09, SHT06]. Knowing which features are available in the system family may help the customer to decide about the features his or her system should support. In particular, knowing which of the desired features are provided by the system family and which have to be custom-developed helps to better estimate the time and cost needed for developing the system.

Currently, there are many variability management methodologies used as follows: feature-based modelling (FBM), scope-commonality-variability (SCV) analysis [CHW98], COVAMOF [SDN+04] and formal concept analysis (FCA) [Sne96]. More recent ones are FAMILIAR (*Fe*Ature *M*odel scr*I*pt *L*anguage for man*I*pulation and *A*utomatic *R*easoning) [CL13] and SPLOT (Software Product Line Online Tools) [SPL09], to name a few.

SCV analysis [CHW98] uses a theory of sets for modelling variability. It defines *commonality* as an assumption held uniformly across a given set of objects (S). Frequently, such assumptions are attributes with the same values of all elements of S. Conversely, *variability* is defined as an assumption true of only some elements of S, or an attribute with different values for at least two elements of S. SCV analysis can be applied with different implementation paradigms, which determine different strategies for implementing variability, e.g. in object-oriented design, S is a collection of classes, C is the code common to all classes in S (this code is placed in the base class), and V is the 'uncommon' code in S (this code is placed in the subclasses).

2. I start dealing with references within this stream from our publications because, to our best knowledge, we were pioneers in suggesting to use the feature diagrams (shortly FDs, they represent feature models) as the useful instrument in e-learning. In the paper [ŠD08], we consider the use of FDs as tools to specify generative LOs first and, then, to implement them using meta-programming techniques. In the paper [ŠDB+08], we analyse the possibility of FDs to specify ontology as a type of knowledge for e-learning. The paper [DS09] discusses the use of FDs as applied to the sequencing problem. In the paper [BS11], we analyse the LO research in the large using feature-based models. Papers of other proponents of feature models within the e-learning research community started to appear only recently [CNC12, DDA12].

The next package of papers deals with the descriptive and modelling aspects in education [BDB+06, CLA06, LC06, PLL+06, RM04]. The paper [RM04], for example, presents a framework with reference to the language PALO as a cognitive-based approach to *Educational Modelling Languages* (EML). The PALO Language, thus, provides a layer of abstraction for the description of learning material, including the description of learning activities, structure and scheduling.

The framework makes the use of the domain and pedagogical ontology as a reusable and maintainable way to represent and store instructional content.

Another paper [BDB+06] reviews the state of the art in the development, application and research concerning the use of design languages in education and e-learning. As a basis for further research, the authors propose a taxonomy of design languages and a framework for possible application of design languages in instructional design and e-learning practices.

The paper [LC06] discusses a teacher-centered approach for the specification of learning scenarios (design), as well as the comprehension of learning scenarios (reuse), by focusing on the application of theory and results from the Model-Driven Engineering and Model-Driven Re-engineering domains. As it is clear from the analysis of the works of the first stream, this approach is, in fact, the other illustration on how SWE approaches are beneficial to e-learning. The paper [CLA06] presents a separation of concerns approach to EML proposing to structure these languages in a way different from the one proposed by the IMS *learning design* (LD) specification, currently considered as the standard EML. The authors argue that the LD specification is too complex to be applicable in and run time applications and to produce EML-educational materials.

The paper [PLL+06] presents a general graphical language and a knowledge editor to support the construction of learning designs compliant with the IMS-LD specification. The authors move up one step in the abstraction scale, showing that the process of constructing learning designs can itself be viewed as a unit of learning (or a 'unit of design'): designers can be seen as learning by constructing learning designs, individually, in teams and with staff support.

The e-learning domain to be modelled with success, it should be first represented explicitly. The paper [KM09] provides a useful framework TRACK with three main components of teachers' knowledge to represent the domain: content, pedagogy and technology. We use this framework for representing CS teaching and learning domain too.

I summarize the analysis with the following basic findings:

1. Researchers within the e-learning community recognize the importance of higher-level modelling on the basis of Educational Modelling Languages and higher-level models. The series of approaches have been proposed for that purpose so far. There are also efforts to introduce model-driven approaches taken from SWE to enhance the modelling capabilities.
2. The feature-oriented modelling concepts and languages represent useful facilities to be applied to the e-learning domain due to the following reasons: simplicity, graphical notation easily transformable to the textual one, intuitiveness to grasp and learn main structures, ability to represent subdomains at different levels of abstraction and the universality of the concept feature to model different aspects of any e-learning subdomain.
3. Feature diagrams can be seen as counterparts of the known Educational Modelling Languages. The following sections will show that in detail.

4.3   Background of the Proposed Modelling Method

As it was stated in Sect. 4.1, our intention is to propose a method suitable for analysis and modelling of the CS teaching and learning domain. Here, modelling means the extraction from the domain a set of higher-level models as input data to enable then the creation of SLOs through transformations. As our method to be proposed is a compound of ideas taken from the different known methods, first it is helpful to state the basic principle on which this compound is built and then to provide the reader with the basics (essence) of the selected methods. After that the proposed method will be described.

4.3.1   Some Principles Used to Construct the Method

We use (as many other researchers do) the dual fundamental principles known in SWE as 'separation of concepts' and 'integration of concepts' to construct our method. The term *dual* means that the principles are typically applied both: separation first and integration next. Most researchers, however, do not emphasize the integration explicitly assuming that this action is a consequence of the first. More generally, the principles perhaps can be treated similarly as *analysis* and *synthesis* used in designing systems.

Note that the previously considered domain analysis methods (FODA, SCV, etc.) are actually built upon the explicit use of separation and integration of concepts. Though in e-learning this term is not so much popular, for the CS researchers, the term is well known and pretty understood.

With what examples (about the concept separation) readers will encounter in further readings? Examples are separation of content features from the pedagogical features, the base domain (say the content features) from the technological features and the base domain from its context, to name a few.

We apply yet another principle – *the analogy*. We see an analogy between the educational course design and the Product Line SW system design. Indeed, the course structure has some resemblance with the SW architecture. The selected features model the SW components within the architecture. In the similar way, a collection of LOs models separate topics within the given course. Furthermore, it is possible to define a smart LO (i.e. SLO) as a set of related LO instances to form different topics. To support the principle of analogy, one can take many other examples.

4.3.2   Basic Requirements

Below we formulate basic requirements (R) for the modelling method to be described later as well as some requirements for feature models themselves:

1. As CS learning and teaching is highly heterogeneous, the scope of the domain, its boundary should be clearly stated.
2. For flexibility reasons, the scope and domain boundaries might be changed depending on analysis objectives.
3. As a result of R1 and R2, the domain should be represented as a set of adequate models relevant to general objectives.
4. Various manipulations on creating models (e.g. merging, splitting, feature counting, etc.) should be taken into account and used.
5. All newly created models and those devised through manipulations should be correct; therefore, the model verification should be at the focus.
6. Drawing of feature diagrams and manipulating operations should be supported by adequate tools.
7. Before creating a feature model, first the objectives and role of the model should be defined.
8. For ease of handling and managing, it is useful to introduce model hierarchies for representing them at the different granularity levels.
9. Knowing the role of context in teaching and learning (perhaps it is true for any other domain), the following vision should be taken into account: it is reasonable to consider a feature model as a pair of the *base model* and its *context model*. In that sense a *priority relation* is a useful mechanism.
10. Context model may appear in two forms: implicit or explicit. Depending on the concrete situation, try to use the explicit context model because the explicit representation is more powerful.

4.3.3 Basics of Methods Used to Construct Our Approach

As it was already stated, we define our domain (i.e. CS learning and teaching) using the TPACK framework [KM09] (see Fig. 4.1). We use, however, additional artefacts taken from other sources so that we could be able to present the framework in more details. Such sources as those to specify teaching objectives, learners' motivation approaches, learner profiles, etc., were discussed in previous chapters.

We apply three basic FODA principles: (1) domain boundaries and context identification, (2) modelling of the context by features and (3) modelling of subdomains within the boundaries of features. We also use the SCV analysis to identify the domain variability in the large. We describe the basics of feature modelling in the next section.

4.3.4 Basics of Feature Modelling

Feature diagrams (FDs) are a graphical language used for representing and modelling variability at a higher level of abstraction, usually at the early design stages,

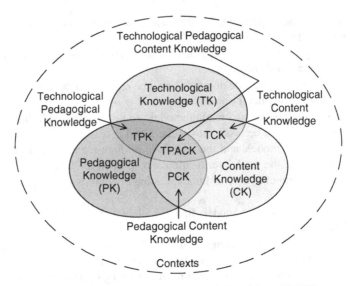

Fig. 4.1 The TPACK framework to define CS domain (Adapted from [KM09])

such as formulation of requirements for software product line designs. As there are slightly different notions and interpretations of elements of FDs, it is possible to consider FDs as a set of graphical languages (though FDs have also a textual representation [ACL+13]). We refer to an FD representing some domain as its feature model. Below, we present basic definitions and syntax and semantics of the conceptualized FDs.

From the perspective of software engineering, it is commonly accepted that a domain can be analysed and modelled at a higher abstraction level using feature-based approaches. Informally, a feature is a prominent characteristic of a system, entity or concept in a domain. Since there is no consensus in the software engineering literature on what a feature is, we deliver some definitions of the term. With regard to different visions, feature is:

1. End-user visible characteristic of a system or a distinguishable characteristic of a concept that is relevant to some stakeholder [KCH+90]
2. A logic unit of behaviour that is specified by a set of functional and quality requirements [Bos00]
3. Qualitative property of a concept [CE01]
4. A functional requirement, a reusable product line (PL) requirement or a characteristic that is provided by one or more members of a software PL [WG04]
5. An increment of program functionality [AK09]

This list is by no means full. The survey [AK09], for example, presents ten slightly different definitions. The fact per se is very important. It actually defines the scope of feature modelling possibilities to interpret the feature concept as the user wants. This is yet another motivation of the benefits of using feature models in the e-learning domain.

Feature modelling is the activity of modelling the common and the variable properties of concepts and their interdependencies in a domain and organizing them into a coherent model referred to as a feature model [CE01]. The intention of a feature model is to represent and model a domain or its subdomains using the feature concept. Specifically, this activity can be seen as part of the domain analysis process, for example, as it is described by FODA [KCH+90]. The advantage of feature models is the provision of an abstract, implementation-independent, concise and explicit representation of the variability present in the software [HHU08].

A feature model represents the common and variable features of concept instances (sub-features) and the dependencies and relationships between the variable features. The model delivers the intention (usually implicitly) of a concept, whereas the set of instances it describes is referred to as an extension, which narrows the meaning and scope of the concept. This extension is often referred to as a hierarchy of features with variability [CKK06]. The primary purpose of a hierarchy is to represent a potentially large number of features into multiple levels of increasing detail. Variability defines what the allowed combinations of features are. To organize a hierarchy as an allowed combination of features, the identification of feature types is essential. *Feature types* are the inherent part of the feature model. They are discussed below.

There are three basic types of features: *mandatory*, *optional* and *alternative*. Mandatory features allow us to express common aspects of the concept (usually they are referred to as *commonality* [CHW98]), whereas optional and alternative features allow us to express *variability*. All basic features may appear either as a *solitary* feature or *in groups*. If all mandatory features in the group are derivatives from the same parent in the parent-child relationship, we can speak about the AND relationship among those features (see also Table 4.1). An optional feature is the one which may be included or not if its parent is included in the feature model. Alternative features, when they appear in groups as derivatives from the same parent, may have the following relationships: OR, XOR, CASE, etc. The XOR relationship also can be treated as a constraint (see Table 4.1) if the relationship is identified for features derived from different parents.

4.3.5 Formal Definition of Features and Constraints

It is possible to express features not only graphically but also formally using the notation of the propositional logic [Bat05, CHE05, TBK09].

Let P be the parent feature and the sets $\{C_1, \ldots, C_n\}$ are children features of P. Then we can specify the feature relationships as follows (see also Table 4.1):

$$(P \Rightarrow \wedge_{i \in M} C_i) \wedge (\vee_{1 \le i \le n} C_i \Rightarrow P); M \subseteq \{1, \ldots, n\} \text{ (AND relationship)}$$

Table 4.1 Feature diagram notation in GPFT [CE01]

Feature types and constraints	Definition	Graphical notation
Mandatory (AND relationship)	If A, then B If A, then B and C	
Optional	If A, then B or none If A, then C or D or none	
Alternative (OR decomposition)	If A, then any of (B, C, D)	
Alternative (XOR decomposition)	If A, then (B but not C) or (C but not B)	
Constraint <mutex>	Feature K excludes feature F and vice versa	
Constraint <Require>	Feature K requires feature F	

© With kind permission from Springer Science+Business Media from [ŠD13]

$(P \Leftrightarrow \vee_{1 \leq i \leq n} C_i) \wedge_{i < j} (\neg C_i \vee \neg C_j)$ (XOR relationship)

$P \Leftrightarrow \vee_{1 \leq i \leq n} C_i$ (OR relationship)

$\neg K \vee \neg F$ (constraint <mutex>)

$\neg K \vee F$ (constraint <Require>)

We have presented the basic features and their formal relationships. More advanced subtypes of alternative features are grouped constraints, attributes, cloning and additional constraints [CKK06]. Though the feature-based representation is attractive from various viewpoints, however, there is also some inconsistency of the graphical notation. The existing discrepancies in representing and interpreting graphical elements of feature models are mostly due to the lack of standardization and inconsistency of the available tools. The next section is about the graphical notation used in [CL13].

4.3.6 FAMILIAR-Based Feature Diagram Notation

Domain modelling is to be supported by the adequate tools. The modelling aim is to build domain models, to be aware of their correctness and to know their basic characteristics. We have selected FAMILIAR feature language and tools [CL13] to provide modelling activities in modelling the CS domain and building models to create SLO. To verify the created models, we use SPLOT tools [http://www.splot-research.org] because they are mutually consistent. Therefore, we need to introduce these notations (see Table 4.2).

4.4 Description of the Proposed Modelling Approach

Figure 4.2 presents an overall view of the modelling methodology. We describe it as a logical sequence of high-level processes along with their outcomes. Here, by the domain we mean CS learning and teaching. We assume that it is highly heterogeneous. Here, in more details, we describe each process as a goal driven input-output relationship, according to the following scheme: *Why-What-How-What*. The interpretation of the scheme is, in fact, the answer to the adequate question as follows:

Why a process is needed?
What are input data?
How does a process work?
What is the outcome of a process?

As here we also speak about the context in modelling, we provide the following definitions of the term:

The context is that 'which constrains something without intervening in it explicitly' [BP99]. The paper [Bre05] extends the previous definition and identifies three main elements being important to the focus of an actor: (1) context is relative to the focus; (2) as the focus evolves, its context evolves too; and (3) context is highly domain dependent.

Process 1

WHY   The aim is to set initial conditions for the remaining processes. As the FODA and SCV methods indicate (see Sect. 4.3.3), the identification of boundaries is the important precondition of modelling because it specifies the scope of the activity.

WHAT   The attribute IN1 is the answer, i.e. external input data IN1 includes FODA instructions, SCV instructions and TPACK framework (see Fig. 4.1).

HOW   This attribute can be fulfilled through analysis of TPACK (the latter is treated as the base domain here) by an analyser (modeller); the basis is his/her competence in the field; the use of some instructional materials and documents such as standard specifications, relevant papers, etc., is important.

Table 4.2 Juxtaposing of FAMILIAR and SPLOT notations

Features and relationships	Notation		Feature tree (XML fail fragment)
	FAMILIAR	SPLOT	
Mandatory (AND)	FM (A : B C ;)	A, ● B, ● C	`<feature_tree>` :r A(_r0) :m B(_r1) :m C(_r2) `</feature_tree>`
Optional	FM (A : [B] [C] ;)	A, ○ B, ○ C	`<feature_tree>` :r A(_r0) :o B(_r1) :o C(_r2) `</feature_tree>`
XOR group [1..1]	FM (A : (D|B|C) ;)	A, ⋀ [1..1], □ D, □ B, □ C	`<feature_tree>` :r A(_r0) :g [1,1] : D(_r1) : B(_r2) : C(_r3) `</feature_tree>`
OR group [1..*]	FM (A : (D|B|C)+ ;)	A, ⋀ [1..*], □ D, □ B, □ C	`<feature_tree>` :r A(_r0) :g [1,*] : D(_r1) : B(_r2) : C(_r3) `</feature_tree>`
Constraint <Exclude >	CONSTRAINTS: (D->!B) FM (A : [D] [B] [C] ;(D -> !B) ;)	A, ○ B, ○ C, ○ D, (¬D ∨ ¬B)	`<feature_tree>` :r A(_r0) :o B(_r1) :o C(_r2) :o D(_r3) `</feature_tree>` `<constraints>` C0:~_r3 or ~_r1 `</constraints>`
Constraint <Requires >	CONSTRAINTS: (B->C) FM (A : [D] [B] [C] ;(B -> C) ;)	A, ○ B, ○ C, ○ D, (¬B ∨ C)	`<feature_tree>` :r A(_r0) :o B(_r1) :o C(_r2) :o D(_r3) `</feature_tree>` `<constraints>` C0:~_r1 or _r2 `</constraints>`

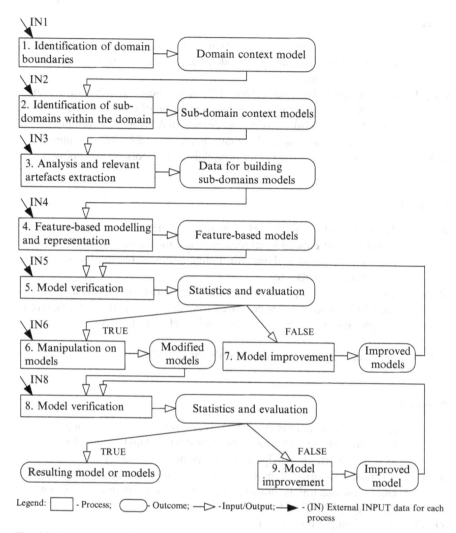

Fig. 4.2 Overall view of the proposed methodology [Bur14]

WHAT   Context model is the outcome here. We can describe the model by
encountering such domains or their influential attributes, which are close
in terms of the importance and their relationships with the base domain.
Having in mind the TRACK framework (see Fig. 4.1), the context model
can be specified as (i) *teaching theories* for the pedagogical knowledge,
(ii) *educational environments* for the technological knowledge and (iii)
CS curriculum for the content knowledge.

Process 2

WHY   The aim is to identify what is within the boundaries and also the context
         model narrowing to simplify modelling. It is an evident application of
         separation of concepts.
WHAT   External input data IN2 includes FODA instructions, SCV instructions,
         TPACK framework and principles (separation of concepts, analogy).
HOW   The process is fulfilled by reconsidering TRACK and by formulating
         aims to modelling each subdomain (pedagogy, technology, content).
WHAT   More narrow (concrete) context models (e.g. robots for technology).

Process 3

WHY   To obtain and extract the artefacts that are relevant to modelling aims.
WHAT   External input data IN3 includes methods, tools and actors (knowledge
         and competence of analyser) for finding artefacts, knowledge, solutions,
         tasks, requirements, etc.
HOW   Through activities performed by analyser on the basis of his/her
         knowledge or knowledge borrowed from domain experts. Activities may
         include reading, collecting, interviewing, classifying, pruning and
         verifying data.
WHAT   Set of data as an initial model of the subdomains.

Process 4

WHY   Aim is to have more abstract and precise representation of models.
WHAT   External input data IN4 includes feature-based language and tools such
         as FAMILIAR, knowledge and competence of the analyser.
HOW   The process is realized through the identification of relationships (parent-
         child) and constraints, drawing and testing feature diagrams (FDs) with
         the help of FAMILIAR tools.
WHAT   A set of output models (FDs).

Process 5

WHY   FM correctness checking and gathering statistics on the models.
WHAT   External input data IN5 includes FM verification tools (SPLOT) and
         modeller knowledge.
HOW   Model validation is achieved through the use of the SPLOT tools.
WHAT   Statistics on model characteristics and properties.

Process 6

WHY	To know for which purposes the combined models will be used.
WHAT	External input data IN6 includes statement of precise requirements for manipulation and FAMILIAR.
HOW	By applying FAMILIAR tools
WHAT	Some combined models.

Process 8 is the same as Process 5, and Process 9 is the same as Process 7 (they ensure the correctness of improved models). In Sect. 4.7, we present and evaluate the models created using the approach.

4.5   Analysis and Evaluation of Created Feature Models

Here, we present some modelling results obtained with the use of the proposed approach to model the CS teaching and learning domain. Some models or their parts are independent upon the teaching subject. For example, the model to describe the learning objective (Fig. 4.3) can be applied (partially or entirely) to any other subject because the model is based on Bloom's taxonomy. Our model was created using the Bloom's taxonomy as it is interpreted in [SMS08]. We treat our model as a concrete because, in our case, the leaves are atomic features, though, in the other context, some leaves might be decomposed in the smallest features (see Property 4.14, in Sect. 4.6).

Another model represents the *motivation* model (see Fig. 4.4). As it largely relates to teaching theories, it is regarded as the important subdomain in e-learning. The model can be treated as independent on the teaching subject too (except the

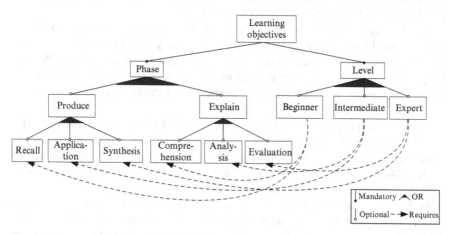

Fig. 4.3 Concrete feature model (FD) to specify learning objectives (created using [SMS08, Bur14])

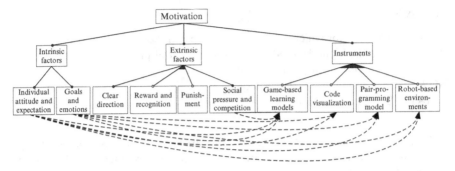

Fig. 4.4 Abstract feature model to specify learning motivation [Bur14]

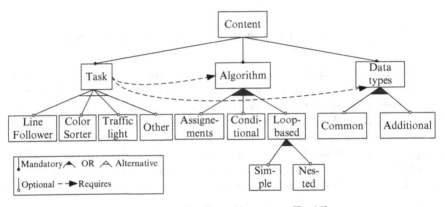

Fig. 4.5 Abstract feature model to specify CS teaching content [Bur14]

children features of the 'instrument' parent feature). The model has been devised on the basis of the following list of papers studied: [Ala12, CAC12, Chu07, DSS+08, HS12, JCS09, LLY10, Pea10, SHL+13, SMG11, Tou12].

The CS content model (Fig. 4.5) is the abstract model because it should be further refined if we aim to implement it in practice as a part of the smart LO. Note that the content model relates to the use of educational robots in teaching CS (see Chap. 12, for more details). Note that this model was devised partially (we mean the features 'algorithm' and 'data types') on the basis of [KP05] and partially (we mean the feature 'task') using [BSM12, ŠBD13].

The next sample model specifies technology (Fig. 4.6). As the feature 'technology' describes a very large domain, this model is abstract too. Therefore, it includes features also relevant to other teaching subjects. This model has been constructed on the following background: [LH10], for 'hardware' features; [KP05], for 'software' features; and [BDB+06], for 'modelling' features (partially).

In Table 4.3, we summarize the syntax-related characteristics of the devised models: pedagogy-oriented, content-oriented and technology-oriented ones. In Table 4.4, we summarize quality-based characteristics of the models. All characteristics were obtained as a result of using FAMILIAR (Table 4.3) and SPLOT

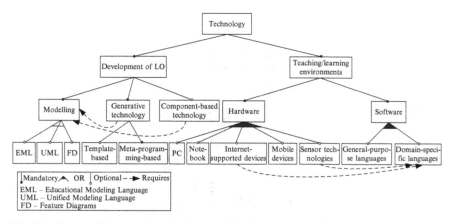

Fig. 4.6 Abstract FD to specify technology used in CS e-learning [Bur14]

Table 4.3 FM statistics obtained using metrics from http://www.splot-research.org/

#	Parameters characteristics	Pedagogy (M, motivation; LObj, learning objectives, TLM, teaching/learning model; A, assessment; L, learner)					Content	Technology
		M	LObj	TLM	A	L		
1	# Features	14	14	37	17	24	13	20
2	# Optional	0	0	0	0	0	0	2
3	# Mandatory	7	2	10	0	5	3	7
4	# Grouped	6	11	26	16	18	9	10
5	# OR groups	2	4	10	4	4	2	2
6	# XOR groups	0	0	0	1	0	1	1
7	# (CTC)	9	6	3	3	3	2	4
8	CTCR (%)	0.50	0.64	0.11	0.18	0.25	0.23	0.30
9	#CTC DV	7	9	4	3	6	3	6
10	CTC CD	1.29	0.67	0.75	1.00	0.50	0.67	0.67
11	Tree depth	3	5	9	6	3	3	4

CTC cross-tree constraints
DV distinct variables
CTCR CTC representativeness calculated as the number of variables in the CTC divided by the number of features in the feature diagram
CTC clause density is the number of constraints divided by the number of variables in the CTC
CTC CD CTC clause density

(Table 4.4) tools. At the bottom, we provide definitions of some derivative characteristics.

Variability degree is the number of valid configurations divided by 2^n, where n is a number of features in the model.

In CS, a *binary decision diagram (BDD)* or *branching program*, like a negation normal form (NNF) or a propositional directed acyclic graph (PDAG), is a data structure that is used to represent a Boolean function. On a more abstract level,

Table 4.4 Analysis of feature models (http://www.splot-research.org/)

| # | Parameters | (M, motivation; LObj, learning objectives; TL, teaching/learning; A, assessment; L, learner) | | | | | | |
		M	LObj	TL	A	L	Content	Technology
1	Consistency	+	+	+	+	+	+	+
2	# Dead features	None	None	None	None	None	None	None
3	# Core features	12	5	1	1	6	4	8
4	Count configurations	3	61	131,071	95	74,803	84	828
5	Variability degree (%)	1.8311 E-2	3.7231 E-1	9.5367 E-5	7.2479 E-2	4.4586 E-1	1.0254 E0	7.8964 E-2
6	#BDD nodes	14	49	103	95	35	16	26

BDD can be considered as a compressed representation of sets or relations. Unlike other compressed representations, operations are performed directly on the compressed representation, i.e. without decompression.

4.6   Properties of Feature Models of CS Teaching Domain

In this section, we generalize our discussion given in the previous sections by presenting some essential properties. We formulate them with the emphasis not so much on syntax-based attributes, but rather on the models' semantics, i.e. as they are seen from the benefits for learning and teaching. Of course, we also provide those properties which we use later, in subsequent chapters.

Property 4.1 As CS learning and teaching (similarly to any other subject) is the heterogeneous domain, we need to use *multiple feature models* aiming to represent the domain at a higher level of abstraction due to (i) ever-increasing requirements, (ii) complexity growth of the domain itself, (iii) needs for reuse enhancement and (iv) automation purposes.

Property 4.2 A set of feature models presented in Sect. 4.5 has the same semantics as the selected papers on e-learning describe, from which the feature has been extracted. The benefits of models are preciseness, correctness, conciseness (if we take into account the ability to present complex models at different abstraction levels) and reusability.

Property 4.3 Feature models are highly reconfigurable items. The following operations (merging, splitting, changing, etc.) enable to perform the adequate reconfiguring on demand.

Property 4.4 From the perspective of the understanding of modelling, two essential types of feature models (*base* and *context* models) and their relationships enable a great deal of flexibility in modelling.

Property 4.5 Context model is treated as having a *higher priority* with respect to its base model. Both models, due to their (re)configurability, can be represented either as the uniform model or as a set of models. What mode to use? It depends on the purpose in a concrete situation.

Property 4.6 In the case of using multiple models, their priority relation can be modelled by the priority levels, e.g. highest, intermediate, low and no priority. Charnecki et al. [CHE05] use the term *staged model* which is the same in meaning as the *prioritized model*.

Property 4.7 Models can change their roles (e.g. context model can become base model and vice versa). This may happen due to the reconfiguration, changes of modelling aims or changing the representation level.

Property 4.8 It is possible to invent the unified *generic model* for the whole CS learning and teaching domain (in terms of predefined scope), for example, for further modelling and better understanding.

As there are some difficulties to represent a large FD (e.g. to be readable, it should be represented onto one page), we can split some nodes, thus splitting the FD into parts. This node should be marked with a reference to the remaining part of the diagram. If there are some splitting points, we can build a *reference FD* to link all separated parts of the FD.

Property 4.9 Mandatory features model the domain *commonality*. Variant points (i.e. grouped alternative features) and variants (i.e. children of a variant point) model the domain *variability*. Constraints among features (such as *requires* and *excludes*) model the feature interaction. Therefore, we are able to specify the domain under consideration *abstractly* or even *formally* (if features and their relationships are expressed using the notion of the propositional logic) by commonality-variability relationships.

Further, we make the difference between two views on the feature model correctness: domain-based and feature-based semantics, meaning adherence to the accepted notion (further we refer to it as semantic correctness).

Property 4.10 The developed feature models are correct with *regard to domain-based correctness* under the following assumptions: (1) the model designer has used initial data to specify models, which were created by domain experts, (2) the designer has applied *allowable manipulations* on the domain initial data (e.g. merging some attributes of initial data to form one representative feature for conciseness, moving attributes from one branch to another for clearness) and (3) relationships and constraints were formed on the basis of expert knowledge.

Property 4.11 The developed feature models are *semantically correct* because the following conditions hold: (1) the models are specified using the notion accepted by the FAMILIAR language and tools; (2) the tool SPLOT we use supports the formal verification of models devised with the help of FAMILIAR.

Property 4.12 There is no unique attribute to characterize feature models; rather multiple characteristics should be applied. The list of characteristics to evaluate models may be as follows: number of models, complexity, *degree of variability*, relevance to the requirements of a specific task such as implementation and characteristics obtained by the tools used.

Property 4.13 The developed models specify and model the CS learning and teaching domain to the extent relevant to the predefined *scope and aims* of modelling.

Property 4.14 We refer to the feature diagram as an *abstract feature model* if there are some leave features that, in the other context, could be further split into smallest ones. We refer to the feature diagram as a *concrete feature model* if all leaves are atomic features. The atomic feature is a value of its parent feature.

Note that the concrete feature model can be derived from a set of abstract features first by selecting the *adequate leaves* from a given set, then splitting them and finally merging sub-models to form a concrete feature model to specify a concrete task. We explain that in detail in Chap. 5.

4.7 Discussion and Evaluation of the Approach

Modelling and model-based approaches are recognized to be a very powerful instrument for extracting knowledge from domains at the early stages in constructing software systems. Now the model-driven approaches prevail in system developments. The benefits of the approaches are evident: they enable to represent designs at a higher level of abstraction. Such a vision makes possible to share design knowledge among groups of shareholders and enables to extend the scope of reuse through automation, meaning *higher productivity*, *better quality* and *shorter time to market*. We were focusing on feature-based modelling aspects, as they are represented within the SWE domain, and some modelling aspects discussed in e-learning. On this basis, we have proposed an approach for analysis and modelling of the e-learning domain. More specifically, the proposed method enables to build feature-based models to support CS teaching and learning.

We have provided feature-based modelling (the methodology has been borrowed from SWE) aiming to create the space of abstract models *within the anticipated scope of modelling* to cover the *most likely situations* in teaching CS. This space specifies feature models at a higher level of abstraction aiming to support wide-scale reuse. We have created and evaluated the models of the following subdomains: *pedagogy* (the latter defines the motivation, learning objective, assessment and learner's social aspects in teaching CS), *CS teaching content* and *technology used*. Though some models within the space may have the concrete feature values, the others usually are *abstract models*. Here, the abstract models should be understood as the ones which represent the most common features without the identification of their concrete values for the concrete situation of use. Therefore, the abstract models are to be *refined* or concretized to the given context of use. We will discuss that in Chap. 5.

The abstract models we have created are *correct models* in terms of the defined feature-related concepts, specified properties, and identified basic characteristics using modelling language and tools (i.e. FAMILIAR) and model verification tools (i.e. SPLOT).

What are the benefits of the approach for different actor (CS researchers, educational system designers, CS teachers, students)?

For all actors, the approach can be seen as a methodological instrument or guidelines to obtain a new knowledge and to represent it in a systematic way. Indeed, the principle 'separation of concepts', the process-based view and the focus on input-output relationships, on which basis the method has been constructed and represented, are general enough to be applicable in many other contexts. The feature models selected to represent the domain artefact could be attractive for all actors too, because of clearness and intuitiveness of the feature concept per se. The possibility of the concept to be interpreted freely enough, on the other hand, might respond to the different actors' flavours.

As feature-oriented modelling is constantly expanding, CS researchers are able to broaden their research topics and themes. They are able, for example, to bring their own contribution to further formalizing and systemizing knowledge in the higher-level modelling and feature-oriented programming. The feature-based modelling may contribute to merging the close research fields such as knowledge representation and reasoning, ontology-based modelling and fuzzy logic-based modelling, to name a few.

The benefits to the educational system designers are also evident – they are able to accept from the SW designers the accumulated experience (e.g. theories, methodologies, approaches and tools) in designing educational software. From the larger perspective, the feature-based approaches might play the same or similar role as UML-based approaches did so far for industry, academia, research and teaching. There are many signs to claim that (industrial support, broad stream of research, variability language [CVL14] with OMG contribution, a variety of tools, initiatives for standardization).

What are benefits for teachers? Teachers should be educated with the focus on higher-level abstractions, models, their transformations and higher-level modelling because (i) all these approaches have evolved incrementally over the long history of computing to reach the current level; (ii) from the pure computing perspective, there is no other way to manage complexity as to use model-based transformations; and (iii) there is an urgent necessity to respond to CS learning and teaching challenges stated in Chap. 1.

The visualization, intuitiveness and syntactic simplicity make the models discussed here acceptable for CS students as well.

What tasks the feature-based approach is able to support? They usually are useful in the requirement statement (formal or semiformal), explicit representation of the learning variability and the task specification at a higher level of abstraction. Having in mind Property 4.14, we can see a feature model as a tool to specify smart LO at a higher level of abstraction. We will discuss all these topics in detail in Chap. 5.

What are bottlenecks of the approach? There are some discrepancies in syntax graphical elements of the notion. That hinders formalization and standardization. The notation is further evolving. There are different textual representations. As so far there are no standard tools to model and verify feature models, one should select the appropriate language notation and available tools.

4.8 Summary and Concluding Remarks

We have introduced the basics of feature-oriented modelling to model the CS learning and teaching domain. To do that systematically with the focus on large-scale reuse, we have combined the artefacts and knowledge from two fields: learning and teaching concepts from CS e-learning and feature-based concepts from SWE. In terms of the general understanding of CS, the first can be viewed as *a task domain*, while the second as a *solution domain*. On this basis, we have proposed a methodology, which formally can be seen as a *mapping* of the *problem domain* onto *the solution domain*. We have represented the methodology on how the CS teaching and learning artefacts are extracted and then represented using the feature-based notation as a solution domain. The methodology was presented as a sequence of the adequate processes to specify the input-output relationships.

As the methodology also includes the use of the proven tools such as FAMILIAR and SPLOT, the refined models are correct. This methodology should be seen as a primary step to define the background of higher-level modelling in creating smart learning objects. We will extend this background in the subsequent chapters.

4.9 Research and Exercise Questions

4.1. Provide a more extensive overview of the Educational Modelling Languages (EMLs), the latter treating as a separate research topic.
4.2. Clarify the meaning and the role of the term 'separation of concepts' (also known as 'separation of concerns') in terms of analysis of EMLs and also in other contexts. If you are a teacher, outline how you can use this term in your practice.
4.3. What is the difference between two terms: *explicit separation of concepts* and *implicit separation of concepts*? Take examples from your field of interest (we also recommend to read Chap. 3 in the book [ŠD13]).
4.4. On the basis of results obtained in Sect. 4.1, invent taxonomy for this area of knowledge.
4.5. Analyse the possible views to essentials of feature modelling by comparing different definitions of the term feature, for example, taken from [AK09].
4.6. Define other terms that are used to specify feature diagrams as graphical modelling language. Focus on feature types, parent-children relations and constrains. Why feature diagrams can be seen as a domain-independent modelling language.
4.7. Provide a comparative study of different modelling languages: EML-, UML- and FODA-based feature diagrams. Draw a distinguishing line among those languages and provide their advantages and drawbacks.
4.8. What is the difference between the abstract feature diagram and the concrete feature diagram?

4.9. What is a variant point, variant within a feature diagram? What is the learning variability in terms of variant points and their variants? (See also Chap. 5.)

4.10. Learn the properties of the abstract and concrete feature diagrams separately.

4.11. Draw the feature diagrams of some process of your everyday activity.

4.12. Discuss the benefits and limitations of feature-based modelling.

4.13. If you have decided that the feature-based notion is your cup of tea, learn and use, say, the FAMILIAR language and tools as a case study for receiving a great pleasure as if drinking your tea.

References

[ACL+13]   Acher M, Collet P, Lahire P, France RB (2013) FAMILIAR: a domain-specific language for large scale management of feature models. Sci Comput Program 78(6):657–681

[AK09]   Apel S, Kästner C (2009) An overview of feature-oriented software development. J Object Technol 8(5):49–8

[Ala12]   Ala-Mutka K (2012) Problems in learning and teaching programming. Codewitz needs analysis. http://www.cs.tut.fi~edge/literature_study.pdf

[Bat05]   Batory D (2005) Feature models, grammars, and propositional formulas. Springer, Berlin/Heidelberg, pp 7–20

[BBC+01]   Butler G, Batory DS, Czarnecki K, Eisenecker UW (2001) Generative techniques for product lines. In: Proceedings of the 23rd international conference on software engineering, ICSE 2001, Toronto, 12–19 May 2001, pp 760–761

[BDB+06]   Botturi L, Derntl M, Boot E, Figl K (2006) A classification framework for educational modeling languages in instructional design. In: 6th IEEE international conference on advanced learning technologies (ICALT 2006), Kerkrade, pp 1216–1220

[Bos00]   Bosch J (2000) Design and use of software architectures, adopting and evolving a product-line approach. Addison-Wesley, Reading

[BP99]   Brézillon P, Pomerol J-Ch (1999) Contextual knowledge sharing and cooperation in intelligent assistant systems. Le Travail Humain 62(3):223–246. PUF, Paris

[Bre05]   Brezillon P (2005) Task–realization models in contextual graphs. Modeling and using context. In: Dey A, Kokinov B, Leake D, Turner R (eds) CONTEXT–05. Springer, LNCS, vol 3554, pp 55–68

[BS11]   Burbaite R, Stuikys V (2011) Analysis of learning object research using feature-based models. In: Rimantas B, Butkiene R (eds) Information technologies' 2011, Proceedings of the 17th international conference on information and software technologies, IT 2011, Kaunas University of Technology, Lithuania, 27–29 Apr 2011, pp 201–208

[Bur14]   Burbaitė R (2014) Advanced generative learning objects in informatics education: the concept, models, and implementation. Summary of doctoral dissertation, physical sciences, informatics (09P), Kaunas University of Technology, Kaunas

[BS99]   De Baud JM, Schmid K (1999) A systematic approach to derive the scope of software product lines. ICSE, Los Angeles, CA, USA, pp 34–43

[BSC10]   Benavides D, Segura S, Cortés AR (2010) Automated analysis of feature models 20 years later: a literature review. Inf Syst 35(6):615–636

[BSM12]   Burbaite R, Stuikys V, Marcinkevicius R (2012) The LEGO NXT Robot-based e-learning environment to teach computer science topics. Electron Elect Eng 18(9):113–116

[CAC12]   Costa CJ, Aparicio M, Cordeiro C (2012) A solution to support student learning of programming. In: Proceedings of the workshop on open source and design of communication, ACM, New York, NY, USA, pp 25–29

[CBS+11]   Campos F, Braga R, Souza AC, Santos N, Matos E, Nery T (2011) Projeto BROAD
           (2011) Busca semântica por objetos de aprendizagem. In: VIII Congresso Brasileiro
           de Ensino Superior a Distância – ESUD 2011, Ouro Preto, pp 1–15
[CE00]   Czarnecki K, Eisenecker UW (2000) Separating the configuration aspect to support
           architecture evolution. In: Proceedings of 14th European conference on object-ori-
           ented programming (ECOOP'2000), International workshop on aspects and dimen-
           sions of concerns, Cannes, 11–12 June 2000
[CE01]   Czarnecki K, Eisenecker U (2001) Generative programming: methods, tools and
           applications. Addison-Wesley, Boston
[CHE05]   Czarnecki K, Helsen S, Eisenecker U (2005) Staged configuration through speciali-
           zation and multi-level configuration of feature models. Softw Process Improve Pract
           10(2005):143–169
[Chu07]   Chudá D (2007) Visualization in education of theoretical computer science. In:
           Proceedings of the 2007 international conference on computer systems and technol-
           ogies, ACM, p 84
[CHW98]   Coplien J, Hoffman D, Weiss D (1998) Communality and variability in software
           engineering. IEEE Softw 15:37–45
[CKK06]   Czarnecki K, Kim CHP, Kalleberg KT (2006) Feature models are views on ontol-
           ogies. In: Proceedings of the 10th international on software product line conference,
           Baltimore, pp 41–51
[CL13]   Collet P, Lahire P (2013) Feature modelling and separation of concerns with FAMIL-
           IAR, CMA@RE, IEEE. Rio de Janeiro, Brasil, pp 13–18
[CLA06]   Caeiro-Rodríguez M, Llamas-Nistal M, Anido-Rifón L (2006) A separation of con-
           cerns approach to educational modeling languages. In: Frontiers in education confer-
           ence, 36th annual, IEEE, San Diego, pp 9–14
[CNC12]   Castro J, Nazar JM, Campos F (2012) EasyT: Apoiando a Construção de Objetos de
           Aprendizagem para uma Linha de Produtos de Software. Conferencias LACLO 3(1)
[CVL14]   Common Variability Language (CVL) standard, http://www.omgwiki.org/variability/
           doku.php. Accessed on January 2014
[CW07]   Czarnecki K, Wasowski A (2007) Feature diagrams and logics: there and back again.
           In Proceedings of SPLC'07, Kyoto, pp 23–34
[DDA12]   Díez D, Díaz P, Aedo I (2012) The ComBLA method: the application of domain
           analysis to the development of e-learning systems. J Res Pract Inf Technol 44(3):331–
           345
[Dij72]   Dijkstra EW (1972) Notes on structured programming. In: Dahl OJ, Dijkstra EW,
           Hoare CAR (eds) Structured programming. Academic, London
[DS09]   Damasevicius R, Stuikys V (2009) Specification and generation of learning object
           sequences for e-learning using sequence feature diagrams and metaprogramming
           techniques. In: Advanced learning technologies, 2009. ICALT 2009. 9th IEEE
           international conference, July, Riga, pp 572–576
[DSS+08]   Dorairaj SK, Singh J, Shanmugam M, Shamini S (2008) Experimenting with
           industry's pair-programming model in teaching and learning programming. In: Pro-
           ceedings of the 4th international conference on information technology and multi-
           media at UNITEN (ICIMU' 2008), Malaysia
[Gre08]   Greer D (2008) The art of separation of concerns. http://ctrl-shift-b.blogspot.com/
           2008/01/art-of-separation-of-concerns.html
[HHU08]   Hubaux A, Heymans P, Unphon H (2008) Separating variability concerns in a product
           line re-engineering project. In: EA-AOSD'08, Brussels, 31 Mar 2008
[HS12]   Hamada M, Sato S (2012) A learning system for a computational science related
           topic. Procedia Comput Sci 9:1763–1772
[JCS09]   Jiau HC, Chen JC, Ssu KF (2009) Enhancing self-motivation in learning program-
           ming using game-based simulation and metrics. Educ IEEE Trans Enhanc Learn 52
           (4):555–562

[KCH+90]   Kang K, Cohen S, Hess J, Novak W, Peterson S (1990) Feature-oriented domain analysis (FODA) feasibility study. TR CMU/SEI-90-TR-21, Software Engineering Institute, Carnegie Mellon University, November 1990

[KM09]   Koehler M, Mishra P (2009) What is technological pedagogical content knowledge (TPACK)? Contemp Issues Technol Teac Educ 9(1):60–70

[KP05]   Kelleher C, Pausch R (2005) Lowering the barriers to programming: a taxonomy of programming environments and languages for novice programmers. ACM Comput Surv 37(2):83–137

[LC06]   Laforcade P, Choquet C (2006) Next step for educational modeling languages: the model driven engineering and reengineering approach. In: 6th international conference on advanced learning technologies, 2006. IEEE, pp 745–747

[LC09]   Laguna MA, Corral JM (2009) Feature diagrams and their transformations: an extensible meta-model. Proceedings of 35th Euromicro conference on software engineering and advanced applications, SEAA 2009, Patras, 27–29 Aug 2009, pp 97–104

[LH10]   Liu GZ, Hwang GJ (2010) A key step to understanding paradigm shifts in e-learning: towards context-aware ubiquitous learning. Br J Educ Technol 41(2):E1–E9

[LLY10]   Law KM, Lee V, Yu YT (2010) Learning motivation in e-learning facilitated computer programming courses. Comput Educ 55(1):218–228

[OMG03]   OMG. MDA Guide Version 1.0.1, 2003. Version 1.0.1, OMG document omg/03-06-01

[Par72]   Parnas DL (1972) On the criteria to be used in decomposing a system into modules. Communications of ACM, December, pp 1053–1058

[Pea10]   Pears AN (2010) Enhancing student engagement in an introductory programming course. In: 40th Frontiers in education conference, ser. Proceedings of the Frontiers in education conference (No. 40)

[PLL+06]   Paquette G, Léonard M, Lundgren-Cayrol K, Mihaila S, Gareau D (2006) Learning design based on graphical knowledge-modeling. J Educ Technol Soc 9(1):97–112

[RM04]   Rodríguez-Artacho M, Maillo MFV (2004) Modeling educational content: the cognitive approach of the PALO language. Educ Technol Soc 7(3):124–137

[ŠBD13]   Štuikys V, Burbaitė R, Damaševičius R (2013) Teaching of computer science topics using meta-programming-based GLOs and LEGO robots. Inform Educ Int J 12(1):125–142

[Sch06]   Schmidt DC (2006) Model-driven engineering. IEEE Comput 39(2):25–31

[ŠD08]   Štuikys V, Damaševičius R (2008) Development of generative learning objects using feature diagrams and generative techniques. Inf Edu 7(2):277–288

[ŠD13]   Štuikys V, Damaševičius R (2013) Meta-programming and model-driven meta-program development: principles processes and techniques. Springer, Heidelberg/New York/Dordrecht/London

[ŠDB+08]   Štuikys V, Damaševičius R, Brauklytė I, Limanauskienė V (2008) Exploration of learning object ontologies using feature diagrams. Proceedings of world conference on educational multimedia, hypermedia & telecommunications (ED-MEDIA 08), 30 June 30–4 July 2008, Vienna, pp 2144–2154

[SDN+04]   Sinnema M, Deelstra S, Nijhuis J, Bosch J (2004) Covamof: a framework for modeling variability in software product families. In: Proceedings of 3rd international conference on software product lines, SPLC. LNCS, vol 3154, Springer, pp 197–213

[SHL+13]   Schäfer A, Holz J, Leonhardt T, Schroeder U, Brauner P, Ziefle M (2013) From boring to scoring–a collaborative serious game for learning and practicing mathematical logic for computer science education. Comput Sci Educ 23(2):87–111

[SHT+07]   Schobbens PY, Heymans P, Trigaux JC, Bontemps Y (2007) Generic semantics of feature diagrams. Comput Netw 51(2):456–479

[SHT06]   Schobbens PY, Heymans P, Trigaux JCh (2006) Feature diagrams: a survey and a formal semantics. In: Proceedings of the 14th IEEE international requirements engineering conference, 11–15 Sept 2006. IEEE CS Washington, DC, pp 136–145

[SMG11]   Salleh N, Mendes E, Grundy J (2011) Empirical studies of pair programming for CS/SE teaching in higher education: a systematic literature review. Softw Eng IEEE Trans 37(4):509–525

[SMS08]   Starr CW, Manaris B, Stalvey RH (2008) Bloom's taxonomy revisited: specifying assessable learning objectives in computer science. ACM SIGCSE Bull 40(1):261–265

[Sne96]   Snelting G (1996) Reengineering of configurations based on mathematical concept analysis. ACM Trans Softw Eng Methodol 5(2):146–189

[SPL09]   SPLOT, http://gsd.uwaterloo.ca:8088/SPLOT/splot_open_source.html

[TBK09]   Thüm T, Batory D, Kästner C (2009) Reasoning about edits to feature models, In: Proceedings of ICSE'09. ACM/IEEE, pp 254–264

[Tou12]   Touretzky DS (2012) Seven big ideas in robotics, and how to teach them. In: Proceedings of the 43rd ACM technical symposium on computer science education. ACM, pp 39–44

[WG04]   Webber DL, Gomaa H (2004) Modeling variability in software product lines with the variation point model. Sci Comput Program 53(3):305–331

Chapter 5
Model-Driven Specification in Designing Smart LOs

5.1 Introduction

In the previous chapter, I have presented a systematic approach to analyse CS learning and teaching as a research domain. The analysis has been provided through modelling of the domain. The result of modelling was a set of the devised models. Those models, in fact, bring an important knowledge, though it is not enough to define and investigate the new kind of LOs called smart LOs. In this chapter, my aim is to extend the theoretical background of smart LOs *directly*.

Here, the word 'directly' means that feature modelling is also a part of the theoretical background, which was presented in Chap. 4 *implicitly*, i.e. without using the term SLO. As computer science (CS) deals with the relevant problem solving, at the very abstract level, the field can be viewed as *the mapping* of the *problem domain* onto the *solution domain*. The reader should not be confused by the use of these two terms again (they have been introduced in Sect. 4.8). Aiming at presenting the reader with the understanding of the topics to be considered here, two questions are important: (1) what is the problem domain? And (2) what is the solution domain in terms of our intention to introduce smart LOs as a basic topic of the book?

The answer to the first question is very clear – CS learning and teaching has been our problem domain already represented by the abstract feature models in Chap. 4. Here, however, the reader should interpret the CS learning and teaching domain also as *learning variability*, i.e. as some model that represents the domain. We will provide the formal definition of the term later.

An attentive reader may give a general answer to the second question easily as follows: the solution domain is a set of approaches used to implement the tasks of the problem domain. In a wider context, this set can be viewed as a methodology, while in the narrow sense, it can be treated as a technology. In our case, *meta-programming* is just the *implementation technology*.

© Springer International Publishing Switzerland 2015
V. Štuikys, *Smart Learning Objects for Smart Education in Computer Science*,
DOI 10.1007/978-3-319-16913-2_5

The aim of this chapter is to present the *model-driven* and *transformation-driven* view in designing smart LOs. This view, in fact, has been borrowed from the SW engineering domain. In our case, the learning variability serves as a *bridge* to connect the *problem domain models* with the *solution domain models* through the adequate *meta-model* and model transformations. Here, the term *meta-model* should be understood as a model that specifies the other models. Therefore, here we present both the problem and solution domains abstractly at three levels: meta-model, model and model elements.

Now, at the very beginning, it is possible to define smart LOs (SLOs) by adding new attributes as complementary to the ones given in Chap. 1.

Definition 5.1 Smart LO is the *meta-level specification* that implements the CS *learning variability* using meta-programming as a technology to automatically generate and adapt the learning content on demand according to the *preprogrammed context* and needs of the user.

This definition better fit to our aim of this chapter. The highlighted terms within the definition require a separate intensive discussion. The latter will be introduced gradually, starting from Sect. 5.2. Therefore, the reader should be patient with respect to the extent of understanding of our approach.

5.2   Literature Review

As usual, after presenting the introduction, I start considering the topic by reviewing the relative work. As it is clear from the given definition, we need to focus on two subjects here: model-driven CS learning variability and relevant implementation technology. The related work of the first subject was thoroughly discussed in Chap. 4, though without the explicit use of the term *learning variability* (in Sect. 4.2, variability was discussed explicitly from the perspective of SW engineering). Therefore, we focus more on the second subject here. As there is a wide spectrum of technological issues, we ignore the standard (well-adapted) technologies, such as the Internet and also technologies needed to build e-learning and teaching environments (in our case robot based).

Two main technologies, namely, the generative and agent-based ones, are treated as most relevant to implement SLOs. As both technologies have a much wider context of use, we restrict ourselves on only those aspects, which are relevant to our aims. Here, by technology, we mean facilities for representing, transferring and processing the content and knowledge to support the SLO concept. Context-based modelling also should be at the focus as the given SLO definition claims. However, this topic is more relevant to Chap. 7. Therefore, this review is restricted because the relevant topics are considered in the other chapters.

First, we analyse some essential features of SLO as compared to the other well-known kinds of LOs as follows:

1. *Similarly* to the generative LO (shortly GLO), introduced by Boyle, Leeder, and Morales [BLC04, MLB05], SLO is the *executable specification*; in [GLO14], for example, GLO is defined as *an articulated and executable learning design that produces a class of learning objects.*
2. *Similarly* to the meta-programming-based GLO (introduced in our papers [ŠD08, DŠ08]), SLO is the *high-level executable* specification.
3. *Similarly* to the agent-based LO [Sto08] and recommended systems for e-learning (introduced in paper [VMO+12]), SLO is the *context-aware specification*, though the context is treated as a static item.
4. *Unlikely* to the GLO [ŠD08], SLO is *a highly reusable specification*, i.e. it implements learning variability using the strategy 'design for reuse and design with reuse' along with modelling and model transformation capabilities.
5. *Unlikely* to the GLO of both kinds [BLC04, ŠD08], SLO is the context-aware specification containing the preprogrammed context for adaptation to the user's needs on demand [BBD+14].

We introduce the additional features (such as a more precise description of context awareness and others) to define the SLO later in Chap. 7, 8 and 12. Next, we present some of the most relevant publications for more extensive studies of the topics we will discuss in this chapter. The book [ABK+14] focuses on the development, maintenance and implementation of product line variability along with a broad classification of tools and techniques for all stages of the development process and a detailed discussion of trade-offs. The reader can learn more about generative programming from the book [CE00]. Meta-programming might be seen as a methodology that combines different views on model and program transformations. More on the topics can be learned from [ŠD13]. A very concise introduction into the GLO context awareness topic can be found in our recent paper [BBD+14]. Our paper [ŠBB+14] deals next with the GLO specialization problem. We present the other related references in the adequate places of this chapter.

5.3   A Framework to Design Smart LOs

The bases of defining and presenting this framework are the following issues: (1) reuse-based design strategy and modelling of learning variability, (2) the modelling approach and the CS teaching domain models devised in Chap. 4 and (3) creating concrete high-level models for both the *problem domain* (i.e. CS teaching and learning in a concrete situation) and the *solution domain* (i.e. meta-programming to specify SLO). Below we discuss the issues in more detail.

5.3.1 Modelling and Reuse-Based Design Strategy

This section is written mainly using the ideas presented in our published papers [ŠBD13, BBD+14], as well as the adequate reuse-oriented papers borrowed from the SW engineering domain.

At the very abstract level, the e-learning process can be identified as an interaction among the following components with the tightly integrated feedback links: (i) *pedagogy-driven activities*, (ii) *technology-driven processes, (iii) knowledge transfer channels with the actors* involved, (iv) a set of *tools* used (they can also be treated as technology) and (v) the *pedagogical outcome* [ŠBD13]. Any form of LO (stand-alone instance, GLO, SLO) stands for an instrument to supply the teaching content. The latter, in fact, enables the interfacing, integrating and functioning of the components as the whole e-learning system. No matter what form we are able to select for representing the teaching content, the whole cycle includes the following processes: to *design*, to *search*, to *adapt* and to *use* the content. With respect to reusability in mind (this vision prevails in e-learning; see Chap. 3), the processes should be handled and managed as effectively as possible. Here, for this purpose, we introduce and apply the *reuse-based framework* as a strategy borrowed from the SWE domain, which is known as *design for reuse* (D*f*R) and *design with reuse* (D*w*R) [Sam97]. We have adapted it to our aims (see Fig. 5.1). Note that there are different terms of the framework (such as a twin life-cycle model [Sam97], product line engineering [PBL05] or software families [Par76]) to express the similar meaning).

Here, we focus mainly on the top level of the framework, i.e. on D*f*R. In fact, the part of this framework called 'learning domain analysis and modelling' (see Fig. 5.1) summarizes the activities we have described in Chap. 4. We will discuss the lower-level part (i.e. D*w*R) of the framework later, in Chaps. 7, 8 and 11. D*f*R aims at understanding the e-learning domain (e.g. CS in our case) through its modelling. The modelling should be guided by the clearly stated goal with the use of the well-defined approach. In our case, the goal is to extract the relevant data and represent them into some generic form (e.g. feature diagram usually considered as a domain model (see Chap. 4) to facilitate the construction of SLOs). At this level, the domain model describes two general aspects: domain *commonality* and domain *variability* (the terms are coined from [CHW98]; see also Property 4.9 in Sect. 4.6). In [ŠBD13], we have introduced the e-learning variability (LV) as a composition of the *pedagogical variability* (PV), *social variability* (SV), *content variability* (CV), *technological variability* (TV) and *interaction variability* (IV). Abstractly, we can express LV as follows:

$$LV = PV \circ SV \circ CV \circ TV \circ IV. \tag{5.1}$$

Here, *variability* is understood as an attribute to indicate the existence of variants in the subject (pedagogy, sociality, etc.), and '$\circ$' means some kind of composition.

Fig. 5.1 A framework to adapt the known reuse paradigm (D*f*R/D*w*R) for e-learning domain (Adapted from [BBD+14])

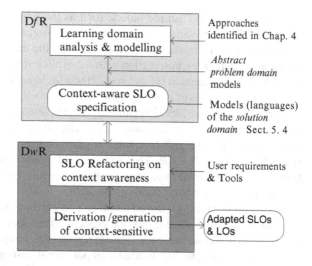

In Eq. (5.1), we consciously omitted the explicit context. The explanation of that is as follows. We define the *context* as an *implicit or explicit factor influencing to delivering the content for teaching*. As the PV and SV, in fact, are those factors, we accept them as a *teaching context* here. The basic assumption is that the context may have variants too (e.g. types of the pedagogical model such as *problem based* and *project based*, student social variability such as *beginner* and *intermediate*, etc.). Therefore, we can speak also about the context variability as well. However, there is also a *specific context* to specify a *relation* among different variability aspects such as content and social issues (we will discuss this later as feature priority).

As any kind of variability we are able to express through higher-level features (see Chap. 4, for details), the D*f*R activity results in context-aware SLO models. As learning variability is a relatively new term, we provide a more extensive discussion on this and related topics (relevant to our context) in the next section.

5.3.2   Analysis of Learning Variability by Example

We do that (using the example taken from [ŠBD13]) because the term is the conceptual basis to understand our approach in general and the further sections in particular. For the CS researchers and, perhaps, for the knowledgeable CS teachers and students, an SLO is a higher-level program. Otherwise, it is a meta-program, because it generates other programs (meaning lower-level ones) automatically (see Definition 5.1 in Sect. 5.1). For less knowledgeable readers (because GLOs and SLOs need still to live up their promises to become more widely accepted in the e-learning domain), we explain the variability concept as a basis to understand the meta-programming-based SLOs more thoroughly.

Let us have a very simple object, such as the linear equation ($y = ax + b$), and interpret it from the variability perspective in different domains (mathematics, CS and e-learning). In mathematics, for example, the equation is a canonical form meaning the general representation with the explicit statement of eligible values for the argument (x), function (y) and coefficients (a, b) is as follows: $x, y, a, b \in \mathbb{R}$. In a particular case, however, some specific variants ($a > 0, a < 0, a = 0, b \neq 0$, etc.) may be excluded and considered separately. All these are variability in that domain, though this term is not exploited here. The function is formally defined as a mapping of the argument (variable) eligible domain D onto the function value space R, that is, $f: D \rightarrow R$. The elegance and beautifulness of the mathematical language is its potential to express the items (objects, categories) uniformly and as general and short representations as possible.

In CS (programming), the equation can be easily transformed into a computer program to calculate y values for the predetermined space of values for x, a and b. The space in this case, however, is much narrower *as compared to the mathematical representation* due to the limited computational resources. Variability (if one realizes the program) could be seen in part explicitly and in part implicitly within the program source code. Now we summarize the discussion (see Table 5.1) and explain the difference between the program and the meta-program-based SLO using some rationale and the same example. From the outcome (i.e. program execution) perspective, a program (if it is correct and terminates) always returns a *concrete value* as a result of the calculation (e.g. $y = 51$ when $a = 2$, $x = 20$ and $b = 11$), while the meta-program returns the *other program (programs)* as a value (e. g. $y := 2*x + 11$;) when both higher-level parameters a and b are equal to 2 and 11 adequately. As the parameters a and b are used to model *variability*, we need to express them through meta-functions (abstractly they are denoted as $f(p1)$ and $f(p2)$ in Table 5.1).

This subtle difference opens the way to extend reusability and generate the program instance on demand and use it as a subject for reuse (use-as-is, transfer for other contexts with or without modification).

E-learning is not a homogeneous domain; rather it is a combination of the following subdomains: pedagogy, information sciences, IT-based technology and sociology, psychology and computer science (sometimes also called informatics; actually it is also a combination of the others). As a consequence, the e-learning variability (*LV*) is also not a homogeneous item; rather it is a set of the constituents as it is defined by Eq. (5.1).

We hope that the introduced framework and provided example to explain the learning variability concept as a basis to develop SLOs will be helpful for the reader to better understand the processes and tasks we consider in the following sections. In the next section, we define the design tasks and processes used within the top-level part (i.e. D/R) of the introduced framework.

Table 5.1 Running example of a smart LO: conceptual level with comparisons

Domain	Domain instance	Objects of the instance	Properties and variability values	Result of manipulation
Mathematics (algebra)	*Function* *y=ax+b*	*Function, variable, constants, operations, relation*	x, y, a, b∈R Algebra laws: Operation priority, commutative law	Representation form; cognition of algebra laws by learners
Programming	*Program* *y:=a*x+b;* *L={y, :=, a, *, x, +, b}* L: program language	*Variable, constants, operations, statement*	a∈[2..10] b∈[11..30] x∈[20..40] *a, b and x are variability for lower-level calculation*	A value of y defined by the computer program, e.g. y=51, when a=2, b=11 and x=20
Meta-programming	*Meta-program* *y:= f(p1)*x + f (p2);* *L1={'y', ':=', '*', 'x', '+'}* *L2={f(p1), f(p2)}* *p1, p2 –* parameters L1: target language L2: meta-language (alphabets)	*Meta-objects: Parameters,* *parameter values, functions (f(p1, f(p2)) substituting a parameter by its value*	Elements of {'y', ':=', '*', 'x', '+'} are *commonality;* a and b are *variability with variants for a∈[2..10]* and b∈[11..30] *for higher-level calculation*	A program instance, defined by the L2 processor, i. e. y:= 2*x +11; when f(p1)=2 f(p2)= 11

5.3.3   Meta-Level Processes and SLO Design Tasks

First, we define the *high-level* (i.e. *meta-level*) *processes* to design SLOs. The modelling process and approaches discussed in Chap. 4 are regarded as the *primary processes* to design SLOs. The primary processes result in creating *the abstract feature models* (see Property 4.14, in Sect. 4.6) applicable to the whole CS topics as it is depicted in Fig. 4.1. To make the abstract models suitable in a concrete situation (i.e. to create SLO), we need to derive the *concrete model* instances. This procedure is based on feature selecting and manipulating on the abstract feature models. In Sect. 5.4, we present the approach to create the concrete model instance for the development of SLO using the model-driven paradigm. Typically, the paradigm can be seen as the process of derivation of (i) a meta-model from its

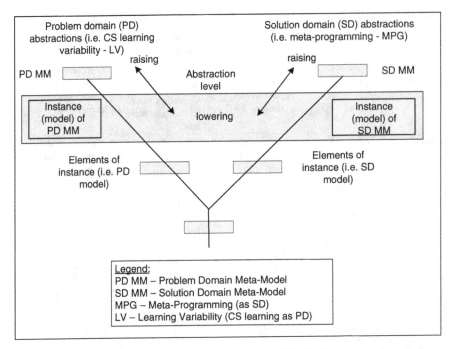

Fig. 5.2 Representation of the paradigm using Y-chart (© With kind permission from Springer Science + Business Media from [ŠD13])

meta-meta-model and (ii) a model element from its meta-model, which we represent by the Y-chart in Fig. 5.2 taken from [ŠD13].

Here, we use the only intermediate part of the Y-chart, which is outlined by the rectangle. The latter describes two common design processes at the model level: *specification of the problem domain model instance* (left branch of the chart; see Fig. 5.2) and *specification of the solution domain model instance* (right branch of the chart). Both processes are the high-level processes. Note that the CS learning variability is the problem domain, whereas meta-programming (MPG) is the solution domain. The concrete languages (meta-language and target language) are treated as instances of the solution domain. Note also that we are able to specify both domains abstractly using the same formalism, i.e. feature-based notation if the basic terms of the domains are predefined (see Sects. 5.4.1 and 5.5). Later we describe the meta-meta models for both problem and solution domains.

Now, using the model-driven paradigm, we are able to formulate the SLO design tasks at the high level of abstraction as follows.

Task 1 is to develop the feature-based specification of the problem domain instance (see Sect. 5.4). The problem domain instance (which is represented by the feature model) is derived from the problem domain meta-model (denoted as PD MM in Fig. 5.2, and its full specification using the meta-meta model is given in Fig. 5.3).

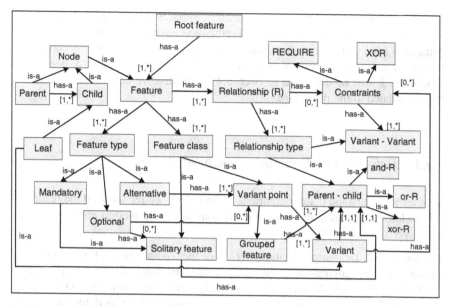

Fig. 5.3 Feature diagram (FD) meta-model (© With kind permission from Springer Science + Business Media from [ŠD13])

Task 2 is to develop the feature-based specification of the solution domain instance (see Sect. 5.5). The solution domain instance (which also should be represented by the feature model) is derived from the solution domain meta-model (denoted as SD MM in Fig. 5.2, and its full specification is the same meta-meta model given in Fig. 5.3).

Task 3 is to map the problem domain model, i.e. the specification defined by *Task 1*, onto the solution domain model, i.e. the specification defined by *Task 2* (see Sect. 5.5). Task 3, in fact, is the transformation task, in which elements of the problem domain model are transformed into the adequate elements of the solution domain model using the prescribed transformation rules. All those issues we will discuss later in detail in Chap. 6.

Now, in the following sections, we continue our discussion on designing the high-level specifications for both domains (problem and solution).

5.4   Feature Selecting and Manipulating to Form Concrete Model Instance for the Problem Domain

The aim is to derive the *concrete model instance* from a set of abstract feature models constructed in Chap. 4 for the problem domain (i.e. CS learning and teaching). As it will be shown later (see Sect. 5.4.1), the concrete model instances have the variant points. The latter is defined by variants that appear in the model as an atomic feature (i.e. terminal node). Furthermore, as the concrete model is to be composed from different abstract models, we also need to describe the composite manipulations on the abstract models. Thus, to do that, we need a systematic procedure. It will be described in Sect. 5.4.2. But first we define the basic terms that are related to the procedure.

5.4.1 Definition of Learning Variability Terms

In order to understand better definitions given below, we recommend the reader to refresh knowledge on more detailed definitions of feature models and their examples given in Chap. 4.

Definition 5.2 Learning variability (*LV*) is the *composition* of the following constituents: pedagogical variability (PV), social variability (SV), content variability (CV), technological variability (TV) and interaction variability (IV) as it is defined by Eq. (5.1) plus *specific context variability* (SCV) to define a relation among other kinds of variability.

Definition 5.3 Pedagogical variability (PV) model is the *concrete feature diagram* (FD_{PV}) constructed using the feature-based language, the adequate *abstract feature models* (such as learning objective, motivation, teaching model; see Sect. 4.5 for the first two) and tools to specify the models and provide modelling.

Definition 5.4 Social variability (SV) model is the *concrete feature diagram* (FD_{SV}) constructed using the feature-based language and tools to specify this kind of variability to support modelling.

Examples are learner's gender (male, female), previous knowledge (low, good, very good) and learner's profile (beginner, intermediate, advanced) to name a few.

Definition 5.5 Content variability (CV) model is the *concrete feature diagram* (FD_{CV}) constructed using the feature-based language and tools to specify this kind of variability to support modelling.

For the concrete example of the content variability (though it is presented informally for three domains), see Table 5.1 in Sect. 5.3.2.

Definition 5.6 Technological variability (TV) model is *the concrete feature diagram* (FD_{TV}) to specify technological characteristics of the educational environment (such as robot based).

Definition 5.7 Interaction variability (IV) model is a part of the concrete feature diagram (FD_{LV}) to specify constraints (*requires* and *excludes*) among other kinds of variability.

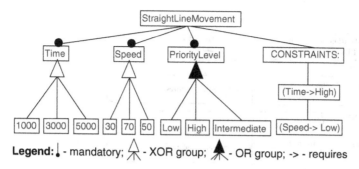

Fig. 5.4 FD instance to specify the robot's straight-line movement task

Definition 5.8 *Specific context variability* (SCV) model is a *concrete node* within the feature diagram FD_{LV} to specify the context along with the constraint *requires* identified among the context node and the adequate nodes (e.g. pedagogical, social or content ones).

We consider the real illustrative example of the models IV and SCV in Fig. 5.4. Here, we present a concrete FD to specify the robot's straight-line movement using the FAMILIAR notation (see Sect. 4.3.6, Table 4.2). The task implements the linear algorithm. Two features *time* and *speed* are the content features. They are also treated as *variant points*, each having three *variants*. The feature *priority level*, in fact, is the SCV model. Thus, we model the context by the priority levels here as follows: {*low, high, intermediate*}. The model IV is described by the feature CONSTRAINTS: *time requires high priority* and *speed requires low priority*.

Note that the model (Fig. 5.4) is the aggregation (composition) of three models: content, context (i.e. SCV) and interaction variability (IV). Note also that we will consider the *context model* more thoroughly in Chap. 7.

Definition 5.9 Learning variability model is the *concrete feature diagram* (FD_{LV}) specifying this kind of variability as it is specified by Eq. (5.2):

$$FD_{LV} = (FD_{PV}) \text{ o } (FD_{SV}) \text{ o } (FD_{CV}) \text{ o } (FD_{TV}) \text{ o } (FD_{SCV}). \qquad (5.2)$$

Here, 'o' means an operator to aggregate (integrate) feature-based models. Note that the interaction variability (IV) has no specific node within the model (if we consider a standard representation, but not the FAMILIAR-based one; see Fig. 5.4). As a result, there is no separate FD in Eq. (5.2). Note also that all kinds of variability components of Eq. (5.2) are modelled by the adequate *variant points* and *variants*.

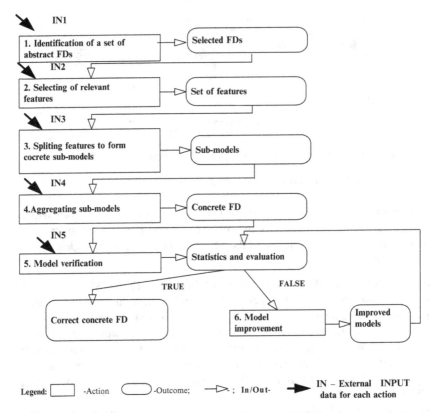

Fig. 5.5 Scheme to derive concrete models from abstract models

5.4.2 A Procedure to Obtain the Concrete Model Instance

We present the procedure as a set of the sequential processes and their outcomes in Fig. 5.5. We provide the description in the similar way as it was done previously in Chap. 4 to devise abstract feature models (see Sect. 4.4 and Fig. 4.2). As now the reader is aware about the form of representing the topic, we omit many descriptive details here.

The external input IN1 (see Fig. 5.5) includes the following items: identification of concrete teaching method, concrete teaching theme, concrete student profile and technology to be used. The external input IN2 includes: task selection and requirements for the concrete tasks. The external input IN3 includes: selected features for concrete tasks (see Figs. 5.6 and 5.4). The external input IN4 includes FAMILIAR tools for manipulating to create a concrete feature model. And finally, the external input IN5 includes SPLOT tools to verify the concrete model.

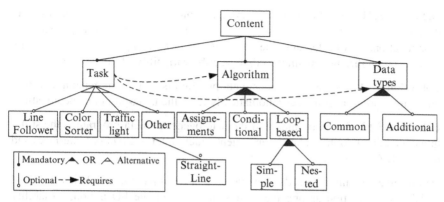

Fig. 5.6 A slightly modified abstract FD given in Fig. 4.6 (see Chap. 4)

5.5 Definitions of the Solution Domain

The aim is to define the solution domain, i.e. heterogeneous meta-programming abstractly at the model level (without specific details), so that the reader could be able to understand the essence of the programming paradigm. We seek that the reader would be prepared for dealing with the deeper insights into the domain to be presented later. In fact, we have already started the introduction of this paradigm (see the conceptual reasoning on meta-programming in Sect. 5.3.2). With regard to the stated tasks in Sect. 5.3.3, this section is about the way of solving Task 2.

Once again, we want to remind the reader the general property of SLO. Syntactically, SLO and meta-program are, in fact, the same items; however, semantically they are quite different structures. SLO specifies the learning variability that describes *heterogeneous features* of the CS learning domain. Meta-programs, on the other hand, if they are treated as abstract entities, specify the *domain variability* without the specific insights into the domain semantics. Next, we start with the definition of the basic terms of heterogeneous meta-programming (He MPG).

5.5.1 Definitions of Basic Meta-Programming Terms and SLO

Definition 5.10 Meta-programming (MPG) is a higher-level programming paradigm to support generative reuse by creating generalized programs called meta-programs.

The generalization can be achieved using the two kinds of meta-programming: homogeneous and heterogeneous (He). One can learn more on homogeneous meta-programming from [ŠD13] or other related sources. As He MPG is the basis to implement SLOs, we define this technology in more detail as follows.

Definition 5.11 He MPG is such a paradigm which uses *at least two languages* to develop meta-programs. The first is a *target language* serving for expressing the base functionality of a domain. The second is a *meta-language* aiming to expressing generalization through parameters that describe variability of the domain.

Definition 5.12 The heterogeneous meta-program is a program generator to produce target program instances automatically from the meta-program specification.

Definition 5.13 Structural model of the heterogeneous meta-program is the structure containing two interrelated components: meta-interface (simply interface) and meta-body (simply body).

Definition 5.14 Interface is the declaration of a set of parameters, their values and variability interaction among the values. In terms of the FD notion, variability interaction is defined as constraints posed on some kinds of features.

Definition 5.15 Meta-body (further body) is the implementation of the declaration given in the interface. The implementation specifies the detailed relationship among the interface items (i.e. parameters) and the base domain functionality using two languages (meta- and target).

Definition 5.16 Meta-program parameters are syntax-driven variables (within the interface and body of a meta-program) to express and represent the *domain variability* independently on the *domain semantics*.

We first remind the given informal definitions (see Table 5.1 in Sect. 5.3.2) and then provide formal definitions of the adequate terms as follows.

Definition 5.17 Computational (behavioural) model of the heterogeneous meta-program is the process within the meta-language environment to process the specification to produce the target program instances.

Definition 5.18 *Meta-programming-based smart LO* (further SLO) is *the heterogeneous meta-program,* assuming that the latter implements learning variability to express the CS learning and teaching concepts and computational model (Definition 5.17).

Definition 5.19 Structurally, SLO is the structure containing two elements: (i) interface expressed through parameters and (ii) meta-body expressed through (meta-) functions of a meta-language to specify the content variants expressed in a target language.

The list of the presented definitions is by no means full. Here, we have defined the only basic terms that are needed to achieve the goal of this section, i.e. to express the terms through features and their relationships. We have omitted, for example, the *contextualization aspects* in defining of SLO here (see Definition 5.18). We will provide a more thorough discussion on context issues later (see Chap. 7, where we focus on adaptation problem). As we have presented the definitions abstractly, some debate on the topic is needed. We provide such a discussion in the next section.

5.5.2   More on Meta-Programming and SLO

For the CS educators and course designers, the following questions are always at the focus: (1) which programming language is to be used in teaching and (2) how it should be delivered to students?

There are many debates on the topics (see, e.g. [KP05]). As SLO is the executable specification, which contains within constructs that are represented by *at least two languages*, the linguistic aspects are extremely important – if not to say more – they predefine both a methodology of creating SLOs and using them as a teaching material. Note that, in terms of SLO and meta-programming, the *target language* is also the *teaching language*. Note also that He MPG is independent upon the use of a target language [ŠD13]. Therefore, this programming paradigm does not restrict in selecting of the teaching language. What is about the meta-language? We have also shown that any programming language (we have investigated C++, Java, C# and PHP) can be used in the role of a meta-language. We will provide a more extensive discussion on the topic in Chap. 9.

Here, we aim to explain the actual meaning of the phrase *at least two languages* (see Definition 5.11) from the learning and teaching perspective. The simplest and most typical explanation might be as follows. Suppose you have an SLO as a meta-program. Now you want to send this SLO to a server (in fact, now all teaching materials and the SLO, as one of that sort, are or should be available online). Before doing so, you need to add yet another specification level by describing the item with HTML. It is just the third language, though its role is quite different as compared to those used within the SLO specification.

The next example is more complicated, but also it relates to the Internet. Say, CS students are studying the Internet-based programming. In order to program the application task, they need to use a set of target languages (HTML, XML, SSL, PHP or the like) to represent the basic domain functionality. If they want to have a *generic specification* for the task, they need to apply a meta-programming-based approach to code the task by a meta-language (for more details, see [ŠD13]).

This short discussion may serve as a hint to considering the following problem: whether or not the multi-language specifications might be the teaching topics in the CS curricular. We left this topic as a research and exercise question (Sect. 5.7).

Now we are ready to discuss the feature-based vision of meta-programming and SLO concepts at the higher level of abstraction by introducing the concept of *meta-model*.

5.5.3   Meta-Model of Meta-Program and SLO

The aim of the feature-based representation is twofold. The first is the understandability issues. As feature models have the well-defined graphical notation (e.g. within accepted and used tools such as FAMILIAR and SPLOT), the models can be grasped and understood intuitively. The visual representation is the *smart repre-sentation*. Therefore, the SLO feature models might be seen as a generalized teaching material at the higher level of abstraction. The users of such models might be the course designers and the adequate educational tool designers in the first place. The models might also be beneficial for the CS teachers, for example, to accept and accommodate 'the higher-level computational thinking', to present, to disseminate the advanced teaching concepts, etc.

The second aim is more concrete: we need to formalize uniformly the solution of the transformation task, i.e. Task 3 (see also Chap. 6, for details). How can we move from the abstract definitions to the feature-based definitions of the solution domain? Again, we need first to return to the definition of the term *feature*. The variety of definitions means universality and independence of the use of the approach in different situations. Next, what we need to do is to analyse the definitions presented in Sect. 5.5.1 (and perhaps the full specification of a meta-program) and then to recognize the aspects to treat them as features. One can identify at least the following aspects: linguistic, structural and relationship based. Finally, we need to decompose the aspects into smaller ones, to treat them as features, to introduce a hierarchy of the features and to present them by the adequate feature diagram. Therefore, the feature-based reasoning can be also applied to the solution domain.

With respect to the model-driven approach, we are able to generalize the solution domain by presenting its meta-model. In fact, this meta-model has already been introduced along with the Y-chart we discussed in Sect. 5.3.3. Here, the meta-program meta-model (MPG MM) is indicated in the right branch on the highest level (see Fig. 5.2). In general, a meta-model specifies the other models. Here, by the meta-model we mean a description that specifies all theoretically possible variants of meta-programs, which are indicated by the meta-model. To specify the meta-model, we use the object-oriented notation proposed by OMG. The notation uses two kinds of items: objects (denoted by rectangular) and relationships (denoted by arrows) along with the explanation text and labels denoted as [. . .]. For example, the label [1, *] means that the object to which the label relates may have at least one item. Note that here we do not make the distinction between the meta-model of SLO and meta-program.

The specification of that meta-model contains two types of entities, i.e. <*meta-interface model*> and <*meta-body model*>, and entities that are used to construct these two models (see Fig. 5.7). For example, the <*meta-interface model*> is constructed of meta-parameters. They are described using meta-constructs derived from a meta-language. The <*meta-body*> is constructed of two parts: modifica-tion/change model and program instance model. The latter is derived from a domain language. The structure of the meta-model should be interpreted as follows. All entities in the description (see Fig. 5.7) are abstractions of the solution domain, i.e. meta-programming per se. By adding the word *model* to any entity, we intend to specify any entity of that kind, but not its concrete instance. For example, the modification/change model describes all possible changes within the meta-model. A set of domain languages means that a concrete target language is yet not specified

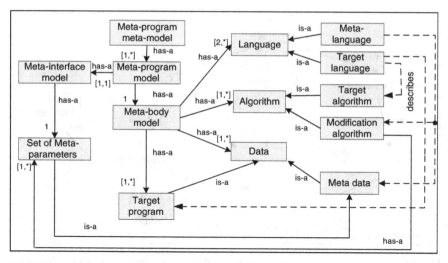

Fig. 5.7 Specification of meta-program meta-model (© With kind permission from Springer Science + Business Media from [ŠD13])

at this level. The same relates to meta-languages. We consider the instantiation of the meta-model in the next subsection.

5.5.4 Instance of SLO Derived from Its Meta-Model

Formally, the model instance of SLO is created through the instantiation process using its meta-model (Fig. 5.7) that is one-level higher than the instance model itself (see also Fig. 5.2). The instance of the SLO meta-model is given in Fig. 5.8. This description differs from the previous one (see Fig. 5.7) in the following: (a) the *target language instance* (in other words, teaching language) is derived from the *set of target languages* (in Fig. 5.7 they are described implicitly as the item *target language*); (b) the *meta-language instance* is derived from the set of meta-language (in Fig. 5.7 they are described implicitly as the item *meta-language*); (c) modification/change model is substituted by the concrete algorithm to implement changes prespecified by the given requirements; (d) SLO instance, parameters and interface are also concretized in the same way.

In order to create an instance of a modification algorithm, however, we need to know the requirements for change in developing SLO. Though the requirements are formulated by the user or/and the domain analyst at the level that is higher than the model, we have included requirements for change in the description of the model for clearness. We describe all that in detail in Chap. 6.

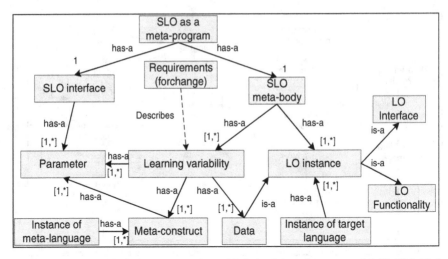

Fig. 5.8 Instance of SLO (meta-program) model derived from its meta-model (© With kind permission from Springer Science + Business Media from [ŠD13])

5.6 Summary, Discussion and Concluding Remarks

We have focused on the high-level design aspects in designing SLO here. By high-level design aspects, we mean the reuse-based *strategy* that, in general terms, has been presented as *design for reuse* and *design with reuse*. We have only discussed the first part of this framework, leaving the space of discussing the second part in the subsequent chapters. We have borrowed this paradigm from the SW engineering (SWE) domain; however, we have applied it with the specific focus on CS learning, aiming to specify SLO for this domain. We have presented the SLO specification tasks abstractly using the model-driven and model-driven transformation concepts, again borrowed from SWE.

The basis of this design vision is the *learning variability* concept. Though this new term (we mean the e-learning domain only, but not SWE) can be grasped and understood intuitively, we have presented the term and related topics from different perspectives: by analysing a simple illustrative example, by defining the term formally and by showing its role to the model-driven transformations.

We have considered SLO specification tasks as the high-level transformations that include, first, the development of the concrete feature models of the problem domain (i.e. CS teaching) and, second, the identification models and base notation for the solution domain (i.e. meta-programming). Our aim was to present both domains as abstractly and generally as possible. Therefore, we have introduced some concepts of meta-modelling (such as meta-meta-model, meta-model and derivation of the lower-level models or their parts from the higher-level ones). We have found the Y-chart representation (taken from [ŠD13]) of the concepts as a relevant means to describe the model-driven transformations. We have specified two model-based specifications in designing SLO: learning variability feature models and meta-programming-based models. What has been left to the further discussion about this approach in Chap. 6 is the *concrete procedure* of mapping CS learning variability feature models onto the meta-programming-based models.

As the complexity of systems or their components grows in all dimensions (technological, methodological, market requirements, etc.), the model-driven perspective in designing the modern systems prevails now. The CS teaching domain with own challenges stated in Chap. 1 should not be departed from the other domains in which the model-driven approaches are widely used and are matured enough. Having in mind this perspective, we hope that the presented approach not only serves for our particular aim to specify SLO at the higher level of abstraction. We believe in the soundness and applicability of the discussed issues in a much wider context of the e-learning community. This expectation is due to the heterogeneity of the e-learning domain in which there are evident signs and efforts to introduce the respective ideas and approaches from more matured domains such as computer science and SW engineering.

5.7 Research and Exercise Questions

5.1. Discuss the actual meaning of the paradigm 'design for reuse and design with reuse' using, for example, the sources [Sam97, ABK+14]. Draw a distinguishing line between design for reuse and design with reuse.

5.2. Define and discuss more thoroughly the actual meaning of the term variability using the following sources [CHW98, CBK13].

5.3. Discuss the commonality-variability issues in your domain of interest.

5.4. Define the basic terms of feature modelling once again.

5.5. What is the difference between the abstract and concrete feature models?

5.6. Define the commonality-variability model in your domain of interest using feature-based notation.

5.7. Draw a distinguishing between the following terms: model, meta-model and meta-meta-model.

5.8. Define the essence of meta-modelling. What is the essence of the model-driven transformative approach?

5.9. Learn more about the Y-chart representation. Might it be useful to represent your problem and solution domain?

5.10. Explain the essence of the statement: *Design as a mapping of the problem domain onto the solution domain.*

5.11. Discuss and present your vision on teaching multi-language specifications in CS courses.

References

[ABK+14]   Apel S, Batory D, Kästner Ch, Saake G (2014) Feature-oriented software product lines: concepts and implementation. Springer, Berlin

[BBD+14]   Burbaitė R, Bespalova K, Damaševičius R, Štuikys V (2014) Context-aware generative learning objects for teaching of computer science. Int J Eng Educ 30(4):929–936

[BLC04]   Boyle T, Leeder D, Chase H (2004) To boldly GLO – towards the next generation of learning objects. In: World conference on eLearning in corporate, government, healthcare and higher education, Washington, DC, November 2004

[CBK13]   Capilla R, Bosch J, Kang KC (eds) (2013) Systems and software variability management (concepts, tools and experiences). Springer, New York

[CE00]   Czarnecki K, Eisenecker U (2000) Generative programming: methods, tools and applications. Addison-Wesley, Boston

[CHW98]   Coplien J, Hoffman D, Weiss D (1998) Commonality and variability in software engineering. IEEE Soft 15:37–45

[DŠ08]   Damaševičius R, Štuikys V (2008) On the technological aspects of generative learning object development. In: Informatics education-supporting computational thinking: third international conference on informatics in secondary schools-evolution and perspectives, ISSEP 2008 Torun, Proceedings, vol 5090. Springer, 1–4 Jul 2008, pp 337–348

[GLO14]   Reusable learning objects. What are GLO's. http://www.rlo-cetl.ac.uk/whatwedo/glos/whatareglos.php. http://www.rlo-cetl.ac.uk/whatwedo/glos/whatareglos.php. Viewed on 16 Apr 2014

[KP05]   Kelleher C, Pausch R (2005) Lowering the barriers to programming: a taxonomy of programming environments and languages for novice programmers. In: ACM computing surveys. New York, NY, USA, vol. 37, No. 2, pp 83–137

[MLB05]   Morales R, Leeder D, Boyle T (2005) A case in the design of generative learning objects (GLOs): applied statistical methods. In: Proceedings of world conference on educational multimedia, hypermedia and telecommunications. AACE, Chesapeake

[Par76]   Parnas DL (1976) On the design and development of program families. Softw Eng IEEE Trans 2(1):1–9

[PBL05]   Pohl K, Bockle G, van der Linden F (2005) Software product line engineering. Springer, New York

[Sam97]   Sametinger J (1997) Software engineering with reusable components. Springer, New York

[Sto08]   Stoilescu D (2008) Modalities of using learning objects for intelligent agents in learning. Interdisc J E-Learn Learn Objects 4:49–64

[ŠBB14]   Štuikys V, Bespalova K, Burbaitė R (2014) Generative learning object (GLO) specialization: teacher's and learner's view. In: Proceedings of 20th international conference ICIST. Springer, Lithuania, 9–10 Oct 2014

[ŠBD13]   Štuikys V, Burbaitė R, Damaševičius R (2013) Teaching of computer science topics using meta-programming-based GLOs and LEGO robots. Inform Educ 12(1):125–142

[ŠD08]   Štuikys V, Damaševičius R (2008) Development of generative learning objects using feature diagrams and generative techniques. Inform Educ 7(2):277–288

[ŠD13]   Štuikys V, Damaševičius R (2013) Meta-programming and model-driven metaprogram development: principles, processes and techniques. Springer, London/Heidelberg/New York/Dordrecht

[VMO+12]   Verbert K, Manouselis N, Ochoa X, Wolpers M, Drachsler H, Bosnic I, Duval E (2012) Context-aware recommender systems for learning: a survey and future challenges. IEEE Trans Learn Technol 5(4):318–335

Chapter 6
Smart LOs Design: Higher-Level Coding and Testing Aspects

6.1 Introduction

So far we have discussed smart LOs (SLOs) mainly from two perspectives: (1) conceptual understanding which focuses on definitions (examples) only (Chaps. 3, 4) and (2) model-driven specification with the focus on variability aspects. Though the model-driven view provides the reader with the fundamental knowledge on SLOs, this knowledge was presented at a higher level of abstraction with many details missed. Knowledge representation and knowledge gaining on SLOs are the different processes. As, according to Bloom's taxonomy, teaching and learning (roughly knowledge gaining) are most effective when learners are involved in doing something, here accordingly we try to involve the reader in the process of constructing SLOs. Therefore, the aim of this chapter is to deliver the *next part* of the design methodology, i.e. how the SLOs should be coded, tested and redesigned (if needed).

The reader should not be confused by the methodological approach we use throughout the book. We try to present items (we treat them as being complex to understand completely at once) for the discussion *gradually*, i.e. to the extent needed to understand the topic in a particular place, with regard to the stated aims. We describe the same topic in the other place later, with some new details or more precisely according to the other aims. For example, in Chap. 6, we re-define the basic terms (e.g. SLO interface, SLO body, learning variability, etc.) which so far (i.e. in Chap. 5) were defined either informally or incompletely.

© Springer International Publishing Switzerland 2015
V. Štuikys, *Smart Learning Objects for Smart Education in Computer Science*,
DOI 10.1007/978-3-319-16913-2_6

6.2   Related Work

Here, we preset a restricted analysis of the related work. The reason of that is simple – the reader can find the adequate references in the other chapters as follows. We have discussed the relevant sources on feature models in Chaps. 4 and 5. We have analysed meta-programming-related issues in Chap. 5. We will provide more on that topic in Chap. 9. Nevertheless, we indicate on the main approaches that are relevant to the topics of this chapter.

The model-driven development and engineering is further evolving. The essence of model-driven development is the use of the following principle: separating the description of abstract properties and logic of an application from a description of its platform-specific implementation and then the automation of the transformation of the former into the latter using model transformation tools. At present, the most mature formulation of this vision is the OMG's model-driven architecture [KWB03]. It refers to a high-level description of an application as a platform-independent model and a more concrete implementation-oriented description as a platform-specific model. The model transformation is at the core of this approach when one or more source models are transformed to one or more target models, based on the meta-models of each of these models. Such transformations are defined by transformation/mapping rules and can be summarized as taxonomy [MCG06, Sch06] that can help developers in deciding which model transformation approach is best suited to deal with a particular problem.

In model-driven development (also known as product line engineering), the feature-based modelling prevails now. The basis of feature modelling is the commonality-variability relationships [CHW98]. The paper [JK07] presents a formalized feature modelling meta-model to support reasoning about feature models, feature trees and their configurations. Another paper [WC09] describes a formal description of multi-variant models, presents transformation processes of such models including change and product configuration and discusses the construction and representation of models incorporating multiple variants. The paper [ECH+09] describes a formal model of change-oriented programming based on feature diagrams, in which features are seen as sets of changes (or high-level transformations) that can be applied to a source program. Another paper [BBC+01] considers the use of generative techniques in designing product lines. The reader can find more on the feature-oriented software product line concepts in [ABK+14] and variability management in [CBK13].

Also the reader can learn more on the model-driven approach as applied to the meta-program development in our book [ŠD13]. Here, we apply this approach too, however with the extension and adaptation to the specific context in designing smart LOs (SLOs).

6.3   Background of SLO Coding and Testing

The framework includes the following topics: (1) formal formulation of the transformation task, (2) conceptual vision of model-driven transformation at the models' element level, (3) formal definition of meta-program elements, (4) parameter-dependency model, (5) formulation of transformation rules, (6) SLO coding rules, (7) SLO testing procedure and (8) SLO redesign with evidence and users.

6.3.1   SLO Design Task (Formal) Formulation

On the basis of the statements and results obtained in Chap. 5, now we are able to formulate the SLO design task formally. Indeed, we already have three items: (1) the model-driven transformation vision as applied to the lowest level (see Fig. 6.1 and also Fig. 5.2 in Chap. 5), (2) feature model instance of an application task (i.e. a task of the problem domain) and (3) feature model instance of the solution domain (i.e. meta-programming).

Here, we are speaking about the designing of SLO at a high level (HL) of abstraction. Taking that and the specified models into account, we can define the

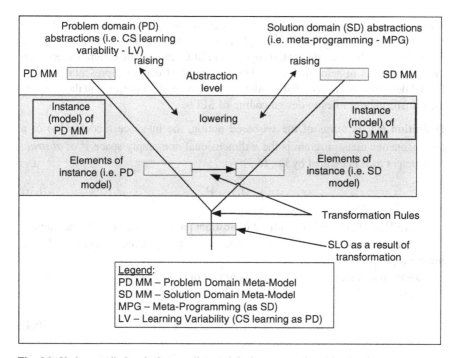

Fig. 6.1 Y-chart applied to the intermediate and the lowest transformation levels (Adapted from [ŠD13] and Fig. 5.2 © Copyright 2013 Springer)

design procedure at this level as the process of mapping the learning variability model(s) onto the heterogeneous meta-programming domain model(s). Formally, we can write

$$SLO_{HL} = FD_{LV} \times FD_{MP} \tag{6.1}$$

where SLO_{HL} is high level SLO model (see Definitions 5.10–5.13); FD_{LV} is learning variability model expressed through the concrete feature diagram (FD) instance, specifying pedagogy, social aspects and content; FD_{MP} is FD to express the meta-program (MP) model; and '$\times$' means mapping.

After mapping, i.e. after the execution of the process defined by Eq. (6.1), we will obtain the meta-programming-based SLO_{MPG}. Its structure is defined by Eq. (6.2):

$$SLO_{MPG} = Interface \times Body \tag{6.2}$$

(Here, MPG means meta-programming and '$\times$' means mapping).

6.3.2   Formal Definition of Meta-Program and SLO Elements

There are two basic elements of a meta-program: *interface* (see Definition 5.14 in Sect. 5.5.1) and *body* (see Definition 5.15 in Sect. 5.5.1). Now we define those terms formally for both items, the meta-program and SLO, though the difference between these terms lies in semantics only, but not in the structural representation. The formal definition is needed, first, to identify the essential properties and then to state the transformation rules to design coding of SLOs.

Definition 6.1 In terms of the set-based notion, the interface model $\mu(M_I)$ of a heterogeneous meta-program is the n-dimensional non-empty space $\mathbf{P}$ of *abstract parameters* as it is defined by Eq. (6.3):

$$\mu(M_I) = \mathbf{P}, \tag{6.3}$$

where $\mathbf{P} = \{P; V\}$, P is the full set of abstract parameter names; n is the number of the parameters, i.e. $n = |P|$; V is the ordered set of *all* parameter values; and M_I is the meta-program interface.

As each parameter $P_i (P_i \in P)$ has its own set of values $\{v_{i_1}, v_{i_2}, \ldots, v_{i_q}\} \subset V$, we can write

$$P_i := V_i = \{v_{i_1}, v_{i_2}, \ldots, v_{i_q}\} \in V, \tag{6.4}$$

where i_q is the number of values of the parameter P_i. The symbol ':=' means 'is defined'.

We explain the actual meaning of the words *abstract parameter* introduced into the definition. This term means that the parameters and their values do not represent any concrete entity and therefore are independent upon the application domain.

Definition 6.2 Structurally, the SLO interface model has the identical structure as it is defined by Eqs. (6.3) and (6.4); however, the parameters and their values have a well-defined semantics – they express different aspects of the learning variability (see Eq. (5.1) in Sect. 5.3.1).

Definition 6.3 Two parameters P_i and P_j $(P_i, P_j \subseteq P \ (i \neq j))$ are said to be *independent upon the choice of their values*, if any pair of values $\{v_{i_d}, v_{j_t}\}$ $(v_{i_d} \in P_i, v_{j_t} \in P_j$, where $d \in [1, i_q]$ and $t \in [1, j_m])$ can be selected to correctly evaluate the *SLO* specification, when it is executed. Otherwise, the parameters are *dependent* upon the choice of their values.

Sometimes dependent parameters are treated as *interacting* (especially in terms of aspects or features [Bat05]). In our case, we use parameter dependency as a means to express the *interaction variability* (see also Eq. (5.1) in Sect. 5.3.1). Note that we provide a more precise definition of the parameter interaction in Chap. 9 (where more details are needed because there we will discuss the SLO tool designer's vision).

Note also that this definition defines the *one-to-one* dependency in making a choice of parameter values. The whole space is used to construct the parameter dependency graph $G(P,U)$ as follows. The set of nodes P of the graph corresponds to the parameters. The set of edges U is defined as follows: for all i and j $u_{ij} = 1$ (meaning the edge exists) *iff* two parameters P_i and P_j are dependable according to Definition 6.3, otherwise $u_{ij} = 0$ (meaning the edge does not exist) $(P_i, P_j \in P, u_{ij} = (P_i, P_j) \in U)$.

Definition 6.4 In terms of the graph-based notion, the graph $G(P,U)$ is the interface model $\mu^*(M_I)$ defined by Eq. (6.3) of both the meta-program and SLO:

$$\mu^*(M_I) = G(P, U) \tag{6.5}$$

Firstly, $\mu^*(M_I)$ is the derivative model that has been derived from Eq. (6.1) (it follows from Definitions 6.3 and 6.4). Secondly, the model $\mu^*(M_I)$ is more precise (as compared to Eqs. (6.3) and (6.4)) because it specifies the parameter dependency explicitly. As it will be clear later, this attribute is the key to identify some useful properties in devising formal transformation rules as well as to state the background of developing the SLO design tool (see Chap. 9). Therefore, the creation of the graph $G(P, U)$ requires a separate attention and explanation with the concrete example. We do that in Sect. 6.3.3.

Now we define the second element of SLO, that is, its body without the explicit referencing to meta-programming.

Definition 6.5 *Body* of the SLO is a pre-ordered set of meta-language functions inserted into some LO-related text (i.e. a teaching program) according to prescribed format and rules, whereas the text is presented by the target (i.e. teaching) language constructs.

Here, we do not provide more details on the SLO body because, from the teacher or learner perspective, it always can be seen as a *black-box entity*. Furthermore, this vision is enough to define SLO here. We will provide more details on the body later (see Chap. 9). Here, however, it is more important to give the possible interpretation of the given SLO definition (see Definition 5.18) as it is stated in the next definition.

Definition 6.6 SLO is the *high-level* specification (i.e. meta-specification) that contains a set of the related LO instances (*structural view*); SLO is also the input data of the meta-language processor; the latter is a generator to automatically generate LO instances on demand, depending on the selected parameter values from the SLO interface (*behavioural or process-based view*).

At this point, the reader should compare Definition 6.6 with Definition 5.1 (see Chap. 5). We leave the comparison result open as a research task (see task 6.1 in Sect. 6.6).

This definition also enables to realize the following vision of using SLOs in practice. Suppose the teacher has a set of the SLOs to cover the whole teaching course. This set can be treated as the *teacher's local library* in which each item is represented in a *compactly packaged way* (we mean the meta-specification) according to the introduced structural view (i.e. as a group of related LO instances to use for a specific topic). Instead of searching the needed LO (if all possible LO instances would be saved as library items), the teacher first identifies what SLO is needed (in fact, the needed topic) and then generates the needed instance on demand from that meta-specification.

6.3.3 Parameter Dependency Model

As it is stated in Sect. 6.3.2 (see Definition 6.3 and also the formal definition of the graph $G(P, U)$), some parameters may interact among themselves while the others not. We express the interaction through the dependencies of the parameter values. The interaction between the parameters may appear in two ways: (1) two parameters are interacting in nature (e.g. when a *prespecified value* of one parameter *requires* of a specific value of the other parameter); (2) by changing the value or adding new ones. As the latter case is more interesting, we present the following illustrative example. Let us have the *generic logic equation* as a very simplified SLO:

$$Y = X1 < logic\,operator > X2 < logic\,operator > \ldots < logic\,operator > Xn.$$

Fig. 6.2 Parameter
dependency: (**a**) no
interaction; (**b**) interaction;
(**c**) mixed case

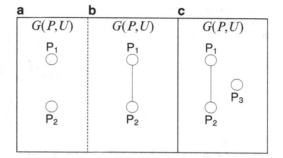

There are two generic parameters: (1) $< logic\ operator >$ (further P_1) and (2) $n -$
the number of arguments (further P_2). Let us have the following values of the
parameters $P_1 = \{AND, OR\}$ and $P_2 = \{2, 3, 4\}$. The parameters are independent, i.
e. not interacting, because any value of P_1 and any value of P_2 can be chosen in
deriving the concrete instance from the generic equation. The possible number of
the instances is equal to 6. They are as follows:

Y = X1 AND X2   Y = X1 OR X2
Y = X1 AND X2 AND X3   Y = X1 OR X2 OR X3
Y = X1 AND X2 AND X3 AND X4   Y = X1 OR X2 OR X3 OR X4.

The parameter dependency graph $G(P, U)$ is the null graph (see Fig. 6.2a).

Now we change the parameter values as follows: $P_1 = \{NOT, AND, OR\}$ and
$P_2 = \{1, 2, 3, 4\}$. As a result, now we have the interaction among the parameters,
because 'NOT' *requires* '1' only. The parameter dependency graph $G(P, U)$ is the
connected graph, i.e. tree in this case (see the graph $G(P, U)$ in Fig. 6.2b). In the
general case, some components of $G(P, U)$ are the null subgraphs while the others
the connected subgraphs (typically trees). For example, if we introduce yet another
parameter $P_3 = \{Y, V, Z\}$ to denote the other name of the equation (function), we
will have the model just of that kind (see Fig. 6.2c).

Here we do not consider how the graph $G(P, U)$ should be constructed formally.
We return to this problem later in Chap. 9.

As a result of this discussion, one can conclude that we express the task
variability aspects through parameters. The parameters are elements of a meta-
program to represent SLO. This observation is very important to understand the
transformation rules to be presented in Sect. 6.3.4.

6.3.4 Transformation Rules to Design SLO

First, we need to return to Fig. 6.1. Here, one can see the conceptual view of
transformations again. We define the design process at the lowest (coding) level as
the process for connecting the elements of the problem domain model with the

Fig. 6.3 An instance of
feature model of the
problem (P) domain

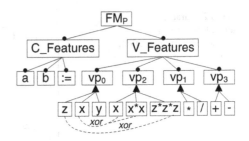

adequate elements of the solution domain model elements according to Eq. (6.1). Now we have the elements of both domains. We have specified the elements for the first domain in Chap. 5. We have identified the elements for the second domain in Chap. 6. Nevertheless, we need to explain that by the examples before stating the transformation rules.

Let we change a bit the example ($y:= a*x+b$) considered in Chap. 5 (see Table 5.1). The variability of the problem domain was expressed through the parameters a and b. Now we want to hold a, b and ':=' as the *commonality features* (C_Features, see Fig. 6.3) and the remaining four items of the equation (y, $*$, x, $+$) as the *variability features* (V_Features, see Fig. 6.3). Typically, to present feature models (FMs), we express the variability features through *variant points* (vp). In Fig. 6.3, the variant points (vp_0, vp_1, vp_2, vp_3) model or represent the items (y, $*$, x, $+$), respectively. We have introduced the following *variants* or values for each variant point adequately: $vp_0 = \{z, x, y\}$; $vp_1 = \{*, /\}$; $vp_2 = \{x, x*x, z*z*z\}$; $vp_3 = \{+, -\}$.

What is the result of this reasoning? First, we have constructed the feature model of the problem domain exposing the elements of the model evidently. Next, we have enlarged the variability space significantly (now it can be defined as $3*3*2*2 = 36$, though there are conflicting variants which we have defined through constraints of the type *excludes* (denoted by the dotted lines and labels *xor* in Fig. 6.3)). Finally, the changed and enlarged variability space enables us to specify the process of deriving equations of the quite different classes (in fact polynomials instead of the linear equations). For example, if we select the following variants for each variant point adequately (y, $z*z*z$, $*$, $+$), we will be able to derive (though intuitively) the following equation from the feature model FM_P: $y:=a*z*z*z + b$;

Now accordingly, we present the feature model of the solution domain, i.e. meta-programming (Fig. 6.4). We treat the model as abstract because neither the parameters and their values nor languages are concrete. Though the basic features of this model have been derived from its meta-model (Fig. 5.7), some features are represented with more details (e.g. abstract parameter values are added, metalanguage (ML) is represented by the base constructs of structural programming, target language (TL) is presented by the set of scenarios). One feature (meta-body) should be discussed separately. Here, we have decomposed this feature into a set of functions $\{f_1, f_2, \ldots, f_m\}$. The parameters and elements of the TL (scenarios) serve as arguments of the functions to implement the meta-program functionality through the modification algorithm indicated in meta-model (see Fig. 5.7 again). In Fig. 6.4,

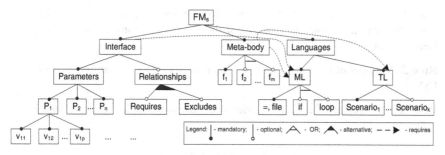

Fig. 6.4 Abstract feature diagram to represent meta-programming as solution domain

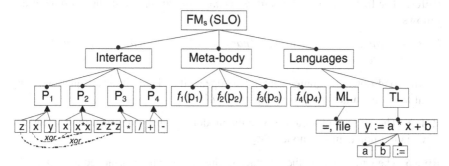

Fig. 6.5 Feature-based SLO specification after mapping of FM$_P$ onto FM$_S$

we represent this relationship by the constraints *requires* (see dotted lines). The following features (any parameter, meta-body, ML, TL) of the model are *variant points* with at least one *mandatory variant* to be selected when transformation rules are applied.

The rules we present below, in fact, describe the mapping of the model *FM$_P$* onto the model *FM$_S$* as it is stated by Eq. (6.1). We present the result of this mapping in Fig. 6.5. Therefore, the reader should interpret the rules along with looking at the mapping result. This result is the model of the concrete SLO (though illustrative). Here, we present the only content or task variability features for simplicity and understandability. What are missed in Fig. 6.5 are the relationships (constraints) among the meta-body and the languages. We can represent those relationships (in fact, SLO model) as follows:

$$f_1(P_1) := a\ f_2(P_2)f_3(P_3)f_4(P_4)b;$$

Here: $P_1 = \{x,\ y,\ z\}$; $P_2 = \{*,\ /\}$; $P_3 = \{x,\ x*x,\ z*z*z\}$; $P_4 = \{+,\ -\}$; f_i = meta-functions (i = [1,4]).

Note also that the rules are formulated for the general case and, as a result, there are some discrepancies as compared to what we see in the represented feature models.

Rule 1 *Variant point* (vp) of the problem domain feature model FM$_P$ (see Fig. 6.3) corresponds to a *parameter name* (P) of the solution domain feature model FM$_S$ (see Fig. 6.4).

Rule 2 Variants of a variant point of FM$_P$ correspond to the parameter values of FM$_S$.

Rule 3 The format of a *simple assignment statement* within the interface is as follows:

$$< parameter >=< parameter\_value\_set > .$$

Rule 4 The format of a *conditional assignment statement* within the interface is as follows:

if   <parameter1><condition><parameter2>   *then*   <parameter1>= <parameter_value_set>

The conditional assignment statement appears if and only if the adequate variant point has constraints $< requires >$ or $< excludes >$.

Rule 5 The number of parameters in the model FM$_S$ must be equal to the number of variation points in the model FM$_P$.

Rule 6 The parameters in the interface of the SLO are to be arranged according to their priorities given in the context model.

Note that we do not illustrate this rule in our example here because of simplicity reasons (the context model we will discuss in Sect. 7.4 and 7.6 (see Chap. 7)).

Rule 7 To form the meta-body, the following set of functions of the meta-language is used:

$$\{assignment(` = `), OPEN\text{-}WRITE\text{-}CLOSE, conditional, loops\}.$$

Note that here we use the full names of the functions as compared to those given in Fig. 6.5.

Having the transformation rules and the models, the SLO designer is able to start the coding procedure. As the models and rules are evident and can be grasped intuitively, the CS teacher or even CS knowledgeable students can be designers of SLOs (we claim that having in mind our practice).

6.3.5 SLO Coding Rules as Recommendations

Again, coding rules are not so much dependable upon the use of the concrete target and meta-language. Therefore, we discuss the coding rules here. We will discuss the topic of selecting languages later in Sect. 9.3.2 (see Chap. 9). The majority of

Fig. 6.6 SLO interface of
our example in PHP after
assignment parameter
values

```
<?
//===================================================
// Begining of the SLO interface in PHP
// Parameters with assigned values and priorities
   $P1 = "z";   // HP - high priority
   $P2 = "x*x"; // HP - high priority
   $P3 = "*";   // LP - low priority
   $P4 = "+";   // LP - low priority
// End of the SLO interface
//===================================================
// Begining of the SLO meta-body
...
// End of the SLO meta-body
//===================================================
?>
```

the rules stated below should be treated as recommendations. They reflect the use of a *good style* in writing programs. Therefore, the rules are enumerated anew.

Rule 1 The description of the target language (TL) and the meta-language (ML) should be represented as the *separate well-designed* documents (in the paper and electronic formats). The documents may include also feature-based representations enriched with the annotated examples.

Rule 2 Parameter names should be meaningful to express the domain semantics explicitly.

Rule 3 Each parameter *must contain* a priority variable or constant (also treated as fuzzy variable to be discussed in detail later in Chap. 8). Parameter priority is coded as the *obligatory comment* followed after the parameter in the SLO interface specification (see Fig. 6.6). In fact, this is the rule, but not the recommendation.

Also note that the parameter priorities are not shown in feature models given in Sect. 6.3.4 (for simplicity reasons, however, the priorities appear in Figs. 6.6 and 6.7 to illustrate Rule 3).

Rule 4 The comments should be supplied by the specific format that enables to distinguish clearly the comments from the machine-oriented commands.

Rule 5 The comments are to be included in only those places where the essential decisions are made.

Rule 6 The comments should be as much clear and concise as possible.

Rule 7 The structural units of SLO (interface and meta-body) should be clearly identifiable in the meta-specification document.

Rule 8 The interface should be coded first and then the meta-body. Parameters should be ordered in the interface according to their roles (priorities, see Fig. 6.6).

Note that the editors (such as Notepad++) that highlight the different language elements with the different colours are highly recommended to use.

Fig. 6.7 SLO interface of
our example with parameter
dependency and HTML
fragments

```php
<?
//===============================================================
// Begining of the SLO interface in PHP
// Parameters with priorities
   $P1 = $_POST[p1]; // HP - high priority
   $P2 = $_POST[p2]; // HP - high priority
   $P3 = $_POST[p3]; // LP - low priority
   $P4 = $_POST[p4]; // LP - low priority
   if(!isset($P1)) {
?>
   <FORM METHOD = POST ACTION = "<?php echo $PHP_SELF;?>">
     <p> <strong> P1 values: </strong> </p>
     <select size="1" name="p1">
        <option value="z"> z </option> <br>
        <option value="x"> x </option> <br>
        <option value="y"> y </option> <br>
     </select>
   <INPUT TYPE = submit VALUE ="Submit" NAME = "submit">
   </FORM>
<? }
   if(isset($P1) && !isset($P2)) {
      if($P1 == "z") {?>
         ...
<? }
      else if($P1 == "x") {?>
         ...
<? }
         else {?>
         ...
<? } }
      if(isset($P2) && (!isset($P3) || !isset($P4))) { ?>
         ...
<? }
// End of the SLO interface
//===============================================================
// Begining of the SLO meta-body
   ...
// End of the SLO meta-body
//===============================================================
?>
```

Rule 9 When the SLO interface is coded, the elements of the representation language HTML should be included (see also Figs. 6.7 and 6.9) in order for us to be able to see the graphical interface in the Internet browser (see Fig. 6.8).

The list of rules we presented here is oriented to the case of manual design (the only ML processor is used). More rules will be added to develop the design tools as it will be done in Chap. 9.

6.3.6   SLO Testing Procedure

As SLO is a meta-program in the syntactical sense, it should be tested similarly to any other computer program. On the other hand, semantically SLO differs from the meta-program because of the pedagogical and social value. Therefore, in the case of SLO, we can speak about *syntactic testing* and *pedagogy-oriented testing*. SLO should be *pedagogically sound*. The pedagogy-oriented aspects have been already introduced in the feature models (see Chap. 4). Those aspects were extracted from

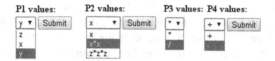

Fig. 6.8 Generated SLO graphical interface with the sequenced (prioritized) parameters and their selected values

the approved sources that take into account teaching-learning theories and expert knowledge. Therefore, the models are *pedagogically sound*. As we then verify the models using the verification tools that are based on the formal background, it is found that our models are also *syntactically sound*.

However, the whole SLO design process (from modelling to coding) is long and complex enough; thus, it requires the human skill. The human's intervention may cause some errors. The source of errors may occur at the model level (e.g. when we are moving from the abstract to concrete models, at the mapping of the models) and at the coding level. How can we obtain the errors and correct the SLO specification?

The use of the tools (such as SPLOT as it was discussed previously; see Chaps. 4 and 5) after each phase of manipulating on models enables to avoid the syntactic errors. Obtaining and removing of the semantic errors of the models is the responsibility of the designer and domain expert (we do not exclude that both actors are or might be the same person). The development of SLO specifications at the lower level (we mean the use of transformation rules and coding) may be performed either manually or using the adequate tools as well. In the first case, errors are unavoidable. However, to minimize their occurrence, we apply two procedures: (1) SLO redesign with evidence (see Sect. 6.3.7) and (2) first deriving LOs from the SLO specification and then analysing their content. In the second case, the use of the SLO design tool enables to facilitate the whole design process, including testing. We discuss the issues in designing SLO in Chap. 9 and the use of the designing tools in Chaps. 11 and 12.

6.3.7   SLO Redesign with Evidence and Users

Here, the basic assumption is that the CS teacher is also the SLO designer. Also, we assume that the use of transformation rules and coding is manual. What is the actual meaning of the phrase "design with evidence"? The meaning is that we need to apply the principle of the evolutionary design (sometimes it also can be seen as a rapid prototyping). In general, developing meta-programs is a hard programming activity. However, it might be simplified significantly if the designer works in the following manner. He/she applies the transformation and coding rules gradually, fully interpreting one parameter at a time, i.e. as if the SLO (meta-program) contains the only one parameter. After that, the testing procedure follows. Next, the designer repeats the full design and testing cycle until all parameters are included into the interface and are implemented within the meta-body.

Such a procedure is very useful, especially for designers who have not so much experience in writing meta-programs. In fact, the procedure specifies the way of getting knowledge and gaining better understanding of meta-programming per se. As a result of using the procedure, the first version of SLO is created. However, the evidence of design correctness should also be tested in the real setting. What is the possibility to change the SLO specification in this case?

There are a few possibilities: (1) deleting some parameter and its values; (2) adding new parameter values without changing the number of parameters; and (3) adding a new parameter and its values without changing the other parameters and their values. The first possibility requires first obtaining the location of the parameter within the interface and its meta-function within the body and then removing both (if the parameter does not interact with the remaining ones, see Sect. 6.3.3). Otherwise, the interaction should be taken into account in removing the needed parts.

The second possibility requires a simple intervention into the interface only (without introducing changes into the meta-body) if, again, the introduced *new value* does not affect the values of the remaining parameters (i.e. there is no interaction among parameters; see Sect. 6.3.3). The third possibility requires a more extensive redesign in both parts (interface and meta-body). This case is the same as one cycle of the procedure discussed above.

Is it possible to involve students into the SLO design process? The answer is no for novices and yes for the advanced students, but not for all. The practice and the experience gained in using the approach (we discuss that in Chap. 13) show that the most knowledgeable students can act as the teacher's apprentices in designing and redesigning SLOs.

6.4   Analysis of SLO Specifications

6.4.1   Analysis of SLO Properties

As this topic (if to consider it fully) is premature, nevertheless we found the necessity to include it here for the completeness of the design procedure. Therefore, here we are able to highlight the most essential aspects from the user perspective only.

The interface (when SLO is used) is treated as a *glass-box entity* visible to the user for selecting parameter values. Meta-body (when SLO is used) is treated as the *black-box* item (the reader will find more on that in Chap. 7 and in the remaining ones). In spite of the fact that the SLO interface and meta-body are separate units, the meta-specification is presented as the one uniform file. This meta-specification is the item of the CS teacher's *local library* accessible online. In fact, there are three

Fig. 6.9 SLO layered
structure

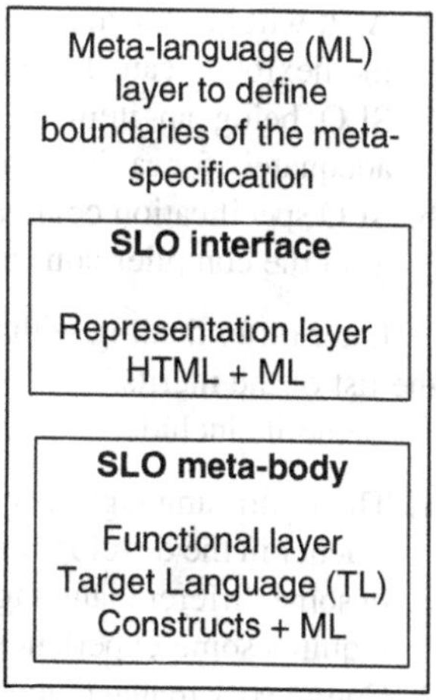

Meta-language (ML) layer to define boundaries of the meta-specification
SLO interface   Representation layer   HTML + ML
SLO meta-body   Functional layer   Target Language (TL)   Constructs + ML

layers in representing SLO (ML boundary layer, representation layer and functional layer as can be seen in Fig. 6.9).

What new aspects can the reader learn from Fig. 6.9? Explicitly multi-linguistic aspects are seen. We need to use *three languages* to specify SLO for the practical use in the real setting: one language (HTML) is the representational language for the Internet browser and the remaining two for implementing meta-programming. We do not consider the issues related to the SLO local library here. We will discuss that in the ending chapters of the book.

6.4.2   Merits and Demerits of the SLO Specifications

At this point of reading Chap. 6, the reader may ask two essential questions: (1) What are the merits of the designed SLOs? (2) What are demerits of those items?
    Merits include:

1. SLO is the teaching content *generator*. The meta-language processor stands for that role. From the reuse perspective, we have the case of generative reuse; therefore, we are able to achieve the highest productivity level in creating the teaching content as compared to component-based reuse.
2. From the user perspective, SLO is used as a black-box item (if there is no need of redesigning). SLO contains the user-friendly graphical interface; therefore, the user's communication with the system is simple and intuitive.
3. No matter that the model-driven and transformation-based approach is complex, it is systematic and there are also designing procedures and tools that make it possible to overcome the design complexity.

4. As it will be shown in Chap. 8, if the SLO is designed properly, it also contains the flexible means for adaptation.
5. SLO being an item of the local library may be also prepared and packed adequately for saving into external repositories (this is not the topic of the book).
6. SLO specification could also be as a *teaching content* for the CS students too (e. g. in the compiler constructing course).

Later (after dealing with topics of remaining chapters) we will be able to extend the list of the merits.

Demerits include:

1. The multi-language specification requires additional efforts of the designer and teacher in the development phase. That means the actor should have competence in some different languages to be able to manipulate them at once. This approach requires some experience in meta-programming.
2. Complexity management in designing (using model-driven approach) and development phases is also an issue to be taken into account. Therefore, the design and development tools are treated as a highly important decision (we will consider that topic later in Chaps. 9 and 10).
3. Deriving the concrete feature models from the abstract ones, there are no supporting tools at the moment (to our best knowledge).
4. In developing specifications, the consequences of the so-called overgeneralization problem might appear in terms of too large number of parameters and the human's restricted ability to remember them for interpreting in terms of the magic 7 problem [Mil56].

6.5 Summary and Concluding Remarks

We have introduced the model-driven and transformation-based approach to design smart LO. We have presented the description of the approach gradually to intensify the cognitive load to the reader in each subsequent chapter, starting from Chap. 4. In fact, the material of this chapter has been delivered to the reader so that it was possible to learn the essence of the approach systematically and get the knowledge to manually design SLO. Therefore, this chapter is regarded as an introduction in developing the tool to design and use SLO. That will be considered later.

Here, we have also introduced the formalism in specifying and describing SLO abstractly and, to some extent formally, using the set-based and graph-based notations. By doing so, we were aiming, first, to prepare the reader for more intensive studies of the topics to be given in Chap. 9 and, next, to provide the background of transformation rules. We have also discussed the testing and redesigning problems in designing SLO along with the analysis and evaluation of the approach. The stated merits and demerits are by no means full. They will be extended later. However, the reader should also know that the use of the development tools enables significantly to diminish the effect of the limitations and demerits of the approach.

6.6 Research and Exercise Questions

6.1. Compare two definitions (Definition 6.6 and Definition 5.1 given in Chap. 5) and draw the discriminating features. Define the value of both.

6.2. Compare the definitions of meta-programming terms given in Chap. 5 with the ones given in this chapter. What is the value of formal definitions?

6.3. Compare two terms: heterogeneous meta-program and SLO. Interpret their semantic difference.

6.4. Compare two generic equations as simple SLOs: *logic* (presented in Sect. 6.3.3) and *algebraic* (presented in Sect. 5.3.2; see Chap. 5). Introduce more variability features (parameters) into the algebraic equation and draw the parameter dependency graph.

6.5. Define the variability interaction formally. What is the value of parameter interaction graph?

6.6. Define once again the relationship among the commonality features and variability features. Learn more on that, for example, from the sources [CHW98, ŠD13].

6.7. Learn more on the feature-based and model-driven development (e.g. using the following sources: [Sch06, TBD07].

6.8. Introduce the problem domain of your interest. Take the simplified examples from your domain and devise feature models for the selected tasks.

6.9. Analyse the feature model to represent the solution domain, i.e. meta-programming (see Fig. 6.4). Learn the way it was created (see Chap. 5).

6.10. Perform the mapping procedure of problem domain model devised in task 6.8 onto the model given in Fig. 6.4.

6.11. Explain the essence of transformation rules and coding rules. What is the style in writing programs? In what aspects the style is different from the meta-program coding style?

6.12. What are testing procedures? Learn more on rapid prototyping in designing computer programs and meta-programs.

References

[ABK+14] Apel S, Batory D, Kästner C, Saake G (2014) Feature-oriented software product lines concepts and implementation. Springer, Berlin/Heidelberg

[Bat05] Batory D (2005) Feature models, grammars, and propositional formulas. Springer, Berlin/Heidelberg, pp 7–20

[BBC+01] Butler G, Batory DS, Czarnecki K, Eisenecker UW (2001) Generative techniques for product lines. In: Proceedings of the 23rd international conference on software engineering, ICSE 2001, Toronto, Ontario, Canada, 760–761, 12–19 May 2001

[CBK13] Capilla R, Bosch J, Kang KC (2013) Systems and software variability management (concepts, tools and experiences). Springer, Berlin

[CHW98]   Coplien J, Hoffman D, Weiss D (1998) Commonality and variability in software engineering. IEEE Soft 15:37–45

[ECH+09]   Ebraert P, Classen A, Heymans P, D'Hondt T (2009) Feature diagrams for change-oriented programming. In: Nakamura M, Reiff-Marganiec S (eds) Feature interactions in software and communication systems X. IOS Press, Amsterdam/Washington, pp 107–122

[JK07]   Janota M, Kiniry J (2007) Reasoning about feature models in higher-order logic. Proceedings of 11th international conference on software product lines, SPLC 2007, Kyoto, pp 13–22, 10–14 Sept 2007

[KWB03]   Kleppe AG, Warmer J, Bast W (2003) MDA explained, the model-driven architecture: practice and promise. Addison Wesley, Boston

[MCG06]   Mens T, Czarnecki K, Van Gorp P (2006) A taxonomy of model transformations. Electron Notes Theor Comput Sci 152:125–142

[Mil56]   Miller GA (1956) The magical number seven, plus or minus two: some limits on our capacity for processing information. Psychol Rev 63(2):81

[Sch06]   Schmidt DC (2006) Model-driven engineering. IEEE Comput 39(2):25–31

[ŠD13]   Štuikys V, Damaševičius R (2013) Meta-programming and model-driven meta-program development: principles processes and techniques. Springer, London/Heidelberg/New York/Dordrecht

[TBD07]   Trujillo S, Batory DS, Díaz O (2007) Feature-oriented model driven development: a case study for portlets. Proceedings of 29th international conference on Software Engineering (ICSE 2007), Minneapolis, pp 44–53, 20–26 May 2007

[WC09]   Westfechtel B, Conradi R (2009) Multi-variant modeling concepts, issues and challenges. European conference on model-driven architecture (ECMDA), Twente, pp 57–67, 24 Jun 2009

Chapter 7
Enhanced Features of SLOs: Focus on Specialization

7.1 Introduction

Smart LOs being reusable items in terms of generative capabilities may also offer new opportunities to create individual and highly adaptable content for learning processes. As it was shown in the previous chapters, reusability is a central topic in LO research. However, reusability cannot be generally understood without the educational context. The main goal of reusability is to adapt the teaching content to the context of use in some learning processes. The adaptive aspects of reusability should be discussed from a wider perspective than it was done so far. We need to have a framework enabling to connect reuse issues with the educational context in order we could be able first *to specialize SLO* and then having the specialized SLO to consider *the adaptability problem* in some well-defined manner. Therefore, the aim of this chapter is to introduce such a framework and discuss the *SLO specialization problem*.

The program specialization (also known as partial evaluation) is a matured subfield in CS research. It deals with the transformation of the program's structure without affecting functionality aiming to achieve some objectives. They might be quite different such as those: automating compiler design, improving program performance and program obfuscation or increasing the communication security. As SLOs are, in fact, also programs (more precisely meta-programs), we are able to apply the theoretical background of program specialization research for the SLO specialization. In our case, specialization aims to make an automatic adaptation of SLO possible. Since both tasks, i.e. specialization and adaptation, are complex enough, we consider them separately. We discuss the first in this chapter and the second in the next.

The main assumption is that the SLO we intend to specialize should be *designed for reuse*, i.e. the following property holds: SLO implements a wide-scale learning variability. We argue that learning variability is a *reuse driver* in the following sense: the more learning features we introduce into a learning specification, the

© Springer International Publishing Switzerland 2015
V. Štuikys, *Smart Learning Objects for Smart Education in Computer Science*,
DOI 10.1007/978-3-319-16913-2_7

wider extent of possible reuse and adaptation we will have. But the reuse space enlargement should be managed adequately because of the negative effect of the *overgeneralization* problem (here meaning excessive learning variability). SLO specialization enables not only to avoid the negative consequences of the overgeneralization problem but also to provide an instrument for adaptation. In general, the specialization problem we discuss here can be called as *specialization for adaptation* that formulates the goal of specialization.

7.2 Literature Review

We present two streams of the related work here. The first deals with program transformation-specialization research. The second considers only those learning aspects which enable to form criteria for the SLO specialization task. We will provide more extensive analysis of the most influential e-learning attributes (e.g. context, cognitive aspects, learner's profile, etc.) as they relate to SLO specialization for adaptation in Chap. 8. Thus, this review is by no means exhaustive. Our aim is to introduce a new terminology and basic principles in order readers would be prepared to understand and be more motivated to accept our approach.

As our approach, in fact, exploits the principles and techniques borrowed from the model and program *specialization* research, we need to introduce basic ideas of this field. There are three interrelated terms (*partial evaluation, specialization* and *refactoring*) that are interchangeably used to determine a specific kind of program and model transformations. At the very general understanding level, their meaning actually is the same or very close. It is the reason why all the terms can be met in three subfields (program manipulation as a subfield of pure CS; see, e.g. [ACM13]), feature modelling and model transformation (both CS and SWE subfields; see, e.g. [CHE05]) and partially in the SW system design and maintenance (pure SWE subfield; see, e.g. [HT08, FBB+99]). Now we present some definitions of the terms.

Program specialization or partial evaluation is the technique that makes it possible to automatically transform a program into a specialized version, according to the context of use (adapted from [JGS93, MLC02]). Initially partial evaluation has been used to the compiler generator's design [JSS85] and later as a source-to-source transformation technique whose aim was to improve *program performance* [Jon96]. Now, however, there are many more applications which include program obfuscation [GJI12], model transformation [HT08, TBK09, GMB11, ACL+12], security improving [Mur12] and many more (see also [MLC02, ACM13]).

Refactoring is the transformation process that takes an existing program and transforms it into an improved new version. Refactoring is changing the program's structure *only*, without affecting its *external behaviour* [FBB+99]. The improvements typically eliminate redundancy and bad smell of code, improve maintainability and may improve performance and reduce space [MT04, Tho05]. This definition manifests the *explicit structural changes, but* preserving the same functionality of a program, while the previous definition focuses on the transformation *aims*. The first definition, however, also implies (though implicitly, e.g. through in-deep analysis of the problem) that both the original program and its specialized version have the same functionality. Now the fact that three terms (specialization, partial evaluation and refactoring) are used interchangeably becomes clear. For consistency, further, we prefer the use of the first term.

Program specialization also relates to *stage programming* and *meta-programming*, especially in logic programming research [She01, TM03]. Shortly, it can be summarized as *multistage* programming, i.e. the development of programs in several different stages. Taha was the first to provide a formal description for a multistage programming language [Tah99, Tah04]. Staging is a program transformation that involves reorganizing the program execution into stages. He treats the use of the formal language MetaML to develop meta-programs as multistage programming. The concept relates to the fundamental principle of information hiding through the introduction of a set of abstraction levels (stages) aiming at gaining a great deal of flexibility in managing the program construction process. In fact, a *program specializer* performs the specialization process in two stages. The first is *early computations* (when some program variables are evaluated at the compile time). The second is *late computations* (when the remaining variables are evaluated at the run time).

As a specialization of SLO should be pedagogically sound, we need to focus on pedagogical reuse, LO design principles and priorities or roles of learning activities. The study [IJL+03] presents the principles and models for designing learning objects (LOs). Among others, this study explicitly formulates some *priorities in designing LOs* such as the one: 'the *learning goals are defined first and then the appropriate principles will be applied*'. Priorities and relations are also seen within the ontology of instructional objects (see Fig. 4.2 on p. 50, in [Ull08]). Even more, they are visible within pedagogical objectives because 'they exist on different levels of abstraction' or at the processes to achieve the objectives using the system PAIGOS to teach mathematics [Ull08]:

Discover: Discover and understand fundamentals in depth.
Rehearse: Address weak points.
trainSet: Increase mastery of a set of fundamentals by training.
guidedTour: Detailed information, including prerequisites.
trainWithSingleExercice: Increase mastery using a single exercise.
illustrate: Improve understanding by a sequence of examples. *illustrateWithSingleExample*: Improve understanding using a single example.

One can also see the priority relation in the intelligent educational environment such as the Intelligent Web Teacher [CGS+11]. Here, this relation, called *concept labelling relation*, labels each concept (of a domain learning model) with one or more contexts. The hierarchic representation of some concept through levels (e.g. context levels: *profile context, preference context, infrastructure context, learning context* [DBC+10]) can be thought of as an implicit priority relation where values are not identified. The discussed issues enable to introduce criteria for managing the SLO specialization as it will be clear later.

7.3　SLO Specialization Task

Here, we formulate the SLO adaptation problem as a meta-program specialization (partial evaluation) task without the *adaptation context* (we will introduce that later). However, first we need to look at the *program specialization task*. Futamura [Fut00], for example, formulates this task as a transformation process π as follows:

$$\pi\left(c_1', c_2', \ldots, c_m', r_1', r_2', \ldots, r_n'\right) = \alpha\left(\pi, c_1', c_2', \ldots, c_m'\right)\left(r_1', r_2', \ldots, r_n'\right).$$

$$(7.1)$$

The left side of Eq. (7.1) presents the state of a program to be evaluated before specialization. Here, the values $(c_1', c_2', \ldots, c_m', r_1', r_2', \ldots, r_n')$ of variables $(c_1, c_2, \ldots, c_m, r_1, r_2, \ldots, r_n)$ of the program are split into two subsets: the *constants* as *compile time values* (denoted by c' with the adequate index) and *variables* as *run-time values* (denoted by r' with the adequate index). The right side of the equation specifies the state of the program after specialization using the 'specialization algorithm' α, which evaluates $(c_1', c_2', \ldots, c_m')$ in the first stage and then evaluates $r_1', r_2', \ldots, r_n'$ in the second stage, though the stages are not defined explicitly. The *higher-level program* that implements the 'specialization algorithm' is called *specializer*. The specializer, in fact, is a meta-program, because it generates a specialized program through the process π.

For clearness, below we present a simple example taken from [Fut00]: (a) the original program and (b) its specialized version with respect to the variable x value $(x = 1)$ of the given function $f[x, y] = x*(x*x+x+y+1) + y*y$, where y varies from 1 to k by step 1.

(a)　$x:= 1$; **for** $y:= 1$ **step** 1 **until** k **do** $f[x,y]:= x*(x*x+x+y+1)+y*y$;
(b)　**for** $y:= 1$ **step** 1 **until** k **do** $f[1,y]:= 1*(3+y)+y*y$;

It is clear that the specialized version (b) is more effective in terms of performance. We are able to interpret the right side of Eq. (7.1) as follows. It is thought of as a function α with two lists of parameters, where the first includes also the computational model π.

Now we are able to formulate the meta-program specialization problem (it is the same as SLO). Let we have a set of parameters $P = \{(p_1, p_2, \ldots, p_m), (p_{m+1}, p_{m+2}, \ldots, p_n)\}$ of a meta-program, where the space P is decomposed into two subsets under the following *constraint: dependent parameters (if any, see Sect. 6.3.3 in Chap. 6) have to appear in the same subset in order to be evaluated correctly*. Similarly to Eq. (7.1), we formulate the problem as *the two-stage specialization* task as follows:

$$\pi\left(p_1, p_2, \ldots, p_m, p_{m+1}, \ldots, p_n\right) = \alpha(\pi, p_1, \ldots, p_m)\left(p_{m+1}, \ldots, p_n\right). \quad (7.2)$$

Here, parameters $(p_1, \ldots, p_m)$ are evaluated in *stage 2*, thus being treated as *constants*, while the remaining parameters $\left(p_{m+1}, \ldots, p_n\right)$ are treated as *variables* (accordingly to x and y in the previous program (b)). By *stage 2* (it is treated as the *highest* here) we mean a subprocess of π. To be evaluated in stage 2, parameters $(p_1, \ldots, p_m)$ have to be *active* (meaning their usual role in the meta-program), while the remaining parameters have to be *passive* (meaning not yet been evaluated). Note that programming languages (e.g. C++, PHP, to name a few) have a very simple mechanism to change the *state* from *active* to *passive*. For example, the record '\p' denotes that the parameter p is *passive* in some context when it is processed or evaluated.

It is the role of a specializer (formally denoted as α), among others, to *preprogram* the change of states so that the parameters $(p_{m+1}, \ldots, p_n)$ would be passive at *stage 2* (which describes evaluation of $(p_1, \ldots, p_m)$ only) and they would *be active* at *stage 1* (which describes evaluation of $(p_{m+1}, \ldots, p_n)$).

Equation (7.2) can be generalized by introducing the concept of multistage (e.g. k-stage) specialization. Indeed, we can 'think' in terms of recursion, i.e. to apply 'specialization' by partitioning the remaining parameters $(p_{m+1}, \ldots, p_n)$ under the stated constraint in two subsets again and again until some of *remaining parameters* will be evaluated $(k-1)$ times. Therefore, we can write:

$$\pi(p_1, p_2, \ldots, p_m, p_{m+1}, \ldots, p_n) = \alpha(\pi, p_1, \ldots, p_m)(p_{m+1}, \ldots, p_n)$$
$$\alpha(\pi, p_{m+1}, \ldots, p_i)(p_{i+1}, \ldots, p_n) \cdots \alpha(\pi, p_{i+1}, \ldots, p_j)(p_{j+1} \cdots, p_n) \cdots \quad (7.3)$$

For increasing readability and stage visibility, we use a column-based representation of staging Eq. (7.4), where the top of the right-side equation represents the highest k-stage, the next represents $(k-1)$-stage and so on till 1-stage.

$$\pi(p_1, p_2, \ldots, p_m, p_{m+1}, \ldots, p_n) = \alpha(\pi, p_1, \ldots, p_m)(p_{m+1}, \ldots, p_n)$$
$$\alpha(\pi, p_{m+1}, \ldots, p_i)(p_{i+1}, \ldots, p_n) \cdots \quad (7.4)$$
$$\alpha(\pi, p_{i+1}, \ldots, p_j)(p_{j+1} \cdots, p_n) \cdots$$

Equations 7.2, 7.3, and 7.4, in fact, describe the specialization not a meta-program itself but its model expressed as a parameter set. According to the realization of the learning variability concept [ŠBD13] (see also Sect. 1.7, Chap. 1), the context and content parameters are expressed uniformly in the initial specification. With respect to specialization through staging, however, the parameters of different types should be evaluated differently. For example, pedagogical context should be evaluated first, the student's context next and then the content [IJL+03]. In the next section, we discuss on how this semantics should be recognized and evaluated.

7.4 SLO Specialization Adaptability Context

In the previous section, the SLO specialization task was formulated without *explicit adaptation context*, i.e. all parameters were treated as being of the same rank. Note that the task itself can be considered in this way; however, the number of solutions would be too large and benefits of that would be unclear. As it was already stated, parameters have quite different semantics despite the fact that they are represented uniformly within the SLO specification. As specialization, in fact, means evaluation, the sequence of parameter evaluation should be strongly ordered.

Now we need to return to learning and teaching domain. Looking at it in the context of the specialization problem in large, we formulate the following hypothesis:

Hypothesis 1 *In general, features extracted from the e-learning domain (i.e. CS teaching) are not always of the same rank (priority); rather there are some strong priority relations that are important to focus with the possible manipulation, such as SLO specialization, in mind.*

(Note that the term *features* is a counterpart to *parameters* within SLOs; see Chap. 5 for details.)

To approve this statement, let us consider principles and models for designing learning objects (LOs) as they are presented in [IJL+03]: 'Learning principles are very close to *the goals of learning*. Learning principles emphasize certain learning activities and these activities support, especially, certain goals. For this reason, applying learning principles in designing LOs means that the *learning goals are defined first and then the appropriate principles will be applied*'. From this cited extract, we are able to derive the following *priority relation* (denoted as '≺' here):

$$< learning\ goals > \prec < learning\ principles > \prec < learning\ activities > \quad (7.5)$$

The meaning of this relation is as follows: learning goals have a higher priority with regard to learning principles, and the latter has a higher priority with regard to learning processes when all these are to be evaluated in the same setting. As learning activities are impossible without the use of content, we can extend Eq. (7.5) as it is presented by Eq. (7.6):

$$< learning\ goals > \prec \ldots \prec < learning\ activities > \prec$$
$$< learning\ content > \quad (7.6)$$

The papers [Ull08, DBC+10, CGS+11] discussed in Sect. 7.2 also serves for motivating the hypothesis. To this end, we can also look at the programming (language) domain in which priorities are well understood, though they are not always expressed explicitly. Take, for example, such features (categories) as *type*, *constant*, *variable*, *statement* or class of arithmetic operations (*, /, +, −). Using the introduced notion, we can write:

$$type \prec constant \prec variable \prec statement \quad (7.7)$$

$$multiplication \equiv division \prec addition \equiv subtraction \quad (7.8)$$

Here, the sign '≡' means the *same priority*. The relationship Eq. (7.7) follows from the logic of using those categories in writing programs. But it, perhaps, has been *rarely* stated explicitly. Another relationship Eq. (7.8) signals that some features may have the same priority. But there are also cases when items with the same priority have to be prioritized in some specific context. A good example of such a mechanism is the use of *parenthesis* in presenting priorities in the arithmetic or other expressions in programming languages.

The previous discussion motivates the need for the explicit prioritizing of parameters within the SLO specification. For this purpose, we introduce a new term, *fuzzy variable* (it has been coined from [BNR+10]), to manage the parameter priority relations. We define a fuzzy variable by its value taken from the set: {*HP*, *IP*, *LP*}, where *HP* means *high priority*, *IP* *intermediate priority* and *LP* *low priority*.

Simply speaking, a fuzzy variable is a weight assigned to the parameter to provide additional information on the *semantic role* of the parameter. As the pedagogical context should be evaluated first, the student's context next and then the content [IJL+03], we are able to prioritize the adequate parameters as follows. The parameters that express the pedagogical context should be weighted by *HP*, and the student context parameters should be evaluated by *IP* and the content parameters by *LP*. Though this reasoning is pedagogically sound, the accuracy may not always be sufficient. There might be various cases and different reasons to provide a more precise interpretation of the fuzzy variables (we explain that in more detail later).

The aim of the further discussion is to show how fuzzy variables are to be coded in the initial SLO specification. Let us consider the task to teach *sequential algorithms* using the NXT robot. The task is to generate the control program in RobotC for the straight-line movement. We introduce fuzzy variables by a *straight-forward comment* written in *the textual interface* of the SLO either *before* the parameter specification *statement* or *after* as it is illustrated below in the textual interface (see the top of Fig. 7.1). Note that there is also the graphical interface (see

Fig. 7.1 Parameters weighted by fuzzy variables (*above*) and selected values (*below*)

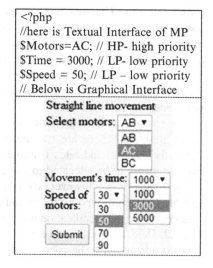

the upper part of Fig. 7.1) used by the user only, while the textual interface is only for the designer's use.

Here, our interest is to consider the technological parameters (motor's type, time and speed) only. In fact, they represent the teaching content. Note that this example is illustrative. It does not include the pedagogical context. Nevertheless, it is clear intuitively from the pure technological viewpoint that the motor's type has *a higher priority* with respect to the remaining parameters (i.e. we are able to evaluate the *time* and *speed* only if the motor's type has been indicated first). It is the content designer's responsibility to specify the fuzzy values for the parameters; however, there might be needed the expert's knowledge to specify the actual values. For example, an expert on the educational robots can confirm that the values of fuzzy variables have been indicated correctly, i.e. *the motors* should be evaluated first and then the *speed* and *time*.

Now we postpone the more deep discussion (till Sect. 7.6) on the role of fuzzy variables to solving the specialization task for adaptation. We do that because we need first to explain the basic idea of the approach to solve the task. In Sect. 7.5, we explain that from the user's perspective without technological details.

7.5 The Basic Idea of the Approach: User's View

We describe the approach from the user's perspective, using the specializer tool (MP-ReTool – stands for 'meta-program refactoring tool') we have developed [BBŠ13]. We will discuss the background on which the tool has been designed later, in Chap. 9. The tool transforms a heterogeneous meta-program (He MP) coded in PHP into the equivalent multistage representation through specialization or refactoring. We are able to use the tool for SLO specialization because they, in fact, are He MPs. We use SLOs to automatically generate LOs to teach CS (programming). The tool accepts the initial SLO specification along with the consistent SLO parameter model as input data. The basic assumption to correctly interpret the approach is that the initial SLO should be designed *for reuse*. The latter means that the SLO implements the *enhanced learning variability* [ŠBD13]. The latter includes *pedagogical, social, content* and *specific technological variability*. Therefore, the concrete context of the SLO use requires its specialization before being adapted and used.

The tool implements the user-tool communication model to solve the specialization problem. There are two modes of using the tool. In mode 1, the user (typically teacher) indicates (through the communication model) on how SLO parameters are to be allocated to stages. In mode 2, the tool works fully automatically. In this case, however, parameters are to be supplied *with nonredundant weights* (for details, see Eq. (7.6) and Table 7.1) introduced by the SLO designer (teacher) when the specification is coded. We explain the approach schematically in Fig. 7.2. Here, SLO_R should be read as 'designed for reuse' and SLO_S as 'specialized for adaptation'. The adequate SLO models are expressed through the set of

Table 7.1 Characteristics of the initial *SLO* (ornament drawing by robot)

Characteristics of SLO	Name of parameters (in bold) and their values (in brackets); for abbreviations and meaning, see legend below
Context-based parameters	**CO** (LN); **LA** (CT; PS); **LL** (BG; IT; AD)
Content-based parameters	**S** (AB; AC; BC); **V1** (10; 30; 50)
	V2 (10; 30; 50); **T** (1000; 3000; 5000)
	P (4; 5; 7); **D1** (10; 30); **D2** (10; 30)
	T1 (200; 500); **P1** (1, 2; 3)
Parameters' interaction model (line means interaction/dependency)	
Bloom's taxonomy levels (BTLs)	
L1: *remember*	
L2: *understand*	
L3: *apply*	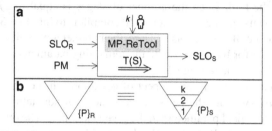
L4: *analyse*	
L5: *evaluate*	
L6: *create*	
HP: highest priority	
IP: intermediate priority as a function of BTLs	
LP: lowest priority	

© With kind permission from Springer Science + Business Media from [ŠBB14]
Legend used in this table Teacher's context: *CO*, curriculum objective (*LN* loops and nested loops), *LA* learning activity (case study (given by *teacher*), *CT* practice (done by *learner*), PS), *S* selected motor (AB, BC, AC), *V1, V2 drawing velocity* of motors (pen on the paper), *T* robot's drawing time, *P* number of ornament's parts, *D1, D2 moving velocity* of motors (pen over paper), *T1* robot's moving time and *P1*, number of ornaments. *LL* learner's previous knowledge level (*BG* beginner, *IT* intermediate, *AD* advanced)

Fig. 7.2 Specialization phase: (**a**) tool's level and (**b**) SLO models before and after transformation (see *right side*) represented as equivalent parameter spaces (© With kind permission from Springer Science + Business Media from [ŠBB14])

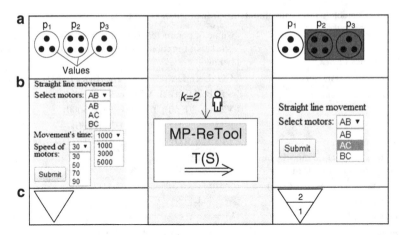

Fig. 7.3 Abstract interfaces of SLO_R and SLO_S models (**a**); user's view of the SLO_R and SLO_S interfaces (**b**); abstract view of specialization (**c**) (© With kind permission from Springer Science + Business Media from [ŠBB14])

parameters $\{P\}$ and outlined graphically in Fig. 7.2a. Here, $T(S)$ should be read as 'transformation through specialization', PM consistent parameter model described as a specific textual data structure, k number of stages, $\{P\}_R$ – SLO model before specialization and $\{P\}_S$ – SLO model after specialization in terms of parameter space.

In Fig. 7.3, we present the simplified real task to explain the approach in some more details. The task has already been introduced (see Fig. 7.1). It is the straight-line movement of the educational NXT robot [Gra03] to model (teach) linear (i.e. sequential) algorithms in RobotC. In terms of meta-programming, the latter is treated as a target (teaching) language. Three parameters (pairs of motors, movement time and speed) along with their values characterize the initial SLO specification of the task (see Fig. 7.3a, b on left side). In general, the weights (fuzzy variables) are not seen for the learners; however, the teacher, working with the tool in mode 1, has the possibility either to change fuzzy variables or to indicate the needed stage for a parameter manually.

The right side of Fig. 7.3 illustrates the state of the task after specialization (i.e. after the use of the tool, when the number of stages is equal to 2). This state is visible through the use of the other tool (PHP compiler) to interpret SLOs when the use of the specialized SLO takes place. Here, the parameter p_1 (pairs of motors) is at stage 2 (it is visible for the user), while the remaining parameters p_2 and p_3 are at stage 1 (they are invisible at stage 2).

We have revealed the only one aspect of our approach, i.e. the essence of the *specialization task* (without the pedagogical context of adaptation, because there are the only technological parameters in the given example). The other aspect is the specialization process itself. In fact, the k-stage SLO is a generator of the other SLO, i.e. $(k-1)$-stage SLO and so on. In this context, the PHP processor is the generator that accepts the k-stage SLO as input and produces a $(k-1)$-stage SLO as output (see Chap. 9, for more details).

We can summarize the task as follows: SLO k-stage specialization is the partitioning of the whole parameter space into k subsets first without intersecting using the adequate prescribed rules, such as prescribed constraints, and then, assigning the subsets to stages with respect to predefined priorities for the parameters. The technological aspects of transformation such as parameter deactivation are hidden for the user.

7.6 Pedagogical Aspects of SLO Specialization for Adaptation

In our approach, we aim at performing specialization so that automatic adaptation of the content to the user's context would be possible. There are two kinds of users (due to SLO reusability): teachers and learners. Therefore, SLO should be specialized for adaptation for both categories of actors. Having a pedagogically sound specialization of an SLO, the teacher should first make the adaptation to his context and later to allow the learners to make the adaptation by themselves in their contexts. The teacher's context has to be separated from the learner's context (such as learner's profile, etc.), when the adaptation takes place. The content adaptation to the learner's context, on the other hand, should be the self-guided process. Such an adaptation is a cognitive process or, more precisely, the *early stage of the knowledge gaining* in the learning process.

In general, Bloom's taxonomy levels [AK01] predefine the cognitive process. We present the levels as L_1, remember; L_2, understand; L_3, apply; L_4, analyse; L_5, evaluate and L_6, create. Now we are able to connect Bloom's taxonomy levels with the needed number of stages from the pedagogical perspective. As it was stated in Sect. 7.4, fuzzy variables $\{HP, IP, LP\}$, being the parameter weights, serve for managing the stage selection. So far, all the variables were treated as constants (see Fig. 7.1). However, this vision is too simplified. Indeed, the value HP is relevant to teacher's context parameters; therefore, HP can be treated as a constant because the teacher knows the teaching context. But this is not the case for the other kinds of parameters.

As we want to make content adaptation to the learner's context as flexible as possible, we need to accept that the values IP and LP are not constants but the functions of Bloom's taxonomy levels. The basis of the assumption is that a learner should have the possibility to *move gradually* (in a step-by-step manner) from the lowest level to the highest, when self-selecting of the content for learning takes place. Thus, we can write:

$$HP = constant; IP = f(\lambda) \text{ and } LP = f^*(\lambda). \tag{7.9}$$

In Eq. (7.9), both f and f^* are different functions, but their arguments are subsets defined on the same set $\lambda \subset \{L_1, \ldots, L_6\}$; L_i is a level of Bloom's taxonomy. Note

Table 7.2 Characteristics of SLO (ornament drawing by robot) obtained by using MP-ReTool

Specialization for teacher			
Teacher's context parameters		CO; LA	Stage 5
Specialization for learner			
Level: category of Bloom's taxonomy (BT)	BT description uses the verb subsets from [MVS+10]	Visible parameters at current stage and already evaluated parameters at previous stages (blacken) as they are seen in the specialized specification	Stages for adaptation by learners
L1: remember	Recognize, recall	$S = \{AB, BC, AC\}^a$	Stage 4
L2: understand	Interpret, exemplify, classify, summarize, infer, compare, explain	S; V1; V2; D1; D2	Stage 3
L3: apply	Execute, implement	S; V1; V2; D1; D2; T; T1	Stage 2
L4: analyse	Differentiate, organize, attribute	S; V1; V2; D1; D2; T; T1; P; P1-LL	Stage 1
L5: evaluate	Check, critique		
L6: create	Generate, plan, produce		

© With kind permission from Springer Science + Business Media from [ŠBB14]
[a]Learner should have previous knowledge about Lego NXT robot

that what levels we need to treat as arguments of the functions depend on the task and teacher's intention. It is the reason why we left the possibility for the teacher to reason about the actual values of *IP* and *LP* (see Table 7.1, in Sect. 7.7) before using the tool MP-ReTool in mode 1. However, the precise definition of *IP* and *LP* values enables first to calculate the needed number of stages and then to assign parameters to stages automatically, when the tool is used in mode 2 (e.g. for our task $k = 5$; see Table 7.2 in Sect. 7.7).

The introduced functions enable us to reason also about the *theoretically possible number* of stages (i.e. the upper bound of stages calculated from the pedagogical perspective). Let us denote it as $k_{max}(p)$. Then we can write Eq. (7.10), taking into account Eq. (7.9):

$$k_{max}(p) = 6 + \text{the number of teacher} - \text{related stages.} \qquad (7.10)$$

In practice, however, there is no need to consider all six levels as separate units to represent the student context and the teaching content (see models (a) and (b) in Table 7.1).

Now we are able to combine technological (t) and pedagogical (p) aspects in calculating the upper bound of stages $k_m(p, t)$ to make specialization correctly as follows:

$$k_m(p, t) = \min\{k_{max}(t), k_{max}(p)\}. \qquad (7.11)$$

Here, $k_{max}(t)$ is the upper bound of stages calculated from the pure technological viewpoint. This bound is equal to the number of independent parameter groups

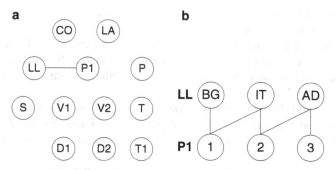

Fig. 7.4 Model of SLO 'ornament drawing by robot': (**a**) parameter model and (**b**) value interaction model of parameters LL and P1 (© With kind permission from Springer Science +Business Media from [ŠBB14])

(e.g. $k_{max}(t) = 11$ in our case study; see Fig. 7.4). For more details on technological aspects of staging, see Chap. 9. To this end, we summarize the main result of this section as follows.

If the number of stages k of the specialized SLO satisfies the following condition $1 < k \leq k_m(p, t)$, then the *specialization is both technologically and pedagogically sound*.

To approve this statement and to introduce the evidence in calculating fuzzy variables according to the extended view on those variables, we need to present the following study of the SLO specialization task.

7.7 Case Study

The aim is to demonstrate the specialization process of the real learning task using NXT robot environment [CCh11] and to reveal more practical details on the SLO specialization. We have selected the 'ornament drawing by robot' task. The learning objective was to teach nested loops written in RobotC [Rob07]. The SLO specification, as teaching content for reuse, has been written manually in advance. PHP has been used as a meta-language and RobotC as a target language. Using the tool MP-ReTool, we were able to extract the dependency (interaction) models from the given specification (see graphs in Fig. 7.4 and in Table 7.1, for more details). The legend below Table 7.1 explains the meaning of all parameters and their values for the task.

In Fig. 7.4, we present the model of the task expressed through parameter names without weights (a) and the value interaction model for parameters LL and P1 (b). The parameters' value interaction model (values are within circles; lines specify the constraints *require* here being defined in terms of feature modelling [CHE05]). The model, for example, should be read as follows: 'It is required to draw the only one ornament with the robot's help for the beginner (BG), while for the advanced learner (AD) it is required to draw 2 or 3 ornaments'. As parameters LL and P1 interact among themselves, they are treated as dependent; while there is no inter-action (or dependency) among the other parameters (see Fig. 7.4a). With regard to the parameter dependency, we have the interaction among the social parameter (LL) and the content parameter (P1) here (cp. this with the interaction given in Fig. 6.2; see Sect. 6.3.3 in Chap. 6).

To understand the task, learners should have previous knowledge on robot architecture and functionality. For example, learners know that there are three motors (A, B, C) used in pairs (AB, AC, BC), and there are two kinds of velocity (drawing velocity and idle move).

In Table 7.1 (see graphs at right), we present the task models in more details. There are two variants (a) and (b) of the SLO model. They differ by the assigned weights introduced by the teacher. Weights are functions of Bloom's taxonomy levels. They describe the semantics for adaptation. The made assignment enables the tool to calculate the number of needed stages. Note that for this task $k_{max}(p) = 6 + 1 = 7$; $k_{max}(t) = 11$ (the number of independent parameter groups – see the model (a)) and $k_m(p, t) = \min\{11, 7\} = 7$ (see Eqs. (7.10) and (7.5)). Thus, the identified numbers of stages (4 and 5) are valid for both models (a) and (b).

For example, for the model (a), five stages are needed (see Table 7.2). For the model (b), four stages are needed (stage 4 contains CP and LA; stage 3 contains S, V1, V2, D1 and D2; stage 2 contains T and T1; stage 1 contains LL-P1 and P). Note that the variants (a) and (b) provide slightly different possibilities for adapta-tion (knowledge levels to be gained already at the adaptation phase). Note that this is the 'surface knowledge' in terms of 'surface learning and deep learning' [SHD09, BPB13]. The more stages we have, the more steps the adaptation includes. But the needed number of stages should be linked with the task semantics. The latter dictates the teacher's intention. For more details on that and adaptation semantics, see Sects. 8.5 and 8.6 in Chap. 8.

Table 7.2 summarizes the specialized task for adaptation (model (a); see Table 7.1) given from the users' viewpoint, where the teacher's and learner's specializations are separated. The criteria for the learner specialization are levels of Bloom's taxonomy. We will provide a more extensive discussion on adaptation semantics in Sect. 8.7 (see Chap. 8).

In Fig. 7.5, we present the results of solving the ornament drawing task: the generated instance, according to the given parameter values (a) and the robot's view to run the task (b). Here, the values of the pure content parameters (P and P1) are 7 and 1 adequately.

7.8 Discussion and Evaluation of the Approach

We have described the specialization task and a process to transform the initial SLO into its multistage format using the specializer tool we have developed. For this purpose, we have applied the theoretical background borrowed from two research

a   b

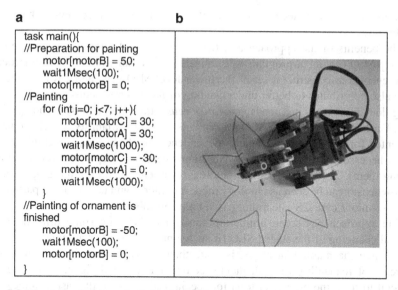

```
task main(){
//Preparation for painting
    motor[motorB] = 50;
    wait1Msec(100);
    motor[motorB] = 0;
//Painting
    for (int j=0; j<7; j++){
        motor[motorC] = 30;
        motor[motorA] = 30;
        wait1Msec(1000);
        motor[motorC] = -30;
        motor[motorA] = 0;
        wait1Msec(1000);
    }
//Painting of ornament is
finished
    motor[motorB] = -50;
    wait1Msec(100);
    motor[motorB] = 0;

}
```

Fig. 7.5 The derived instance in RobotC (**a**); (**b**) the ornament drawing task by NXT robot (© With kind permission from Springer Science + Business Media from [ŠBB14])

fields: program partial evaluation and stage-based meta-programming. The aim of specialization through staging is to let flexible (automatic) adaptation when the specialized SLO specification is used.

Our domain is not homogeneous and includes subdomains such as CS teaching content (curricular), pedagogy, programming languages, educational robotics, etc. We specify the domain abstractly as learning variability. As by using meta-programming techniques, we are able to uniformly and explicitly express the essential variability aspects through parameters (with regard to teaching aims), and we treat the developed initial SLO specification as the product of *design for reuse* (to support that, we have developed the other tool; see Chap. 10). As the initial SLO may preprogram a large number of possible variations (LOs), first SLO should be *specialized for adaptation*. To make the learning variability easy manageable in the stage-based specialization, we have enriched parameters with *priorities* using fuzzy variables (*HP*, *IP*, *LP*). The variables enable to separate roles of parameters (pedagogical from social, social from content, etc.) and, in this way, to manage the process.

The practical needs for specialization have come from our extensive experiments in using the NXT and other educational robots in the real setting (school) to teach CS topics. Aiming at the efficiency to preparing the content and ensuring flexibility of its continuous changes (by both teacher and students), we have described the SLOs as meta-programs. Because of the extremely wide e-learning context (social, pedagogical, etc.), SLOs may contain a large number of parameters. Because of the necessity of managing changeability and adaptation of the teaching content to the context of use, we have found the specialization through staging as a relevant and beneficial technology, though the details of this technology have not yet been revealed.

The benefits of the approach are: (a) it provides a theoretical background to develop SLO (i.e. meta-program) specializers, or in other words refactoring tools; (b) it enables to construct a set of the lower-level SLO generators; (c) staging of SLO also contributes to better understanding of the heterogeneous meta-programming domain; and (d) it extends *generative reuse*, though in a narrow and specific way. Furthermore, the initial SLO implements learning variability, which we have presented formally by the parameter dependency graph. In fact, the graph represents the essential domain knowledge (fundamental concepts and relationships among them). In terms of domain ontology (see, e.g. [VIK13]), the graphs (in a narrow sense) can be seen as ontology models to model and understand a particular domain (in our case CS e-learning based on using robots).

The approach has some limitations too. First, there are some difficulties in manual changing of the staged SLO (if such a need arises after automatic specializing when the number of stages is more than 3). The reason is the significant decrease of readability of such meta-specifications (meta-designer's view). It is difficult to form the precise criteria for specialization due to the task complexity, context and content dependency and fuzzy variable identification. Some debates may arise due to the identification of fuzzy variables for the parameters. In the simplest case, they are constants with three values (*HP*, for teacher's parameters; *IP*. for student's parameters; and *LP*, for content's parameters). As the adaptation of teaching content should be oriented to students' needs, a more precise specification is needed. Though Bloom's taxonomy levels are helpful in this case; however, such an approach requires additional efforts and expert's intervention in defining the more precise values.

7.9 Summary and Conclusion

The graph-based approach enriched by concepts and principles of program partial evaluation research has been found as a relevant theoretical basis for approving the solution of the SLO specialization problem. The problem itself has been formulated taking into account the CS learning variability and parameter priorities so that the solution, being also the input specification of the *SLO adaptation problem*, enables the automatic content adaptation. Fuzzy variables are an instrument to make assignments of parameters to stages automatically in the specialization process. The variables enable to discriminate the context-based parameters from the rest (i.e. content based). Therefore, they introduce context awareness in managing the specialization process for adaptation. In fact, fuzzy variables specify criteria (requirements) for SLO adaptation at the specialization phase.

We have developed the tool and are using it to specialize (automatically) the real SLOs for teaching CS topics within the robot-based environment. From the user's (i.e. teacher's and learner's) perspective, SLO specialization raises the abstraction level of transformations because, at a higher stage, he/she uses a less amount of information to be presented in the user-friendly manner.

As SLOs, in fact, are meta-programs, it is possible to evaluate the approach in the broader context, i.e. from different perspectives as follows: (i) specialization by staging is *design with reuse*, while meta-program developing to provide input data for the specialization is *design for reuse*; (ii) the specialization is a generalization process *by narrowing*, while the meta-program development is a generalization process *by widening*; (iii) the specialization is a partial evaluation of a heterogeneous meta-program in terms of the program partial evaluation research in CS; and (iv) specialization is also *refactoring* of a heterogeneous meta-program in terms of the software refactoring research.

7.10   Research and Exercise Questions

7.1. Define the following terms: program specialization, partial evaluation and program refactoring. In what aspects are they similar? In what aspects are they different?

7.2. Provide a more extensive overview of research in two fields: software refactoring and program partial evaluation.

7.3. What is heterogeneous meta-programming? What is stage-based meta-programming? Explain the role of languages and parameterization in those paradigms (use [ŠD13] as a guide). Provide simple examples of meta-programs and SLO.

7.4. Explain the similarity and difference between two terms: SLO and heterogeneous meta-program.

7.5. Why is SLO specialization needed?

7.6. What is stage-based specialization of SLO (meta-program)?

7.7. Explain the essence of SLO specialization.

7.8. What is the SLO model? What is the parameter dependency model? How can it be specified? What is the constraint required?

7.9. What is the role of fuzzy variables in the stage-based specialization of SLO? How can values of fuzzy variables be specified?

7.10. Why can we use Bloom's taxonomy levels in defining fuzzy variable values?

7.11. What are influential factors in defining the number of stages in stage-based specialization of SLO?

7.12. How can the upper bound of stages for a given (initial) SLO be defined?

7.13. Select some examples of SLO from previous chapters or from [ŠD13] extend them with fuzzy variables {HP, IP, LP} and then using the tool MP-ReTool provide specialization with different number of stages.

References

[ACL+12]   Acher M, Collet P, Lahire P, France RB (2012) FAMILIAR: a domain-specific language for large scale management of feature models. Sci Comput Program 78 (6):657–681

[ACM13]   PEPM 2013 – ACM SIGPLAN (2013) Workshop on partial evaluation and program manipulation (PEPM'13)

[AK01]   Anderson L, Krathwohl D (2001) Taxonomy for learning, teaching and assessing: a revision of Bloom's taxonomy of educational objectives. Longman, New York

[BBŠ13]   Bespalova K, Burbaite R, Štuikys (2013) MP-ReTool tools. http://proin.ktu.lt/ metaprogram/MP-ReTool/

[BNR+10]   Bagheri E, Noia TD, Ragone A, Dragan Gasevic D (2010) Configuring software product line feature models based on stakeholders' soft and hard. In: 14th international software product line conference. Springer, Berlin

[BPB13]   Bhattacharya T, Prasath R, Bhattacharya B (2013) Qualitative learning outcome through computer assisted instructions. In: Mining intelligence and knowledge exploration. Springer, Tamil Nadu, pp 567–578

[CCh11]   Castledine A, Chalmers C (2011) LEGO robotics: an authentic problem-solving tool? Des Technol Educ Int J 16(3):19–27

[CGS+11]   Capuano N, Gaeta M, Salerno S, Mangione GR (2011) An ontology-based approach for context-aware e-learning. In: 2011 third international conference on intelligent networking and collaborative systems (INCoS). IEEE, Fukuoka, pp 789–794

[CHE05]   Czarnecki K, Helsen S, Eisenecker U (2005) Staged configuration through specialization and multilevel configuration of feature models. Softw Process Improv Pract 10 (2):143–169

[DBC+10]   Das M, Bhaskar M, Chithralekha T, Sivasathya S (2010) Context aware E-learning system with dynamically composable learning objects. Int J Comput Sci Eng 2 (4):1245–1253

[FBB+99]   Fowler M, Beck K, Brant J, Opdyke W, Roberts D (1999) Refactoring: improving the design of existing code. Addison Wesley, Westford, Massachusetts. http://www. refactoring.com/

[Fut00]   Futamura Y (2000) Partial evaluation of computation process – an approach to a compiler-compiler. Higher-Order Symb Comput 12(4):381–391

[GJI12]   Giacobazzi R, Jones ND, Mastroeni I (2012) Obfuscation by partial evaluation of distorted interpreters. In: Proceedings of the ACM SIGPLAN 2012 workshop on partial evaluation and program manipulation, PEPM'12. ACM, New York, pp 63–72

[GMB11]   Gheyi R, Massoni T, Borba P (2011) Automatically checking feature model refactorings. J Univ Comput Sci 17(5):684–711

[Gra03]   Gray JA (2003) Toeing the line: experiments with line-following algorithms. Technical report. http://www.fll-freak.com/misc/01-jgray_report.pdf

[HT08]   Hartmann H, Trew T (2008) Using feature diagrams with context variability to model multiple product lines for software supply chains. In: Software product line conference, 2008. SPLC'08. 12th international. IEEE, pp 12–21

[IJL+03]   Ilomäki L, Jaakkola T, Lakkala M, Nirhamo L, Nurmi S, Paavola S, Rahikainen M, Lehtinen, E (2003) Principles, models and examples for designing learning objects (LOs). Pedagogical guidelines in CELEBRATE. A working paper for the European Commission, CELEBRATE Project, IST-2001-35188, May

[JGS93]   Jones ND, Gomard CK, Sestoft P (1993) Partial evaluation and automatic program generation. Peter Sestoft

[Jon96]   Jones ND (1996) An introduction to partial evaluation. ACM Comput Surv 28 (3):480–503, September

[JSS85]   Jones ND, Sestoft P, Søndergaard PH (1985) An experiment in partial evaluation: the generation of a compiler generator. In: Jouannaud JP (ed) Rewriting techniques and applications, Dijon. Lecture notes in computer science, vol 202 Springer, Berlin, pp 124–140

[MLC02]   Le Meur AF, Lawall JL, Consel Ch (2002) Towards bridging the gap between programming languages and partial evaluation. PEPM'02, 14–15 Jan 2002

[MT04]   Mens T, Tourw T (2004) A survey of software refactoring. IEEE Trans Softw Eng 30 (2):126–139

[MVS+10] Martin S, Vallance M, van Schaik P, Wiz C (2010) Learning spaces, tasks and metrics for effective communication in Second Life within the context of programming LEGO NXT Mindstorms™ robots: towards a framework for design and implementation. J Virtual Worlds Res 3(1)

[Mur12]   Murakami M (2012) An application of partial evaluation of communicating processes to system security. Int J Found Comp Sci Technol (IJFCST) 2(4):15–27

[Rob07]   RobotC – Improved movement (2007) Robotics Academy. http://www.doc.ic.ac.uk/ ~ajd/Robotics/RoboticsResources/ROBOTC%20%20Improved%20Movement.pdf, p 19

[ŠBB14]   Štuikys V, Bespalova K, Burbaitė R (2014) Generative learning object (GLO) specialization: Teacher's and learner's view. In: Proceedings 20th international conference, ICIST, Druskininkai, Lithuania, Springer, 9–10 Oct 2014

[ŠBD13]   Štuikys V, Burbaitė R, Damaševičius R (2013) Teaching of computer science topics using meta-programming-based GLOs and LEGO robots. Inf Educ 12(1):125–142

[ŠD13]   Štuikys V, Damaševičius R (2013) Meta-programming and model-driven meta-program development: principles, processes and techniques. Springer

[SHD09]   Shuhidan S, Hamilton M, D'Souza D (2009) A taxonomic study of novice programming summative assessment. In: Proceedings of 11th Australasian computing education conference (ACE 2009), Wellington, pp 147–156

[She01]   Sheard T (2001) Accomplishments and research challenges in meta-programming. In: Proceedings of 2nd international workshop on semantics, application, and implementation of program generation (SAIG'2001), Florence. Lecture notes in computer science, vol 2196. Springer, pp 2–44

[Tah04]   Taha W (2004) A gentle introduction to multi-stage programming. Domain-specific program generation. Lecture notes in computer science, vol 3016, pp 30–50

[Tah99]   Taha W (1999) Multi-stage programming: its theory and applications. Ph.D. thesis, Oregon Graduate Institute of Science and Technology

[TBK09]   Thum T, Batory D, Kastner C (2009) Reasoning about edits to feature models. In: Software engineering. ICSE 2009. IEEE 31st international conference on (pp 254–264). IEEE

[Tho05]   Thomas D (2005) Refactoring as meta programming? J Object Technol 4(1):7–12

[TM03]   Tourwe T, Mens T (2003) Identifying refactoring opportunities using logic meta programming. In: 7th European conference software maintenance and reengineering, IEEE, Benevento, Italy

[Ull08]   Ullrich C (2008) Pedagogically founded courseware generation for web-based learning: an HTN-planning-based approach implemented in PAIGOS. Springer, Berlin

[VIK13]   Vesin B, Ivanović M, Klašnja-Milićević A, Budimac Z (2013) Ontology-based architecture with recommendation strategy in java tutoring system. Comput Sci Inf Syst 10(1):237–261

Chapter 8
Context-Aware Adaptation of Smart LOs

8.1 Introduction

We consider adaptation as a bridge to connect generative reuse aspects with the educational context to create opportunities for adaptive personalized learning. To achieve this aim, we have already made an essential move – we have created conditions for that. Indeed the learning variability discussed at the modelling level in Chap. 4 can be seen also as the conceptual background (in terms of creating a space of possible variants) for adaptive personalized learning on the basis of using SLOs. Even more, the specialized SLO considered in the previous chapter is the methodological background for automatic adaptation.

This chapter starts dealing with supplementary generative features such as adaptability, which make a given SLO actually smart. In general, adaptability is the ability to change the LO's structure or behaviour (or both) under the change of external conditions such as context or agent. Adaptability is the property that also pertains with reusability. If a resource is easy to adapt, this also means the support for reusability. Here, we focus on the automatic preprogrammed adaptation. It is possible if we have the already specialized SLOs prepared using the approach discussed in Chap. 7. This approach was evaluated in the previous chapter as *specialization for adaptation*. The approach we consider in this chapter can be treated as *adaptation with specialization*. This framework we continue to discuss here is, in fact, the modified paradigm known in SWE as *design for reuse* and *design with reuse* [Sam97].

Furthermore, the adaptation in our approach is self-guided for both teacher and student, if SLO specialization has been made adequately. Indeed, specialization through staging enables to distribute (classify) teacher-oriented parameters at the highest stages and student context parameters at intermediate stages, while content parameters are allocated at the lowest stage. Because of this property, adaptation is a multilevel process. First, the teacher makes adaptation to his/her teaching context, and then learners are able to manage self-adaptation of the content to own context of use.

© Springer International Publishing Switzerland 2015
V. Štuikys, *Smart Learning Objects for Smart Education in Computer Science*,
DOI 10.1007/978-3-319-16913-2_8

8.2 Literature Review

As LO reusability issues were extensively discussed in the previous chapters, here we focus to the larger degree on pedagogical context awareness and adaptability problems. In general, the adaptability problem is not as simple as it might be thought of. There are many attributes to characterize the problem such as context, learner's profile, capabilities of a system used, etc. There are also a variety of factors influencing its understanding (e.g. content representation forms, cognitive aspects, structure and model of LO, etc.). As a result, one can meet a diversity of related terms in the literature to characterize the problem: *adaptive learning*, *personalized learning* [MKS10, BVV+10], *adaptable LO*, *personalized LO* [BCW+08], *adaptive granularity* [MJ10], *adaptive learning scenarios* [BS08], *adaptive learning path* [BSS+12], etc.

All above-stated facts require introducing a scheme to review the related work in some systematic way. As this research field is indeed very broad, we restrict ourselves presenting the review with our vision and our approach in mind only. First, we focus on context issues as the most influential factor to adaptability. Next, we analyse the adaptability problem from the *external* (i.e. the environment) and *internal* (i.e. the content model) views. Finally, in the next section, we summarize the analysis by introducing a framework which, in our view, gives the better understanding the essence, broadness and complexity of the problem.

We start from definitions and interpretations of the term *context* as it is understood in general and in the e-learning literature in particular. Context-related issues have been intensively researched, especially in the computer-human interaction and technology-enhanced learning. As it is emphasized by Zimmermann et al. [ZLO07], in the area of CS, there are a number of definitions of the term *context* and *context awareness*. The vast majority of the earliest definitions of the term *context* can be categorized into two groups: definition by synonyms (e.g. application's environment context or situation context) and definition by example (e.g. enumeration context elements like location, identity, time, temperature, noise and the beliefs and intentions of the human).

Dey [Dey01] defines context as 'any information that can be used to characterize the situation of an entity'. In the other paper [DAS01], Dey et al. extend the previous definition by stating that context is 'a person, place, or object that is considered relevant to the interaction between a user and an application, including the user and applications themselves'. This can be viewed as an application-centric definition which clearly states that the context is always bound to an entity and that information that describes the situation of an entity is context. The paper [LCW +09] defines the learning context as 'information to identify the state of the item, i.e. learner's location, learning activities, the used tools and LOs'. Dourish [Dou04] emphasizes a dual origin of the context: technical and social based aspects. From a social viewpoint, the author argues that context is not something that describes a setting or situation, but rather a feature of interaction. From a technical viewpoint, researchers try to define context in a more specific way as an *operational term*

[Win01, ZLO07, VMO+12], i.e. by enumerating categories of the term. The main contribution of the paper [ZLO07] is the introduction of a context definition that comprises three canonical parts: a definition per se in general terms, a formal definition describing the appearance of context and an operational definition characterizing the use of context and its dynamic behaviour.

The paper [VMO+12] provides extensive analysis of context definitions with regard to designing recommendation systems to support technology-enhanced learning (TEL). The latter aims to design, develop and test socio-technical innovations that will support and enhance learning practices of both individuals and organizations. With respect to our aims, one important result of this paper is the framework that summarizes the known so far definitions of the term context and presents how these definitions relate to each other.

We formulate the following finding of this short analysis as follows:

1. Context is a multidimensional category that, in general, may include the following features: *special time, physical conditions, computing, resource, user, activity* and *social*.
2. As many of these features are overlapping (see [VMO+12]), it is reasonable to combine some of them in a concrete situation such as teaching with the use of SLOs. Thus, we will focus on three context dimensions: computing/resource, user (learner/teacher)/social and activity/task/content. Comparing these dimensions with pedagogical reusability as it is proposed in [PS04], we are able to connect a learning situation with the three context categories we will use later respectively: *technical context, pedagogical context* and *content context*.
3. Context, in fact, creates conditions or brings important information to provide actions for adaptation.

Now we move more closely to the adaptability problem. It can be analysed and understood at least from two perspectives: *external* and *internal*. The first approach means constructing an adaptive system to make LOs adaptive or contributing to the adaptability problem in somewhat way. The second approach focuses on incorporating adaptive features within the structure of LO itself. To support the first vision, Pitkanenen and Silander [PS04] propose the criteria for pedagogical reusability of LOs as a basis for designing an adaptive system or for the use within a learning content management system. The paper [HMM+05] describes the ontology-based system, *OntAWare*, which provides an environment comprising a set of software tools that support learning content authoring, management, the semi-automatic generation of standard e-learning and other courseware elements (learning objects), adaptation and delivery.

The approach [AAB+06] enriches the content context, thereby allowing e-learning platforms to dynamically compose, reuse and adapt educative content provided by third parties (learning objects). Three context models are presented together with a multi-agent-based e-learning platform that composes and adapts extended learning objects according to learner's context changes. The paper [AGL11] proposes ontological representations of learning environment and a memetic distributed problem-solving approach to generate the best learning presentation and, at the same time, minimize the computational efforts necessary to compute optimal learning experiences.

Assuming that learning style is a useful model for quantifying user characteristics for effective personalized learning, the paper [BBF+09] presents two case studies that provide rigorous and quantitative evaluations of learning-style-adapted e-learning environments. These studies indicate a limited usefulness in terms of learning styles for user modelling and suggest that alternative characteristics or techniques might provide a more beneficial experience to users.

There are efforts to adapt system functionality, e-learning scenarios or learning styles to learner's behaviour [EAJ+10, FLD+12, KVI+11]. Some systems provide recommendation on how to create adaptive learning objects by modelling ant colony behaviour [YW09] (more on recommendation systems can be learnt from [VMO+12]), by adaptive retrieval of LOs through learning styles [MS06].

The next package of papers discusses some aspects of *internal adaptation*. As internal adaptation directly relates also with design, Boyle and Ravenscroft [BR12] suggest combining the context with the so-called deep design in designing the reusable content. Jones [Jon05] proposes to use *patterns* to support adaptability in constructing LOs. He states that requirements for reusability may be in conflict with those for effective learning. So the proposed patterns must ensure that the LOs constructed are adaptable to different contexts and remain pedagogically sound within those contexts. Patterns can be used to create learning resources that are both reusable and adaptable. Han and Kramer [HK09] propose generating interactive learning object produced from configurable samples.

Internal adaptation also relates to *visualization*. Visualization-based approaches have been shortly discussed in Sect. 7.2 (see Chap. 7). In general, *visualization* is defined as a transformation process that takes abstract data and gives it a form suitable for visual presentation [CBK13]. What is the role of visualization in the case of SLO, reader had the opportunity to learn from examples given in Chap. 7.

How all those briefly discussed topics relate to our approach in more details will be clear later. In the next subsection, we extend the discussion on adaptability problem.

8.3 Understanding the Adaptation Problem in Large

Here, we are aiming to extend and summarize analysis of the relevant work given before. For this reason, we present a framework by formulating some related questions along with possible answers in order we could be able first to better understand the adaptation problem itself and then to tackle it with respect to the capabilities of our approach. We do that because, as it is also clear from the previous analysis, adaptation is the *cross-disciplinary problem*. It is why we need also to look at this problem from different perspectives (e.g. SWE, CS and e-learning). Some questions raised below, in some other context, can also be regarded as separate research questions. We do not pretend to give an exhaustive explanation or answer the questions posed; rather we seek to show the relationship of crosscutting aspects and a holistic nature of the adaptation problem.

1. *What is adaptation in large* (e.g. *in SWE and CS) and in e-learning?*

   In SWE, adaptation is conceived of as 'any process which modifies or extends the implementation or behaviour of a subsystem to enable or improve its interactions, or synonymously, its communication with the surrounding parts of the system (which is its environment)' [Kel08]. Here, 'communication' is understood not only as dynamic interactions at run time but also as interactions occurring statically, at compile time. In CS, the term *adaptation* refers 'to a process, in which an interactive system adapts its behaviour to individual users based on information acquired about its user(s) and its environment'. Furthermore, the term *adaptability* 'refers to users that can substantially customize the system through tailoring activities by themselves' [see free encyclopaedia]. In e-learning, *adaptation* is thought of as the customization of the system 'to the cognitive characteristics of the students and implies the study and conjunction of *technical and pedagogical aspects*' [RDS+08]. Based on earlier research, the paper [BMM+05] defines adaptation as 'the adjustments in an educational environment aiming to (1) accommodate learners' needs, goals, abilities, and knowledge, (2) provide appropriate interaction, and (3) personalize the content'. Further, we accept both definitions as the most relevant to our approach. The definitions, in fact, identify the *holistic nature* of the adaptation problem, because those indicate on the explicit integration of technological, pedagogical, social and content-based aspects and consequences of the integration such as interaction.

2. *What are adaptation objectives in e-learning?* There is no unified or single objective, rather a set of different objectives as follows:

   (a) Increasing learning outcome and learning performance and attractiveness and minimizing time spent by students in learning [CG10]

   (b) Easing understandability of the content and its presentation

   (c) Enriching the adaptation functionality of e-learning environments being able to evaluate context data from personal profiles, learning domain and technological situation [PDM+12]

   (d) Accommodation of the educational environment to learners' needs, goals, abilities and knowledge [BMM+05]

   (e) Enhancing learning content interoperability and creating learning design spaces (e.g. through meta-design [FGS+04, FG06])

   However, all these can be combined under the same umbrella – the efforts by the research community to *enhance reuse* through adaptability [Qui07, BS11].

3. *What are or might be strategies for adaptation?* Here, by strategy we mean the far-reaching objectives. Thus, the answer has much in common with the previous question: e-learning domain modelling for extending reuse dimension (e.g. modelling with learning variability in mind [ŠBD13]), meta-design and participatory design in creating e-learning systems [FGS+04], moving from the

traditional classroom-based learning paradigm to the learner's centred and collaborative learning, enhancing the capabilities of active learning [GD95] and contributing to STEM initiatives [Kri14].

4. *Who are or might be adaptation providers?* This question is due to understanding the relationship among other stated questions. Therefore, on the basis of the previous analysis, we are able to state: all actors involved in the process (i.e. learning domain experts, designers of educational environments, instructional designers, teachers and learners) are or might be adaptation makers; however, their possibilities to do that are quite different and depend on many factors which are implicitly or explicitly seen in other questions. We do not neglect that teachers and even learners could also be adaptation makers.

5. *What are items or objects among which adaptation should be provided?* The adaptation item might be (i) e-learning system to learners' behaviour ([GMB +04] defines an adaptation system as 'an environment of software modules, which comprises a set of features for adaptivity and adaptability'), (ii) content to environment, (iii) content to tool's characteristics (such as robots, smartphones), etc.

6. *What are types of adaptation?* The comprehensive answer can be found in [BTK06]. Some types of adaptation are considered in [CG10]: system-driven adaptation and user-driven adaptation, static (i.e. at compile time) and dynamic (i.e. at run time).

7. *What criteria should be used for adaptation?* The answer is (i) user's profile, (ii) learning styles, (iii) user's motivation measurements [ERB12], content visualization, content (program) transformation into the physical process such as the educational robot movement, etc. Again, all these can be combined under the same umbrella – *context in large*, meaning to support teachers' and learners' needs, though to the different extent.

8. *When adaptation has to be started: at the design time as a specific requirement, at the use time only or at the whole life cycle (meaning design and use)?* There is no a single answer. That depends mainly upon the strategy and goals and technological capabilities. This requires a separate investigation.

9. *What is the scope or granularity level of adaptation: the whole educational environment, some system/tool, either stand-alone LO, course-level LOs or some combination of items enumerated above?*
   There might be various cases as it was previously discussed. This question requires a specific altitude and separate investigation too.

10. *What are possible mechanisms and techniques to support adaptation?* Again, a variety of possibilities may support that, including *pure technological* (e.g. interfaces, parameterization, LO models [Jon05], program specialization [BN02], program transformation to name a few), *pure social* (e.g. frameworks for social learning [Jar10]) and *mixed* ones (e.g. methods for learning path (i.e. sequence of LOs and learning activities used to achieve predefined learning goals) identification [BM07], REAL – Rich Environments for Active Learning [GD95]). Though the discussion on REAL has been provided two decades ago, the raised problems there are still of great importance nowadays, especially in

the context of STEM solutions and the needs for improving CS education [Kri14]. In our context, the use of specialized SLO within education robot environments might be seen as a way for implementing active learning and contributing to STEM solutions in teaching CS.

We summarize the discussion as follows. Adaptation in e-learning is a holistic cross-disciplinary process. It can be also seen as a reuse-based activity within some educational environment aiming at changing the structure, the functionality (behaviour) of an item (LO) or both so that the predefined objectives or requirements of the learning context can be fulfilled. The provided analysis enables us to outline the scope of the adaptation problem to be considered in the next sections.

8.4 Adaptation Task Using SLO and Educational Robots

Now we are able to formulate the adaptation task in our context using SLO and NXT robots as a part of the educational environment as follows. Let be given the educational environment that includes the following components: (*i*) *specialized* SLO oriented to using NXT robots (see Sect. 7.7), (*ii*) PHP processor to interpret the SLO, (*iii*) RobotC programming environment and (*iv*) ready-for-use NXT hardware. The task is to *initiate* and *perform* the user-guided multistage *processes* that include (*i*) the preprogrammed content (i.e. specialized SLO) *adaptation* to user's (i.e. teacher's and learner's) needs through selecting the adequate parameter values, (*ii*) monitoring and evaluating the result of adaptation through the feedback, (*iii*) adapting the intermediate result to the robot's environment and (*iv*) creating *active learning* through monitoring and evaluating robots' actions with respect to teaching goals as well as through discussions and experience exchange.

Before explaining the essence of the solution of the task, first we need to highlight the main properties of the specialized SLO (further SLO$_S$) once again because they predefine the capabilities for adaptation. Below we make the distinction between properties that, to a larger extent, represent syntactic features and those which focus more on semantic features. The properties of the first category are as follows.

1. The stage-based SLO$_S$ is a specialized version of the initial (original) SLO that was designed for reuse. The initial SLO implements a large scale of e-learning variability that may include pedagogical variability, social variability, technological variability and content variability.
2. We express all kinds of variability uniformly through parameters and their possible values. The parameter space predefines the reusable variants of LOs derivable from the original SLO. It is supposed that among those variants there is the most *suitable* LO in the *preprogrammed context of use*. Such a variant is treated as a result of adaptation. As the number of LO variants may be very large, it is difficult to generate the *needed* LO from the original SLO. Specialization for adaptation enables to tackle this problem.

3. Specialization is the structural transformation of the original SLO into its specialized form without affecting the overall functionality of the original SLO. Structural transformation is to be performed so that to facilitate the search of the suitable variant as a result of adaptation.
4. Both the design of the original SLO and then its specialization are supported by the adequate tools. Therefore, the user (typically teacher) can focus mainly on managing issues in dealing with the processes.
5. The specialization process results in creating the *multistage executable specification* SLO$_S$ that is coded as the k-stage heterogeneous meta-program. A particular stage defines a subspace of the whole variability space.
6. There is a strong technological support of a meta-language to implement staging at the current stage through deactivating of only those parameters that are to be evaluated later, in the subsequent stages. The evaluated parameters at the current stage yield the *increment* in specifying the subset of variants for adaptation. The other increments are added in the subsequent stages.
7. The k-stage SLO specification (i.e. SLO$_S$) along with the supporting tool is also a $(k-1)$-stage SLO generator. In fact, $(k-1)$-stage SLO represents the narrowed space for adaptation.
8. The processor of the meta-language in which the SLO$_S$ (and also the original SLO) is coded is *the generation tool* as well as the *adaptation tool*.
9. The specification SLO$_S$ has the following important property due to the specializer [BBŠ13]: after executing of SLO$_S$ at stage i $(1 < i < k)$, it is possible to return to any previously executed stage j $(i < j \leq k)$, to select the other parameter values at this stage and then to continue the generation process, thus creating *a new path for adaptation*.

The semantic-based properties are as follows.

1. Stages of SLO$_S$ differ not only structurally (syntactically) but also semantically. Fuzzy variables carry this semantic load. They are added as parameter weights within the original specification to reason about the semantic role of parameters. We have linked fuzzy variables with Bloom's taxonomy levels which define the cognition process in knowledge gaining (see Sect. 7.6). Thus, fuzzy variables enable to make the distinction between types of parameters.
2. Fuzzy variables, *being the user invisible items*, serve for managing information to assign parameters to stages and, in this way, provide a means for managing stage-based specialization.
3. Fuzzy variables indicate on the priorities of parameters and hierarchy of stages to manage adaptation process. Typically, according to defined rules (semantics of teaching), teacher-oriented parameters are at the top of the hierarchy (at the highest stage). Learner-oriented parameters describing his/her context reside in the middle stages. Content-based parameters are at the lowest stage.
4. Content adaptation is the user-guided process that includes user's actions and automatic processing by the tool. User (teacher or learner) exams the given interface to recognize and supply his/her context parameter values. Then the

automatic processing follows yielding more *specialized variants* to support needs for adaptation.

5. Content adaptation is a part of the whole learning process being included 'surface learning' (along with its feedback) and 'deep learning' (along with its feedback) (the terms will be defined later).
6. Technologically, the adaptation process is the staged forward transformation with respect to the specialization process (the latter might be seen as the reverse transformation).

8.5 Processes to Solve the Adaptation Task

At this point, we need to introduce and define some new terms such as *surface learning*, *deep learning* and *active learning*.

In the paper [Hou04] Houghton defines surface learning as 'accepting new facts and ideas uncritically and attempting to store them as isolated, unconnected items'. The same source defines deep learning as 'examining new facts and ideas critically, and tying them into existing cognitive structures and making numerous links between ideas'. Active learning, as defined by [CRLT14], 'is a process whereby students engage in activities, such as reading, writing, discussion, or problem solving that promote analysis, synthesis, and evaluation of class content'. The use of educational robots promotes active learning due to the possibility of combining cooperative learning, problem-based learning, the use of case studies and simulations.

Now we are able to present our approach to solving the adaptation task in more detail. In Fig. 8.1a, we outline the approach schematically as a multiple process with different sorts of adaptation and feedbacks. There are three kinds of adaptation scenarios: (i) stage-based (see also property 9 in Sect. 8.4), (ii) technological and (iii) adaptation at the active learning phase.

According to the given definition, the stage-based content adaptation is a surface learning because the user selects the parameter values (see 'User action' in Fig. 8.1b on left) as 'isolated, unconnected items' (see also user interface in Fig. 8.2). We present the overall stage-based content adaptation in Fig. 8.1b. Here, the user action is combined with the automatic processing phases $(P_1, \ldots, P_k)$ performed at each stage by the PHP processor. The result of the processing at a higher stage is the lower-level specialized SLO (denoted, e.g. as $SLO_{S(i)}$). The result of the phase P_k is the concrete LO as an intermediate result of adaptation.

Within each stage, the stage-based adaptation is automatic. It is also the user-guided process running within the meta-language environment (PHP processor in our case). The higher stages are for the teacher. The lower stages are for learners. Here, however, we do not make the distinction between the teacher's and learner's adaptation activities (we will focus on those actions later, see case study, Sect. 8.6). The adaptation process as surface learning may follow two modes. In mode 1, there is no feedback. The process goes through phases (stages) resulting in narrowing the

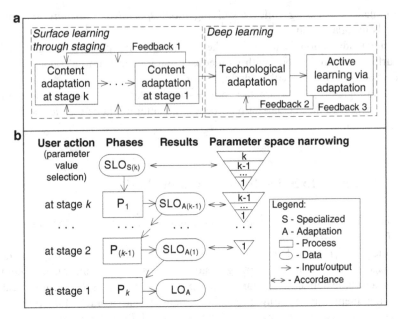

Fig. 8.1 Adaptation scenarios (**a**) and stage-based adaptation subprocesses (**b**)

space of variants smoothly (see Fig. 8.1b). In mode 2, it is possible to return to the previous stages through feedback 1 for selecting the other parameter values for adaptation, if the previous values do not satisfy the user's needs. The tool that performs specialization ensures the functionality of mode 2.

By technological adaptation we mean the compilation of the adapted LO (i.e. robot's control program (CP)) and uploading it into the robot's flash memory. After that, the robot is ready to solve the prescribed task, and learners are able to monitor the robot's actions and evaluate the characteristics comparing them with selected parameters. Even more, the learners are able to analyse the CP and to investigate the correspondence among the abstract parameter values (those that were previously defined as the staging process) with the physical characteristics of the robot's actions. What is most important is the possibility to change the CP by the *short* feedback 2 (meaning the change of CP and its recompilation and reloading) or by the *deep* feedback 2 (meaning the selection of the other parameter values at the stage-based adaptation).

Therefore, we have presented the whole adaptation process abstractly as a sequence of the *surface* learning and *deep* learning with the multiple feedbacks. In fact, surface learning is the user-guided *content preparation-adaptation* through gradual staging and feedback between stages (i.e. user-oriented parameter selection). The adapted content and possible feedbacks enable to happen the active (deep) learning. However, we are able to describe the whole adaptation process in detail through a case study.

8.6   A Case Study: Adaptation and Learning Paths

As the adaptation task is driven by the specialization process (i.e. using specialized SLO), this case study should be connected to the one considered in Chap. 7. Therefore, we have to consider the same task, the 'ornament drawing by robot', though slightly modified. The learning objective is also the same – to teach nested loops written in RobotC [Rob07]. The aim of this case study is to demonstrate the adaptation process of the real learning task using NXT robot environment [CCh11] and to reveal more practical details on the surface and deep learning through SLO adaptation.

In Fig. 8.2, we present two different models of the same task aiming once again to highlight that adaptation is dependent on specialization. Furthermore, here we have slightly changed the task as compared to the one given in Chap. 7 (here, curriculum objective (CO) is missed and time for the task (TT) is added). For simplicity reasons, we also consider the parameter priorities as constants here. The model (Fig. 8.2a) contains three stages. They might be interpreted, for instance, as follows. The dependent parameters LA and TT represent the teacher's context (are at stage 3). The dependent parameters LL (the pure learner's context) and P1 and P (the pure content parameters) must appear on the same stage (stage 2 in this model).

An attentive reader can also notice some discrepancies of the parameter dependency interpretation here as compared to the one given in Chap. 7 (see Sect. 7.7). The rest parameters are pure technological parameters (representing the content in the case of using robots). They are independent (there are no edges between nodes). They are ordered according to the Bloom's taxonomy levels (see Chap. 7) and be shown for the learner at stage 1 in this order. Due to the large number of parameters, however, there might be difficulties to ensure a flexible adaptation.

The second model (Fig. 8.2b) is more flexible because there is the additional stage (i.e. the user's interface) to select values for technological parameters. Using

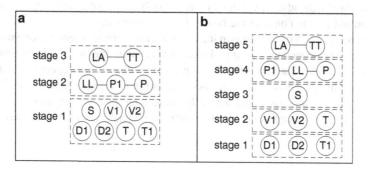

Fig. 8.2 Three-stage (**a**) and five-stage (**b**) models of the task 'ornament drawing by robot' *LA* learning activity, *CT* case study (given by *teacher*), *PS* practice (done by *learner*), *TT* time for the task; *S* selected motor (AB, BC, AC); *V1, V2 drawing velocity* of motors (pen on the paper), *D1, D2 idle moving velocity* of motors (pen over the paper), *T* robot's drawing time, *T1* robot's moving time for the next action, *LL* learner's previous knowledge level (beginner (BG), intermediate (IT), advanced (AD)), *P1* number of ornaments, *P* number of ornament's parts

this model, it is also possible to present the other interpretation of the context as follows. If we allow students themselves to make a choice of learning activity (LA) variants (CT, PS), as well as variants of the time for the task (TT), then the dependent parameters LA and TT (stage 4) can be seen as the *learner's context*. Therefore, we have two stages (4 and 3) for the learner's context (though stage 3 is mixed due to the parameter dependency, i.e. it contains the context and content parameters) and two stages (2 for the operating move and 1 for the idle move) to represent the content parameters.

Further, we have selected the second model for more detailed analysis. Parameters at stages 2 and 1 are pure technological parameters, but they are transformed into content-based ones, when the stage-based adaptation through generation takes place. We illustrate this transformation in Fig. 8.3 (see right column). The second column shows the user's (learner's) graphical interface to perform the adaptation actions at each stage. The submission of user-defined values initiates the process, and then, the processing tool creates the intermediate result of the adaptation at the adequate stage. The third column illustrates on how the model of the task is interpreted at each stage. The hidden parameters are not evaluated at the current stage.

At stage 1, we have the LO, i.e. two nested loops written in RobotC. It is the robot's control program to be compiled into the executable code and downloaded into the robot's memory. The surface learning path starts at the stage-based adaptation of the content to be generated by the learner's initiative and guidance. Next, the robot performs the preprogrammed actions which were coded within the generated and compiled specification. Robot's actions enable involving the learner into deep learning through the series of activities. First, the learner is able to follow and observe what is going on the robot's action space. As there are a few robots within the classroom with slightly different control programs, learners can communicate among themselves. It is possible to measure/evaluate visually (roughly) the speed of robots and to observe how robots' actions are changing from the drawing state to the idle state. Students are not only able to observe the task solution in action but also to compare the results (produced drawings).

Even more, it is possible to provide experimentation and research, for example, to estimate the dependency among the robot speed and drawing accuracy. For this purpose, of course, learners need to go through feedbacks and repeat the learning path accordingly depending on the new scenarios (see Figs. 8.1a, 8.4 and 8.5). However, the adaptation-based active learning path analysis requires a separate attention and more deep focus. We present such an analysis in the next section.

8.7 Analysis of Active Learning Paths and Adaptation

On the basis of the previous analysis, below we present two possible scenarios of adaptation-based learning that combines both surface and deep learning into the whole process with the deep feedbacks. The first scenario (Fig. 8.4) includes the

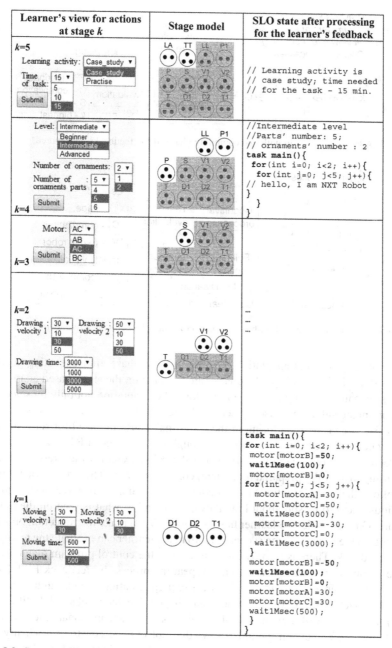

Learner's view for actions at stage k	Stage model	SLO state after processing for the learner's feedback

$k=5$
Learning activity: [Case_study ▾]
[Case_study]
[Practise]
Time of task: [15 ▾]
5
10
15
[Submit]
	LA TT LL P1
	P S V1 V2
	T D1 D2 T1
		``
		// Learning activity is
		// case study; time needed
		// for the task - 15 min.
		``

Level: [Intermediate ▾]
[Beginner]
[Intermediate]
[Advanced]
Number of ornaments: [2 ▾]
Number of ornaments parts: [5 ▾] 1
2
4
5
6
$k=4$ [Submit]
	LL P1
	P S V1 V2
	T D1 D2 T1
		``
		//Intermediate level
		//Parts' number: 5;
		// ornaments' number : 2
		task main(){
		  for(int i=0; i<2; i++){
		    for(int j=0; j<5; j++){
		// hello, I am NXT Robot
		}
		  }
		}
		``

Motor: [AC ▾] [AB] [AC] [BC] **$k=3$** [Submit]	S V1 V2 T D1 D2 T1	
$k=2$ Drawing velocity 1 [30 ▾] Drawing velocity 2 [50 ▾] 10 10 30 30 50 50 Drawing time: [3000 ▾] 1000 3000 5000 [Submit]	V1 V2 T D1 D2 T1	... ...

$k=1$
Moving velocity 1 [30 ▾] Moving velocity 2 [30 ▾]
10 10
30 30
Moving time: [500 ▾]
200
500
[Submit]
	D1 D2 T1	```
		task main(){
		for(int i=0; i<2; i++){
		  motor[motorB]=50;
		  wait1Msec(100);
		  motor[motorB]=0;
		  for(int j=0; j<5; j++){
		    motor[motorA]=30;
		    motor[motorC]=50;
		    wait1Msec(3000);
		    motor[motorA]=-30;
		    motor[motorC]=0;
		    wait1Msec(3000);
		}
		  motor[motorB]=-50;
		  wait1Msec(100);
		  motor[motorB]=0;
		  motor[motorA]=30;
		  motor[motorC]=30;
		  wait1Msec(500);
		}
		}
		``

Fig. 8.3 Stage-based adaptation through parameter value selection and intermediate adaptation result without feedback

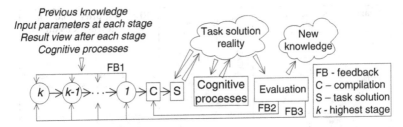

Fig. 8.4 Adaptation scenario with one compiling phase (if the feedbacks are ignored)

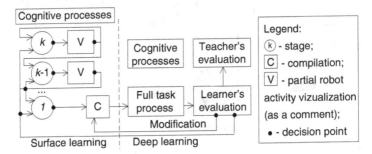

Fig. 8.5 The advanced adaptation-based scenario to define the paths of active learning

only one technological adaptation (i.e. compilation phase after executing generation at stage 1). The multiple feedbacks are possible on the stage-based adaptation
process because the learner is able to perform the adaptation not only by selecting
the parameter values but also by seeing the result of stage-based processing (see
Fig. 8.3). The visual monitoring of the result may cause the need for selecting the
other values and repeating the process through the feedbacks FB1.

Deep, i.e. active, learning starts when the robot executes the prescribed task
according to the fully prepared (complete) control program. The learner's activity is
to follow the robot's action, to remember what parameters have been chosen
previously and to reason about how they correspond to what is seen on the drawn
picture. On the whole, the learner has the possibility to make the reflection on what
is going on the robot's action scene. After that, the learner can evaluate the reality of
the solved task. There is the possibility to change the control program manually (if
some inconsistency was observed) and repeat the process by feedback FB2. Even
more, it is possible to provide a wide-scale experimentation and research using the
deep feedback FB3. Taking into account all possible feedbacks (FB1, FB2 and
FB3), there is indeed a great deal of learning paths to accommodate the learner's
adaptation preferences in gaining knowledge not only to construct gradually (in
step-by-step manner) the nested loops but also to be convinced on how the control
program constructs are transformed into physical entities such as velocity, time,
idle move, operating move to draw line fragments, etc.

The second scenario (see Fig. 8.5) provides much more capability as compared
to the first one. Those capabilities are due to the multiple compilations (executed

after each adaptation stage) resulting in the partial robot's actions followed by the increased number of decision points and feedbacks at the surface learning phase. By the partial robot action (denotes as RA in Fig. 8.5), we mean the state of SLO after the adequate stage execution and then the compilation of the staged SLO and, finally, the execution of the compiled code (i.e. RobotC). Physically, a partial robot's action shows a fragment (such as pen lifting, idle move, etc.) of the whole task solution. In fact, the use of this scenario blurs the boundaries between the surface learning and deep learning because of the deep fragmentation of processes at the staging phase. Furthermore, the use of this scenario enables to perform the examination and research of the processes using the feedbacks FB2 and FB3; however, in this case, it is possible to exclude the multiple compilations (this path is indicated by the adequate decision points on circles and broken arrowed lines in Fig. 8.5). Note that the path that includes the broken arrows in fact indicates the surface learning as it is described in the first scenario.

We treat the second scenario as advanced because of two reasons. One reason has been already stated (the second scenario includes the first). The next reason is that we have enriched the scenario by the teacher's evaluation. The evaluation, for example, can be done using the students' 'engagement levels' as described by the methodology given in [UV09]. This methodology evaluates the students' engagement levels through the following cognitive processes (ordered by cognitive deepness from the lowest to the highest): *viewing, responding, changing, constructing and presenting.*

In our case, *viewing* means the student's passive monitoring of the robot's actions; *responding* means the student's ability to answer a question given by the teacher or the formulation of a question for the teacher; *changing* means the student's ability to modify the control program directly (i.e. using FB2; note that this possibility can also be treated as a *practice* (PC), the learning activity (LA) value; see Fig. 8.2); *constructing* means the conscious adaptation (through the use of feedbacks FB2 or FB3; see Figs. 8.4 and 8.5); and finally, *presenting* means the student's ability to explain, to discuss with the teacher or other students on the topics and to present the obtained and researched results either orally or in the written form. The teacher's task is to identify the *length of cognition process path* for each student according to [UV09], i.e. to identify how many students are able to go through all cognitive processes and how many students failed (at which point and why).

8.8 Summary and Evaluation of the Approach

In this chapter, we have discussed the adaptation problem from two perspectives: general and specific. The aim of the first was to better understand the essence of the problem itself and, in this way, to outline the context for considering the second. Indeed, our approach is specific. It is based on the internal structure of SLO, which was identified as a *multistage specialized specification* for adaptation. We have described the approach from the user's viewpoint (i.e. teacher's and learner's perspective). In our case, adaptation is a user-guided semi-automatic generation process with multiple feedbacks. We have made a distinction between three kinds of adaptation (though they are related): the pure content adaptation, technological adaptation and learning process adaptation. The multistage generation process (along with feedbacks to higher stages) supports the user-guided content adaptation. The content adaptation goes through stages so that the learner is able to monitor *gradually* the result in creating the content through adaptation. Therefore, this kind of adaptation can be also treated as a *surface learning*.

The technological adaptation is needed to link different environments (PHP and NXT robots). The learning process adaptation is due to the robot's operating actions and the learner's ability to monitor, to understand and to react to the robot's action through feedbacks to previous phases. The process is active, and we are able to identify it as deep learning because of the presence of different learning paths. This possibility is a background for the 'smart learning' to be considered later, in Chap. 12.

Here, we evaluate the approach from two perspectives: methodology (i.e. taking into account analysis presented in Sect. 8.3) and technology. Note that in the overall evaluation, the pedagogical view should be included. We will provide that later as a part of 'smart learning' in Chap. 12. We summarize the first evaluation in Table 8.1.

Table 8.1 Characteristics as requirements for SLO adaptation

Characteristics	Supported aspects in SLO	Explanation
SLO adaptation objectives	Enhancement reuse and active learning	See our case study
Strategy used	Design for reuse	For more details, see Sect. 7.4
	Design with adaptation	
Adaptation makers	Course designers, teachers, students	
What-to-what is adapted?	SLO (LO) content to the contexts of use	Pedagogical context: teacher's context, learner's profile
Adaptation type	Automatic through generation	User guided
Criteria used	A set of stages $\{k, k\text{-}1, \ldots 1\}$	The user selects one for his/her context
When to start considering adaptation problem?	At learning variability modelling	See Chap. 4.
What is granularity level?	Covers low and middle granularity levels	To cover at least one or more topics
Mechanisms used	Parameterization, parameter priority relation expressed through fuzzy variables	See Chaps. 5 and 7.3 in Chap. 7
Technologies applied	Meta-programming, program specialization techniques	See Chaps. 5 and 7
Adaptation kind	External (Ext)	Ext: user's view, compiler time; Int: designer's view
	Internal (Int)	
Supported processes	Selecting, meta-generation and generation	See Fig. 8.1

The technological evaluation includes the statement of properties and capabilities of the approach from the SWE and SC perspective. The basic assumption to correctly interpret the approach is that SLO_R should be design *for reuse*. As reuse in designing of LO and in e-learning in general plays indeed the significant role, the interpretation of this term might be different in the concrete context. In the context of the proposed approach, design for reuse has the following meaning:

(a) SLO implements the *enhanced learning variability*; the latter includes *pedagogical variability*, *social variability*, *content variability* and *specific technological variability*.

(b) Variability features (parameters) are extracted through the use of the systematic approach such as *feature-based modelling* adapted from the product line engineering, the well-known approach in SWE as well in CS.

(c) The result of modelling is the *verified feature models* that represent the learning variability abstractly at the higher level of abstraction.

(d) The devised model (models) may be general enough, thus the narrowing of the variability scope might be needed for the concrete case of use; it is possible to implement through model specialization.

(e) The *anticipated scope* for each kind of variabilities (can be also treated as reuse scope) should be clearly (explicitly) stated in the requirements for designing SLO_R and then implemented when the SLO_R is coded.

The above stated can be achieved only if the adequate technological support is available (a more thorough discussion on tools for learning variability model constructing and SLO_R design will be given in Chaps. 9 and 10). The SLO_R specification is a value per se because (a) it is the executable specification, (b) it is pedagogically sound (i.e. SLO inherence to well-defined principles, learning theories, models and requirements in designing LOs) and (c) it is socially oriented (i.e. learner's profile, learning activities, etc. are taken into account).

8.9 Conclusion

We have considered the teaching content (i.e. SLO) adaptation problem using the concept of the preprogrammed stage-based adaptation. At the core of this adaptation is the use of the program (meta-program) specialization techniques. The latter uses the staged parameterization and predefines the capabilities of the approach. The specialized SLO represents such a specification that enables the learners to guide the adaptation process themselves. The process includes three phases: staging (parameter selection for the required content generation), technological adaptation and active learning driven by generating the user-guided content. The process contains within multiple feedbacks (within staging) and as well within an active learning to enable different adaptation paths. The staging phase is supported by the meta-language processor which performs interpretation of the specialized SLO under the user's guidance. The learner's task is to select the one that is most relevant to his/her context. Staging (which is expressed through parameter sequences and the latter being shown to the learner) can also be seen as the *internal sequencing of knowledge chunks* to be learned. Therefore, the proposed approach can be viewed as a framework to generate paths (i.e. sequences of knowledge chunks) for adaptive and active learning.

8.10 Research and Exercise Questions

8.1. Describe the framework to characterize the adaptation problem by identifying (a) the scope of the problem and (b) the most influential factors and their interactions.
8.2. Provide a specific insight and investigation into the role of the context to the adaptation problem.
8.3. Draw the links (conceptual, model based) between reusability and adaptability of the teaching and learning content.
8.4. Define the terms adaptation and adaptability using the results of previous questions. Clarify what might be the object of adaptation.
8.5. What kinds of adaptations might be?
8.6. Draw the links among the learning process and content adaptation.
8.7. Consider the content adaptation problem from the pure technological perspective and provide the relevant technologies that might be helpful.
8.8. Provide research on program partial evaluation (specialization) for the purpose of CS teaching.
8.9. Model the presented approach using the tool [BBŠ13] along with test cases given there and identify the main properties of the approach.
8.10. Clarify how can model-driven and generative technologies contribute to adaptation problem?

References

[AAB+06] Abarca MG, Alarcon RA, Barria R, Fuller D (2006) Context-based e-learning composition and adaptation. In: On the move to meaningful internet systems 2006: OTM 2006 workshops. Springer, Berlin/Heidelberg, pp 1976–1985

[AGL11] Acampora G, Gaeta M, Loia V (2011) Combining multi-agent paradigm and memetic computing for personalized and adaptive learning experiences. Comput Intell 27(2):141–165

[BBF+09] Brown EJ, Brailsford TJ, Fisher T, Moore A (2009) Evaluating learning style personalization in adaptive systems: quantitative methods and approaches. IEEE Trans Learn Technol 2(1):10–22

[BBŠ13] Bespalova K, Burbaite R, Štuikys (2013) MP-ReTool tools. http://proin.ktu.lt/metaprogram/MP-ReTool/

[BCW+08] Brady A, Conlan O, Wade V, Dagger D (2008) Supporting users in creating pedagogically sound personalised learning objects. In: Nejdl W et al (eds) Adaptive hypermedia 2008, LNCS 5149 Springer, pp 52–61

[BM07] Brusilovsky P, Millán E (2007) User models for adaptive hypermedia and adaptive educational systems. . In: Brusilovsky P, Kobsa A, Nejdl W (eds) The adaptive web. Springer, Berlin/Heidelberg, 4321, pp 3–53

[BMM+05] Bednarik R, Moreno A, Myller N, Sutinen E (2005) Smart program visualization technologies: planning a next step. http://www.google.lt/url?

[BN02] Bobeff G, Noy J (2002) Molding components using program specialization techniques. http://research.microsoft.com/en-us/um/people/cszypers/events/wcop2003/14-bobeff-noye.pdf

[BR12] Boyle T, Ravenscroft A (2012) Context and deep learning design. Comput Educ 59 (4):1224–1233

[BS08] Boticario JG, Santos OC (2008) A standards-based modelling approach for dynamic generation of adaptive learning scenarios. J Univ Comput Sci 14(17):2859–2876

[BSS+12] Bargel BA, Schröck J, Szentes D, Roller W (2012) Using learning maps for visualization of adaptive learning path components. Int J Comput Inf Syst Ind Manage Appl 4(1):228–235

[BTK06] Burgos D, Tattersall C, Koper R (2006) How to represent adaptation in eLearning with IMS learning design. Interact Learn Environ 15(2):161–170

[BS11] Burbaite R, Stuikys V (2011) Analysis of learning object research using feature-based models. Information technologies' 2011: proceedings of the 17th international conference on information and software technologies, pp 201–208

[BVV+10] Butoianu V, Vidal P, Verbert K, Duval E, Broisin J (2010) User context and personalized learning: a federation of contextualized attention metadata. J Univ Comput Sci 16(16):2252–2271

[CBK13] Capilla R, Bosch J, Kang KC (2013) Systems and software variability management (concepts, tools and experiences). Springer, Heidelberg

[CG10] Cristea AI, Ghali F (2010) Towards adaptation in E-learning 2.0. citeseerx.ist.psu.edu/viewdoc/download?doi=10.1.1.185.980&rep=rep1&type=pdf

[CCh11] Castledine A, Chalmers C (2011) LEGO robotics: an authentic problem-solving tool? Des Technol Educ Int J 16(3):19–27

[CRLT14] Center for Research on Learning and Teaching (2014) Active learning. http://www.crlt.umich.edu/tstrategies/tsal

[DAS01] Dey A, Abowd G, Salber D (2001) A conceptual framework and a toolkit for supporting the rapid prototyping of context-aware applications. Hum Comput Interact 16:97–166

[Dey01] Dey AK (2001) Understanding and using context. Pers Ubiquit Comput 5(1):4–7

[Dou04] Dourish P (2004) What we talk about when we talk about context. Pers Ubiquit Comput 8:19–30, Feb. 2004

[EAJ+10] Essalmi F, Ayed LJB, Jemni M, Graf S (2010) A fully personalization strategy of E-learning scenarios. Comput Hum Behav 26(4):581–591

[ERB12] Endler A, Rey GD, Butz MV (2012) Towards motivation-based adaptation of difficulty in e-learning programs. Aust J Educ Technol 28(7):1119–1135

[FG06] Fischer G, Giaccardi E (2006) Meta-design: a framework for the future of end user development. In: Lieberman H, Paternò F, Wulf V (eds) End user development: empowering people to flexibly employ advanced information and communication technology. Kluwer Academic Publishers, Dordrecht, pp 427–457

[FGS+04] Fischer G, Giaccardi E, Ye Y, Sutcliffe AG, Mehandjiev N (2004) Meta design: a manifesto for end-user development. Commun ACM 47(9):33–37

[FLD+12]   Fernandes MA, Lopes CR, Dorca FA, Lima LV (2012) A stochastic approach for automatic and dynamic modeling of students' learning styles in adaptive educational systems. Inform Educ Int J 11(2):191–212

[GD95]   Grabinger RS, Dunlap JC (1995) Rich environments for active learning: a definition. Res Learn Technol 3(2):5–34

[GMB+04]   Gütl Ch, Manuel V, Barrios VMG, Mödritscher F (2004) Adaptation in E-learning environments through the service-based framework and its application for AdeLE. In: Proceedings of E-learn 2004 conference, Washington, DC, pp 1891–1898

[HK09]   Han P, Kramer BJ (2009) Generating interactive learning object from configurable samples. In: Proceedings of international conference. On mobile, hybrid and on-line learning, pp. 1–6, IEEE

[Hou04]   Houghton W (2004) Engineering subject centre guide: learning and teaching theory for engineering academics. HEA Engineering Subject Centre, Loughborough. http://www.engsc.ac.uk/er/theory/learning.asp

[HMM+05]   Holohan E, Melia M, McMullen D, Pahl C (2005) Adaptive e-learning content generation based on semantic web technology. In: International workshop on applications of semantic web technologies for E-learning

[Jar10]   Jarche H (2010) A framework for social learning in the enterprise. http://www.jarche.com/2010/02/a-framework-for-social-learning-in-the-enterprise/

[Jon05]   Jones R (2005) Designing adaptable learning resources with learning object patterns. J Digit Inf 6(1). https://journals.tdl.org/jodi/index.php/jodi/article/view/60/62

[Kel08]   Kell S (2008) A survey of practical software adaptation techniques. http://www.cl.cam.ac.uk/~srk31/research/papers/kell08survey.pdf

[Kri14]   Krigman E (2014) Standards for computer science education need improvement http://usnewsstemsolutions.com/conference

[KVI+11]   Klašnja-Milićević A, Vesin B, Ivanović M, Budimac Z (2011) E-learning personalization based on hybrid recommendation strategy and learning style identification. Comput Educ 56(3):885–899

[LCW+09]   Liu L, Chen H, Wang, H, Zhao C (2009) Construction of a student model in contextually aware pervasive learning. In: Pervasive computing (JCPC), 2009 joint conferences on PC, pp 511–514, IEEE

[MJ10]   Man H, Jin Q (2010) Putting adaptive granularity and rich context into learning objects. In: 9th international conference on Information technology based higher education and training (ITHET), pp 140–145

[MKS10]   Mbendera AJ, Kanjo Ch, Sun L (2010) Towards development of personalized knowledge construction model for e-learning. 2nd international conference on mobile, hybrid, and on-line learning, IEEE, pp 29–35

[MS06]   Mustaro PN, Silveira IF (2006) Learning objects: adaptive retrieval through learning styles. Interdiscipl J Knowl Learn Objects 2:35–46

[PDM+12]   Pernas AM, Diaz A, Motz R, Oliveira JPM (2012) Enriching adaptation in e-learning systems through a situation-aware ontology network. Interact Technol Smart Educ 9 (2):60–72

[Qui07]   Quinton SR (2007) Contextualisation of learning objects to derive meaning. In: Koohung A, Harman K (eds) Learning objects: theory, praxis, issues, and trends. Informing Science Press, Santa Rosa, CA, pp 113–179

[PS04]   Pitkanen SH, Silander P (2004) Criteria for pedagogical reusability of learning objects enabling adaptation and individualised learning processes. In: Proceedings of IEEE international conference advanced learning technologies, pp 246–250

[RDS+08]   Ruiz MPB, Díaz MJF, Soler FO, Pérez JRP (2008) Adaptation in current e-learning systems. Comput Standards Interface 30:62–70

[Rob07]   RobotC – Improved movement (2007) Robotics academy. www.doc.ic.ac.uk/~ajd/Robotics/RoboticsResources/ROBOTC%20%20Improved%20Movement.pdf, p 19

[Sam97] Sametinger J (1997) Software engineering with reusable components. Springer, New York

[ŠBD13] Štuikys V, Burbaitė R, Damaševičius R (2013) Teaching of computer science topics using meta-programming-based GLOs and LEGO robots. Inform Educ Int J 12:125–142, ISSN 1648–5831

[VMO+12] Verbert K, Manouselis N, Ochoa X, Wolpers M, Drachsler H, Bosnic I, Duval E (2012) Context-aware recommender systems for learning: a survey and future challenges. Learn Technol IEEE Trans 5:318–335

[Win01] Winograd T (2001) Architectures for context. Hum Comput Interact 16(2):401–419

[YW09]   Yang YJ, Wu C (2009) An attribute-based ant colony system for adaptive learning object recommendation. Expert Syst Appl 36(2):3034–3047

[ZLO07] Zimmermann A, Lorenz A, Oppermann R (2007) An operational definition of context. In: Proceedings of the sixth international and interdisciplinary conference modeling and using context (CONTEXT'07), pp 558–571

[UV09]   Urquiza-Fuentes J, Velázquez-Iturbide JÁ (2009) Pedagogical effectiveness of engagement levels–a survey of successful experiences. Electron Notes Theor Comput Sci 224:169–178

Fundamentals of Authoring Tools to Design SLOs, Environments and Smart Education Case Study

So far, in Part I, our focus was given mainly to the context of the emerging e-learning technology based on the smart LO (further SLO) concept. We were aiming to provide the concept so that it would be *understandable* to those who are or might be potential users (researchers in e-learning, CS teachers and to some extent students studying CS-related courses). Here, the word 'understandable' has the following meanings: the structural aspects (i.e. SLO models, including those with multifaceted views such as pedagogy and social aspects along with content and other features being represented at the high abstraction level), supporting technology (such as heterogeneous meta-programming), properties and capabilities of SLO (such as the ones for wide-scale reuse and adaptation) and use cases for practice as they are seen, or might be seen, from the user perspective.

In Part II, we focus on three main topics: (1) background to design SLO, i.e. how the concept of SLO looks like from the content and tool designer's perspective; (2) description of authoring tools to support the design, the adaptation and the maintenance of SLOs; and (3) analysis of *integrative and usage* aspects of SLOs to provide the whole CS-related and robot-oriented teaching course, including the 3-year experience of using the approach in the real teaching setting.

Note that the modelling of the CS learning domain (which we have discussed in Part I) is also a part of the theoretical background to support the development of SLOs (mainly related to the specification of SLOs). We have included the modelling aspects in Part I because they are, to a larger extent, relevant to general and intuitive understanding of both CS learning domain and SLOs. On the other hand, the concrete feature models are the input specifications to design SLO with the aid of the adequate authoring tools. Thus, to understand feature models as they are applied to the CS teaching domain, the reading of Chaps. 4 and 5 might be very helpful for the designer, no matter what level of knowledge in feature modelling the designer had so far.

Though the authoring tools were used in previous chapters, we provide an in-depth study of the topics here. Mostly, we focus on the design process with the tool support and provide architectures and functioning algorithms along with their main capabilities. Since we have discussed SLO as a separate (single) item throughout the previous chapters, we also focus on the content sequencing problem (though implicitly) to form the learning paths of the whole course here. We provide a framework of the possible solution of the problem through the local (personal) library concept. The latter enables to extract the needed content through the generation process (because SLO is a content generator) and then to integrate the entire CS course.

Chapter 9
Background to Design Smart LOs and Supporting Tools

9.1 Introduction

Here, by the designer's perspective, we mean the representation of the data and processes related to the functioning and design of smart LOs (SLOs) as fully and abstractly as possible. As we use the model-driven approach for designing SLOs, a formal definition and representation of the adequate models play a significant role. Thus, our focus is directed to the precise and complete representation of the SLO models here. The aim is to provide the motivated and sound background of the approach. However, the educational software designers typically tend to work with the informal scenarios of an application domain for its implementation. To resolve this contradiction, we also use informal scenarios (motivating example) to explain the essential details of the approach. Therefore, we hope that different forms of representing the design models at the different level of abstraction are helpful for a variety of designer flavours.

Apart from the educational software developer, who yet might be the SLO designer or the adequate tool designer? We do not exclude the possibility that e-learning researchers with the adequate technological background, computer scientists or even knowledgeable CS teachers can act as SLO designers or as designers of the authoring tools to support the SLO design processes. The designer's vision, in contrast to the user's vision, should reveal all details needed to implement the SLO-based approach. Indeed, when we were considering SLOs in the previous chapters, the internal structure of SLOs has been hidden. In fact, the only interface of the SLO was visible to the user.

Thus, the models and theoretical background we have considered so far were incomplete and now should be extended. To do that, we need to repeat and extend some definitions given in the previous chapters as well as to add new ones here. Therefore, the reader should not be confused by some replication of the rules (they are common for the manual design of SLOs as well for designing the design tool).

© Springer International Publishing Switzerland 2015
V. Štuikys, *Smart Learning Objects for Smart Education in Computer Science*,
DOI 10.1007/978-3-319-16913-2_9

We do that also due to the methodological reasons in order this chapter would be complete for the independent reading.

The main tasks we consider in this chapter are as follows: (1) literature review with the focus on linguistic aspects of representing SLO and LO to teach CS topics; (2) SLO design preliminaries with motivating example, as well as the statement of the design principles and requirements; and (3) model-driven theoretical background to design tools for developing SLO, including the *stage-based design* perspective to support the context-aware adaptation.

9.2 Literature Review

In this review, we focus mainly on the linguistic aspects. We start with the categorization of programming languages. There are two large categories of computer programming languages: general purpose or conventional programming languages (shortly CPLs) and domain-specific languages (shortly DSLs). In the history of programming languages, there were efforts to keep the count of the languages in each category. As it is stated in [IEEE99], in 1991 there were known about a hundred and a half of CPLs and about two thousand of DSLs (published in the approved issues throughout the world). But later it was a very difficult task to keep and maintain the list of the languages as precise as possible due to their rapid evolution. Perhaps this is not so much important. What is more important is the general trend of their evolution because programming languages have been under development for years and will remain so for many years to come.

The evident fact is that over the time the scope of research and use of DSLs were constantly increasing [IEEE99, Ous98, Hud98, DKV02]. There are a few reasons for that. First, the ever-increasing technological potential requires the adequate linguistic support with new capabilities (the evident example is the Internet-based programming and a set of languages of that domain). Second, the software content within modern systems is steadily increasing (due to the technology advances) with the ever-growing computational potential in a variety of applications; therefore, we need to cover the needs of end users of the extremely wide applications. Third, there are two extreme trends in designing and using systems: (1) *unification* with the focus on general solutions and standardization (e.g. UML standard) and (2) *specialization* with the focus on the specific domains (e.g. VHDL for hardware design). Typically, specialization enables to better satisfy the diverse needs of the very large communities of end users.

Finally, taking into account various studies on DSL (e.g. earlier works [Ous98, Hud98, DKV00, DKV02] or more recent works [KLB+08, OPH+09, KOM+10]), it is possible to summarize the above-stated arguments by the following observation. Today, as a rule, any matured domain of great importance has own DSL or even a set of DSLs (e.g. Internet (HTML, XML, etc.), hardware design (Verilog, VHDL, SystemC, etc.), robotics (BasicRobot, RobotC, etc.). The educational community has also own languages known as the *educational programming languages* (EPL)

[WLL11, MRR+10, SI11, BBH+13, Köl10]. The languages can also be viewed as DSLs because they are primarily designed as a learning instrument, but not so much as a tool for writing the real-world programs.

What are the main similarities and differences among DSLs oriented to the professional use and those dedicated for education? The similarity is that the great deal of DSLs of both categories is created on the basis of the conventional languages such as C, C++, FORTRAN, etc. However, there is the essential difference between those categories. Typically DSLs for the professional use are extensions of CPL languages [Hud98], though there are languages designed from scratch and have a specific functional model [DKV00, DKV02]. The CPLs and DSLs for education, on the other hand, are used in the simplified manner (typically the basic subset of a language) with the focus on visualization capabilities. The extensions of DSLs include the constructs needed to cover the specific requirements of a particular domain to be more understandable and useful to the domain users. Another important discriminating feature of EPLs is their orientation on the learner's age (for more details, see [Wiki14]).

Therefore, both categories of languages (CPLS and DSL) are researched and studied not only by the researchers and professional users. The educational community also focuses on both categories of languages, however, with a specific educational view. Here, we speak about both categories of the languages because they are directly related to our approach. We use PHP as a meta-language and RobotC as a target or teaching language (the first can be treated partially as a CPL and partially as DSL, while the second is the DSL derived from the CPL C).

In teaching CS-related courses, the student profile and previous knowledge are the main attribute in selecting the language. At the university level, the main focus should be taken not so much to programming languages per se but to the algorithmic skill, the programming paradigms (such as structural, object-oriented or component-based, parallel and distributed programming) and the tool construction (such as compilers, processors, debuggers, graphical editors, etc.).

In this regard, Rodríguez-Cerezo et al. [RHS14] present a platform for the development and debugging of language processors based on *attribute grammar* specifications. They propose the visual debugger enabling students to design their own language processors, solve design problems, improve the effectiveness and efficiency of their language processors and understand their operations. Pereira et al. [POC+13] propose a strategy based on DSLs where students have to develop a language processor for a DSL for a specific domain attractive to the students. Students develop the tool incrementally, in the step-by-step manner. Hu and Fred [XL06] provide an approach of teaching compilers with the help of the embedded robot controller. We do not provide a more extensive analysis on the topics of tool design because (1) we use standard tools (PHP processor) and (2) the reader can find more on the topic in Chaps. 3 and 7.

9.3   Preliminaries to Design SLO

We will start from the initial point, formulating a summary of what we have learned so far. Therefore, we enumerate the basic properties of SLOs. Those properties as seen from the *user perspective* are as follows:

(i) Smart LO is meta-programming-based generative LO (GLO) with extended features to support reusability.

(ii) The extended *reuse features* are either *pure technological, pure pedagogical, pure content* or their *combination* also treated as *learning variability* (see Chap. 5).

(iii) Smart LOs may implement a wide scale of learning variability.

(iv) With respect to the pure technological view, SLO is a hierarchical structure to support both component-based and generative reuse. This structure should be understood as follows: (1) SLO is the executable specification enabling (with the aid of the adequate tools) to produce the LO instances (i.e. components) automatically on demand; (2) SLO enables to represent the domain under consideration with the wide scale of variability (due to parameterization).

(v) The extended reuse features also mean the flexibility for semi-automatic adaptation of the learning content to the different contexts of use.

(vi) In the SLO model, the learning variability (i.e. pedagogical, social, content and technological aspects or features) is represented *uniformly* through parameters; the parameter semantics is defined and interpreted by the user (learner or teacher) through the context, i.e. through the reading and interpreting parameter values supplied by the system (meta-language processor) via the SLO interface.

(vii) SLO is a domain-specific meta-program that is oriented to implement CS learning variability. The latter can be represented as the *one-stage* or *multistage* structure. The multistage structure enables to implement the flexible adaptation of the content in the different context of use.

9.3.1   Statement of Design Principles and Requirements

Now we are able to formulate the basic principles and requirements to develop a single SLO. The principles are as follows:

(a) *Adhere* to the adequate teaching and learning theories of instructional design such as the ones presented in [JH07, KRS+09].

(b) *Tolerate* the existing standards (internal, local and worldwide) within the domain.

(c) *Analyse* the possible scenarios for clear understanding of the properties and capabilities of SLO such as those considered in Sect. 9.2.

(d) *Apply* the model-driven strategy through the use of analysis methods and modelling approaches for representing the CS teaching domain and its subdomains (i.e. content, pedagogy, technology, social context, etc.) at the relevant abstraction level (see Chap. 4).

(e) *Use* the formal approaches (where they are applicable) to approve and verify the design processes and models.

(f) *Analyse* the capabilities of the relevant technology or technologies that enable to realize the SLO.

(g) *Try* to automate the design process with the aid of available tools as widely as possible.

(h) *Analyse* various case studies for extracting the new knowledge and requirements for the improvement and redesign.

The *virtual* requirements as guidelines to design a single SLO might be as they are described below. Here, we use the term 'virtual' because of immaturity of the approach and, as a result, a wide scale of experiments and research yet to be provided.

1. With regard to (a), the teaching goal should be identified first. The goal should be related to the social context (student's previous knowledge, abilities to learn, preferences of learning, etc.), the organizational context (strategy of education within the organization, its relevance to the governmental strategy of education within the country, role of the course with respect to the others) and the pedagogical context (e.g. methods and theories).

2. The teaching model should be predefined in accordance with the identified teaching and learning goals.

3. The functionality of a single SLO should cover not a single topic but a series of the related topics (due to the managing aspects, such as producing, storing, sharing, etc.).

4. The identification of the scope of CS teaching and learning subdomains and then extracting (or creating) *models separately* for each subdomain with respect to the needs of the variability extent to support reuse should be provided. The basic requirement is the use of the *feature models* and feature modelling approaches. The identification of the *concrete feature models should be given* with respect to the identified modelling scope (use the methodology described in Chap. 4).

5. A specific focus should be taken in choosing of languages (meta-language and target) to realize the SLO as a meta-program. The selection should be provided in accordance with the requirements of the teaching strategy, goals and models. Those requirements (to a higher extent) relate to the choice of the *target language* because it is also the *teaching language* in which LOs (teaching content) are specified (for details, see Sect. 9.3.2).

6. Requirements for the choice of the meta-language are less restrictive. The reason is that any programming language or a dedicated language may be used as a meta-language [ŠD13]. The requirements should or might be also connected to teaching goals, teacher's preferences and availability of the tool support (see Sect. 9.3.2).

7. Guidelines for coding SLO specifications with regard to the chosen languages should be developed. Two cases should be taken into account: manual coding and semi-automatic coding with the aid of adequate tools. A special focus should be taken to the SLO interface coding. Many aspects of good coding can be inherited from the software domain. The basic requirement is clearness (keeping the coding rules, where comments are at the focus).

8. Apart from the requirements of the functionality, the specific requirements of coding the SLO interface should be also taken into account.

9. Guidelines for testing, packaging and storing for dissemination also might be provided.

10. The adequate design paradigms that take into account reusability, adaptability and related aspects such as complexity issues and tool support should also be provided (see Sects. 9.3.3, 9.3.4 and 9.3.5).

9.3.2 Choice of Languages to Specify SLO

The linguistic aspects in teaching CS courses are of great importance. What language to teach and how in the concrete situation? This is a wide topic for debate. Some issues can be found in the short discussion given in Sect. 9.2. And there is no uniform answer. The preference should be taken to the capabilities of the language to realize teaching goals and models. The most influential factors might be the functionality of the language to realize the visualization and active learning and the possibility to deal with the real-world tasks. In that sense, the preference should be taken to the domain-specific languages (DSLs), such as robot programming languages.

On the other hand, the modern programming paradigms (such as object oriented, component based, graphical, etc.) cannot be ignored too. Thus, in general, teaching should be harmonized with the trends of computing technology. Where is the key for making the solution? In our view, the meta-programming paradigm, as the basis to realize SLO, may provide the acceptable solution. In essence, meta-programming is the multi-language paradigm with respect to two aspects. The first is a standard definition of the paradigm. We define heterogeneous meta-programming as the paradigm that uses at least two languages (meta- and target) to code a meta-program. The second aspect is more interesting in the case of choosing the target language. We can, in many cases, use a few target (teaching) languages for coding the *same algorithm*. This is possible, for example, to realize the computational tasks, data manipulation and other tasks using different languages that support different paradigms (Java, C++ – object-oriented and Pascal – structured programming). The realization (through the use of SLO approach) of the same algorithm by a few target languages might be seen as one aspect of the *content variability* realization.

The most influential factor in choosing the target (teaching) language is the educational environment because it predefines the learning strategy and models.

Thus, the target language within the SLO specification should conform to (be the same) as the one used for teaching within the given educational environment. There might be a variety of educational environments to support different teaching models and tasks (computational, control based, etc.). Therefore, in general, a wide spectrum of target languages can be chosen to realize the SLO approach, when used. As, in the most case studies, we have provided in the book the educational environments are robot oriented, it is easy to understand why we use RobotC as a target language. In other words, the selection of the target language depends on the domain we try to automate.

The choice of the meta-language is independent upon the domain. As it has been shown by the study [ŠD13], any programming language in the mode of *structured programming* can be used as a meta-language. In practice, however, a decisive point might be the authoring tools to design meta-programs (SLO in our case). The tools are highly dependable on the language the tools are implemented. For example, we use the authoring tools that are specifically targeted for PHP. Thus, we use PHP as a meta-language to code SLO specifications.

The following questions may also be the topic for debate: can the meta-language be used as a teaching language? Should the meta-programming paradigm be taught and in which cases? We have left the answers as separate research and exercise questions (see Task 9.12 in Sect. 9.6).

9.3.3 SLO Design Paradigms

As it was discussed in Chap. 3, nowadays the reuse vision prevails in e-learning in general and in the content design in particular (see, e.g. [JH07]). The key reuse processes are as follows: to *design*, to *search*, to *adapt* and to *use* the content. Therefore, with respect to reusability in mind, the processes should be handled and managed as effectively as possible. Here, for this purpose, we apply the *reuse-based framework* borrowed from the SWE domain, which is known as *design for reuse* (DfR) and *design with reuse* (DwR) [Sam97]. This framework has been already introduced in Chap. 7, however, here we have extended the representation of the framework with added details (see Fig. 9.1). Note that there are different terms of the framework (such as a twin life-cycle model [Sam97], product line engineering [PBL05] or software family [Par76]) to express the similar meaning). Note that similarly to software families, SLO can be also viewed as a family of the related LOs.

DfR aims at understanding the e-learning domain (e.g. CS) through its modelling. The modelling should be guided by the clearly stated goal. In our case, the goal is to extract the relevant data and represent them into some generic form (e.g. feature diagram usually considered as a domain model to facilitate the construction of SLOs; for details, see Chap. 4). The initial models are to be designed with the expert's knowledge using some well-defined scheme such as TPACK (should be read as Technological, Pedagogical and Content Knowledge [KM09]).

Fig. 9.1 A reuse-based
framework adapted to
design and specialize SLOs

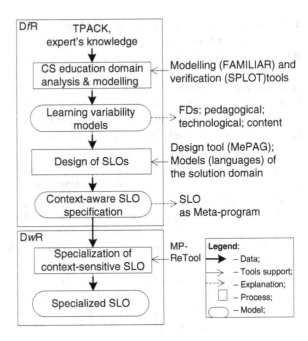

At this level, the domain model describes two general aspects: domain *common-ality* and domain *variability*. In the context of SLOs, we consider *the learning variability*. The latter has been already discussed in Chap. 5 where it was defined as a composition of pedagogical (PV), social (SV), content (CV), technological (TV) and interaction (IV) variability:

$$LV = PV \circ SV \circ CV \circ TV \circ IV.$$

Here, the learning *variability* is understood as an attribute to indicate the existence of variants in the subject (pedagogy, sociality, etc.), and '∘' means some kind of composition (see also our papers [ŠBD13, BBD+14]). Both the *learning commonality and learning variability* are components that characterize reusability, though differently. Here, by the learning commonality, we mean those learning aspects that have no tendency to be changed in a given context. As an example of learning commonality, we may consider the *priority relations* (such as those considered in Chap. 8: 'perhaps always, the *pedagogical aspects* have a higher priority with respect to the teaching content'). It is clear from the common sense that the learning commonality poses less reusability problems as compared to the learning variability. That is due to the following fact: once defined, the learning commonality can be applied in the mode 'use-as-is' in the different use contexts, whereas the learning variability is more influential on generative reuse aspects and potential for adaptations. Note that in practice there is no neither *pure* commonality nor *pure* variability. Typically, they coexist and appear together to represent the domain models.

We define the *context* as an *implicit or explicit factor influencing to delivering the content for teaching*. As the PV and SV, in fact, are those factors, we accept them as a *teaching context* here. The basic assumption is that the context may have variants too (e.g. types of the pedagogical model such as *problem based* and *project based*, student social variability such as *beginner* and *intermediate*, etc.). Therefore, we can speak also about the context variability as well. We are able to model the context variability, for instance, through the use of fuzzy variables {HP, IP, LP}. In the simplest case, the variables are constants. We can gain a much more flexibility and expressive power in the context representation, when the fuzzy variables are treated as functions of Bloom's taxonomy levels (see Chap. 8, for details).

As we are able to express any kind of variability through higher-level parameters, the D*f*R activity results in designing the context-aware SLOs. Further, when it is appropriate, we refer to context-aware SLOs as the SLOs for simplicity.

In fact, the first part of the framework (i.e. D*f*R) summarizes all activities that are needed to create a smart LO. Those activities are complex undertakings with the use of a variety of methods, models and tools. The activities result in the creation of the executable specification along with the *preprogrammed context* to support wide-range reuse and context-aware adaptation. Within the introduced framework, we treat this specification as the context-aware SLO. As, indeed, it is a complex structure, its complexity should be measured and evaluated in somewhat way in the course of design. We will describe that later (see Sect. 9.3.4).

The second part of the framework (i.e. D*w*R, see Fig. 9.1) is about adaptation. In general, the content adaptation is a big problem in e-learning. Even the well-designed content, for example, extracted from digital libraries, requires adaptation to the new context of use. There are many reasons for that as follows: rapidly changing the social context and the need to introduce innovations in the syllabus, to transfer the content from one learning environment to another, to be a more competitive teacher/educator, to enforce the students' engagement, etc. Especially it is true for CS teaching.

Our adaptation model has two phases. We implement the first phase using the automatic refactoring tool MP-ReTool managed by the context. It aims at narrowing the context-aware SLO by refactoring or specializing (structural transformations only) it into the so-called multistage SLOs. This phase, in fact, is the adaptation to the teacher's context. We refer to the *stage* as an abstraction to rearrange the structure of an SLO so that to enable its partial evaluation by staging when processed. The teacher, before using the tool, identifies the number of stages needed, i.e. identifies a *strategy* for adaptation. The tool, on the basis of *the preprogrammed context for staging* and preliminary teacher's needs, produces the k-stage SLO. The k-stage SLO is a $(k-1)$-stage SLO generator, i.e. a high-level specification containing information to support the adaptation by staging, i.e. narrowing the space for selecting variants (for more details, see Sect. 9.4.3).

In the second phase, using a refactored SLO (we can also use the term *specialized SLO*; to motivate that, see Sect. 8.2) as an input of the meta-language processor (PHP compiler in our case), the teacher or student is able to automatically derive the needed LO. Before doing that, the adequate parameter values should be identified and submitted by the user. Therefore, the adaptation is a two-phase process: firstly, we create a multistage SLO which is seen as a higher-level (or *deep* [BR12]) adaptation to the teacher's needs, and secondly, the lower-level adaptation by deriving the concrete LO to the student's needs.

At the end, we are able to present the following concluding observation: (1) D*f*R is the higher-level activity to design the highly reusable structures such as context-aware SLOs. (2) D*w*R is the low-level activity or process to design highly adaptable SLOs for teachers and adaptable LOs for students. (3) There are the following tools (FAMILIAR, SPLOT, MePAG) available to support the D*f*R processes. There are the following tools (MP-ReTool, PHP processor, target language compiler) available to support the D*w*R processes.

9.3.4 Complexity Issues in Designing SLO

As it has been stated previously, when we try to extend the reuse dimension, typically, this action results in the growth of complexity of the product designed for reuse. Therefore, the designer has to have measures to evaluate the complexity of SLOs. As they, in fact, are meta-programs, it is possible to apply the methodology and metrics presented in [ŠD13]. Those metrics include: (1) relative Kolmogorov complexity (in fact measuring the content variability), (2) meta-language richness (measuring the complexity of the meta-level specification), (3) cyclomatic complexity (measuring the interface complexity), (4) normalized difficulty (it is the algorithmic complexity of a meta-program) and (5) cognitive difficulty (CD) (meaning the cognitive understandability of a meta-program). The latter is defined as follows: $CD = max\ (|P|, N1, N2)$ (where $|P|$ is the number of parameters, N_1 is the number of meta-functions and N_2 is the number of the respective arguments of the functions within a meta-program). It has been devised using Miller's work [Mil56] (stating that humans hold 7 ($\pm$2) chunks of information in their short-term memory at one time) and Keating's observation [Kea00], who claims that the number of modules at any level of the software hierarchy must be 7 ($\pm$2).

Therefore, the introduced metrics enable to define the complexity boundaries, such as *simple, moderate, complex* and *overcomplex*, from various perspectives in designing SLOs.

9.3.5 Staging and Context Awareness: A Rationale for Adaptation

Before introducing the formal definition and a methodology for designing tools, we first aim at presenting a rationale to understand the *technical aspects* of adaptation here. This, in fact, is the motivation of the adaptation concept and the key for the primary understanding of the functionality of the adaptation tools. Staging can be viewed as a process to define stages, either logically (when multistage SLO is specified) or physically (when user is working with the MP-ReTool). Staging is also seen as splitting the whole into pieces, i.e. *categorizing* the learning variability. As 'there is nothing more basic than categorization to our thought, perception, action and speech' (Lakoff, taken from [Dav97]), it is much easier to understanding the role of staging for adaptation. It is so because, by staging, we are able to diminish the complexity in interpreting the SLO interface by the user, when he/she works with the stage-based specification (which has been shown in Chap. 8).

On what ground we are talking about the splitting or categorization here? More formally, it is about the parameter assignments to stages within the interface and making the adequate changes within the meta-body, as it will be discussed in more detail later. What is the base mechanism to provide the meaningful assignments? Here, we describe this mechanism as context awareness (expressed by the parameter context model). As it was already stated, we express the context by the fuzzy weights to interpret the parameters within the interface meaningfully. Our context model is simple: it is based on parameter priorities. The pedagogy-oriented parameters have the highest priority (HP). The social-oriented parameters have the intermediate priority (IP). This group of parameters may have a priority to be represented as a constant (imply IP – intermediate priority) or as a function with arguments that are levels (from 1 to 6) of Bloom's taxonomy. The pure content and technological parameters have the lowest priorities (LP). In the case of interacting parameters, however, their priority is defined by the special rules.

Note that the context model should be predefined in advance, along with the SLO, and integrated within this specification. As the context model, in fact, describes the domain expert's knowledge, it is not the designer's responsibility to change or modify the model. For the tool designer, this model is the input data to be used 'as-is'. However, the designer of tools has to foresee the possibility for the teacher to adapt the context model to his/her needs.

Technologically, the SLO adaptation tool should implement the adequate connection (among stages, parameters and context model) to make the adaptation possible. As indeed this connection is not a simple task, we need first to define and study more thoroughly the basic concepts, models, properties and rules (restrictions). Therefore, the next two subsections provide the background to support the SLO design and adaptation processes and tools.

9.4 Background of Smart LOs to Develop Authoring Tools

Here, by authoring tools, we mean the two: (1) tool for developing SLOs (semi-automatic or even automatic) and (2) tool for transforming (refactoring) an initial SLO (developed for reuse either manually or with the aid of the first tool) into its multistage representation for the adaptation purposes. As it was stated before, we are proponents of the model-driven design. We apply the approach in designing both tools. The approach focuses on creating and dealing with models at the different levels of abstraction. In the first case (i.e. in designing the first tool), we exclude two base levels of the models: SLO *design specification* and *coding*. We use the feature-based models to specify SLO at the specification level. The formal and semiformal definition of the models has been already discussed (see Chap. 4). Two important kinds of feature models should be highlighted here: *abstract* and *concrete* models. Abstract feature models describe the CS teaching domain for general representation and analysis. The concrete models are *derivatives* from the abstract models. The basis for the SLO specification is the concrete models. Thus, the theoretical background of the specification level is *a feature-based modelling* (i. e. model creation, aggregation and verification).

The theoretical background of the coding level is meta-programming, computational models, transformation rules and algorithms for implementing the models and rules. Below, we define meta-programming as a base technology/methodology to implement SLO using the formal notations. We use, in fact, three notations for representing meta-programming concepts: the set-based one (for concise representation and general understanding because this form is more popular in the mathematical sense), the graph-based one (for visual representation of interdependencies among the adequate items) and the feature-based one (for *connecting* the specification and coding tasks through model transformations). The reader should not be confused by the use of those notions because they are not so much different (feature models, in fact, are graphs with adequate semantics and both use the set formalism).

In the second case (i.e. in designing the second tool), we use also the feature models to specify the meta-programming level concepts, meta-program specialization (in other words, partial evaluation or refactoring) techniques, graph theory and stage meta-programming as a theoretical background. For better understanding the main concepts of the background, we illustrate them with the same example that was already introduced in Chap. 5 (see Table 5.1). Here, however, we introduce new features into this illustrative example, according to the specific context.

9.4.1 Definition of Meta-Programming Concepts and SLO

In this section, we define the meta-programming and SLO-related concepts more precisely as it was done so far (see Sect. 6.3.2 in Chap. 6). To illustrate them, we also provide illustrative examples. We use the same examples (generic Boolean equation and generic algebraic equation as simplified instances of SLOs) that were already introduced in Chap. 6. Here, however, the examples are extended in order we could be able to explain the additional aspects. For readability and conciseness, we use a simplified representation of the languages (meta- and target).

Definition 9.1 Heterogeneous meta-program (He MP) is the higher-level executable specification, which is coded using *at least* two languages (meta-language L_M and target language L_T) to specify and generate a set of the target program instances.

Table 9.1 Running example of a meta-program as SLO: conceptual level with comparisons

Domain	Domain instance	Objects of the instance	Properties and values	Result of manipulation
Programming	*Program:* $y:=a*x+b;$ $L=\{y, :=, a, *,$ $x, +, b\}$ L: program language	*Variable, constants, operations, statement*	$a\in[2..10]$ $b\in[11..30]$ $x\in[20..40]$	A value of y defined by the computer program, e.g. $y=51$, when $a=2, b=11$ and $x=20$
Meta-programming	*Meta-program:* $y:= af(p1)f(p2)f$ $(p3)b;$ $L1=\{a, b, y, :=\}$ $L2=\{f(p1), f(p2),$ $f(p3)\}$ L1: target language L2: meta-language (in fact, alphabets)	*Meta-objects: parameters, parameter values, functions substituting a parameter by its value*	$f(p1)\rightarrow p1\in$ $\{*, /\}$ $f(p2)\rightarrow p2\in$ $\{x, x*x,$ $z*z*z\}$ $f(p3)\rightarrow p3\in$ $\{+, -\}$	A program instance, defined by the L2 processor, i.e. $y:=a*z*z*z$ $+b;$ when $f(p1)=$'*' $f(p2)=z*z*z$ $f(p3)=$'+'

Further L_T and L_M stand for the formal notation (L1 and L2 stand for the informal notation; see Table 9.1) of the target and meta-languages, respectively. Note that the L_M processor is the transformation tool to generate programs in L_T from the He MP (MP for short).

Definition 9.2 MP model $\mu(M)$ is the structure $\mu(M) = \mu(M_I) \cup \mu(M_B)$, where $\mu(M_I)$ and $\mu(M_B)$ are the interface and meta-body models, respectively.

Definition 9.3 In terms of the set-based notion, interface model $\mu(M_I)$ is the n-dimensional non-empty space of parameters and their values defined as: $\mu(M_I) = \{P; V\}$, where P is the full set of n parameter names, i.e. $n = |P|$, and V is the ordered set of *all* parameter values.

As each parameter $P_i (P_i \in P)$ has its own set of values as follows: $\{v_{i_1}, v_{i_2}, \ldots, v_{i_q}\} \subset V$. Thus, we can write: $P_i := V_i = \{v_{i_1}, v_{i_2}, \ldots, v_{i_q}\} \in V$, i_q – the number of values of parameter P_i. The symbol ':=' means 'is defined'.

Definition 9.4 Two parameters P_i and P_j ($P_i, P_j \subseteq P$ $(i \neq j)$) are said to be *dependent upon the choice of their values*, if there exists a pair of values (v_{i_d}, v_{j_t}) $(v_{i_d} \in P_i, v_{j_t} \in P_j,$ where $d \in [1, i_q]$ and $t \in [1, j_m]$; q, m – the number of values adequately) such that the following condition holds:

$$\left(v_{i_d} \text{ requires } v_{j_t}\right) \textbf{or} \left(v_{i_d} \text{ excludes } v_{j_t}\right) = \textbf{true} \tag{9.1}$$

Otherwise (i.e. if Eq. (9.1) is *false* for all values of P_i and P_j), the parameters are *independent upon the choice of their values*.

Definition 9.4 as compared to Definition 6.4 expresses the interaction formally by Eq. (9.1). This enables us to formulate the property using which it is possible to define rules of constructing the parameter dependency graph $G(P,U)$.

In general, the graph $G(P,U)$ is defined as follows: P is the set of parameters; U is the set of parameter dependency, i.e. $u_{ij} = 1$ if and only if P_i and P_j are dependent according to Definition 9.4 and $u_{ij} = 0$ otherwise ($P_i, P_j \subseteq P$ ($i \neq j$)).

How the graph is constructed? For this purpose, we need to return to the *generic Boolean equation* that was given in Sect. 6.3.3. Two cases were discussed here: *Case 1* when $P_1 = \{AND, OR\}$ and $P_2 = \{2, 3, 4\}$ (parameter P_1 specifies generic operation and P_2 specifies the number of arguments for the generic operation) and *Case 2* when $P_1 = \{NOT, AND, OR\}$ and $P_2 = \{1, 2, 3, 4\}$ (there parameter values are slightly changed as compared to *Case 1*).

Now we illustrate (see Fig. 9.2) how the parameter dependency graph $G(P,U)$ is actually constructed for our generic equation, using the *value interaction graph*. The latter is the *bipartite graph* defined as $H((V_i, V_j), E)$, where V_i is the set of values of parameter P_i, V_j is the set of values of parameter P_j ($P_i, P_j \subset P(i \neq j)$) and E is relationships among V_j and V_j.

In Fig. 9.2a, we illustrate *Case 1*. Here, the parameters P1 and P2 are *independent* (graph $G(P,U)$ is the null graph), because the value interaction graph H is the *complete bipartite graph* (meaning Eq. (9.1) is *false*). In Fig. 9.2b, we illustrate *Case 2*. Here, on the contrary, the parameters P1 and P2 are dependent (graph $G(P, U)$ is the connected), because the value interaction graph H is the *non-complete bipartite graph* (meaning Eq. (9.1) holds, i.e. *true*).

Therefore, we are able to describe the interface model using either the set-based notion (Definitions 9.3 and 9.4) or the graph-based notion (i.e. the parameter

Fig. 9.2 Example illustrating the construction of parameter dependency graph $G(P,U)$: (**a**) *Case 1* (*H* is the complete bipartite graph) and (**b**) *Case 2* (*H* is non-complete)

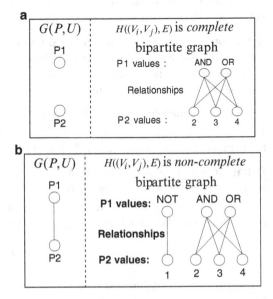

Table 9.2 Meta-program specification level: SLO interface model

Domain instance	Meta-program (MP) represented by feature diagram	Interface elements	Interface model without the context
Meta-program f(p0):= af(p1)f (p2)f(p3)b; L1 = {*a, b,* :=} L2 = {*f(p0), f (p1), f(p2), f (p3)*} L1: target language L2: meta-language (In fact, alphabets of the languages)	$f(p0) \rightarrow p0 = \{y, x, z\};$	p0 p2 ● ● ● ● ● ● p1 p3 ● ● ● ●	

dependency graph G and parameter value interaction graph H; the latter serves for constructing the first). As the graph-based representation is complete, we use it in the subsequent formal reasoning.

Definition 9.5 The meta-body model is an *ordered* set of functions: $\mu(M_B) = \{f_k(a_j)\}$, where $f_k(a_j) \in L_M$; $a_j \in P$ or/and fragments of L_T.

Note that the ordering of the functions depends on the syntax and semantic of the target language L_T and requirements of the meta-program itself. All these can be learnt from our running example (see Table 9.1).

Definition 9.6 SLO is the heterogeneous meta-program that specifies the *learning variability* along with the *preprogrammed context* to express the variability semantics for adaptation.

The reader can also interpret the given formal definitions along with informal or semiformal examples taken in Table 9.1 (note that here the meta-program example is interpreted in the same way as it was done in Chap. 6). As the MP (i.e. SLO) model can be also defined using the feature-based notation, we provide this representation in Table 9.2. Note that, in terms of features, the interacting parameters are typically expressed through the constraints of the type *excludes* or *requires* (see Table 9.2) and the meta-body is expressed through functions (cp. Definition 9.5 and adequate features in Table 9.2).

We illustrate the meaning of Definition 9.5 in Table 9.3. Note that here the learning variability is presented by two components (content and context) only. The pedagogical context is missed due to the reasons of simplicity.

Next, we present the formal definition of feature models.

Table 9.3 SLO as a meta-program specification with the context-aware interface model

Domain instance	SLO feature diagram, where the *feature p4* models the context (here, p means priority)	Interface model with the context
SLO as a meta-program without pedagogical features $f(p0):= af(p1)f(p2)$ $f(p3)b$ $L1 = \{a, b, :=\}$ $L2 = \{f(p0), f(p1),$ $f(p2), f(p3), p4\}$		

9.4.2 Fundamentals of Feature Models

Definition 9.7 *Base* domain feature model is the compound: $FM = \langle G, E_{mand}, G_{xor}, G_{or}, REQ, EX \rangle$,

where $G = (F, E, r)$ is a rooted tree, F is a finite set of features, $E \subseteq F \times F$ is a finite set of edges, $r \in F$ is the root feature, $E_{mand} \subseteq E$ is a set of edges that define mandatory features with their parents, $G_{xor} \subseteq P(F) \times F$, and $G_{or} \subseteq P(F) \times F$ define alternative and optional feature groups and are sets of pairs of child features together with their common parent feature, and *REQ* and *EX* are finite sets of constraints *requires* and *excludes* (adopted from [ACL+13], see also Table 9.3).

Definition 9.8 Priority feature model (*PFM*) is *the context model* expressed through fuzzy variables that are treated as features taken from the set {HP, IP, LP} along with adequate constraints of the type *requires*, where HP is high priority, IP is intermediate priority and LP is low priority (see the node-feature p4 in Table 9.3).

Note that priorities are defined at the analysis phase by a domain expert. In fact, fuzzy variables are parameter weights helpful to sequencing parameters in constructing the MP interface (see Property 9.2 in Sect. 9.4.5).

Definition 9.9 Extended domain feature model (*EFM*) is the aggregation of the base feature and priority models: $EFM = FM \oplus PFM$, '$\oplus$' means the aggregation operator (in Table 9.3, in fact, there is shown the aggregated model).

Definition 9.10 Meta-program feature model is defined by *Definition* 9.7 so that all components of *FM* are taken from the meta-programming domain (see concepts definition in Sect. 9.4.1).

9.4.3   Stage Meta-Programming and Stage SLO Concepts

This part gives the formalized background to develop tools (see Chaps. 8 and 10) for designing the highly adaptive SLOs. This background is rooted on the stage-based meta-programming concept. The latter is about the specification of meta-meta-programs [ŠBB14]. To specify the functional model in designing meta-meta-programs, we need to introduce additionally new technological terms such as the ones: *deactivating label, active/passive meta-construct, deactivating index, stage* and *k-stage meta-program.* Their definitions follow.

Definition 9.11 Deactivating label is the sign (usually denoted as '\') written before a language construct.

Note that modern high-level languages (such as Java, C++, PHP, etc.) have the deactivating labels to control and change the role of the language constructs during their compilation. Here, we use the label in the other context – to change the role of meta-constructs of the meta-language, when it is interpreted by the meta-language *processor.*

Definition 9.12 Meta-construct of a meta-language is the *parameter*, the *function* or *both*. The meta-construct is said to be *active* if it performs the prescribed action defined by the meta-language at the current stage of meta-program execution. Simply, the active meta-construct has no deactivating label.

Definition 9.13 Meta-construct is said to be *passive* if it contains the deactivating label (labels) written before the meta-construct (e.g. the construct $x = a$ is active; the construct $\backslash x = a$ is passive; here, $x is treated as a variable of PHP (i.e. meta-language) and a as a variable of a target language).

Note that the passive meta-construct is treated as a target language text at the current stage of meta-program execution.

Definition 9.14 *Deactivating index* is the adequate number of deactivating labels written before a meta-construct. The value of the index depends on the meta-construct's stage and meta-language used (Rule 12 to be considered in Chap. 11, Sect. 11.3.4 indicates how to calculate the index value).

Definition 9.15 Stage is the state of the meta-program defined by the active meta-constructs.

Definition 9.16 *Deactivating process* is the multistage process (in terms of k-stage processing) to reducing the deactivating index by 1 or changing the state of a meta-construct from the passive state to the active state.

The meta-language processor performs the deactivating process reducing the deactivating index by 1 at the given stage. Note also that the deactivating process does not affect semantics (functionality or behaviour) of the meta-construct. The process affects its state only.

Definition 9.17 A k-stage meta-program is the specification, where parameters are assigned to stages so that the following conditions are valid:

(i) Each stage has at least one parameter.
(ii) At stage j $(1 \leq j \leq k)$, all parameters assigned to this stage and all functions of the stage are *active*, while the remaining *meta-constructs* (i.e. parameters and functions of the meta-language) are *passive*.
(iii) There are specific rules and constraints to support the deactivating mechanism at the adequate stage.

Definition 9.18 Structural model of the stage meta-program is the hierarchic structure, where j stage $(1 \leq j \leq k)$ has the interface and meta-body that both are embedded into the $j + 1$ stage (see Fig. 9.3).

Definition 9.19 *Stage-based meta-program* is the meta-meta-program. If there are k stages, we treat the meta-meta-program as the k-stage meta-program.

Note that the initial meta-program is the *one-stage* meta-program.

Definition 9.20 *Stage-based SLO* is the stage-based meta-program that represents learning variability through stages of the model (Fig. 9.3).

How looks the complete implementation of the stage-based SLO in PHP, one can learn from the running example (see Fig. 9.4a, b). Here, for simplicity reasons, we present the two-stage SLO (Fig. 9.4b) to specify the *generic Boolean equation* (see also Sect. 6.3.3 in Chap. 6) with three parameters (P1 = {∧, ∨} defines a set of possible operations; P2 = {2, 3, 4} defines the number of arguments; the arguments are represented as $X1, X2, \ldots$; P3 = {Y, Z} defines the set of names of the right side function (equation)). Parameters are prioritized according to their role in the equation.

In this section, we continue the discussion on the designer's view and present a background that may contribute to *context-aware adaptation tool development* using the SLO approach. Here, we discuss the SLO model aspects in more details along with most significant properties that enable to develop and validate the tool.

Fig. 9.3 Structural model of the k-stage meta-program and SLO

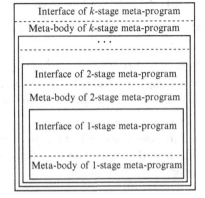

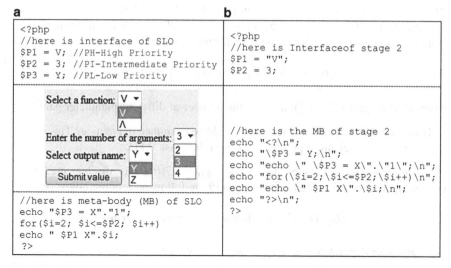

Fig. 9.4 Initial one-stage SLO coded in PHP (**a**), two-stage SLO specification in PHP (**b**)

9.4.4   Properties of SLO-Based Models

Property 9.1 In terms of the graph-based notion, the graph $G(P, U)$ is the interface model of a meta-program (or SLO).

This property follows from the *Definition* 9.3 and *Definition* 9.4 (see Sect. 9.4.1). This property defines the interface model more precisely because it, in fact, combines the *Definition* 9.3 and *Definition* 9.4 and, additionally, explicitly states the interaction among the parameter values with the aid of the graph H. The next property generalizes the issues discussed in Sect. 9.4.3 (see Figs. 9.3 and 9.4).

The model is said to be weighted and denoted as $G(P^w, U)$ if a parameter within the specification is labelled by the fuzzy variable $w \in \{HP, IP, LP\}$. The latter represents *a priority* of the parameter (see also Sect. 7.5, for more details). Fuzzy variables play two roles: (1) they are a helpful instrument to make parameter sequencing in designing interfaces of SLO because parameters differ in semantics, and (2) they represent *the context of adaptation* to allocating parameters to stages when the task of creating the multistage SLO is considered.

Property 9.2 *Context-aware* interface model of SLO is the weighted graph $G(P^w, U)$ whose nodes are labelled by the fuzzy variable w ($w \in \{HP, IP, LP\}$) to represent *the context for adaptation*.

As the weights are not influential to the properties considered below, for simplicity, we omit the symbol w in representing the model here.

Property 9.3 The parameter dependency graph $G(P, U)$ of the SLO specification is the null graph *iff* for each pair of parameters $P_i, P_j \in P$ $(i \neq j)$ their value interaction graphs are complete bipartite graphs, i.e. formula (9.2) holds:

$$\forall_b\left(H_b\left((V_i, V_j), E\right) \text{ is complete}\right) = \textbf{true}, \tag{9.2}$$

where $(b \in [1, |B|]; |B| = C_n^2)$; and B – the number of different parameter pairs.

How many different parameter pairs should be examined in practice? This is left to the reader as a scientific problem (see Sect. 9.6, task 9.11).

Property 9.4 The parameter dependency graph $G(P, U)$ is disconnected (i.e. containing a set of connected components) *iff* the following relation holds:

$$\exists_b\left(H_b\left((V_i, V_j), E\right) \text{ is non} - \text{complete}\right) = \textbf{true}. \tag{9.3}$$

The parameter dependency graph can be expressed as:

$$G(P, U) = \overset{g}{\underset{i=1}{\cup}}\, G_i, \left(G_i \cap G_j = \varnothing;\ G_i, G_j \subseteq G\right) \tag{9.4}$$

$(i \neq j)$, g is the number of connected components, including isolated nodes $(g > 1)$.

Property 9.5 The connected components $G_i \subseteq G(P, U)$ and $(i = [1, g])$ (see Eq. (9.4) represent the groups of independent parameters.

Property 9.6 The upper bound of the eligible number of stages k_{max} to perform specialization of the *given correct* SLO specification into its k-stage format is defined by inequality (formula (9.5)):

$$k_{max} \leq g \tag{9.5}$$

To illustrate *Property* 9.5 and *Property* 9.6, in Fig. 9.5, we present an abstract example (adapted from [ŠBB14]) that contains possible variants of $G_i \subseteq G(P, U)$.

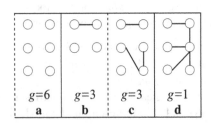

Fig. 9.5 Variants of $G_i \subseteq G(P, U)$: (**a**) G_i as 6 isolated nodes; (**b**) G_i as two isolated nodes and one group of dependent parameters; (**c**) two groups of dependent parameters and one isolated node; (**d**) one dependent group

Property 9.7 *Property* 9.4 and *Property* 9.5 hold also for the graph $G(P^w, U)$ and its components $G_i^w \subseteq G(P^w, U)$. As a result, all nodes (i.e. parameters) of a connected subgraph G_i^w have the same weight w.

9.4.5 Formal Statement of SLO Design and Refactoring Tasks

Here, we formulate two tasks. *Task 1* is to design a *reusable context-aware* SLO (in terms of the paradigm D*f*R, see Fig. 9.1). *Task 2* is to apply the *refactoring transformation* and to produce (from the context-aware SLO) the *stage-based specification for the purposes of adaptation*. Task 2 is seen as a result of using the D*w*R paradigm (again, see Fig. 9.1).

Typically, computer scientists define a design task as the process of mapping the *problem domain* onto the *solution domain* [CBK13]. In our case, CS teaching and learning is the problem domain, and meta-programming is the solution domain. In terms of the model-driven design, we represent each domain by the adequate feature models. Furthermore, it is possible to express our problem domain through the learning variability (see Chap. 5). Thus, we are able to reformulate the SLO design task *at the feature model* level as follows:

The Task 1 is to map the learning variability feature model onto the meta-programming feature model.

Formally, we can write:

$$FD_{SLO} = FD_{LV} \times FD_{MPG}, \tag{9.6}$$

where *FD* (feature diagram) is the adequate feature model, *LV* is the learning variability and *MPG* is the meta-programming.

In Chap. 10, we will discuss *how to develop the authoring tools* and how to solve *Task 1* and *Task 2* (semi-)automatically using the tools. Note that we apply the model-driven design approach, where the model *transformation rules, computational models* and *algorithms* to realize them are at the focus (Chap. 10).

Task 2, in fact, has been already stated in Chap. 7 as the *SLO specialization task* through the *formal permutation* of parameters within stages. That was enough to the user to understand the essence of the task. Some important details to realize the stage-based SLO, however, were omitted there. Now, we are able to fulfil this gap, because we have specified more precise models here. Note that here we use the term *refactoring* instead of *specialization* as it was previously. Though both have the same meaning (see discussion in Sect. 7.2), the first is more relevant to the SW engineering domain (we treat the SLO design tools as a subject just of this domain). The second is more relevant to the CS domain (we treat the use of SLO as a subject of CS as it follows from Sect. 7.2).

Suppose, we have a correct initial SLO_R specification (here, R means reuse, i.e. design for reuse; see Fig. 9.1). We seek to obtain the stage-based specification, denoted as SLO_S (here, S stands for *stage* or *specialization through staging*; see also Fig. 9.1). Now the formal statement of Task 2 is as follows:

To perform refactoring transformation according to the relationship 9.7:

$$SLO_R \overset{T(S_k)}{\rightarrow} SLO_S, \tag{9.7}$$

where $\overset{T(S_k)}{\rightarrow}$ stands for refactoring transformation by staging (S_k) and k – the number of required stages.

Now we are able to formulate the theoretical statement important to design SLO_S. The statement formulates the *existence of the solution* to the problem.

Statement   Transformations $SLO_R \overset{T(S_k)}{\rightarrow} SLO_S, (1 < k \le k_{max})$ exist *iff* the parameter dependency graph $G(P^w, U)$ of SLO_R is disconnected, i.e. it is defined by Eq. (9.4).

The proof is based on *Properties* 9.1, 9.2, 9.3 and 9.4 (see also Fig. 9.5d).

In practice, however, the graph $G(P^w, U)$, as a rule, is disconnected, and there are many possible solutions. The interesting question is how much? Theoretically, i.e. if we neglect the role of the weights w and consider the model $G(P, U)$, the number of possible solutions depends on two variables k and g (k is the number of required stages and g is the number of disconnected components of $G(P, U)$). Therefore, the number of possible transformations can be calculated by Eq. (9.3) (when $k = 2$) and by Eq. (9.4) (when $k = 3$) as follows [ŠBB14]:

$$|T(S_k)| = 2^g - 2, \tag{9.8}$$

$$|T(S_k)| = 3^g - \sum_{i=1}^{g} 3*2^{(i-1)}. \tag{9.9}$$

Here, $|T(S_k)|$ is the number of possible transformations. The number defines the *adaptation space*. For example, there are 130 transformations or possible variants of adaptations, when $k = 3$ and $g = 5$ (the case of a simple SLO in terms of complexity measures, see Sect. 9.3.4). In practice, however, the real tasks have a much larger space of adaptation. Therefore, the weights provide the context-aware information, enabling to narrowing the search space in dealing with the adaptation problem, as it will be discussed later in Chap. 10.

Now, we summarize the basic result of this chapter as follows.

9.5   Summary, Discussion and Conclusion

In Chap. 9, first, we have outlined the *preliminary statements* that are important to the SLO designers and to the designers of authoring tools. We have formulated the basic principles and requirements to design smart LOs (SLOs). We have treated those requirements as being virtual, i.e. independent upon a concrete situation as much as possible. We have also focused on the linguistic aspects, i.e. on the problem of choosing languages (meta- and target) in coding the SLO specifications. s. We have described the reuse-based design paradigms (i.e. *design for reuse* and *design with reuse* that we have adopted from SW engineering) as they are applied in our case to design and adapt SLOs. Note that we have also considered those paradigms, however, in another context in Chap. 4. As designers, before starting their activities, should be aware the complexity issues, we have also shortly discussed the complexity measures to evaluate the designs.

Next, we have provided the *theoretical background* to design smart LOs and transform them to the stage-based specifications aiming to adapt them to the user's contexts of use. We have specified more precise models (as it was done so far, for example, in Chap. 7) for the motivated solving of the tasks. We have used the set-based (graph-based), feature-based and meta-programming-based concepts and notions to specify our models. We have formulated the *basic properties* of the analysed models. The properties are the basis to *define the other* (i.e. realization-level) *properties, transformation rules, computational models* and algorithms to specify the functioning of the authoring tools.

9.6 Research and Exercise Questions

9.1. Describe the framework to characterize the adaptation problem by identifying (a) the scope of the problem and (b) the most influential factors and their interactions.

9.2. Provide a specific insight and investigation into the role of the context to the adaptation problem.

9.3. Draw the links (conceptual, model based) between reusability and adaptability of the teaching and learning content.

9.4. Define the terms adaptation and adaptability using the results of previous questions. Clarify what might be the object for adaptation.

9.5. What kinds of adaptations might be?

9.6. Draw the links among the learning process and content adaptation.

9.7. Consider the content adaptation problem from the pure technological perspective and provide the relevant technologies that might be helpful.

9.8. Provide research on program partial evaluation (specialization) for the purpose of CS teaching.

9.9. Model the presented approach using the tool [BBŠ13] along with test cases given there and identify the main properties of the approach.

9.10. Clarify how can model-driven and generative technologies contribute to adaptation problem?

9.11. Investigate the parameter value interaction model specified by the bipartite graphs in Sect. 9.4.4 (see Properties 9.3 and 9.4) as a separate research task.

9.12. Investigate the linguistic aspects of the meta-programming paradigm. Motivate the need of multilinguistic teaching in CS courses.

References

[ACL+13]   Acher M, Collet P, Lahire P, France RB (2013) FAMILIAR: a domain-specific language for large scale management of feature models. Sci Comput Program 78 (6):657–681

[BBD+14]   Burbaitė R, Bespalova K, Damaševičius R, Štuikys V (2014) Context-aware generative learning objects for teaching computer science. Int J Eng Educ 30(4):925–936

[BBH+13]   Black AP, Bruce KB, Homer M, Noble J, Ruskin A, Yannow R (2013) Seeking grace: a new object-oriented language for novices. In: Proceedings of the 44th ACM technical symposium on computer science education. ACM, pp 129–134

[BR12]   Boyle T, Ravenscroft A (2012) Context and deep learning design. Comput Educ 59 (4):1224–1233

[BBS13]   Bespalova K, Burbaite R, Štuikys V (2013) MP-ReTool tools. http://proin.ktu.lt/ metaprogram/MP-ReTool/

[CBK13]   Capilla R, Bosch J, Kang KC (eds) (2013) Systems and software variability management (concepts tools and experiences). Springer, Berlin/New York

[Dav97]   Davenport TH (1997) Information ecology. Oxford University Press, New York

[DKV00]   van Deursen A, Klint P, Visser J (2000) Domain-specific languages: an annotated bibliography. SIGPLAN Not 35(6):25–35

[DKV02]   van Deursen A, Klint P, Visser J (2002) Domain-specific languages. In the encyclopedia of library and information science. Marcel Dekker Inc, New York

[Hud98]   Hudak P (1998) Modular domain specific languages and tools. In: Proceedings of the 5th international conference on software reuse. IEEE Computer Society Press

[IEEE99]   Special issue on domain-specific languages. IEEE transactions on software engineering, 25(3), May/Jun 1999

[JH07]   Johnson K, Hall T (2007) Granularity, reusability and learning objects: theory, praxis, issues, and trends, pp 181–207

[Kea00]   Keating M (2000) Measuring design quality by measuring design complexity. In: Proceedings of the 1st international symposium on quality of electronic design (ISQED) 2000), IEEE, Washington, DC, pp 103–108

[KLB+08]   Kosar T, Lopez PEM, Barrientos PA, Mernik M (2008) A preliminary study on various implementation approaches of domain-specific language. Inf Softw Technol 50(5):390–405

[KM09]   Koehler M, Mishra P (2009) What is technological pedagogical content knowledge (TPACK)? Contemp Issue Technol Teach Educ 9(1):60–70

[Köl10]   Kölling M (2010) The greenfoot programming environment. ACM Trans Comput Educ 10(4):14

[KOM+10]   Kosar T, Oliveira N, Mernik M, Pereira MJV, Črepinšek M, da Cruz D, Henriques PR (2010) Comparing general-purpose and domain-specific languages: an empirical study. ComSIS 7(2):247–264, Special issue

[KRS+09]   Koohang A, Riley L, Smith T, Schreurs J (2009) E-learning and constructivism: from theory to application. Interdiscip J E-Learn Learn Object 5:91–109

[Mil56]   Miller G (1956) The magic number seven, plus or minus two: some limits on our capacity for processing information. Psychol Rev 63(2):81–97

[MRR+10]   Maloney J, Resnick M, Rusk N, Silverman B, Eastmond E (2010) The scratch programming language and environment. ACM Trans Comput Educ 10(4):16

[OPH+09]   Oliveira N, Pereira MJV, Henriques PR, da Cruz D (2009) Domain-specific languages: a theoretical survey. http://inforum.org.pt/INForum2009/docs/full/paper_86. pdf

[Ous98]   Ousterhout JK (1998) Scripting: higher level programming for the 21st century. IEEE Comput 31(3):23–30

[Par76]   Parnas DL (1976) On the design and development of program families, software engineering. IEEE Trans 2(1):1–9

[PBL05]   Pohl K, Bockle G, van der Linden F (2005) Software product line engineering. Springer, New York

[POC+13]   Pereira MJ, Oliveira N, Cruz D, Henriques P (2013) Choosing grammars to support language processing courses. In: Proceedings of the 2nd symposium on languages, applications and technologies. Open Access Series in Informatics (OASIcs)

[RHS14]   Rodríguez-Cerezo D, Henriques PR, Sierra JL (2014) Attribute grammars made easier: EvDebugger (A visual debugger for attribute grammars). In: SIIE'14 (Actas del XVI Simposio Internacional en Informĩtica Educativa, Logroño, La Rioja), 12–14 Nov 2014, pp 45–50

[Sam97]   Sametinger J (1997) Software engineering with reusable components. Springer, New York

[ŠBB14]   Štuikys V, Bespalova K, Burbaitė R (2014) Refactoring of heterogeneous metaprogram into k-stage meta-program. Inf Technol Control 43(1):14–27

[ŠBD13]   Štuikys V, Burbaitė R, Damaševičius R (2013) Teaching of computer science topics using meta-programming-based GLOs and LEGO robots. Inform Educ 12(1):125–142

[ŠD13]   Štuikys V, Damaševičius R (2013) Meta-programming and model-driven metaprogram development: principles, processes and techniques. Springer, London/Heidelberg/New York/Dordrecht

[SI11]   Salcedo SL, Idrobo AMO (2011) New tools and methodologies for programming languages learning using the scribbler robot and Alice. In: Frontiers in education conference (FIE), IEEE, p F4G-1

[Wiki14]   Wikipedia.   http://en.wikipedia.org/wiki/List_of_educational_programming_ languages

[WLL11]   Watson C, Li FW, Lau RW (2011) Learning programming languages through corrective feedback and concept visualisation. In Advances in web-based learning-ICWL 2011. Springer, Berlin/Heidelberg, pp 11–20

[XL06]   Xu L, Fred G (2006) Chirp on crickets: teaching compilers using an embedded robot controller. In: Proceedings of the 37th SIGCSE technical symposium on computer science education, ACM, pp 82–86

Chapter 10
Authoring Tools to Design Smart LOs

10.1 Introduction

Nowadays the teaching and learning processes are widely supported by the adequate authoring tools. In general, the aim of using the tools is to gain the technological value in the first place, i.e. efficiency, flexibility, etc. (of course, the pedagogical value comes together if the tools are applied properly). Our approach is different in many aspects from those analysed throughout the book. The main distinguishing feature is the realization of the concept of *producing* and *adapting* the teaching content automatically. The automation, however, never comes for free. The process of developing smart LOs (SLOs) is the time-consuming and error-prone activity. It requires specific knowledge, competency and some experience of working with meta-programming. Of course, it is possible to write the meta-programming-based SLO specifications manually (by the knowledgeable CS teacher or even by knowledgeable students). Our practice shows that, at the initial phase of adoption of the approach, it is even recommended to apply the manual development. On the other hand, the human efforts are highly dependable on the complexity of SLOs (simply, it might be measured by the number of parameters and their dependency, i.e. model complexity). The more complex SLOs are, the more efforts to develop them are needed. In this case, the use of the adequate tools is highly desirable. Such a situation is with the development of SLOs.

With regard to the redesign and refactoring (i.e. specialization of SLOs for the adaptation purposes), however, the situation is quite different. The refactoring of SLOs, aiming to support the needs for adapting the content to the context of use, is a much more complicated task to the user. This is because of the complexity issues, i.e. due to an extremely low level of readability and understandability in analysing the meta-program texts. Especially it is true, when the number of stages of adaptation is larger than 2. Therefore, in the course of the provided research activities in the field, we found the necessity to develop the experimental tools to support both processes – the SLO design and refactoring (i.e. specialization for adaptation).

© Springer International Publishing Switzerland 2015
V. Štuikys, *Smart Learning Objects for Smart Education in Computer Science*,
DOI 10.1007/978-3-319-16913-2_10

In this chapter, we address tasks related to the development and functioning of the tool, namely, MePAG (*Me*ta-*P*rogram *A*utomatic *G*enerator). Though the theoretical foundation and conceptual framework to develop the tools have been suggested by the book's author, the practical implementation has been completely provided by my Ph.D. student, Kristina Bespalova. Again, my sincere thanks for her nice work.

10.2 Literature Review

As, in this chapter, we focus on presenting processes and tools specifically oriented to support teaching and learning in CS with regard to using an SLO, we categorize the related work into two groups: A, authoring tools used in CS teaching but not so much related to our approach, and B, processes and tools that relate to the development of an SLO.

Group A   Here, we focus on the more general aspects of tools such as their taxonomies, their attributes that support teaching in programming, visualization capabilities, etc. Kelleher and Pausch [KP05], for example, categorize environments in teaching programming (the main topic of CS) into two groups: *teaching systems* and *empowering systems*. The first group focuses mainly on the *programming mechanics*. To deal with the problems of this sort, the following techniques are applied: (1) simplifying the programming language to be learned, (2) applying the language to the specific domain problems, (3) introducing automatic syntax error detection and eliminating, (4) using graphical objects to construct programs, (5) applying a means to support program's structuring and (6) using facilities to observe the program's running process. Typically, the teaching process is supported through the networked interaction.

The second group of facilities and tools have more capabilities in constructing and realizing programs. The main attributes of these systems are as follows: (1) support of the programming style, (2) representation of the code, (3) construction of programs, (4) support to understand programs, (5) preventing syntax errors, (6) designing accessible languages and (7) communication support.

The paper [GM07] provides the main characteristics of environments and tools that have the essential effect on learning and teaching. They are as follows: (1) identification of the learner's previous knowledge and indicating on the adequate learning style, (2) use of programming models, (3) introduction of elements of gaming and (4) use of facilities to create algorithms. Dillon et al. [DAB12] categorize the systems to teach programming according to their *assistive level* taken to the learner. There are the *low assistive*, *moderately assistive* and *highly assistive* systems. In the first case, the learner writes the textual code and uses independent compilation, processors and text editors. The debugging of the program is manual. In the second case, there are additional facilities such as *syntax highlighting*, *error highlighting, autocompletion* and *integrative debugging*. In the third case, there are already *means of visualization*.

The learning and teaching tools also follow the main technological trend such as *mobility*. Therefore, there are systems enabling learning and teaching programming with the use of mobile devices [MP10, TMH+12]. The program visualization and game-based learning of programming are specific topics which are not considered here. Note that the program visualization tools are discussed in [SFP+12]. The reader of this paper, for example, can learn more on the taxonomy of such tools and systems.

Finally, one kind of tools should be mentioned with particular respect and attention. We have in mind the authoring tools *GLOMaker*. The system has been developed to support the design of the teaching and learning content based on the original concept of GLO proposed by Boyle, Leeder and Morales et al. [LBC04], the pioneers of the concept. The tool has been built using the template-based generative technology. Though the GLOMaker is not specifically dedicated to teaching CS, it has played and continues to play a significant role in the formation and consolidation of the new direction in LO research. We have accepted this new concept and connected it with the meta-programming-based approach to develop a new kind of GLOs, more suitable to teach CS topics. Further, our research on the meta-programming-based GLOs has paved the way to the arrival of smart LOs – the main topic of this monograph.

Group B As we use the model-driven approach in designing SLO, we focus more on processes to transform models and code. Furthermore, as the tool design is not so much related to the teaching process itself, we need to focus more on research in relative domains, i.e. CS and SWE.

It is commonly agreed that the analysis and manipulation of a program source code are regarded as one of the most important computing aspects [Har10]. At present, however, there is an evident shift from the *program code* transformation towards the *program model* transformation, i.e. computational models are to be considered at a higher level of abstraction [BMR11]. The reasons for that are at least two: the ever-increasing *software content* within modern IT-based systems and the *continuous growth of complexity* of both programs and systems [Men12]. As a response to the complexity challenges, model-driven approaches have been proposed and widely researched in recent years. Among those approaches, feature-based modelling prevails now with the focus on software product line (SPL) engineering (also known as software families) to a larger extent enabling reuse and automation [CBK13].

The basic idea is first to determine the features that are domain abstractions relevant to stakeholders and, then, to devise feature models to support modelling and high-level transformations. In Chap. 10, we have adopted feature-based modelling to build the tools for the semi-automatic development of heterogeneous meta-programs. They are, in fact, domain program generators [ŠD13]. Though they cannot be created in any case and for any domain, their role is growing continuously. The ability to design program generators should be directly connected with a domain variability modelling and managing. As variability modelling is the main focus now [CBK13], the meta-programming-based approaches follow the same trend too.

A great deal of the reviewed papers considers the *feature* concept as the basis for feature-oriented modelling. There is no unified definition of the term feature [AK09]. Slightly different definitions, in fact, mean *universality* of the approach. As a result, the intensive research and developments around formal semantics, reasoning techniques and tool support make feature models (FMs) a de facto standard to model and manage variability now [AK09, CL13, SHT06, CW07, TBK09]. Furthermore, the OMG standard for variability modelling [OMG13], the common variability language, is also based on FMs [CVL14]. Acher et al. [AHC +13] present a comprehensive, tool-supported process for the reverse engineering architectural FMs to extract and combine different variability descriptions of the architecture along with alignment and reasoning techniques to integrate the architect knowledge. The paper [ACL+13] proposes a DSL FAMILIAR (*Fe*Ature *M*odel script Language for man*I*pulation and *A*utomatic *R*easoning) that is dedicated to the management and manipulations of FMs to realize a non-trivial scenario in which multiple SPLs are managed.

Mendonca et al. [MBC09] introduce SPLOT, a Web-based reasoning and configuration system for SPLs. The system benefits from mature logic-based reasoning techniques such as SAT solvers and binary decision diagrams to provide efficient reasoning and interactive configuration services to SPL researchers and practitioners. Abbasi et al. [AHH11] address the issues of complex FM configuration processes, enabling to extend a feature-based configurator with multi-view support and by integrating it with a workflow management tool.

Meta-programming (MPG) is a higher-level programming paradigm which deals on how to manipulate programs as data. The result of the manipulation is the lower-level programs. There are many different views to understand and study this approach. For example, meta-programming can be viewed as a technology to implement the domain variability given by feature models (for details, see [ŠD13]). According to Veldhuizen [Vel06], MPG can be seen as a program generalization and generation technique. The MPG taxonomies [ŠD13, Pas04, She01] provide a systemized knowledge on the topic. In large, the MPG is the domain to research model transformations too. Mens et al. [MCG06] state in this regard that the term 'model transformation' encompasses the term 'program transformation' since a model can range from the abstract analysis models, over more concrete design models, to very concrete models of the source code. Visser [Vis05] presents a taxonomy that considers two major groups of transformations: translation and rephrasing. Winter [Win04] identifies seven major bidirectional goals of program transformation: clarity, efficiency, computability, simplicity, functionality, translation and computation. Cordy and Sarkar [CS04] demonstrate that meta-programs can be derived from higher-level specifications using second-order source transformations. Trujillo et al. [TAD07] describe ideas to generate meta-programs from abstract specifications of synthesis paths. Finally, Batory [Bat06] formulates fundamental ideas and vision to connect the following fields: multilevel models in

MDE, product lines and MPG. Guerra et al. [GLW+13] propose a declarative language for the specification of visual contracts, enabling the verification of transformations defined with any transformation language.

With respect to refactoring transformations, a specific interest should be taken to multistage programming and multistage meta-programming. One can learn more about that from [Tah99, Tah04, TBD06, ŠD13].

Though we have analysed only the small part of the available sources on the transformation processes and tools, we hope that the presented ideas create a pretty good context to discuss the topics in the remaining sections.

10.3   Process-Based Framework of the Design Tools

First, we present a framework that gives the general understanding of the proposed approach for developing SLO design tools. Here, we focus on describing the structural and functioning aspects of the series of tools (selected and newly developed) along with the processes the tools support. Later we present more details (such as functioning algorithm) on how to develop the tools to design SLOs. Note that the material of Chaps. 4 and 9 stands for the theoretical basis of the framework.

To understand the structural and functioning aspects, it is convenient to apply the process-based view. Therefore, the framework includes a series of transformative processes with possible feedbacks as it is presented in Fig. 10.1. Processes are driven either by the external data to be supplied by the user or the internal data created by the processes themselves. Data are also the source to create models as it will be discussed in detail later. As there are different models, the processes differ also.

We consider two kinds of processes: *general* and *task-specific* ones. General processes include the specification and verification of the developed feature models. Task-specific processes include model transformation to produce meta-programs (i.e. SLOs) and generation of target program instances (i.e. LOs). The processes are to be supported by the adequate tools. As it is not an easy task to develop new tools, designers and researchers typically prefer to use the well-proven existing tools in the first place. However, such a selection is not always possible either due to the task specificity or due to the unsatisfactory characteristics and functionality of the existing tools. Very often, the solution is in the middle as it is in our case. To support more general processes, we use the known and proven tools, whereas to support the task-specific processes, we have developed new tools.

The selection of tools highly depends on the processes and models used. As we use feature models to model our tasks, we have selected the freely available feature-oriented tools FAMILIAR [ACL+13] and SPLOT [MBC09]. The first supports the specification and modelling of feature models. In terms of model transformations, the FAMILIAR tools enable to perform two types of model-to-model (M2M) transformations: (1) transformation lowering the abstraction level and (2) transformation preserving approximately the same abstraction level. The FAMILIAR tool's

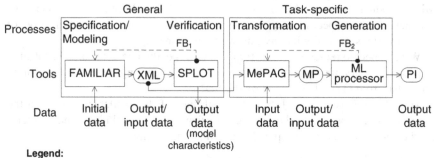

Fig. 10.1 Process-based framework to understand SLO (LO) creation

editor supports the first transformation that, in fact, is the specification process, in which the input model is described by the informal requirements of a domain task and the output model is represented formally by feature diagrams. The FAMILIAR modelling facilities support the modelling process in which we are able to perform some needed manipulations (e.g. feature aggregation, merging, etc.) on input models that were created through the specification process (see Chap. 5). Manipulations do not change the abstraction level the models are presented.

The important property of the used tools is that the specification yields the graphical representation of the output model(s), whereas the modelling processes use the textual language and yield the textual representation of the output model (s) in the XML format (in fact SXML- an alternative syntax for writting XML data). As both tools (FAMILIAR and SPLOT) are compatible (i.e. they use the same textual representation of feature models), we are able to use the straightforward connection of the tools (see Fig. 10.1). We use SPLOT tools for the verification in creating models. Furthermore, the SPLOT tools possess facilities to provide modelling metrics. The latter is regarded as very helpful information to reason about the models' properties and correctness.

Now we put some ideas on the task-specific processes. There are also two processes (see right part of Fig. 10.1): *transformation* and *generation*. The tool MePAG (*Me*ta-Program Automatic Generator) supports the *model*-to-*meta-program* transformation (shortly M2MP). This kind of transformation lowers the abstraction level. The transformation process uses the semiformal model, because not all input data used we are able to present formally. The reason is that we use the heterogeneous meta-programming (MPG) paradigm [ŠD13], in which the metalanguage (ML) and the target language (TL) are both abstract (not formal). Furthermore, not always it is possible (or reasonable) to synthesize a meta-program (MP) fully automatically.

A standard ML-processor (e.g. PHP-processor in our case, though other languages such as C++ and Java can be used in the role of an ML (see, e.g. [ŠD03])) serves as a generating tool to provide the experimental validation of the synthesized MP. This process may be multicycle with a possible feedback. This may happen due to some semantic or syntactic inconsistency introduced by the designer, when such an interleaving is needed. The technique enables to develop a higher-level executable specification (i.e. meta-program) from which the target program instances are generated on demand automatically at the use phase.

10.3.1 The Extended Process-Based Description

The tool MePAG implements the model-driven approach in designing meta-programs (i.e. SLOs). At the core of the approach are models and model transformation processes. In Fig. 10.2, we present the *model-process relationship* the tool implements. This relationship can be also seen as architecture, because processes are created by the adequate components. The tool enables to realize two functional modes: *automatic* (Fig. 10.2a) and *semi-automatic* (Fig. 10.2b). The *ASM engine* is the central component that performs the transformation processes (ASM stands for abstract state machine).

The tool synthesizes heterogeneous meta-programs from two *input feature models* and supplementary data, such as constructs of the meta-language (ML) and the target language generic instance (TLGI). Two feature models, namely, FM_P and $TLGI_P$ (see Fig. 10.2a), represent the *problem domain* (PD), whereas the other feature models, namely, FM_S and ML functions or MLF_S (see Fig. 10.2a), represent the *solution domain* (SD). Thus, we formulate our task formally as mapping the problem domain onto the solution domain: $PD \rightarrow SD$ (see also Eq. (9.5) in Sect. 9.4.6). Both feature models are correct because they have passed through the formal verification (see Fig. 10.1). Here, the model FM_S should be conceived as a *meta-program structural model*. The model consists of the interface and meta-body models that do not contain linguistic features. Those are being delivered by the models MLF_S and $TLGI_P$. Two additional properties of the input models are important to state: (1) it is possible to create $TLGI_P$ easily (for not complex tasks) and (2) there are difficulties in creating $TLGI_P$ for the real-world tasks since the efforts of developing the model $TLGI_P$ are roughly the same as manual coding of the meta-body. We present the model later along with the full implementation of the running example that was constructed using the tool.

Typically, the first mode means that we are able to develop the relatively simple meta-programs (i.e. SLO) automatically. The second mode is more general and specifies the real-world tasks for which we are not always able to develop MPs automatically, or such a case is merely unreasonable due to the complexity issues as defined previously. We depict this situation graphically in Fig. 10.2a.

There is some difference among the models FM_P and FM_S in terms of their mode of use. The first model is created *anew* for each new problem task to be solved, whereas the second model is common for all domain tasks considered in the given context. Because of this property, we are able to represent the model FM_S within the transformation engine as a *fixed data structure* while the model FM_P should be always supplied to the engine as the external input model (see Fig. 10.2a, b).

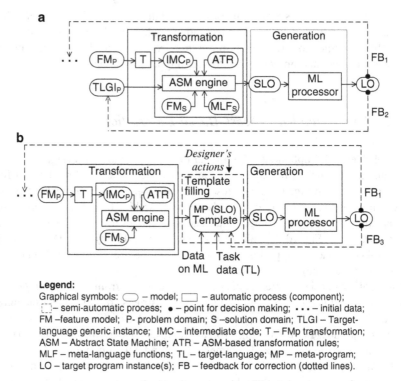

Legend:
Graphical symbols: ◯ – model; ▢ – automatic process (component);
⬚ – semi-automatic process; ● – point for decision making; ••• – initial data;
FM –feature model; P- problem domain; S –solution domain; TLGI – Target-
language generic instance; IMC – intermediate code; T – FMp transformation;
ASM – Abstract State Machine; ATR – ASM-based transformation rules;
MLF – meta-language functions; TL – target-language; MP – meta-program;
LO – target program instance(s); FB – feedback for correction (dotted lines).

Fig. 10.2 Two modes of MePAG functioning: (**a**) automatic; (**b**) semi-automatic MP synthesis

Yet another fact is important to highlight here. The format of the internal representation of models within the MePAG might be compatible with the internal/external format of FAMILIAR (SPLOT) or not. As the latter format has yet not been standardized, here we have accepted that those formats are incompatible; thus the additional transformation (T) is needed. This transformation results in transforming the format of FM_P into the intermediate model code (IMC_P) of the problem domain.

The remaining components of the transformation engine are the abstract state machine (ASM) engine and ASM-based transformation rules (ATR). We present more details on that as well on some meta-programming-based and feature model aspects in Sect. 10.3.3. In the next section, we provide more details on LO generation process.

10.3.2 LO Generation Process from SLO

As it is depicted in Fig. 10.2, the designer goes through the generation processes to validate the SLO to be designed. When the design is complete, the correct SLO

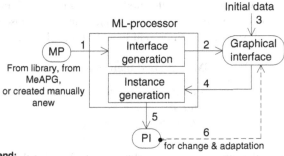

Legend:
MP – meta-program; ML – meta-language; PI – target program instance(s); paths:
1-2-3-4-5 – typical, without change; 1-2-3-4-5-6-3-4-5-6... – with possible changes.

Fig. 10.3 Functional model (user's perspective): instance generation paths

serves as the input data to produce LO on demand automatically. In Fig. 10.3, we explain the generation process from the user's perspective. The user, by reading the graphical interface and introducing initial data, is able to specify what LO features are most relevant to his/her context. The generation process is similar to the one the SLO designer provides; however, the aims of the process and actions to be performed are quite different. If the designer, in fact, is able to make any changes within the internal structure of SLO, the user cannot provide the changes. He/she is able to manage the different paths in creating LOs only.

From the user's perspective, there are seen two subprocesses (see Fig. 10.3): (1) interface generation and (2) instance generation. The meta-language processor reads the textual MP (SLO) interface and transforms it into the user-friendly graphical representation. Next, the user's actions follow, i.e. the user selects (from the graphical boxes) the parameter values needed. After that, the instance generation follows. The typical generation path is 1-2-3-4-5. If there is the need to change parameter values, the feedback follows and the new path follows to create a more relevant LO.

10.3.3   ASM-Based Transformation Rules

As it was stated previously, two key formalisms (i.e. feature models of the problem domain and feature models of the solution domain) form the background of the developed tools. But we need to use yet another formal model in order to combine the first two models into the coherent structure. This action has been identified as the mapping of the problem domain onto the solution domain (see Sect. 9.4.5 in Chap. 9). Therefore, the mapping procedure requires of using some computational model. We have selected the *abstract state machine* (ASM) as the computational model to specify the behaviour and functionality of our tool. Though there are many slightly different interpretations of this computational model (e.g. in mathematics and especially in CS), we have adapted the model viewing it as *FSM* (interpretation in CS as the most suitable in our case). Following the notation proposed in [Bör99] and extending it for all states, we can present the ASM model as follows:

$$\underset{i,\,j(i\neq j)}{\forall}\Big(\mathbf{FSM}(i,\ \mathbf{if}\ cond\ \mathbf{then}\ rule,\ j)\ =$$
$$\mathbf{if}\ ctl\_state = i\ \mathbf{and}\ cond\ \mathbf{then} \tag{10.1}$$
$$rule$$
$$ctl\_state := j\Big),$$

where i is the current state, j is the next state, $i, j \in \Sigma$ is a set of all possible deterministic states, *ctl_state* is the variable to denote a control state, *cond* is a set of conditions affecting the rule selection and *rule* is the *transformation rule* used at the current stage to produce an adequate element of the meta-program.

To implement this computation model, we need to use the full list of transformation rules. Note that the model and the transformation rules are also presented in [ŠBB14]. ©2014 IEEE. *Reprinted, with permission, from* [ŠBB14].

Note that there are some methodological issues: we need to repeat the same examples given before for clearness. Below we present the set of transformation rules to define ASM.

Rule 1 *Variant point* in the feature model FM_P (see Fig. 10.4) corresponds (is equal) to a *parameter name* in the feature model FM_S (see Fig. 10.5b).

Rule 2 *Variants* of a variant point within the feature model FM_P correspond (are equal) to parameter values in the feature model FM_S (see Fig. 10.5a).

Property 2 The *priority* feature within the model FM_P plays the specific role to define the priorities to sequencing parameters in designing the MP interface. The constraints *'requires'* indicate the correspondence among the variant points and priority values (see feature *pf* in Fig. 10.4 and also *Rule 1*).

Rule 3 The format of a *simple assignment statement* within the interface of the meta-program is as follows:

<parameter>=<parameter_value_set>;

Rule 4 The format of a *conditional assignment statement* within the interface is as follows:

<parameter1>   <condition>   <parameter2>   <parameter1>   =
   <parameter_value_set>;

The conditional assignment statement appears if and only if the adequate variant point has constraints *requires* or *excludes*.

Note that the assignment statements can be also substituted by *input statements* of the selected meta-language. The full list of meta-language constructs (i.e. PHP) to realize the task is defined by the feature *'ML constructs'* (see Fig. 10.5b).

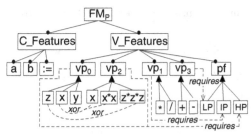

Legend: C –commonality V- variability, vp –variant point, pf –priority feature; LP – low priority; IP – intermediate priority; HP – high priority; xor – the constraint '*excludes*'

Fig. 10.4 Feature model of the problem domain task $y:=a*x+b$ (see Table 9.1 in Sect. 9.3)

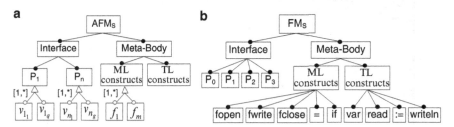

Fig. 10.5 Solution domain models: (**a**) abstract feature model (AFM) and (**b**) concrete feature model as applied to the given task

The used target language constructs (in our case Pascal is used as a TL) are defined by the feature '*TL constructs*' (see Fig. 10.5b).

Rule 5 The number of parameters extracted from the model *FM*s is equal to the number of variation points extracted from the model *FM*$_P$ to be transferred to the engine to form the interface according to Rule 3 or Rule 4.

Rule 6 The ASM engine orders parameters (identified by Rules 1, 2 and 5) according to their priorities (note that the priority feature is represented as a parameter weight but not as the parameter itself; see Rule 1).

Rule 7 The ASM engine presents the values of the priority parameters as a comment (/* ..*/) before each simple assignment statement (see lines 3–5 in Fig. 10.6).

Rule 8 The ASM engine builds the MP interface according to Rules 1–7 (see lines 2–53 in Fig. 10.6).

Rule 9 To form the meta-body, the following set of functions of the meta-language is used: {Operation (assignment ('='), OPEN-WRITE-CLOSE), conditional, loops} (see Definition 9.5, Chap. 9).

Meta-program of the task y:=a*x + b to implement variability

```
1   <?
2   //-------------------(Meta-)interface---------------------
3   $p0=$_POST[p0]; //HP - High Priority: context of using p0
4   $p2=$_POST[p2]; //HP - context of using p2
5   $p1=$_POST[p1];//IP - Intermediate Priority: context of using p1
6   $p3=$_POST[p3]; //LP - Low Priority: context of using p3
7   if (!isset($p0) && !isset($p2) && !isset($p1) && !isset($p3)) {
8   ?>
9   <FORM METHOD = POST ACTION = "">
10  Select parameter $p0 value:
11  <select name="p0">
12  <option value="x"> x </option>
13  <option value="y"> y </option>
14  <option value="z"> z </option>
15  </select> <br>
16  <INPUT TYPE = submit VALUE ="Submit" NAME = "submit" style="height:
17  28px">
18  </FORM>
19  <?
20  }
21  if (isset($p0) && !isset($p2) && !isset($p1) && !isset($p3)) {
22  ?>
23  <FORM METHOD = POST ACTION = "">
24  Select parameter $p2 value:
25  <select name="p2">
26  <? if("$p0"=="x"){ ?>
27  <option value="z*z*z"> z*z*z </option>
28  <? } if("$p0"=="y"){ ?>
29  <option value="x"> x </option>
30  <option value="x*x"> x*x </option>
31  <option value="z*z*z"> z*z*z </option>
32  <? } if("$p0"=="z"){ ?>
33  <option value="x"> x </option>
34  <option value="x*x"> x*x </option>
35  <? } ?>
36  </select> <br><br>
37  Select parameter $p1 value:
38  <select name="p1">
39  <option value="*"> * </option>
40  <option value="/"> / </option>
41  </select> <br><br>
42  Select parameter $p3 value:
43  <select name="p3">
44  <option value="+"> + </option>
45  <option value="-"> - </option>
46  </select> <br><br>
47  <INPUT TYPE="hidden" name="p0" value="<?php echo $_POST[p0];?>">
48  <INPUT TYPE = submit VALUE ="Submit" NAME = "submit" style="height:
49  28px">
50  </FORM>
51  <?
52  }
53  if (isset($p0) && isset($p2) && isset($p1) && isset($p3)){
54  //---------------------Meta-body----------------------
55  $myFile = "result.pas";
56  $fr = fopen($myFile, 'w');
57  fwrite($fr, "program Function; \n");
58  if($p0==x or $p0==z ){
59    fwrite($fr, "var x, z, a, b : integer; \n");
60  }else if($p2=='z*z*z'){
61    fwrite($fr, "var y, z, a, b : integer; \n");
62  }else if($p2!= 'z*z*z') {
63    fwrite($fr, "var x, y, a, b : integer; \n"); }
64  fwrite($fr, "begin \n");
65  if($p2=='z*z*z'){
66    fwrite($fr, "read(z, a, b); \n");
67  }else if($p2!= 'z*z*z'){
68    fwrite($fr, "read(x, a, b); \n");}
69  fwrite($fr, "$p0:= a $p1 $p2 $p3 b; \n");
70  fwrite($fr, "writeln ($p0); \n");
71  fwrite($fr, "end. \n");
72  fclose($fr);
73  echo" <br> <a href=\"result.pas\">Program
74  file</a></span></span></strong><br>";
75  }?>
76  //--------------------END---------------------------
```

Fig. 10.6 Full specification of SLO in PHP and Pascal

Rule 10 Target language generic instance ($TLGI_P$, if any) should be always written by the designer with the clear specification of the location, where parameters have to appear (see Fig. 10.7).

Rule 11 In the case of the $TLGI_P$ presence, the ASM engine performs parsing, i.e. syntactic analysis of the item, and builds the meta-body automatically (see Figs. 10.2a, 10.7).

Rule 12 If there is no $TLGI_P$, ASM provides the meta-body template for its filling in by the designer (see Fig. 10.2b).

Now, having the transformation rules, we are able to present the algorithm of the tool MePAG.

10.3.4 ASM-Based Functioning Algorithm of the Tool MePAG

The following algorithm determines the tools implementation on the ASM basis. Note that the ASM states are modelled by steps as it is described below.

Algorithm ©2014 IEEE. *Reprinted, with permission, from* [ŠBB14]

Step 1. **if** <IMC_p exists> **then** Read data; /* *Rule 5; value of n ($n \geq 1$) is defined* */

Step 2. **if** n >1 **then** Sort parameters according to their priorities; /
**Rule 6* */

Step 3. Create the MP file /*MP.php*/ to store MP's statements;

Step 4. Write a comment to denote the beginning of the interface; /* *for template filling in*/

Step 5. **for** $i = 1$ to n **do**

    Read data for the parameter i; /*Rule 1 & Rule 2*/

    if <parameter independence exists> **then** Create the parameter value selection form; /* *Rule 3 & Rule 7*/

    else Create the parameter value selection form with the conditional branching; /* *Rule 4 & Rule 7*/

  end;

Step 6. Create a comment to denote the beginning of the meta-body; /* *for template filling in*/

Step 7. **if** <$TLGI_p$ not exists> **then do** Create comments for the user; Create the MP completion statements; **end do;** /*Rule 12 */

    else do Read the $TLGI_p$ and make the parser's initialization; /*Rule 10; value of m ($m >1$) is defined* */

        for $i = 1$ to m **do**

        Perform parsing the line i within $TLGI_p$;

```
    Find the parameter locations in the line and create parameter
    variables; /*Rule 11*/Create the meta-body line; /*Rule 9*/
  end;
    Create the MP completion statements;
  end do;
Step 8. end.
```

10.4   An Example of Meta-Program Constructed Using the Tool MePAG

We present the same example (task) as it was given in Sect. 6.3.5 (see Fig. 6.6, in Chap. 6). Here, the tasks has been solved not manually but using the tool to design meta-programs. We use the term *meta-program* (instead of SLO) because (1) there are no pedagogy-based features and (2) the tool is not oriented for the e-learning domain only: it enables to construct meta-programs for any other domain in which PHP is used as a meta-language. We present the example in Fig. 10.6. It was developed using the tool MePAG in the automatic mode. For doing so, the target language generic instant ($TLGI_P$, see Fig. 10.2a) has to be constructed first. It always is constructed manually (see Fig. 10.7). We present the graphical interface of the task along with the derived LO (i.e. the program in Pascal which was used as a target language) in Fig. 10.8.

As it was already highlighted in Sect. 10.3.1, there are some issues with the model $TLGI_P$. The first is the manual effort needed. The second is the representation language. It should be a simple descriptive language that fits for both the internal (i.e. system) and the external (i.e. designer) representation. For this purpose, we have adapted the Pascal-like language. The language contains only conditional and loop operators specified as follows:

```
@ if <condition> then begin
<TL constructs>
@ end

@ for <variable name> = <initial value> to <end value> div <step>
do begin
<TL constructs>
@ end
```

Figure 10.7 presents the model, which is described using the language. By comparing this model with the meta-body specification (see lines 58–71 in Fig. 10.6), it is easy to conclude that both are of a similar complexity. In other words, the efforts of manual coding of the meta-body (in semi-automatic design

Fig. 10.7 TLGI_P model to
support automatic SLO
design of the task (*legend*:
@ – the mark to denote the
beginning of a meta-
language construct; var_ –
the placeholder for a
parameter)

```
@ if var_p0 = x || var_p0 = z then begin
var x, z, a, b : integer;
@ end
@ else if var_p2 = 'z*z*z' then begin
var y, z, a, b : integer;
@ end
@ else if var_p2 != 'z*z*z' then begin
var x, y, a, b : integer;
@ end
begin
@ if var_p2 = 'z*z*z' then begin
read(z, a, b);
@ end
@ if var_p2 != 'z*z*z' then begin
read(x, a, b);
@ end
var_p0:= a var_p1 var_p2 var_p3 b;
writeln (var_p0);
```

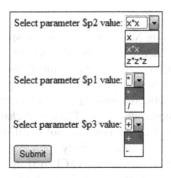

a

```
Select parameter $p0 value:  y  ▼
  Submit                       x
                               y
                               z
```

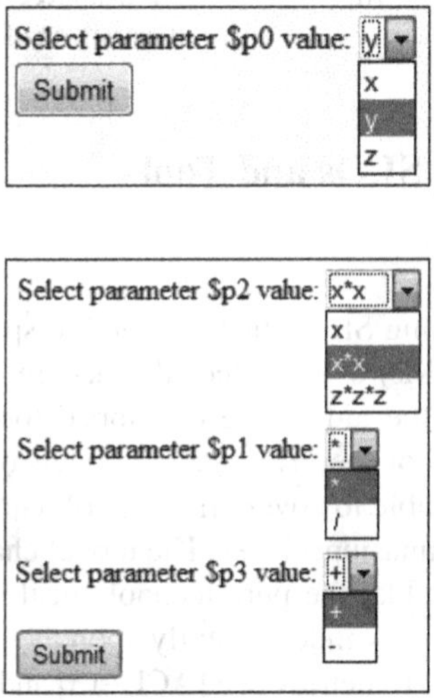

b

Instance:
```
program Function;
var x, y, a, b : integer;
begin
read(x, a, b);
y:= a * x*x + b;
writeln (y);
end.
```

```
Select parameter $p2 value:  x*x   ▼
                             x
                             x*x
                             z*z*z
Select parameter $p1 value:  *   ▼
                             *
                             /
Select parameter $p3 value:  +   ▼
                             +
  Submit                     -
```

Fig. 10.8 SLO interface (**a**) and LO instance in Pascal (**b**) derived from the SLO specification

mode) are roughly the same as to develop the TLGI_P model. It is so, because the
TLGI_P model is, in fact, the meta-program.

10.5   Main Characteristics of the Tool

In Table 10.1, we summarize the main characteristics of the developed tool.

Table 10.1 Main functional characteristics of the tool MePAG

#	Characteristics	Value	Relationships	Evaluation metrics
1	Status	Experimental	All	Low maturity
2	Design languages and OS	PHP, HTML Windows	3–7	Conventional, widely approved
3	Design approach	Model driven	4–8	# of processes and tools
4	Input models and data	Domain variability, target language-based scenarios	2, 3	Complexity
5	Output data	MP and MP template	2–4, 6–7	Complexity measures [ŠD13]
6	Theoretical background	Feature models, MP- models, meta-programming	2–5	Conciseness, precision, consistency
7	User interfaces	User-friendly	2, 4	Intuitiveness, readability
8	Other tools used	FAMILIAR, SPLOT Dream viewer	3	# of supplied characteristics
9	Functionality	Transformation on the basis of the ASM computational model	All	Expressed by the stated requirements
10	Use modes	Semi-automatic, automatic	All	For real tasks, for illustrative tasks

10.6   Experimental Validation of the SLOs and Tool MePAG

As we use the model-driven approach in designing SLOs, first we need to specify tasks at the model level. The feature models (FMs) of the selected tasks are input data to design SLOs either manually or with the aid of the developed tool. In Table 10.2, we present the main *characteristics* of the investigated models of the real tasks. Real tasks were selected so that to enable to cover all topics of teaching CS (programming) at the secondary school (gymnasium) level. The model characteristics obtained using the adequate tools look like the pure technological ones, because all features of SLOs are expressed uniformly independently upon their role and meaning. For details on the feature model (FM) metrics, see [ACL+13] and also Chap. 4. Note also that those FMs are concrete models derived from the abstract subdomain models (see Tables 4.3 and 4.4 in Chap. 4) and aggregated with the content models of tasks.

Next, we present *a methodology* of the provided experiments and results obtained applying the manual development and using the developed tool. We carried out experiments with the real tasks to investigate both SLO and the tool. The used methodology includes the following activities:

(i)   Identification of actors involved in the experiments provided
(ii) Identification of the aim and scope of experiments
(iii) Formulation of activities and methodology for the manual development

Table 10.2 Characteristics of problem domain FMs obtained using FAMILIAR and SPLOT

Task	Robot calibration	Line follower	Ornament design	Scrolling text on LCD	Light follower	Traffic light
Model metrics	1	2	3	4	5	6
# of features	38	44	51	27	41	44
# of mandatory features	11	10	15	7	10	12
# of core features	15	14	20	8	11	14
# of XOR groups	8	8	11	5	7	8
# of OR groups	1	1	2	2	1	2
# of cross-tree constraints	18	12	21	12	7	14
CTCR, %	0.53	0.57	0.43	0.63	0.24	0.39
Tree depth	3	3	3	3	3	5
Valid configurations	1,296	8,640	62,208	1,440	87,480	97,200
Variability degree, %	4.7148	4.9113	2.7626	1.0729	3.9781	5.5252
	E-7	E-8	E-9	E-3	E-6	E-7

©2014 IEEE. Reprinted, with permission, from [ŠBB14]

Table 10.3 Characteristics of actors being involved in the experiments

# of designer	Domain knowledge (domain expertise)	Programming experience in years	MPG experience in years	Initial robot CP created by	IMC created by	TLGI and MePAG created by	Experimentation	
							Manual	Using MePAG
1	Yes	20	5	Yes	Yes	No	Yes	Yes
2	No	18	4	No	Yes	Yes	Yes	Yes
3	No	5	No	No	No	No	No	Yes

Legend: *CP* control program, *IMC* intermediate code that represents problem domain FM after transformation (see Fig. 10.2 a), *TLGI* target language (i.e. RobotC, the teaching language) generic instant (see Fig. 10.2a), *MePAG Meta-Program* (i.e. SLO) *Automatic Generator*

(iv) Creation of instructions for using the tool MePAG in the SLO development
(v) Collection, analysis and evaluation of the outcomes

First we characterize the actors being involved in the experiments (see Table 10.3). Three designers carried out the experiments. One of them is characterized as a *domain expert* in robot-based programming and CS teaching. Her experience was about 20 years in teaching programming and about 5 years in robot-based programming and meta-programming. The other two experimenters were the experienced and inexperienced programmers. The activities provided by the actors are also outlined in Table 10.3.

Note also that TLGI, in fact, is a generalization of the initial robot control program (CP) written in RobotC to specify the learning content variability.

Next, we outline the aim, scope, modes and some results of experiments provided (see Table 10.4). The aim was twofold: to test the correctness of SLOs and to test the correct functionality of the tool MePAG through solving real-world tasks (i.e. SLOs used in the real setting to teach CS topics). Furthermore, from the scientific point of view, it was very interesting to obtain the experimental data to compare the efforts needed in the manual, semi-automatic and automatic SLO design activities.

Though it was enough to consider six tasks (6 SLO) in order to cover the whole CS curriculum (secondary/gymnasium level), the scope of experiments was about 45 slightly different SLO versions created and tested only during the years 2013–2014. In Table 10.4, we also present the size of the latest SLO versions for all tasks (separately for interface (I) and meta-body (MB)). The size of a program or meta-program (i.e. SLO), which is typically measured by code lines or KB, is the practical metric to evaluate the complexity. However, the internal complexity of meta-programs has more accurate metrics. We will return to the complexity issues later to discuss the technological and pedagogical (cognitive) complexity in Chap. 12 in more detail.

As the intermediate code (ITC) and target language generic instance (TLGI) play a significant role for implementing the design automation (see Fig. 10.2a), we also provide the size (see Table 10.5) and efforts needed to develop those items (see Table 10.6).

In Table 10.6, we have provided the *average efforts* expressed by the time dimension. The actual meaning of the term 'average' should be interpreted with respect to the designers' activities indicated in Table 10.3. For example, the average efforts for creating TLGI should be interpreted as the evaluation of some trials needed by the same designer to develop the model for the same task. Therefore, we found the necessity to split the efforts into three parts: (1) those needed for input models (IMC and TLGI), (2) those needed for the pure manual development and (3) those needed to design SLOs using the tool. Note that the input models are part of the tool itself (IMS is used in both modes of the tool; TLGI is used in the automatic mode only). Note that the manual development of SLOs was provided under the following conditions: (1) there was used the *consistent feature models* prepared in advance; (2) there was used the SLO evolutionary design methodology

Table 10.4 Size of SLOs of the *latest version* developed manually and using MePAG

Task	SLO attributes				
	# of versions created manually by two designers	Interface (I) created manually (LOC/KB)	Meta-body (MB) created manually (LOC/KB)	Interface (I) generated by MePAG (LOC/KB)	Meta-body (MB) generated by MePAG (LOC/KB)
Robot calibration	5 + 2	190/7.74	69/2.68	194/8.11	71/2.69
Line follower	6 + 4	279/12.8	138/4.81	287/13	144/4.94
Ornament design	11 + 2	328/14.5	131/5.5	336/14.8	134/5.5
Scrolling text on LCD	4 + 1	125/5.19	74/2.86	125/5.32	76/2.87
Light follower	4 + 1	176/7.54	109/2.89	176/7.71	112/2.91
Traffic light	4 + 1	221/9.98	91/3.33	221/10.2	93/3.34
Scope of tool testing (total SLO)	45				

Legend: *LOC* lines of code in PHP; the tool MePAG is available to test from the Website (see [BBŠ14])

Table 10.5 Size of IMC and TLGI models for *the latest versions* of SLO

Task	SLO attributes	
	IMC (LOC/KB)	TLGI for automatic mode only (LOC/KB)
Robot calibration	14/0.6	62/1
Line follower	19/0.8	137/4.5
Ornament design	21/0.7	128/3.6
Scrolling text on LCD	8/0.3	67/2.3
Light follower	10/0.4	100/2.3
Traffic light	12/0.4	85/2.1

treated as 'SLO redesign with evidence' (see Sect. 6.3.7 in Chap. 6); (3) the only two designers were involved in the manual development with the different intention. The practical intention of the domain expert (she is identified as designer 1 in Table 10.3) was to create the real SLOs for the real use in teaching before the tool design is completed. The practical intention of designer 2 was twofold: to better understand the domain and to better understand the requirements of the tool to be designed. For both the designer 1 and designer 2, there was a great scientific interest to repeat the design process also using the tool.

Table 10.6 Efforts needed to create models (IMC and TLGI) and SLOs (*the latest versions*): the manual development vs. the use of MePAG

Task	SLO attributes		Average efforts needed to create SLO (in minutes)		
	Average efforts needed to create input models (in minutes)		Manually (I + MB)	By MePAG (semi-automatic) (I + MB)	By MePAG (automatic) (I + MB)
	IMC	TLGI			
Robot calibration	6	34	74 (34 + 40)	About (2 + 40)	About 2
Line follower	9	64	112 (43 + 69)	About (2 + 69)	About 2
Ornament design	11	45	125 (71 + 54)	About (2 + 54)	About 2
Scrolling text on LCD	4	20	43 (19 + 24)	About (2 + 24)	About 2
Light follower	5	34	68 (29 + 39)	About (2 + 39)	About 2
Traffic light	7	25	64 (36 + 28)	About (2 + 28)	About 2

Note also that the task specification (i.e. feature models) was developed by the domain experts using also adequate modelling and verification tools. The given effort estimations do not include the efforts needed for the task specification and modelling. Typically the latter efforts highly exceed the efforts needed for the SLO design and coding. On the other hand, however, the task specification feature models are highly reusable items diminishing efforts in redesigning and reusing.

In Table 10.7, we present the needed efforts to design SLO in three modes (manual design, semi-automatic design and automatic design) for the same (latest) version for all selected tasks.

What main conclusion can be made from the provided experiments and outcomes obtained? We are able to summarize the discussed results as follows:

1. The use of the model-driven approach (partially for the manual design and fully in the tool design and design with the tool) as well as the well-defined methodology has ensured the reliability and correct SLO specifications.

2. For all tasks, there was obtained the increase of the SLO size by using the tool as compared to the pure manual SLO design. The increase is about (2–4) %. Furthermore, the increase of the interface size as compared to the size of the meta-body is more notable (see Table 10.4). The increase is due to the human's ability to optimize the code by not duplicating the repeating fragments of the code while the tool lacks of that possibility.

3. With respect to the automation issues and the scientific value, we have obtained the comparative evaluation of the needed efforts in three categories: (i) the semi-automatic development of SLOs is more efficient by 30–46 % as compared to the

Table 10.7 Efforts needed to create models (IMC and TLGI) and SLO of *the latest version* manually vs. the use of MePAG

| Task | Operating mode | | | | | |
| | Total efforts, in minutes | | | Comparison | | |
	Manual (M)	Semi-automatic (S)	Automatic (A)	M vs. S (%)	M vs. A (%)	S vs. A (%)
Robot calibration	74	48	42	35	43	13
Line follower	112	80	75	29	33	6
Ornament design	125	67	58	46	54	13
Scrolling text on LCD	43	30	26	30	40	13
Light follower	68	46	41	32	40	11
Traffic light	64	37	34	42	47	8

pure manual development (see Table 10.7); (ii) the automatic development is more efficient by 33–54 % as compared to the automatic development; (iii) the automatic mode gains vs. the semi-automatic mode is evaluated by 6–13 %.

Note also that the figures in Table 10.7 were estimated under the following condition: the previously developed versions for each task were not used. It is expected that the efficiency of using the tool in the *reuse mode* (for introducing changes and redesigning) should be always higher.

10.7   Summary, Discussion and Conclusion

We have presented the main issues *on how*, using the well-founded background, to develop the experimental tool that supports the SLO design. We have also discussed the main characteristics of the developed and investigated tool. The theoretical background introduced and discussed here consists of the following components: *feature-based models* of both the problem and solution domains and the *FSM-based computation model* to connect the domains on the basis of trans-formation rules. Though we were using the development tool in designing SLO, the tool is not specifically dedicated to this application only. The tool is oriented to the wider use – to develop heterogeneous meta-programs coded in PHP, which could be applied to other domains too. The use of PHP as a meta-language is not a restriction of using the tool in other domains because the target language (it defines the selected domain) can be any. In other words, the tool is not only application domain independent, but it is also meta-language dependent. That was the reason why we were using more frequently the term meta-program rather than SLO throughout Chap. 10.

In fact, we have discussed the outlined topic at two levels of abstraction: fundamental (i.e. model based) and process based. The latter, being based on the first, is oriented to the designer (fully) and user (partially). The approach has been developed using the following well-grounded principles:

(i) *Conceptual analogy* among the software product line approach (where product feature variability and configurability management are the main focuses) and heterogeneous meta-programming (where parameter-driven variability to specify a family of related program instances is the main focus)

(ii) *Explicit separation of concerns* at multiple levels (domains, domain models, features within a model, roles of languages, meta-program structure)

(iii) *Adaptation of the abstract state machine* as a computational model to specify model-to-model (M2M) and model-to-meta-program (M2MP) transformation rules in designing the tools.

The theoretical value of the approach is the lifting of meta-programming to the meta-meta level using feature-based models and the ASM-based computational model. The practical value is the extension of the generative reuse dimension by semi-automatic generation of program generators, i.e. meta-programs (smart LO in our case).

The approach has some limitations too: (1) though the developed tool is independent upon the target language, it is meta-language dependent (in our case the developed tool is specifically targeted to PHP); (2) the maturity level of the approach is low and more extensive research is needed.

Therefore, model-driven transformations by mapping problem domain models onto the solution domain model is a higher-level computational meta-programming. The ASM computational model has been proven as a relevant abstraction at both feature model and meta-program levels. The effectiveness of the approach (tools) has been proven not only through scientific experiments we have carried out but also in the real use (in the robot-based educational settings, where meta-programs are smart learning objects to provide the content for teaching CS topics as it will be discussed in detail later in Chap. 12).

10.8   Research and Exercise Questions

10.1. Define the following terms (model, feature, feature model, model-driven design) on the basis of your current knowledge. Compare yours definitions with the ones taken from the references [ACL+13, CBK13].

10.2. Define the meta-programming terms, analyse the example of the simplified meta-program and then write another simplified meta-programs.

10.3. Clarify the role of the variability concept in model-driven design.

10.4. Learn more on the feature-based model-driven design approaches from the references [ACL+13, CBK13].

10.5. Explain the statement '*At the model level, design is the mapping of the problem domain model onto the solution domain model*'. Illustrate that using a concrete example.

10.6. Learn the transformation rules to support the model mapping.

10.7. What is the computational model in programming? What is the computational model in model transformations? Define abstract state machine (ASM) as a computational model.

10.8. How does the ASM model relate to the algorithm that performs model transformations?

10.9. Define input models needed to construct the SLO (meta-program).

10.10. Learn the structure and functionality of the MePAG tool.

10.11. Use the tool MePAG to create meta-programs of your tasks using the instructions given in [BBŠ14].

References

[ACL+13] Acher M, Collet P, Lahire P, France RB (2013) FAMILIAR: a domain-specific language for large scale management of feature models. Sci Comput Program 78 (6):657–681

[AHC+13] Acher M, Heymans P, Cleve A, Hainaut JL, Baudry B (2013) Support for reverse engineering and maintaining feature models. In: Proceedings of the seventh international workshop on variability modelling of software-intensive systems, p 20

[AHH11] Abbasi EK, Hubaux A, Heymans P (2011) A toolset for feature-based configuration workflows. In: 2011 15th international SPL conference, Jakarta, vol 11, pp 65–69

[AK09] Apelm S, Kastner C (2009) An overview of feature-oriented software development. J Object Technol 8(5):49–84

[Bat06] Batory D (2006) Multilevel models in model-driven engineering, product lines and metaprogramming. IBM Syst J 45(3):527–539

[BBŠ14] Bespalova K, Burbaitė R, Štuikys V (2014) MePAG tools. http://proin.ktu.lt/metaprogram/MePAG/

[BMR11] Basha NMJ, Moiz SA, Rizwanullah M (2011) Model based software development: issues & challenges. Spec Issue Int J Comput Sci Inform II:226–230

[Bör99] Börger E (1999) High level system design and analysis using abstract state machines. In: Applied formal methods – FM-trends 98. Springer, Berlin/Heidelberg, pp 1–43

[CBK13] Capilla R, Bosch J, Kang KC (2013) Systems and software variability management. Springer, Berlin

[CL13] Collet P, Lahire P (2013) Feature modeling and separation of concerns with FAMILIAR. In: Comparing requirements modeling approaches workshop, 2013 international, IEEE, pp 13–18

[CS04] Cordy JR, Sarkar MS (2004) Metaprogram Implementation by second order source transformation. In: Software transformation systems workshop, p 5

[CVL14] Common Variability Language (CVL) standard (2014) www.omgwiki.org/variability/doku.php. Accessed January 2014

[CW07] Czarnecki K, Wasowski A (2007) Feature diagrams and logics: there and back again. In: Software product line conference, SPLC 2007. 11th International, pp 23–34

[DAB12] Dillon E, Anderson M, Brown M (2012) Comparing feature assistance between programming environments and their effect on novice programmers. J Comput Sci Colleg 27(5):69–77

[GLW+13] Guerra E, de Lara J, Wimmer M, Kappel G, Kusel A, Retschitzegger W, Schönböck J, Schwinger W (2013) Automated verification of model transformations based on visual contracts. Autom Softw Eng 20(1):5–46

[GM07]   Gomes A, Mendes AJ (2007) An environment to improve programming education. In: Proceedings of the 2007 international conference on computer systems and technologies, ACM, p 88

[Har10]   Harman M (2010) Why source code analysis and manipulation will always be important. In: Source code analysis and manipulation (SCAM), 10th IEEE working conference on, pp 7–19

[KP05]   Kelleher C, Pausch R (2005) Lowering the barriers to programming: a taxonomy of programming environments and languages for novice programmers. ACM Comput Surv (CSUR) 37(2):83–137

[LBC04]   Leeder D, Boyle T, Chase H (2004) To boldly GLO – towards the next generation of learning objects. Symposium presented at world conference on eLearning in corporate, Government, Healthcare and Higher Education, Washington, DC, November 2004

[MBC09]   Mendonca M, Branco M, Cowan D (2009) SPLOT: software product lines online tools. In: Proceedings of the 24th ACM SIGPLAN conference companion on object oriented programming systems languages and applications, ACM, pp 761–762

[MCG06]   Mens T, Czarnecki K, Van Gorp P (2006) A taxonomy of model transformations. Electronic notes in theoretical computer science, vol 152, pp 125–142

[Men12]   Mens T (2012) On the complexity of software systems. Computer 45(8):79–81

[MP10]   Mahmoud QH, Popowicz P (2010) A mobile application development approach to teaching introductory programming. In: Frontiers in education conference (FIE), 2010 IEEE, IEEE, pp T4F-1

[OMG13]   OMG (2013) Model driven architecture. http://www.omg.org/mda/. Accessed August 2013

[Pas04]   Pasalic E (2004) The role of type equality in meta-programming, Ph.D. thesis, The Evergreen State College

[ŠBB14]   Štuikys V, Bespalova K, Burbaitė R (2014) Feature transformation-based computational model and tools for heterogeneous meta-program design. In: CINTI 2014, Budapest, IEEE, 19 Nov 2014

[ŠD03]   Štuikys V, Damaševičius R (2003) Metaprogramming techniques for designing embedded components for ambient intelligence. In: Ambient intelligence: impact on embedded system design, Springer, pp 229–250

[ŠD13]   Štuikys V, Damaševičius R (2013) Meta-programming and model-driven meta-program development: principles, processes and techniques. Springer

[SFP+12] Stephen M, Franklin W, Patrick O, Peter A, Elizabeth A (2012) Classifying program visualization tools to facilitate informed choices: teaching and learning computer programming. Int J Comput Sci Telecommun 3(2):42–48

[She01]   Sheard T (2001) Accomplishments and research challenges in meta-programming. In: Semantics, applications, and implementation of program generation, pp 2–44

[SHT06]   Schobbens P, Heymans P, Trigaux JC (2006) Feature diagrams: a survey and a formal semantics. In: Requirements engineering, 14th IEEE international conference, pp 139–148

[TAD07]   Trujillo S, Azanza M, Díaz O (2007) Generative metaprogramming. In: Proceedings of the 6th international conference on generative programming and component engineering, pp 105–114

[Tah04]   Taha W (2004) A gentle introduction to multi-stage programming. Domain-specific program generation. Lecture notes in computer science, vol 3016, pp 30–50

[Tah99]   Taha W (1999) Multi-stage programming: its theory and applications. Ph.D. thesis, Oregon Graduate Institute of Science and Technology

[TBD06]   Trujillo S, Batory D, Diaz O (2006) Feature refactoring a multi-representation program into a product line. In: Proceedings of the 5th international conference on generative programming and component engineering, ACM, Portland, Oregon, pp 191–200

[TBK09]   Thum T, Batory D, Kastner C (2009) Reasoning about edits to feature models. In: IEEE 31st international conference on software engineering (ICSE2009), Vancouver, pp 254–264

[TMH+12]   Tillmann N, Moskal M, de Halleux J, Fahndrich M, Bishop J, Samuel A, Xie T (2012) The future of teaching programming is on mobile devices. In: Proceedings of the 17th ACM annual conference on Innovation and technology in computer science education, ACM, pp 156–161

[Vel06]   Veldhuizen TL (2006) Tradeoffs in metaprogramming. In: Proceedings of the 2006 ACM SIGPLAN symposium on partial evaluation and semantics-based program manipulation, pp 150–159

[Vis05]   Visser E (2005) A survey of strategies in rule-based program transformation systems. J Sym Comput 40(1):831–873

[Win04]   Winter VL (2004) Program transformation: what, how and why. In: Wah BW (ed) Wiley encyclopedia of computer science and engineering. Wiley, Hoboken

Chapter 11
Authoring Tools to Specialize and Adapt Smart LOs

11.1 Introduction

The main distinguishing feature of the smart LO approach is the realization of the concept of *producing* and *adapting* the teaching content semi-automatically, or even automatically. The automation never comes for free. On the other hand, the use of the SLO design tool enables us to develop the highly reusable entities. At the development stage, for example, we are able to ensure reusability due to the use of the design paradigm known as *design for reuse* and *design with reuse* (see Chap. 9). In this chapter, design with reuse can be technologically interpreted as the *SLO adaptation problem*. As the designed SLO, in fact, is the context-driven meta-specification implementing a wide scale of learning variability, indeed there is a large space for adaptation. In the pure technological sense, the adaptation is a specific transformation process. In the case of using SLO specification, we are able to carry out adaptation through refactoring or specialization (see the discussion on the term issues in Sect. 7.2).

Refactoring of SLOs, aiming to support the needs for adapting the content to the context of use, is a much more complicated task to the user as compared to the design of SLO itself. This is because of the complexity issues, i.e. due to an extremely low level of the readability and understandability issues in analyzing the meta-program texts. Especially it is true, when the number of stages of adaptation is larger than 2. Therefore, in the course of the provided research activities in the field, we found the necessity to develop the experimental tools to support both processes – the SLO design and refactoring (i.e. specialization for adaptation).

In this chapter, we address tasks related to the development and functioning of the tool, namely MP-ReTool (*Meta-Program Refactoring Tool*). Though the theoretical foundation and conceptual framework to develop the tool has been suggested by the book's author, the practical implementation has been completely provided by my Ph.D. student, Kristina Bespalova. Again, there are my sincere thanks for her nice work.

© Springer International Publishing Switzerland 2015
V. Štuikys, *Smart Learning Objects for Smart Education in Computer Science*,
DOI 10.1007/978-3-319-16913-2_11

Here, we extend the discussion on the adaptation problem (already initiated in Chaps. 7 and 8), however, now from the designer's perspective. The tasks we consider in this chapter are presented in the similar way as that was done so far. First, we provide the literature review aiming to bring the basic knowledge to the reader (and as well as to the designer) to motivate and understand our approach. Next, we provide a more extensive discussion on our context-aware model which, in fact, is the basis of the context-driven adaptation. We also extend the theoretical background of the stage-based refactoring. The latter enables us to formulate the adequate refactoring transformation rules, to apply them within the ASM-based computational model and to realize the model through the rule-based computational algorithm to specify the tool's functionality. Finally, we discuss the architectural aspects, main characteristics, processes within the tool and experiments we carried out with the aid of the tool.

11.2   Literature Review

Here, we have selected two research topics, which, in our view to a larger extent, are relevant to that we will discuss in this chapter. The first topic (further identified as Group A) is the context awareness in teaching in general and learning and teaching in CS in particular. The second topic (further identified as Group B) is the processes and tools that relate to SLO refactoring and specializing. This review is by no means comprehensive. There are a few reasons for that: (1) both topics are wide enough and deserve a separate discussion in another context; (2) we have already started this discussion in Chaps. 7 and 8; and (3) meta-program refactoring is a specific case of the model and program transformations, and the latter has been discussed in Sect. 10.2.

Group A   At the very beginning, the following observation is important to state. *Any entity, any process, any design* and *any system* we want to study or explore have the *base part* and *its context.* The context typically enables us to extract the additional knowledge to better understand the base system. Such a vision can be gained by studying the related literature from different domains (see [BR12, LK10] to name a few). Our topic is not the exclusion from this general rule. Therefore, we start this review from the context-related analysis. The next note is pure methodological: we have already analyzed the context in Chap. 7. To make the reading of this chapter independent on the previous ones, we have included some works already analyzed and added also the others relevant to this topic.

As it was stated previously, there are many attributes to characterize the context. There are also a variety of factors influencing its understanding (e.g. content representation forms, cognitive aspects, structure and model of LO, etc.). Furthermore, a diversity of related terms characterizes the context-related problem in learning: *adaptive learning, personalized learning* [MKS10, BVV+10], *adaptable*

LO, personalized LO [BCW+08], *adaptive granularity* [MJ10], *adaptive learning scenarios* [BS08], *adaptive learning path* [BSS+12], etc.

All above-stated facts require an introduction of a scheme to review the related work in some systematic way. As this research field is indeed very broad, we restrict ourselves presenting the review with our vision and our approach in mind only. First, we focus on context issues as the most influential factor to adaptability. Next, we analyze the adaptability problem from the *external* (i.e. the environment) and *internal* (i.e. the content model) views. Finally, in the next section, we summarize the analysis by introducing a framework which, in our view, gives the better understanding of the essence, broadness and complexity of the problem.

We start from definitions and interpretations of the term *context* as it is understood in general and in the e-learning literature. Context-related issues have been intensively researched, especially in the computer-human interaction and technology-enhanced learning. As it is emphasized by Zimmermann et al. [ZLO07], in the area of CS there are a number of definitions of the term *context* and *context awareness*. The vast majority of the earliest definitions of the term *context* can be categorized into two groups: definition by synonyms (e.g. application's environmental context or situation context) and definition by example (e.g. enumeration context elements like location, identity, time, temperature, noise, as well as the beliefs and intentions of the human).

Dey [Dey01] defines context as 'any information that can be used to characterize the situation of an entity'. In the other paper, Dey et al. extend the previous definition by stating that '*an entity is a person, place, or object that is considered relevant to the interaction between a user and an application, including the user and applications themselves*'. This can be viewed as an application-centric definition which clearly states that the context is always bound to an entity and that information that describes the situation of an entity is context. The paper [LCW +09] defines the learning context as 'information to identify the state of the item, i.e. learner's location, learning activities, the used tools and LOs'. Dourish [Dou04] emphasizes a dual origin of the context, i.e. technical and social-based aspects. From the social viewpoint, the author argues that context is not something that describes a setting or situation, but rather a *feature of interaction*. From the technical viewpoint, researchers try to define context in a more specific way as an *operational term* [Win01, ZLO07, VMO+12], i.e. by enumerating categories of the term. The main contribution of the paper [ZLO07] is the introduction of a context definition that comprises three canonical parts: a definition per se in general terms, a formal definition describing the appearance of context and an operational definition characterizing the use of context and its dynamic behaviour. The paper [HSK09] presents a literature review of the context-aware systems from 2000 to 2007 and a classification framework on the topic using a keyword index and article title search. Dey defines the context-aware system as follows: 'A system is context-aware if it uses context to provide relevant information and/or services to the user, where relevancy depends on the user's task'.

The paper [VMO+12] provides extensive analysis of context definitions with regard to designing recommendation systems to support technology-enhanced learning (TEL). The latter aims to design, develop and test socio-technical innovations that will support and enhance learning practices of both individuals and organizations. With respect to our aims, one important result of this paper is the framework that summarizes the known so far definitions of the term context and presents how these definitions relate to each other.

As it was stated previously, the feature-based models are the core of a great body of research in domain analysis and modelling, especially as applied to PLE. The feature commonality-variability modelling is at the focus, where context plays also a significant role [LK10]. One important aspect of variability modelling is also the use of ontology and context to model the base domain features. Ontology enables to extract and represent variability dependencies and interaction [LKS+07]. The paper [LK10], for example, uses the context to configure and select features for the product family of embedded software. Sometimes context modelling is treated as a service. The paper [TLL10] proposes the context-based ontology whose property is to reason and describe the rules in e-learning using Protégé software. The paper [JGK+07] presents an ontological framework aimed at the explicit representation of context-specific metadata derived from the actual usage of learning objects and learning designs.

The paper [BBH+10] provides an extensive study on context modelling along with reasoning techniques. Here, the authors discuss the requirements, a variety of context information types and their relationships, situations as related to abstractions of the context information facts, histories and uncertainty of the context information. This discussion also provides a comparison of the current context modelling and reasoning techniques and a lesson learned from this comparison. Based on the existing context-aware e-learning systems, the paper [DBC+10] presents a model and taxonomy of context parameters from the learner's situation.

We reformulate the following finding of this short analysis taken from Chap. 7 as follows:

1. Context is a multidimensional category that, in general, may include the following features: *special time, physical conditions, computing, resource, user, activity* and *social.*
2. As many of these features are overlapping (see [VMO+12]), it is reasonable to combine some of them in a concrete situation such as teaching with the use of SLOs. Thus, we will focus on three context dimensions: computing/resource, user (learner/teacher)/social and activity/task/content. Comparing these dimensions with pedagogical reusability as it is proposed in [PS04], we are able to connect a learning situation with the three context categories we will use later, respectively, *technical context, pedagogical context* and *content context.* All these were the basis to propose our context model to be further discussed in Sects. 11.3.1, 11.3.2 and 11.3.3.

Group B Source code analysis and manipulation is an important topic in program transformation research [Har10]. Refactoring is a specific kind of program transformation aiming at improving the program's structure. The reader can learn more on this topic from the book [FBB+13] and a comprehensive survey [MT04].

Thomas [Tho05] tries to identify links between refactoring and MPG in using the object-oriented paradigm. The paper [TBD06] considers the refactoring problem at the level of feature models. Another paper [RSA10] presents a novel approach based on *role models* to specify *generic refactorings*. Role models support the declaration of roles which have to be played in a certain context. Assigned to generic refactoring, the contexts are different refactorings and roles are the participating elements. The approach is supported by the Refactory tool using the Eclipse Modelling Framework and is evaluated using multiple modelling languages and refactorings.

Mens et al. [MTR07] represent refactorings as graph transformations and propose the technique of critical pair analysis to detect the implicit dependencies between refactorings. The results of this analysis can help the developer to make an informed decision of which refactoring fits best in a given context and why. Porres [Por05] discusses how to define and execute model refactorings as rule-based transformations in the context of using the UML and MOF.

Lopez-Herrejon et al. [LME11] present some experience in refactoring features based on the requirement specifications and identify eight refactoring patterns that describe how to extract the elements of features which were subsequently implemented using the Feature-Oriented Software Development (FOSD). As refactoring often requires non-trivial program analysis, the tool support to deal with this task is highly desirable. A wide discussion on this topic can be found in [ACM08]. The paper [KF09], for example, compares some refactoring tools with respect to the automation and coverage, reliability, configurability, scalability and discoverability, thus providing guidelines for the appropriate tool selection. The paper [KKB07] proposes a tool that helps automating tedious tasks of refactoring legacy applications into features, as applied to the PLE approach.

The theoretical basis of meta-program transformation (refactoring) can be tracked from the early works of Taha [Tah99, Tah04] on multistage programming (see also Chaps. 7 and 9). Thus, the extracted facts, ideas, models and approaches form a pretty good background to extend the refactoring concept to the MPG domain as follows.

11.3 Models and Processes to Develop Refactoring Tool for SLO Adaptation

In this section, we present the second tool already introduced in Chap. 7. Here, however, we will discuss it from the designer's perspective. Note that Chap. 9 is the background for such a discussion. We present the discussion in a similar way as it was done in Sect. 10.3. We need, however, first to highlight two additional issues: (1) to put more light on the context model and (2) to describe informally the tight relationship between the context-aware parameters and meta-program stages. We do that in Sect. 11.3.1 and Sect. 11.3.2, respectively. Next, in Sect. 11.3.3, we formulate the rules to support refactoring transformation. They form the basis of the ASM-oriented computation model, the algorithm and the tool itself.

11.3.1 More About the Model to Realize Context Awareness

In general, context modelling is an extremely important and a very complicated issue in learning. Therefore, there are multiple views and models proposed (see Sect. 7.2). In our case, the context modelling plays also a significant role in both the design and use of SLOs. In Chaps. 7, 8 and 9, we have already introduced the context-related models as applied to our approach. In the previous discussion, however, we were focused more on the syntactic aspects of the context model, though we have outlined the connection between the context-related weights (identified as fuzzy variables) and the cognitive levels (identified from the Bloom's taxonomy; see Chap. 7).

Here, we continue this discussion and present more details on the context model semantics. So far, assuming that weight values $\{HP, IP, LP\}$ are constants, we have presented the context along with the SLO interface model as the weighted graph G $(P^w, U), w \in \{HP, IP, LP\}$ (see Property 9.2). As the weight w models the context of dependent parameter groups, we can rewrite Eq. (9.4) (see Chap. 9) as follows:

$$G(P^w, U) = \overset{g}{\underset{i=1}{\cup}} G_i^w, \left(G_i^w \cap G_j^w = \varnothing, G_i^w, G_j^w \subseteq G(P^w, U)(i \neq j)\right) \qquad (11.1)$$

g is the number of connected components, including isolated nodes $(g > 1)$.

What is the semantics of this model? In other words, a few questions should be raised for analysis as follows: (1) How to select the weight from the list $w \in \{HP, IP, LP\}$ aiming to assign the weight to a group of the dependent parameters (i.e. subgraph G_i^w)? (2) What is the actual meaning of parameter dependency? (3) Who is responsible to take this activity in designing SLO?

The values HP, IP and LP (meaning high, intermediate and low priority, respectively) have been introduced to model the three different groups of domain features (or parameters): pedagogy related, social related and content related. In the case of using robots, there are also technology-related features (such as velocity, moving time, etc.); sometimes, e.g. for simplicity, we can treat them as content-related features because they, in fact, are closely related. We present the possible cases of the relationship among the priority weights and domain features (parameters) in Fig. 11.1. There are four groups of domain parameters or features (in terms of feature models): P, pedagogy related (e.g. teaching goal, teaching model such as problem based, project based, etc.); S, social related (e.g. student's profile, previous knowledge, gender, etc.); T, technology related (e.g. robot's speed, moving time from point A to point B, etc.); and C, content related (e.g. data, operations, fragments of an algorithm, etc.).

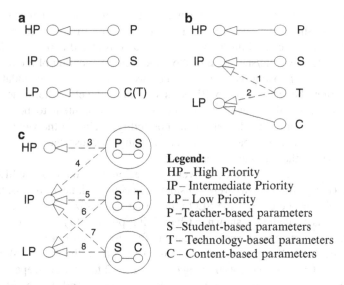

Fig. 11.1 Context models as a parameter-weight relation: case of independent parameters (**a, b**) and dependent parameters (**c**)

The context models (see Fig. 11.1a, b) represent the ideal case, i.e. we assume that there is no interaction among the parameters P, S, T and C. Why P is modelled by HP, S is modelled by IP and T (C) is modelled by LP? It is clear from the general understanding of the domain and the thorough discussion (see Chap. 7). Where such models are helpful? That is helpful for sequencing parameters within the interface in designing SLO, i.e. the parameters should appear as the sequence P→S→T→C (such is the learning and teaching logic). As the SLO is typically used by the teacher, the relation P→HP can be seen as the *teacher's context* with respect to the remaining part of the interface, i.e. (S→T→C). Similarly, the relation S→IP can be seen as the *student's context* with respect to the remaining part of the interface, i.e. (T→C). Therefore, the context information is evaluated first, and only after that, it is possible to evaluate the content. The latter leads to the creation of a concrete LO according to the teacher's and learner's contexts being specified a priory.

The context model (Fig. 11.1c) specifies the case when the parameters from the different groups interact among themselves (i.e. they are dependent). Three of the most typical variants of interacting are in the focus: P and S, S and T and S and C. We admit that the interactions (P and C (T) or P and S and C) are not the case. What context weights are to be allocated to the adequate groups of parameters in constructing the context model? There are two alternatives for each group of parameters. Which is most relevant (see Fig. 11.1c): 3 or 4 to the group P and S, 5 or 6 to the group S and T and 7 or 8 to the group S and C?

The solution (3, 5 and 8) looks like the best. But we need to take into account three extra facts: (a) there might be also solitary parameters in each group (to those parameters the relationship *parameter-weight* is clear; see Fig. 11.1a); (b) the SLO is to be used in the mode 'use-as-is', i.e. without refactoring; and (c) most likely the designed SLO should be specialized later (at use time) aiming at more flexible adaptation. In our view, taking into account what was stated above, the designer should act as follows. He/she should follow the recommendation of the teacher or domain expert in choosing the context-related weights. This recommendation, for instance, might be connected to Bloom's taxonomy levels, where the highest cognitive levels (analyze, evaluate, create) require the content to be presented explicitly. On the other hand, there is the possibility to change the weights at *use time* easily without the impact on the functionality, because they are written as comments within the interface specification.

So far, we have discussed the relatively simple context models of the SLO to be designed. Though the weights were considered as constants, nevertheless, they are applicable also in the case of the SLO refactoring (specializing) for deeper adaptation. As it has been already shown in Chap. 7, it is possible to gain more flexibility in adaptation if we express some weights as functions whose arguments are the cognitive levels of Bloom's taxonomy. Here, we return to the model (b) given in Table 7.1 (see Chap. 7) and present it again in Fig. 11.2 to provide deeper analysis.

The parameters CO and LA are of the type P (see legend in Fig. 11.1). The parameter LL is of the type S. The parameters S*, V1, V2, D1, D2, T* and T1 are of the type T. Finally, the parameters P* and P1 are of the type C (i.e. they define the pure content stating the tasks explicitly). The solution has been made by the expert (i.e. by the teacher with the 3-year experience of using educational robots in teaching CS). It is possible to achieve higher or the highest cognition levels in learning if the learner works with the content explicitly. This happens at the final stage of producing LO from the SLO specification. As it was difficult to take a

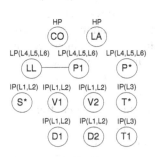

Legend: **Teacher's context: CO** – curriculum objective (LN – loops and nested loops), **LA** – learning activity (Case study (given by *Teacher*)- CT; Practice (done by *Learner*) – PS); **S*** – selected motor (AB, BC, AC), **V1, V2**– *drawing velocity* of motors (pen on the paper), **T*** – robot's drawing time, **P *** – number of ornament's parts, **D1, D2** – *moving velocity* of motors (pen over paper), **T1** – robot's moving time, **P1** – number of ornaments **LL** – learner's previous knowledge level (Beginner-BG; Intermediate – IT; Advanced – AD). **L1:** *Remember (the lowest cognition level)*, **L2:** *Understand* **L3:** *Apply*, **L4:** *Analyze*, **L5:** *Evaluate*, **L6:** *Create (the highest cognition level according to Bloom's taxonomy)*

Fig. 11.2 Context-aware model as a part of the SLO interface model
Legend – teacher's context: CO curriculum objective (LN, loops and nested loops), *LA* learning activity (case study (given by *teacher*), CT; practice (done by *learner*), PS), *S** selected motor (AB, BC, AC), *V1, V2 drawing velocity* of motors (pen on the paper), *T** robot's drawing time, *P** number of ornament's parts, *D1, D2 moving velocity* of motors (pen over paper), *T1* robot's moving time, *P1* number of ornaments and *LL* learner's previous knowledge level (beginner, BG; intermediate, IT; advanced, AD). *L1 remember (the lowest cognition level), L2 understand, L3 apply; L4 analyse, L5 evaluate* and *L6 create (the highest cognition level according to Bloom's taxonomy)*

priority to the levels L4, L5 and L6, the context-related weights for the parameters LL, P1 and P* have been defined as a function of all the levels. The remaining functions have been defined taking into account (1) the models given in Fig. 11.1 and (2) the parameter relevance to Bloom's taxonomy levels.

On the other hand, there might be some debates on how to define the context weights as functions with arguments of the Bloom's taxonomy levels. Indeed, this has been already shown as the variant (a) in Table 7.1 (see Chap. 7). Here, it is recommended for the reader to compare variants (a) and (b) given in Table 7.1 once again.

Furthermore, it is not always evident the fact of the parameter interaction if the parameters belong to the different types (categories). The reason is that there is the difficulty in defining relationships (*exclude* or *require*) among different values of parameters. Very often (especially in the case of the relationships P-S, P-C), the *intuitive decision* can be made by the expert. What will happen if the decision would be questionable from the other viewpoint? As it is not a pure content relationship, perhaps, there would be the other *semantic interpretation* of SLO, but *not the syntax error* of the generated program. Of course, if the interaction has been missed in designing meta-programs, that most likely will cause an erroneous program (i.e. LO).

11.3.2   Relationship Among Stages and Context-Aware Model

At this point, the reader should have a clear understanding of two items: (1) what is *a meta-specification* (i.e. meta-program or SLO) and (2) in which aspects it differs from the *stage-based meta-specification* of the same functionality. Heterogeneous meta-programming is such a paradigm that aims at developing the executable meta-specification, in which we express the domain variability through parameters and the higher-level manipulations on those parameters using meta-functions. When processed, all parameters are evaluated and processed along with the adequate meta-functions at once, in the same processing phase or stage. On the contrary, the stage-based meta-program is such a meta-specification, in which the parameter or parameters and its (their) meta-functions are evaluated and processed not at once but rather gradually, i.e. strictly in the sequential phases, called stages. Such an approach brings a great deal of flexibility and variation in interpreting meta-specifications. From the user perspective, for example, it is easier to understand the stage-based meta-specification. Typically, by splitting the whole into pieces, we are able to diminish the complexity and achieve a better understanding of the whole.

In learning, there is a specific term such as the *content granularity* to fix and manage the content complexity. In our case, on the other hand, we are able to achieve even more – we can deal with the content adaptation problem to the context of use automatically, or almost automatically. For this purpose, however, we need to focus on the context model we have already discussed. Here, our aim is to outline the relationship among stages and the weighted parameters of the context-aware model. This is important to better understand the functionality of the processes within the tool and the tool itself.

The main question is the knowing of how many stages the user (i.e. the teacher or learner) needs and which parameters might be allocated to the particular stage from the pedagogical viewpoint. That is, the relationship model should be *pedagogically sound*. The theoretical background of stage-based programming (mostly from the technology viewpoint) has been outlined in Chap. 9. Here (see Fig. 11.3), we present the stage-context relationship model. The feasible stages are numerated in the order from the highest (k) to the lowest (1), i.e. as the sequence: k, $(k-1)$, ...,1 ($k > 1$). This sequence is always the same, except the fact that the value k may vary. There are two possibilities: either the user indicates the value (*mode* 1) or the system (i.e. the tool) calculates it on the basis of the context information (*mode* 2, see Fig. 11.3). There are two modes, because it is not always easy to define as precisely as possible the weights that define the context awareness. This is especially true in the case when the weights are functions of the Bloom's taxonomy levels. Note that L6 is the *highest cognitive* level and L1 is the *lowest cognitive* level (see Fig. 11.3).

11.3.3   Strength and Weakness of the Parameter Context Model

As context models are of the immense importance, we need to evaluate our model too. First, we define the features that might be considered as strengths of the model. They are as follows:

(s1) Explicit representation of the model.
(s2) The model is easily separable from the base functionality.

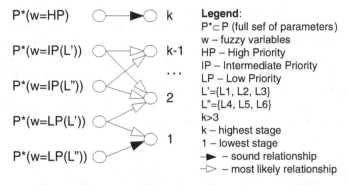

Fig. 11.3 Possible relationships between stage and priority, the latter being expressed as a function of Bloom's taxonomy levels (L1–L6)

(s3) Representation of the model is simple.

(s4) It is both computer readable and human readable.

(s5) It is easy to express both the teacher-related and student-related aspects.

(s6) It is a preprogrammed entity to carry out adaptation automatically.

(s7) It is easy to change and modify the model according to the use cases.

(s8) It is pedagogically sound in terms of using Bloom's taxonomy levels to express the student's ability to achieve the adequate cognition in interpreting the content pieces.

(s9) Formal representation of the model by weighted graphs makes it possible to consider the model for representing knowledge.

There are also a few limitations that we present as the *weaknesses* of the model here. They are as follows:

(w1) It is too specific to be applicable to other tools in the mode 'use-as-is', though conceptually it might be helpful in other situations as well.

(w2) It is not an easy task to define fuzzy variables as functions of Bloom's taxonomy levels; there might be a few reasons for that: dependability on the task, different interpretations of the task by different actors and high abstraction level of representing the content aspects by parameters to which we need to supply the context weights.

(w3) It is difficult to compare the model with other models due to the specificity, e. g. relationship among context variables and the prespecified hierarchy of stages.

(w4) There is a gap between the designer's technological knowledge to develop the tool and representing the context model as the pedagogically sound entity; to close the gap, the expert's knowledge is needed; as a result, it is not always possible to carry out the adaptation automatically.

(w5) The context model is locked within the SLO specification and, therefore, the model serves for the internal transformation, but not for the external communication among different SLOs.

11.3.4   Rules to Perform Refactoring Transformation

Rule 1 Checking the condition defined by Eq. (9.4) (see Property 9.6 in Chap. 9). If the condition holds, the refactoring transformation is valid; otherwise, the refactoring is impossible (see also the *Statement* on the problem solvability in Sect. 9.4.5).

Rule 2 The parameters and their context information are extracted from the context-aware interface model $G(P^w, U), w \in \{HP, IP, LP\}$ (see Property 9.2, Property 9.4 and Eq. (9.4) in Chap. 9 and also Eq. (11.1) in Sect. 11.3.1). The information is to be represented in a *separate file*.

Rule 3 The structure of the file has to represent the parameter-dependent parts separately as it is specified by Eqs. 9.1, 9.2 and 9.3 (see Properties 9.3–9.5 in Sect. 9.4.4, Chap. 9).

Rule 4 Parameters of the dependent (interacting) group always should appear on the same stage (it is based on Properties 9.3–9.5 given in Chap. 9).
  As a result of this rule, the following property holds:

Property All nodes within the connected subgraph $G_i(P^{w_0}, U)$ must have the s*ame weight* w_0 (see also *Property 9.7* in Sect. 9.4.4).

Rule 5 A stage is not empty, i.e. it has at least one parameter group or a separate parameter.

Rule 6 The group of parameters with the highest priority (HP) should appear at the *higher stages*.

Rule 7 The group of parameters with the intermediate priority (IP) or with the lower priority (LP) should appear at the *lower stages*.

Note that the stage which should be treated as higher or lower is to be either calculated by the system on the basis of the values of weights or identified by the user of the tool (system).

Rule 8 The number of stages and the parameters' group allocation to stages are performed automatically according to the context information (i.e. according to the parameter priorities). If the context information is not sufficient, or the context model is incorrect, the model should be corrected manually by the designer (domain expert). This rule is used in mode 1 (see Fig. 11.4).

Rule 9 The number of stages and the allocation of the parameters to stages can be also performed by the user. This rule is used in mode 2 (see Fig. 11.4).

Rule 10 *Rule 8* and *Rule 9* are mutually exclusive.

Rule 11 When the parameter allocating process runs at the stage i (*Rule 8* or *Rule 9*), all parameters are to be deactivated by the deactivating index at stages $(i-1) \ldots 1$ (see *Rule 12 and Rule 14*).

Rule 12 Deactivating index is defined by the following formula [ŠBB14]:

$$Index = 0 \text{ for stage } i; 1 \text{ for stage } (i\text{-}1), \text{ etc.; and } \sum_{a=0}^{i-2} 2^a \text{ for stage } 1.$$

  We explain the use of this rule with examples (see Table 11.1). Here, PHP is the meta-language to code the 3-stage specification, where parameter P1 appears in stage 3, parameter P2 in stage 2 and parameter P3 in stage 1.
  Note that *Rules 1–12* are used to perform refactoring of the meta-program interface.

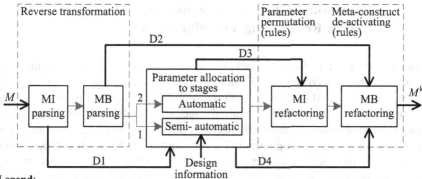

Legend:

M – Meta-program, MI – (meta-) interface, MB – meta-body, M^k – k-stage meta-program
→ data, ⟶ control (sequence), working modes: 1- semi-automatic; 2- automatic
D1– parameter dependency graph and contextual information (parameter priority)
D2 – parameter – meta-construct dependency; meta-construct location (addres)
D3 – transformed MI model into k-stage model
D4 – transformed MB model into its k-stage model

Fig. 11.4   Refactoring-based architecture of the tool MP-ReTool

Table 11.1   Examples of calculating and using deactivating index for PHP

Where applied	Examples in PHP	Index value
In stage 3	`$P1 = "AND";`	0
In stage 2	`echo "\$P2 = 3;";`	1
In stage 1	`echo "echo \"\\\$P3 = Y;\";";`	3

Table 11.2   State of stages 2 and 1 after processing 3-stage meta-program

After processing at stage 3	Examples in PHP	Index value
Stage 2	`$P2 = 3;`	0
Stage 1	`echo " \$P3 = Y;";`	1

Rule 13   Each deactivated parameter *requires* the deactivating of the meta-function (within the meta-body) with the same deactivating index, in which this parameter appears.

Rule 14   Processing of the k-stage meta-program at stage i $(k > i > 1)$ results in diminishing the deactivating index by the value defined for this stage.

In Table 11.2, we illustrate Rule 14 with the same example.

11.4   Process-Based Architecture and Algorithm to Perform Refactoring Transformation

We describe the refactoring process along with the simplified architecture. The input data are (1) a correct initial meta-program designed either manually or with the aid of the MePAG tool and (2) design information supplied by the user. The latter may include the number of required stages or a pre-allocation of parameters to stages if the user wants to prespecify his/her refactoring strategy for adaptation. The output is the k-stage meta-program (k – the number of stages). It can be created either semi-automatically (if the user wants to introduce the adaptation strategy anew and, perhaps, aims to change the context model) or fully automatically (if the user accepts the context model as the *use-as-is structure*, i.e. as a preprogrammed entity).

The architecture (Fig. 11.4) consists of five basic components. Two first components implement parsing of the given meta-program. There are two components to implement refactoring. One component is responsible for managing the parameter allocation to stages. As the structure of the (meta-) interface and meta-body differs, there are needed two separate components for parsing, as well as for refactoring. The parsing results in extracting two different models D1 and D2 (see legend in Fig. 11.4). The first model supplies the information to provide the parameter allocation to stages, whereas the second gives the adequate information to perform refactoring of the meta-body.

The parameter allocation to stages enables to realize two operating modes: semi-automatic (mode 1) and automatic (mode 2). Mode 1 ensures (1) flexibility of the process because of some weakness of the context model (see Sect. 11.3.3) and (2) feedback if there is the need to repeat the refactoring process of the same initial meta-program.

Below we present an algorithm that implements the functionality of the tool. The basis to implement the algorithm and the tool itself is as follows:(1) the previously formulated rules, (2) the concept of multistage meta-programming (see Chap. 9 and [ŠD13]) and (3) the ASM model [Bör99], in fact, the same as it was presented in Sect. 10.3.3 (see also Eq. (10.1)).

Step 1. *Choose* the operating mode; /* *mode 1* or *mode 2**/

Step 2. *Read* the (meta-)interface model; /* *Rule 2, Rule 3; the model is created by MePAG* */

Step 3. *Read* the meta-body;

Step 4. **if** <*mode 1*> **then do** *Initiate* parameters' assignments to stages; /* Using *Rule 8* */

    if n >1 **then** *Sort* parameters according to their priorities; /*n – the number of parameters*/

    Identify the number of required stages; /*according to the priority values from the set: {HP; IP (L1); IP (L2); IP (L3); LP (L4, L5, L6)} see Fig. 11.2*/

Allocate parameters to stages; /* according to the parameter priority values; *Rule 4; Rule 5; Rule 6; Rule 7*/*

If <there is no refactoring feasibility> **then** *Print* error message 'correct the model, i.e. change the priority values and start from the beginning*/

        end;

Step 5. **if** <*mode 2*> **then do** *Initiate* parameters' assignments to stages; /*Rule 9 */

Choose the number *k*; /* *k* is # of required stages */

if *k* >*g* **then** *Print* message 'refactoring impossible: *reduce k* ';

   /* *Rule* 1; *g* – the maximum number of stages*/

if n >1 **then** *Sort* parameters according to their priorities;

Allocate parameters to stages; */ according the user's choice; the priority values from the set: {HP; HP or IP; IP; IP or LP; LP}; *Rule 4, Rule 5, Rule 6, Rule 7* */

If < allocation is incorrect> **then** *Print* error message: allocate parameters anew;

        end;

Step 6. *Perform* the meta-interface refactoring as follows;

  for *i* = 1 to *n* **do**

Read data of the parameter *i*;

Fix the parameter to the given stage (which will be used);

if <parameter *i* is independent > **then** *Create* the *simple* interface form for this stage; /* the parameter *i* de-activation; *Rule 11 and 12* */

  else *Create* the *branching* interface form for this stage; /* the parameter *i* de-activation; *Rule 11 and 12* */

  end;

Step 7. *Perform* the meta-body refactoring as follows;

for *j* = 1 to *m* **do** (*m* — the number of meta-body code lines)

  Perform parsing of the meta-body line *j*;

  if <any parameter in the line *j* exists> **then**

    Fix the parameter stage from the *staged interface*; /* it has already been formed at *Step 6* */

  if <the parameter stage is less (<) than *k*> **then**

De-activate the parameter and its all functions; /* *Rule 12, Rule 13**/

   else *Rewrite* the line *j* without changes;

  else; *Rewrite* the line *j* without changes;

  end;

Step 8. **end.**

Note. Rule 14 (see Sect. 11.3.4) is not the entity of this algorithm. The rule has the sense in the generating process only.

11.5   Main Characteristics of the Tool

Again, we need to remind the reader that the tool has been designed not only to support SLO refactoring. As SLOs, in fact, are meta-programs, we can use the tool for the refactoring of the PHP-based heterogeneous meta-programs taken from other applications. To do that, we need to change the context model within the meta-specification. As the context model is presented as PHP comments, the change does not affect the functionality. Furthermore, the simplest case of the context model (when it is expressed through fuzzy variables as the constants of the set {HP, IP, LP}) is general enough and is not so much dependable on applications.

We present the main functional characteristics of the tool MP-ReTool in Table 11.3.

11.6   Experimental Validation

The aim of the experiments was (1) to test the tool MP-ReTool by creating the specialized SLOs for adaptation (i.e. stage-based meta-programs), (2) to test the created items and (3) to obtain some characteristics of the specialized SLO designed with the help of the tool. The scope of experiments (we have carried out during the writing of this chapter) in terms of tested variants was $273 = (225 + 48)$ (see also Table 11.3, line 15). The majority of created variants were real tasks. The initial one-stage SLOs were created either manually or using the tool MePAG (see, Sect. 10.6 and Table 10.4 in Chap. 10).

In Table 11.4, we present the characteristics of the *line follower task* for the NXT robot. The task was implemented as a meta-program with the indicated character-istics (read legend to understand the meaning of parameters). In Fig. 11.5, we present the context-based interface model. In Fig. 11.6, we outline the parameter value interaction model. The latter serves to construct the first model. The initial meta-program is the input of the refactoring tool.

In the development phase, we have presented the context-based information at two abstraction levels: *learning process* (a higher abstraction level) and *implemen-tation* (a lower abstraction level). We treat the context at the first level as a set of pedagogical approaches to be delivered to learners along with the content. We have selected five basic parameters from [DCS10] as the most relevant ones to our objectives to define the context at this level. We present the context model at the process specification level using the feature-based notation (see Fig. 11.7).

At the implementation level, we have presented the context as priority-based relations within the weighted parameter dependency graph. Note that this graph represents also the context-aware interface model. We have constructed the graph and priority relations on the basis of the physical task semantics and designer's knowledge of the domain. For example, from the e-learning understanding

Table 11.3 Characteristics of MP-ReTool and their relationships

#	Characteristics	Value	Relationships	Evaluation metrics
1.	Status	Experimental (number of users, 5)	15	# of user
2.	Accessibility	Free online network tools	9, 10	No
3.	Theoretical background	Feature models, meta-programming, program specialization, design *for* reuse (D*f*R), design *with* reuse (D*w*R), ASM computational model	6, 7, 8, 13	Complexity metrics [ŠD13]
4.	Refactoring basis	Context awareness, stage meta-programming, user needs	3, 7, 9	# of stages
5.	Design language and OS	PHP, HTML, Windows	9, 10, 13, 14	No
6.	Design approach	Model-driven transformation	3, 4	No
7.	Input models and data	Meta-interface model, MP model, MP	3, 4, 8, 9	Variability level
8.	Output data	k-stage MP (specialized SLO)	All	Complexity measures
9.	User interfaces	User-friendly graphical interfaces (≤ 7)	4–7	# of interfaces
10.	Other tools used	Dreamweaver, Web browser	Indirect	No
11.	Constraints	Only for PHP as meta-language, max # of stages = 5	5, 8, 9, 12	# of constraints
12.	Refactoring characteristics	# of stages, parameter priority values, preprogrammed context model	9	Numbers and values
13.	Complexity of tool's algorithm	$O(m)$ m – the number of code lines of a meta-program	Internal	Linear complexity
14.	Compatibility with other tools	MePAG, PHP processor, TL tool independent, Web browser	5, 10	# of tools
15.	Current maturity level[a]	(45*5 = 225) variants of SLO (3*4*2*2 = 48) variants of other meta-programs	All: 1–14	# of explored items

[a]The current maturity level means the time of writing this chapter; figures are continually varying in the course of extending the scope of experiments; here, (see line 15) 45, the number of variants of real SLO tasks tested (see Table 10.4, Column 2); 5, the number of variants of stage-based SLOs for each variant of tested real tasks

viewpoint, it is clear that context-based parameters (such as pedagogical approaches) are of higher (or at least of the same) priority as compared to the content-based parameters. Furthermore, all nodes of a subgraph have the same weight (priority relations) due to Property 9.7 (see Sects. 9.4.4 and 11.3.4). The priority-based relations serve for allocating parameters to stages automatically by the refactoring tool.

Table 11.4 Line follower task: meta-level characteristics of the initial SLO

MP (SLO) characteristics	Name of parameters (in bold) and their values (in brackets); for abbreviations and meaning, see legend below
Context-based parameters	**CO** (LC); **LA** (CT; PS; AK); **LL** (BG; IT; AD); **M** (PR, PB); **LP** (SL, MD, F)
Content-based parameters	**A** (OI; OB; ST; TI) [Gra13]; **L** (S1; S2; S3; S4; S1 and S2; S1 and S3; S1 and S4; S2 and S3; S2 and S4; S3 and S4); **S** (AB; AC; BC); **V** (10; 20; 30; 40)
Parameters' dependency model (see Fig. 11.5; Line means an interaction/ dependency)	Parameter value interaction model (values within circle; line, the relationships, e.g. SL-BG is of type *requires* and SL-IT is of type *excludes*; see Fig. 11.6)
Possible # of target programs (i.e. RobotC programs as LO)	1*3*2*32*3*4 = 2,304

Legend. Learning process context-based parameters: *CO* curriculum objective (loop-based and conditional algorithms, LC), *LA* learning activity (case study (given by *Teacher*), CT; practice (done by *learner*), PS; assessment of knowledge, AK), *LL* learner's previous knowledge level (beginner, BG; intermediate, IT; advanced, AD), *LP* learning pace (slow, SL; medium, MD; fast, F) and *M* learning method (project based, PR; problem based, PB). *Content-based parameters*: *A* algorithm (one inside, OI; one bounce, OB; straddle, ST; two inside, TI) [Gra13], *L* light sensors' inputs, *S* selected motor and *V* velocity of motors in %. *Other characteristics*: MI_T/MI_G textual and graphical meta-interface, respectively, *MB* meta-body and *LOC* lines of code (practical complexity measure)

Fig. 11.5 Graph $G (P^w, U)$ as context-based interface model (Note: LP within circle means 'learning pace', whereas LP out the circle means 'lower priority')

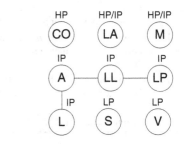

Fig. 11.6 Parameter value interaction

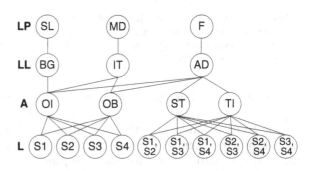

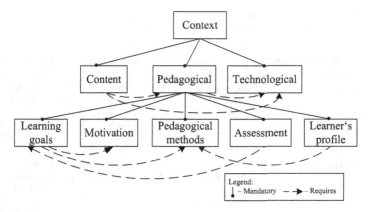

Fig. 11.7 Feature-based context model at the specification level

To identify physical characteristics of educational robots, that is, content-based parameter values, we need to provide an experimental investigation of the robot's behaviour (in fact to solve the robot's calibration task), a prior to designing its meta-specification (see Sect. 12.5.1 in Chap. 12, for details). Parameters may interact among themselves. The interaction depends on the tasks, i.e. on parameters and their values. For example, for the line follower task, the interaction is among parameters A, LL, LP and L (see also Table 11.4). To identify the interaction among context-based parameters as precisely as possible, the designer (if he/she is not a teacher) should rely on the expert's (teacher's) knowledge and experience.

In Table 11.5, we present size-related characteristics of the stage-based SLOs for adaptation that were obtained using the refactoring tool MP-ReTool for the selected task. In fact, there is reflected the size dependency of the specialized SLO for *adaptation* upon the number of stages and the number of parameters within stages. The more stages are required, the larger created items are. The more parameters are at the highest stage, the shorter created items are.

In Table 11.6, we present data that illustrate some structural characteristics of the same task (line follower), but from the adaptation perspective. The overall number of instances (target programs in RobotC) that could be generated from any stage-based specification (4 stage, 3 stage and 2 stage) is the same (see the ending line in Table 11.6) because the refactoring is semantic-preserving transformation. What is different is the other location of an instance within the whole space.

In Fig. 11.8, we present the results of solving the line follower task: the robot's view to run the task along with the specified parameter values (Fig. 11.8a) and the generated instance (Fig. 11.8b) according to the given values.

Note also that we have presented the partial results of our experiments. More results (for all tasks and other characteristics) will be provided in Chap. 12.

Table 11.5 Line follower *specialization task* results obtained using MP-ReTool: SLO size dependency on the number of stages and parameter allocation

Parameters	CO, LA, M, LP, LL, A, L, S, V		
Initial stage 1 SLO size (COL/KB)	431/17,4 (see Table 10.4 Line 2 in Sect. 10.6 (431 = 287 + 144))		
Variants of parameter allocation to stages (k = 4)	Stage 4: CO Stage 3: LA, M Stage 2: LP, LL, A, L Stage 1: S, V	Stage 4: CO, LA Stage 3: M Stage 2: LP, LL, A, L Stage 1: S, V	Stage 4: CO, LA, M Stage 3: LP, LL, A, L Stage 2: S Stage 1: V
Stage 4 SLO size (KB)	39	38, 8	31, 8
Variants of parameter allocation to stages (k = 3)	Stage 3: CO Stage 2: LA, M, LP, LL, A, L Stage 1: S, V	Stage 3: CO, LA, M Stage 2: LP, LL, A, L Stag 1e: S, V	Stage 3: CO, LA, M, LP, LL, A, L Stage 2: S Stage 1: V
Stage 3 SLO size (KB)	27, 6	25, 5	22, 5
Variants of parameter allocation to stages (k = 2)	Stage 2: CO Stage 1: LA, M, LP, LL, A, L, S, V	Stage 2: CO, LA, M Stage 1: LP, LL, A, L, S, V	Stage 2: CO, LA, M, LP, LL, A, L Stage 1: S, V
2 stage SLO size (KB)	25, 5	22, 6	18, 4

Legend: *k* the number of stages, *COL* code of lines in PHP and *KB* kilobyte, for the parameter name and meaning, see the legend below Table 11.3

11.7   How Does the Tool Support Paradigm Change in E-Learning?

The tool enables to specializing the given SLO to the context of use. The initial SLO is to be designed for reuse and adaptation. Adaptation, in fact, is a specific kind of the reuse process. The tool provides a technological support for adaptation only through the specialization of the initial SLO according to the predesigned context model. The context model, in fact, defines the capability to provide adaptation. The model is seen as the adaptation driver: to which extent it specifies the teacher's and learner's context and to the same extent the adaptation is possible with the aid of the tool. Therefore, the raised question in the title should be answered as follows.

The tool supports the technological side of adaptation only. Which side of adaptation, either teacher's or learner's should be stronger, depends on the context model and the needs of adaptation. Bringing all together, i.e. the tool's capability, the selected task, the SLO predesigned features for reuse and adaptation and the embedded context model within the original (initial) SLO specification, we will have a means of the flexible choice to ensure the shift from teacher-centric learning to student-centric learning.

Table 11.7 presents a comparison of the paradigms: teacher centred vs. learner centred. The criteria are adapted from [All04] (1–6 criteria) and [HF00] (7–14 criteria).

Table 11.6 Line follower *adaptation task*: some characteristics obtained using PHP processor as *generating* and *specializing* tool

Meta-programs (MPs) and their characteristics	# of stages $k = 4$				# of stages $k = 3$			# of stages $k = 2$	
	Parameters at stage				Parameters at stage			Parameters at stage	
Line follower characteristics	4	3	2	1	3	2	1	2	1
Line follower parameters	CO	LA, M	A, LL, LP, L	S, V	CO, LA, M	A, LL, LP, L	S, V	CO, LA, M	A, LL, LP, L, S, V
MI_S/MB_S LOC in PHP	11/321	22/269	43/193	58/36	30/267	43/193	58/35	40/230	88/114
# of MPs (SLOs)	1	6	6	12	6	32	12	6	384
# of instances	$1*6*32*12 = 2{,}304$				$6*32*12 = 2{,}304$			$6*384 = 2{,}304$	

Note that parameter names are the same as in Table 11.4 (see Legend used, for their meaning). MI_S (meta-) interface of the specialized (staged) MP (SLO), MB_S meta-body of the specialized, i.e. stage-based meta-program (SLO)

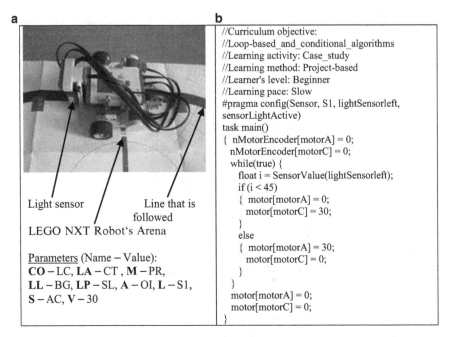

a

b

```
//Curriculum objective:
//Loop-based_and_conditional_algorithms
//Learning activity: Case_study
//Learning method: Project-based
//Learner's level: Beginner
//Learning pace: Slow
#pragma config(Sensor, S1, lightSensorleft,
sensorLightActive)
task main()
{ nMotorEncoder[motorA] = 0;
  nMotorEncoder[motorC] = 0;
  while(true) {
    float i = SensorValue(lightSensorleft);
    if (i < 45)
    { motor[motorA] = 0;
      motor[motorC] = 30;
    }
    else
    { motor[motorA] = 30;
      motor[motorC] = 0;
    }
  }
  motor[motorA] = 0;
  motor[motorC] = 0;
}
```

Light sensor   Line that is
                          followed
LEGO NXT Robot's Arena

Parameters (Name – Value):
CO – LC, LA – CT , M – PR,
LL – BG, LP – SL, A – OI, L – S1,
S – AC, V – 30

Fig. 11.8 NXT robot in operating mode with specified parameter values (**a**) and the derived instance in RobotC (**b**)

11.8   Summary, Discussion and Conclusion

We have presented the main issues *on how,* using the well-founded background, to develop the meta-program refactoring tool that supports the adaptation of smart LOs to the context of their use. In fact, we have discussed the outlined topic at two levels of abstraction: fundamental (i.e. model based) and process based. We have started the presentation of the first level already in Chap. 9, where we have specified the fundamentals of meta-program transformations. In this chapter, we have focused on those models which are close to the refactoring tool realization. Those models include (1) transformation rules as a part of the ASM-based computational model and (2) the extended specification of the context model.

The process-based view gives the essential information to design the tool. The information includes the (1) architecture consisting of the base components to realize the adequate processes and (2) algorithm that implements the computation model to describe the functionality of the tool. We have also discussed the main characteristics of the developed and investigated tool. The tool (MP-ReTool) uses meta-programs as input data to provide the adaptation through refactoring. The latter is driven by the *preprogrammed parameter context information.* The preprogrammed context predefines the functionality to enable the refactoring trans-formations flexibly. The flexibility comes from two sources: (1) the user is able to

Table 11.7 Teacher-centred vs. learner-centred paradigm comparison

#	Criteria	Teacher-centred learning	Learner-centred learning
1.	Teaching goals	*T1* Cover the subject	*L1.1* How to use subject *L1.2* How to integrate subjects *L1.3* Core learning objectives: communication and information literacy skills
2.	Organization of curriculum	*T2* Courses in catalogue	*L2* Cohesive program with opportunities to synthesize, practise and develop new ideas and skills
3.	How students learn	*T3.1* Listening *T3.2* Reading *T3.3* Independent learning	*L3.1* Learners construct knowledge by integrating new learning into what they already know *L3.2* Learning is a cognitive and social act
4.	Pedagogy	*T4* Based on delivery of information	*L4* Based on engagement of students
5.	Course delivery	*T5.1* Lecture *T5.2* Assignments and exams	*L5.1* Active learning *L5.2* Assignments for formative purposes *L5.3* Collaborative learning *L5.4* Community service learning *L5.5* Cooperative learning *L5.6* Self-directed learning *L5.7* Problem-based learning
6.	Faculty role	*T6* Sage on the stage	*L6* Designer of learning environments
7.	Knowledge transmission	*T7* From teacher to learners	*L7* Learners construct knowledge through gathering and synthesizing information and integrating it with the general skills of inquiry, communication, critical thinking, problem solving
8.	Learners' role	*T8* Passively receive information	*L8* Are actively involved
9.	Teacher's role	*T9* To be the primary information supplier and the primary evaluator	*L9.1* To be the coach and consultant *L9.2* To be the team to evaluate learning together
10.	Context role	*T10* Acquisition of knowledge outside the context in which it will be used	*L10* Using the communicating knowledge to address enduring and emerging issues and problems in real-life contexts
11.	Teaching and assessing	*T11* Are separate	*L11* Are intertwined
12.	Assessment's role	*T12* To monitor learning	*L12* To promote and diagnose learning
13.	Emphasis	*T13* Right answers	*L13* Generating better questions and learning from errors
14.	Focus	*T14* A single subject	*L14* Interdisciplinary learning

change the parameter context model either by selecting more relevant values of context-based fuzzy variables or by indentifying the number of suitable stages and their content for adaptation in his/her context and (2) all crucial transformations are carried out by the tool itself automatically.

Furthermore, we have provided an intensive discussion on the parameter context model. The context role is important, for example, for the parameter sequencing in designing the interface of a meta-program (SLO). In the case of the meta-program refactoring, however, the context role is much higher because, in fact, refactoring is the context-driven transformation.

Our parameter context model introduced and discussed here is based on using fuzzy variables to mark the parameter's role, such as HP (high priority), IP (intermediate priority) and LP (low priority). Our vision is that the context should be preprogrammed in advance along with the problem domain (i.e. learning variability) within the SLO meta-specification. In the simplest case, i.e. when we need to use two or three refactoring stages (e.g. for the content adaptation purposes), it is enough to have the context model with three-valued fuzzy variables (the values are regarded as constants). To provide means of the deeper adaptation, however, we need to have a more complex parameter context models. We have suggested also the extended context-based model, which exploits fuzzy variables as functions of the Bloom's taxonomy levels.

A majority of experiments we have carried out with the tool were dedicated to the learning and teaching CS using educational robots and SLOs. As SLOs are, in fact, meta-programs, the tool is applicable to other applications as well if their two main constraints are held: (1) the specification is written using PHP as a metalanguage and (2) the parameter context model is expressed through fuzzy variables which are treated as constants. There are the following consequences of refactoring transformations: (1) transformation changes the complexity of the resulting specifications; (2) as there are different complexity metrics, the complexity changes of the resulting specification also differ; for example, cognitive difficulty of the stage-based specification increases when the number of stages is increased; and (3) adaptation is a sequential process that is modelled through stage-based manipulations – first the user makes self-adaptation by selecting the relevant parameters at all stages starting from the highest k followed by processing to produce $(k-1)$ specification; then the process repeats until the final product (adapted program or LO) is received.

11.9   Research and Exercise Questions

11.1. Address the following terminological issues: What is the similarity between the terms *partial evaluation* (of a program or meta-program), *specialization* and *refactoring*? What is the difference between these terms? Find and discuss the relevant papers on the topics.

11.2. Motivate why the adequate research findings in program partial evaluation (specialization, refactoring) are adaptable to meta-programming domain.

11.3. Research the specialization and refactoring transformations at the level of feature models in your domain of interest.

11.4. Make the juxtaposition of the following terms: design *for* reuse *vs.* design *for* adaptation and design *with* reuse *vs.* design *with* adaptation.

11.5. Analyze the *context definitions* taken from [VMO+12] and select the one which is most relevant to your domain or domains of interest.

11.6. Build a context model with respect to the aims of your research domain.

11.7. Analyze the presented context models (usability, strength, weakness).

11.8. Learn the basic terms, rules and models related to meta-program refactoring.

11.9. Devise a meta-program as simple as possible (say, having the only two parameters to making two changes within a bit string or text string). Introduce a context model to this specification. Rewrite (manually) the devised meta-program as a two-stage specification, using PHP as the meta-language.

11.10. Lean more on how to use the MP-ReTool from [BBŠ14].

11.11. Use MP-ReTool to obtain the two-stage specification automatically for the task 11.9.

11.12. Research and solve more refactoring tasks using the MP-ReTool.

References

[ACM08]   Second ACM Workshop on Refactoring Tools (WRT'08). http://refactoring.info/ WRT08/. Accessed August 2013

[All04]   Allen MJ (2004) Assessing academic programs. Anker Publishing, Boston

[BBH+10] Bettini C, Brdiczka O, Henricksen K, Indulska J, Nicklas D, Ranganathan A, Riboni D (2010) A survey of context modelling and reasoning techniques. Pervas Mob Comput 6(2):161–180

[BBŠ14]   Bespalova K, Burbaitė, R, Štuikys V (2014) MP-ReTool: user guide. http://proin.ktu. lt/metaprogram/ MP-ReTool/

[BCW+08] Brady A, Conlan O, Wade V, Dagger D (2008) Supporting users in creating pedagogically sound personalised learning objects. In: Nejdl W et al (eds) Adaptive hypermedia 2008, LNCS 5149 Springer-Verlag, pp 52–61

[Bör99]   Börger E (1999) High level system design and analysis using abstract state machines. In: Applied formal methods – FM-trends 98, Springer, Berlin/Heidelberg, pp 1–43

[BR12]   Boyle T, Ravenscroft A (2012) Context and deep learning design. Comput Educ 59(4):1224–1233

[BS08]   Boticario JG, Santos OC (2008) A standards-based modelling approach for dynamic generation of adaptive learning scenarios. J Univers Comput Sci 14(17):2859–2876

[BSS+12] Bargel BA, Schröck J, Szentes D, Roller W (2012) Using learning maps for visualization of adaptive learning path components. Intern J Comput Inf Syst Ind Manag Appl 4(1):228–235

[BVV+10] Butoianu V, Vidal P, Verbert K, Duval E, Broisin J (2010) User context and personalized learning: a federation of contextualized attention metadata. J Univ Comput Sci 16(16):2252–2271

[DBC+10] Das M, Bhaskar M, Chithralekha T, Sivasathya S (2010) Context aware e-learning system with dynamically composable learning objects. Intern J Comput Sci Eng 2(4):1245–1253

[DCS10] Das MM, Chithralekha T, Sivasathya S (2010) Static context model for context aware e-learning. Int J Eng Sci Technol 2(6):2337–2346

[Dey01] Dey AK (2001) Understanding and using context. Pers Ubiquit Comput 5(1):4–7

[Dou04] Dourish P (2004) What we talk about when we talk about context. Personal Ubiquit Comput 8:19–30

[FBB+13] Fowler M, Beck K, Brant J, Opdyke W, Roberts D (2013) Refactoring: improving the design of existing code, Addison Wesley. http://www.refactoring.com/. Accessed August 2013

[Gra13] Gray JA (2013) Toeing the line: experiments with line-following algorithms. Technical report [Online]. Available: http://www.fll-freak.com/misc/01-jgray_report.pdf. Retrieved on 10 Jun 2013

[Har10] Harman M (2010) Why source code analysis and manipulation will always be important, In: 10th IEEE working conference on source code analysis and manipulation (SCAM), pp 7–19

[HB00] Huba ME, Freed JE (2000) Learner centered assessment on college campuses: shifting the focus from teaching to learning. Commun Coll J Res Pract 24(9):759–766

[HSK09] Hong JY, Suh EH, Kim SJ (2009) Context-aware systems: a literature review and classification. Expert Syst Appl 36(4):8509–8522

[JGK+07] Jovanović J, Gašević D, Knight C, Richards G (2007) Ontologies for effective use of context in e-learning settings. Educ Technol Soc 10(3):47–59

[KF09] Katić M, Fertalj K (2009) Towards appropriate software refactoring tool support. In: WSEAS international conference on applied computer science, pp 140–145

[KKB07] Kästner C, Kuhlemann M, Batory D (2007) Automating feature-oriented refactoring of legacy applications. In: Proceedings of the ECOOP workshop on refactoring tools (WRT), Berlin

[LCW+09] Liu L, Chen H, Wang, H, Zhao C (2009) Construction of a student model in contextually aware pervasive learning. In: Pervasive computing (JCPC), 2009 Joint Conferences on PC, IEEE, pp 511–514

[LK10] Lee K, Kang KC (2010) Usage context as key driver for feature selection. In: Bosch J, Lee J (eds) SPLC Software product line conference. LNCS, vol 6287. Springer, Berlin, pp 32–46

[LKS+07] Lee SB, Kim JW, Song CY, Baik DK (2007) An approach to analyzing commonality and variability of features using ontology in a software product line engineering. In: 5th ACIS international conference on Software Engineering Research, Management & Applications, SERA 2007, IEEE, pp 727–734

[LME11] Lopez-Herrejon RE, Montalvillo-Mendizabal L, Egyed A (2011) From requirements to features: an exploratory study of feature-oriented refactoring. In: Software Product Line Conference (SPLC), 2011 15th international, IEEE, pp 181–190

[MJ10] Man H, Jin Q (2010) Putting adaptive granularity and rich context into learning objects. In: Information Technology Based Higher Education and Training (ITHET), 2010 9th international conference on, pp 140–145

[MKS10] Mbendera AJ, Kanjo Ch, Sun L (2010) Towards development of personalized knowledge construction model for e-learning. In: 2nd international conference on mobile, hybrid, and on-line learning, IEEE, pp 29–35

[MT04] Mens T, Tourwe T (2004) A survey of software refactoring. IEEE Trans Softw Eng 30(2):126–139

[MTR07] Mens T, Taentzer G, Runge O (2007) Analysing refactoring dependencies using graph transformation. Softw Syst Model 6(3):269–285

[Por05]   Porres I (2005) Rule-based update transformations and their application to model refactorings. Softw Syst Model 4(4):368–385

[PS04]   Pitkanen SH, Silander P (2004) Criteria for pedagogical reusability of learning objects enabling adaptation and individualised learning processes. In: Proceedings of IEEE international conference advanced learning technologies, pp 246–250

[RSA10]   Reimann J, Seifert M, Aßmann U (2010) Role-based generic model refactoring. In: Model driven engineering languages and systems. Springer, Berlin/Heidelberg, pp 78–92

[ŠBB14]   Štuikys V, Bespalova K, Burbaite R (2014) Refactoring of heterogeneous meta-program into k-stage meta-program. Inf Technol Control 43(1):14–27

[ŠD13]   Štuikys V, Damaševičius R (2013) Meta-programming and model-driven meta-program development: principles, processes and techniques. Springer, London/New York

[Tah04]   Taha W (2004) A gentle introduction to multi-stage programming. Domain-Specif Progr Gener Lect Note Comput Sci 3016:30–50

[Tah99]   Taha W (1999) Multi-stage programming: its theory and applications. PhD thesis, Oregon Graduate Institute of Science and Technology

[TBD06]   Trujillo S, Batory D, Diaz O (2006) Feature refactoring a multi-representation program into a product line. In: Proceedings of the 5th international conference on generative programming and component engineering, ACM, pp 191–200

[Tho05]   Thomas D (2005) Refactoring as meta programming? J Object Technol 4(1):7–11

[TLL10]   Tong MW, Liu QT, Liu XN (2010) A service context model based on ontology for content adaptation in e-learning. In: Frontiers in education conference (FIE), the following terminological issues IEEE, pp S1D–1

[VMO+12]   Verbert K, Manouselis N, Ochoa X, Wolpers M, Drachsler H, Bosnic I, Duval E (2012) Context-aware recommender systems for learning: a survey and future challenges. Learn Technol IEEE Trans 5(4):318–335

[Win01]   Winograd T (2001) Architectures for context. Hum-Comput Interact 16(2):401–419

[ZLO07]   Zimmermann A, Lorenz A, Oppermann R (2007) An operational definition of context. In: Proceedings sixth international and interdisciplinary conference modeling and using context (CONTEXT '07), pp 558-5

Chapter 12
Robot-Based Smart Educational Environments to Teach CS: A Case Study

12.1 Introduction

First, the term 'smart educational environment' should be defined. There are *standard* educational environments that are based on using the Internet-based technology along with some e-learning-oriented systems such as Moodle. In *the widest* sense, the word 'environment' should be understood as the overall technological support (hardware, software and networking with remote terminals) and the infrastructure of the methodological support, including databases or digital libraries with the teaching content, management facilities and teaching instructions (for teachers and students) to support e-learning. The base actors (teachers and students), maintenance facilities and personnel might be also treated as components of the environment. In the *narrow sense*, by the educational environment, we mean the facilities for functioning e-learning processes to achieving teaching goals within the teaching organization. Using the *m*-learning paradigm, for example, on the smartphones basis, one can treat as being the smart environment too.

In our case, however, the *smart educational environment* means much more: the use of smart LOs integrated along with the 'smart' educational robotic facilities. The facilities, being the highly reconfigurable structures, enable to devise the variety of usage modes. For example, in terms of the *use logic*, there might be a variety of tasks with the pedagogical value (such as achieving teaching objectives easier) and practical value (such as modelling the real-world situations). In terms of the *architectural choices*, there might be the single robot with a PC, the robot connected to the Internet, the ensembles of robots with sensors for the enlargement of the functional capabilities, etc. We provide also a vision of the smart robot-based

© Springer International Publishing Switzerland 2015
V. Štuikys, *Smart Learning Objects for Smart Education in Computer Science*,
DOI 10.1007/978-3-319-16913-2_12

educational environments as being the *Thing of the Internet*. Note also that the acronym SMART in [Pro14] has a quite different meaning (student-centred, multicultural, active, real-world teaching).

The aim of this chapter is to present and analyse the robot-based smart educational environments that have been *constructed, tested and used* in the real teaching setting to teach programming (the basic computer science course) by the second author of this chapter.

12.2   Literature Review

Robotics is an exciting multidisciplinary area that is going to dominate in the twenty-first century. The robotics industry is entering a new period of rapid growth [SS12]. For example, the year of 2011 has been named as the most successful year for industrial robots since 1961 [IFR12]. The current high school and university students will live in a highly technologized society surrounded by industrial and service robots at work, educational robots at educational institutions, assistive robots at hospitals and care facilities and domestic/entertainment robots at home. As we are living in an increasing digital world, children should be taught how it works. Therefore, the educational priorities must shift toward teaching students how to manipulate all digital devices (computers, robots, smart TVs, high-tech gadgets, etc.) that surround them for their own needs [Bri11].

On the other hand, robots can be viewed as specialized computers with both computational and mechanical facilities to perform physical movement-oriented tasks. Robots allow demonstrating the capabilities of electronics technology and providing students with opportunities for project-based learning. In the context of e-learning, robots are increasingly seen as a means for enforcing engagement, excitement and fun in learning; promoting interest in mathematics, engineering and science career [PR04], increasing student achievement scores [BA07], encouraging problem solving [Mau01], and promoting cooperative learning [BCD99].

Recently, with the advance of technology, new technology-based models of teaching and learning are becoming more popular. Learning is being transformed from the traditional classroom-centred education to the education based on Web-based resources (e-learning) [Wil00] and mobile devices (m-learning) [HTK02], immersive learning in a context-aware ubiquitous learning environment (u-learning) [JJ04], a context-aware environment able to offer ubiquitous personalized content (i-learning) [KSY11] and a context-aware system that overlays virtual educational information on the real world based on the learner's location and needs (augmented learning) [Klo08, TKS14].

New learning models are usually based on the concept of a learning object (LO). The latter is defined as 'any digital entity, which can be used, reused or referenced during technology-supported learning' (adapted from [IEEE00]). In most cases, an LO is a directly usable educational resource or a resource with the adaptation for computer-aided teaching, such as an educational applet or a self-teaching module to be obtained from a DVD or a Web site. In a wider context, an LO per se is a model to support reusability across large e-learning communities [Lib05], including mechanisms to support automation of reuse [S-VNK+08]. With the advances in learning technologies, however, traditional LO models such as metadata-content or hierarchical models based on content granularity [BMB08] – are not enough. That is because (1) e-learning is rapidly advancing and we need to have more flexible, more adaptable, more personalized and more contextualized LOs to support advanced e-learning and (2) e-learning has very wide choices of IT support (mobility, networking, tools, etc.) which so far have been underutilized.

In the last two decades, educational robots offer new benefits by implementing the most effective active learning methods and supporting tools for the teaching of science, technology, engineering and mathematics (STEM).

As it is stated in [Ben12], researchers deal with problems of the field such as the (a) use of robotics as an educational tool, (b) empirical testing of the effectiveness of robots and (c) defining of future perspectives of the use of the robots. The paper also summarizes the educational potential of robotics in schools and concludes the following issues: (a) 'most of the studies found are concentrated in areas related to robotics' per se (meaning robot construction, mechatronics, robot programming); (b) a predominance of the use of Lego robots is observed (90 %); and (c) with regard to the STEM concept, robotics tend to increase the learning achievements, especially in schools – a great deal of applications is 'descriptive in nature, based on reports of teachers achieving positive outcomes with individual initiatives'.

The other publications consider the following topics: (1) a learner-centred robotic-enhanced environment based on the constructivist approach and a methodology to involve students to knowledge construction [FP09], (2) a simple programming environment AiboConnect for robotics [CFW+06], (3) an introductory programming environment based on the use of Lego Mindstorms robots designed for CS learning to program in C++ [Has08] and (4) a game-based learning system using robots, which enhance students' learning motivation and effectiveness [CLL+11].

This short analysis confirms the prediction that the constructing, testing and using of the robot-based environments are the main focus in the case of interdisciplinary-oriented teaching such as STEM. On the other hand, it should be recognized that there is a lack of publications about the learning environments associated with the use of robots for advanced learning. Therefore, our research aims at fulfilling this gap to some extent. Therefore, we consider the robot-based smart learning environments along with SLOs as an important area of research.

12.3 Principles and Requirements for Creating Smart Learning Environments

The learning environment (if it is properly constructed or chosen) helps to achieve learning objectives. However, constructing the smart environment is not an easy task. It requires the use of a systematic approach. Therefore, we start formulating

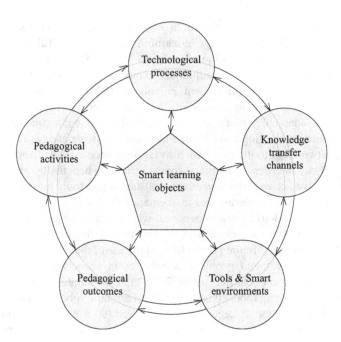

Fig. 12.1 CS learning and teaching conceptual model (Revised from Fig. 1.1)

some principles and requirements. But to do that, we first need to know the context. We outline the context by introducing a slightly modified conceptual model (see Fig. 12.1). In our case, smart LOs are treated as the root of the CS learning and teaching conceptual model. Under the use of adequate tools, it is possible to ensure the interaction of SLOs with pedagogical activities, technological processes, knowledge transfer channels, tools and pedagogical outcomes.

Pedagogical activities are closely related to learning objectives, content, teaching model, selection of the tools, formulation of the task and evaluation of the pedagogical outcomes. Technological processes start with choosing the task. Those processes allow creating SLO, but they depend on tools, programming languages and algorithms that cover topics of the course. After the creation or selection of SLOs from the library, the parameters' selecting and content generating processes occur. The user compiles and executes the generated program and performs the control of the task's solution.

Knowledge transfer channels connect pedagogical activities and technological processes. The feedbacks among components ensure the flexibility of the content regeneration, modification and knowledge extraction through learning scenarios.

Now we are able to formulate the basic principles and requirements to develop the smart learning environment. Those principles and requirements were defined on both the approved knowledge in the domain (extracted through the thorough literature analysis) and our practical experience as follows:

(a) *Analyse* main components of the smart learning environment (the audience, goals, resources and tools, relationships and networks, training and education, the company and supervisor support aspects [LOM08]).
(b) *Consider* the possibility of incorporating all necessary components.
(c) *Treat* SLO as the obligatory component of the smart learning environment.
(d) *Apply* the verified teaching and learning methods and models [Sch02, Had09, LY11, CAL12, SHL+13].
(e) *Ensure* an individualized learning as much as possible.
(f) *Support* the formal learning activities and active interpersonal connections with respect to the learning context.
(g) *Define* the roles of actors in the ongoing feedback and coaching.
(h) *Use* collaborative technologies and other rapid development techniques [Lom08].
(i) *Identify* priorities of each type of components.
(j) *Evaluate* the smart learning environment as a whole using technological [KD09] and pedagogical [KSV04] evaluation criteria.

12.4 Architectural and Functional Aspects

12.4.1 A Generalized Framework

The smart learning environment includes three interrelated parts: teacher's component, learner's component and server (see Fig. 12.2a). The teacher's component consists of the teacher's computer with the software for creating SLOs (such as FAMILIAR, SPLOT, MePAG, Mp-ReTool and PHP processor; see Chaps. 4, 10 and 11) and software of general use that ensures communication with the server (Browsers, Client–server programs to transfer SLOs to/from the server, etc.) (see Fig. 12.2b). Created SLOs are transferred to the SLOs repository located in the server. We install software of general use on the learner's computer to enable to generate the LO according to the user's needs. Moreover, programming language environments that create an executable specification to be transferred to the educational robot or microcontroller must reside in the learner's computer too (see Fig. 12.2b).

In Fig. 12.2c, we present a behavioural model of the proposed environment. Firstly, we create SLO's specification and transfer it to the repository. The designer can modify SLO at any moment.

The learner can find SLO in the repository by using software of general use. He/she selects the values of parameters in the user's meta-interface (SLO interface) and generates LO. Later, the learner uploads it to the programming language environment and creates executable specification and after that transfers it into the robot or a microcontroller.

The teacher ensures monitoring and flexible feedback.

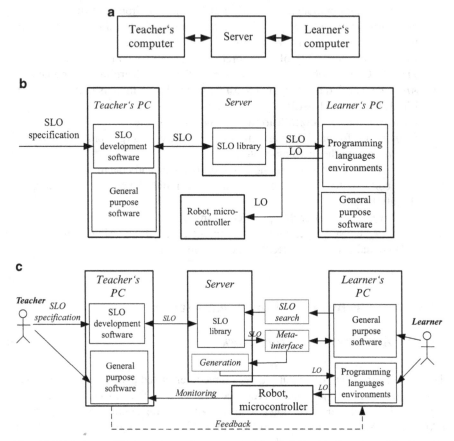

Fig. 12.2 The generalized structure of smart environment: (**a**) – conceptual model, (**b**) main components, (**c**) behavioural model (Adapted from [Bur14])

12.4.2   One-Robot System

When creating the smart one-robot environment, we highlight two stages: (1) preparation for the operating mode and (2) creation of the working mode (see Fig. 12.3).

In the first stage, we construct the educational robot that will solve the predefined task. The next important step within the process is the measurement of technical parameters of the robot, because these parameters are used for the robot control program.

In the second stage, we create the robot control programs automatically and transfer them into a robot, and then we implement visualization of the task.

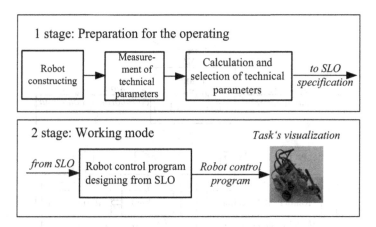

Fig. 12.3 Designing stages of educational one-robot environment

12.4.3   Collaborative Robot-Based Architecture

The architecture of the collaborative robot-based learning environment refers to a classical master-slave model and includes additional components required for robot orientation in its environment (sensors, wireless cameras), communication channels to ensure the exchange of messages between communicating robots and support for different communication protocols (Bluetooth, WiFi) and control hardware/software (PC). In the master-slave model, slaves perform parallel computations and the master does sequential computations. We control subprocesses using communication between the master and slaves either by a single node broadcast from the master or by send/receive messages exchanged between the master and any slave. The principle is similar to task decomposition so that the master-slave model itself can be used as an illustrative example of practical implementation of task decomposition.

Figure 12.4 presents a four-tiered framework to construct the collaborative robot-based environment as follows:

1. *Deliberative layer:* Central Coordinator (CC) receives initial tasks for robots from the teacher and then decomposes tasks into sub-tasks and uploads generated robot control programs (RCP) to the student PCs. In the simplest case, each task is divided into two sub-tasks (Master → Slave), and also we have two independent groups of students (GROUP1, GROUP2) assigned to work with the same task.
2. *Physical layer:* tangible mobile robots with wheels driven by servo motors.
3. *Reactive layer:* sensors allow a robot to receive information about its environment and react to it changes.
4. *Communication layer:* exchange of messages between robots and provision of feedback to teacher's PC for monitoring and evaluation.

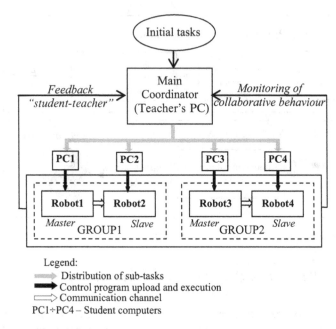

Fig. 12.4 Framework of collaborative robots based environment for e-learning (Adapted from [BSD13])

On real setting, the number of collaborating robot groups depends on the technical capabilities (the number of available robots and PCs in the classroom) and educational needs (the number of students, teaching and learning objectives). In order to ensure satisfaction of educational needs and improvement of technical reliability, we provide a real-time 'student-teacher' feedback and monitoring of collaborative behaviour of robots.

12.5   Case Study: A Support of Teaching/Learning Process Using SLOs and Robot-Based Smart Learning Environments

12.5.1   One-Robot-Based Smart Environment

The case study demonstrates the ability to solve and visually represent a set of related graph-based tasks (given as LOs) in teaching programming (i.e. in informatics or computer science). A particular LO adapted to the learning context is derived from the SLOs automatically. We summarize the overall process below as follows:

1. Learning/teaching subject: *computer science*.
2. CS topic: *loops and nested loops in a computer program*.

3. E-learning environment: *Lego-based drawbot (drawing robot).*
4. Learning content: *an LO derived from SLOs.*
5. Learners: *10th–11th grade secondary school students.*
6. Pedagogical model used: *constructivist*
7. Learning objectives: *visualization of the process and learning content.*
8. Process description by the teacher: *(a) design and testing of the e-learning environment, (b) testing of an existing SLO (or modifying if needed) and designing of the new SLO (if needed, see* http://www.proin.ktu.lt/metaprogram/MePAG/help.pdf*) and (c) testing-generating of LO instances from the SLO to apply them in a different context of use.*
9. A learning activity by students: *(a) design of the robot mechanics under the teacher guidance, (b) identification of robot characteristics relevant for teaching tasks and (c) participation in the development of SLOs, including robot control programs as SLOs and content visualization programs as LOs.*
10. Learning evaluation: *(a) the teacher observes and records the students' activity actions and feedback and on this basis evaluate the gained knowledge.*

We analyse two SLOs here. The first is 'robot calibration' (see Fig. 12.5), because these parameters are used for the robot control program. Motors are controlled for specifying a power level to apply to the motor. The programming language RobotC uses a parameter named 'power level'. Power levels range from −100 to +100. Negative values indicate reverse direction and positive values indicate forward direction. For example, to move motor A forward at 30 % of full power, we would use the following statement: motor[motorA] = 30;

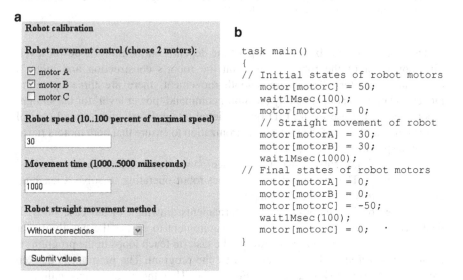

Fig. 12.5 (**a**) (Meta-)interface of SLO 'robot calibration', (**b**) generated instance as LO (© Copyright 2013 by VU IMI)

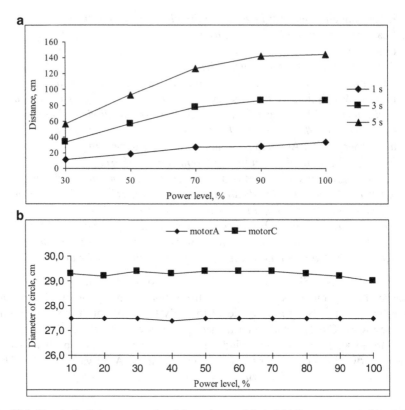

Fig. 12.6 Drawbot's distance-power level dependences: (**a**) straight line movement; (**b**) rotation movement (full circle) (© Copyright 2012 by KTU)

The distance driven by the robot per time depends on the motor's power level. The movement of the robot depends on the robot's construction and motor's technical parameters. To ensure smooth movement, there are three operating modes: (1) manual adjustment by the motor command 'power level' for the straight robot's move, (2) use of the PID (proportional-integral-derivative) speed control algorithm and (3) use of the motor synchronization to ensure that both motors run at the same speed.

Figure 12.6 presents drawbot's distance-power level dependencies obtained experimentally. They are needed for correct robot operating to solve a teaching task (e.g. to smoothly make drawings).

Now we consider the second SLO, 'ornaments drawing', of our case study. It deals with the task that responds to the requirement to ensure the possibility for better students' engagement in learning. The task (to teach loops in the program) is about *visualization* of the result created by the program. The program is derived from the SLO as an LO instance (see Fig. 12.7a). Then the instance runs within the robot environment that makes drawing to realize the visualization (see Fig. 12.7b).

a
```
task main()
{
//-----------------------------------
// Preparation for drawing
    motor[motorB] = 50;
    wait1Msec(100);
    motor[motorB] = 0;
    //-----------------------------
    // Drawing
    for (int j = 0; j < 4; j++) {
        motor[motorC] = 50;
        motor[motorA] = 50;
        wait1Msec(1000);
        //-------------------------
        motor[motorC] = -50;
        motor[motorA] = 0;
        wait1Msec(1000);
    }
    //-----------------------------
    // Drawing is finished
    motor[motorB] = -50;
    wait1Msec(100);
    motor[motorB] = 0;
    //-----------------------------
}
```

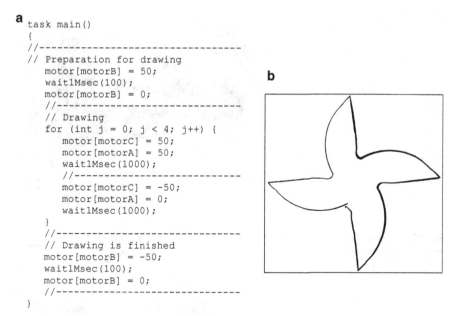

Fig. 12.7 (**a**) Generated LO instance (from SLO 'ornaments drawing') as motivating example to cover 'loops-teaching', (**b**) result of LO execution as a material introduced by teacher for learning at initial phase through problem solving (© Copyright 2013 by VU IMI)

12.5.2 Collaborative Robot-Based Smart Environment

This section has been written on the basis of our two papers [BSM12] and [BSD13]. However, here we present much more detail, including new experiments. Furthermore, the figures of the papers were revised and adopted to the book's format. This section presents the e-learning environment that was elaborated in the high school for teaching the CS course. The environment includes hardware, software and communication facilities.

Hardware It includes educational robots, wireless Internet cameras and computers. We use the heterogeneous Lego Mindstorms NXT robots, i.e. robots with different sensors. There are two collaborative robots. In Fig. 12.8, we present their general view. The robots are named according to the tasks to be performed as follows:

1. Line follower (Fig. 12.8, left) is the *master robot*. Its function is to solve the line follower task physically. The robot uses one colour sensor to follow a black line on the *arena* and one ultrasonic sensor to observe the distance to any obstacle. When an obstacle is obtained, the master sends a message to another robot called drawbot.
2. Drawbot (Fig. 12.8, right) is the *slave robot*. Its function is to draw lines. On this basis, it is possible to construct more complex drawings such as ornaments. The latter action requires the use of an algorithm to be implemented, for example, as

Fig. 12.8 A full view of line follower and drawbot

Fig. 12.9 Example of environment with two collaborating robots

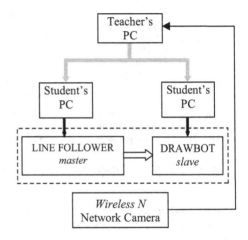

the loops or nested loops within the robot control programs to teach programming. The slave robot receives messages from the line follower and draws lines on the arena. Note that this new environment, in fact, is an extension of the one described in [BSM12]. Therefore, both robots enable to demonstrate visually the solution of the CS teaching tasks.

The teacher's computer (see Fig. 12.9) is used for the delivery of the teaching tasks, which include formulating the general task, splitting it into sub-tasks and then distributing the sub-tasks to the student computers. Furthermore, the teacher's computer is equipped by the *mydlink-enabled Wireless N Network Camera* DCS 932-L to monitor the collaborative behaviour of the robots. Also the camera enables to receive a qualitative 'student-teacher' feedback when students perform tasks within the environment.

Software The software part of the system includes the (1) facilities for the general use (they are in both teacher's and student's PC); (2) facilities to manage the resources of the personal library where the SLOs reside (see Chap. 13, Sect. 13.5), the tools to adapt SLO to the educational context (MP-ReTool, see Chap.

11), the task decomposition and allocation software (all facilities are in the teacher's PC); and (3) RobotC environment and robot control programs as LOs derived from the SLOs (both are in the student PCs).

Communication To carry out the communication activities, the NXT robots use the Bluetooth application protocol called Serial Port Profile (SPP). It is implemented on the top of a low-level RFCOMM (radio frequency communication) protocol, which provides a simple reliable data stream to the user. The Bluetooth protocol is used to ensure the following communication modes: (1) to ensure the connection between PCs and Lego robots (up to three, but only with one at a time), (2) to link the teacher and students' PCs and (3) to connect the other Bluetooth-enabled devices (e.g. mobile phones, tablet PC) into the educational environment. When multiple robots or/and devices are connected together, a master-slave relationship is established. The master always creates the Bluetooth connection and initiates communication. To ensure reliability of the Bluetooth connection, we apply the rules formulated in [Tol06].

The architecture of the collaborative educational environment is shown in Fig. 12.9. It presents how the components discussed previously interact among themselves. The scenario of using the environment is as follows.

Using the line follower and drawbot, we have created a collection of the robot-based SLOs for teaching and learning of the CS course topics such as 'conditional branching statements', 'loops', 'nested loops', 'task decomposition' and 'sub-task aggregation'.

For the line follower robot, the students can select the line-following algorithms out of the two (*One Inside, One Bounce* [Gra01]). Then students test the task and observe the behaviour of the robot. After that, they need to modify the robot control programs by adding new functions to ensure the communication between the line follower and drawbot. The One Inside and One Bounce algorithms use one colour sensor that detects the edge of the line.

For the drawbot, the students can select the preprogrammed ornament templates (i.e. LOs) from the library, and then they need to choose the values of the template parameters to generate the ornament drawing program, while the robot executes the program and draws a figure on the arena using the pencil mounted into its gripper.

We illustrate the use of the environment to implement the tasks described below (see Fig. 12.10).

Below we illustrate the pedagogical outcomes, using the collaborative learning model. This model has been adapted from Reid et al. [RFC90]. The outcomes include six phases as follows.

1. *Engagement*. The learners are introduced with the idea of the behaviour in solving complex tasks. Typically, those tasks require the decomposition, allocation and coordination among tasks in the process. We present the line follower robot that has to follow a line and avoid obstacles at the same time. Using this task, we are able to explain the principle of the task decomposition as a method to solve complex problems. We are also able to explain the constraints and conditions such as static obstacles vs. dynamic obstacles, priority of tasks, etc.

Fig. 12.10 Collaborating
robots: drawbot (*centre*) and
line follower (*above*)

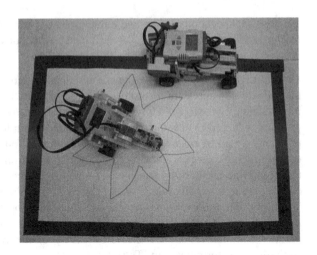

2. *Elaboration*. The learners are working in groups. The groups are formed either by
   the teacher or by themselves. The students within the group elaborate the task
   using the information given by the teacher. The subproblems are identified by
   students and required sub-tasks are formulated for the master and slave robots. The
   tasks are as follows: line following, obstacle detection and message sending for the
   master robot, roaming, message receiving and stopping for servicing the robot.
3. *Transformation*. Then the students analyse SLOs taken from the library. Therefore, students generate the robot control programs as LOs and adapt their
   suitable functions for implementing the sub-tasks. For example, the LO 'obstacle
   searching' is adopted for the obstacle avoidance sub-task, and the LO 'ornament
   drawing' is adopted for the roaming sub-task. Also the students select and adapt
   the variant of the line-following algorithm and perform research on the robot's
   behaviour.
4. *Research*. Figure 12.10 presents the view of the researched environment.
   Drawbot (in the centre) draws a selected ornamental figure bounded by a black
   line, while line follower follows the black line and at the same time observes the
   distance to drawbot. If the distance between robots becomes too big or too small,
   line follower sends a message to drawbot to stop. Two different routes are used
   (see Fig. 12.11): the elliptical (its radii are 21 and 32 cm) and rectangular
   (lengths of the sides are 42 and 70 cm). A dotted line presents the real path of
   line follower obtained experimentally. When the robot's speed is 10–30 % of full
   power, the robot trajectory coincides with the black line. When the robot's speed
   is larger than 40 % of full power, it is unable to follow the black line exactly and
   consequently the robot deviates from it.
5. *Presentation*. After the task solving, students present the results of their team-
   work. They are discussing on researching outcomes. Therefore, they receive the
   feedback from the teacher and colleagues. As an example, Fig. 12.12 presents
   the results of the accuracy comparison of the line-following algorithms. The
   accuracy is calculated by estimating what part of the robot path overcomes
   without leaving the black line while following the routes of different shape

Legend:
▰ Robot movement's start and finish position
➡ Robot movement's direction
- - Real robot's movement's trajectory, when speed is 40÷100 % of full power

Fig. 12.11 Elliptical and rectangular routes followed by line follower

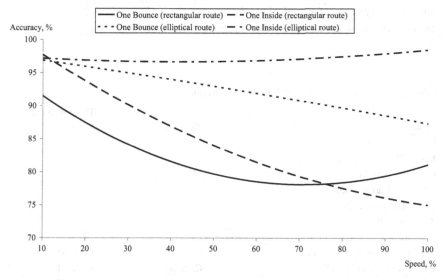

Fig. 12.12 Results of research on the line-following algorithm using elliptical and rectangular routes

and driving at different speeds (speed is expressed as a percentage of the max power level of servomotors controlling the rotation of the robot wheels).

6. *Reflection.* Finally, students fill the surveys provided by the teacher and evaluate the advantages and disadvantages of the course topic and its pedagogical delivery methods.

12.6   Evaluation of Learning Environments

In Tables 12.1 and 12.2, we present the evaluation (i.e. technological and pedagogical) of the quality of created environments. The quality's criteria are adapted from [KD09] (technological) and [KSV04] (pedagogical).

Table 12.1 Learning environments' technological evaluation[a] [Bur14]

Criteria \ Environment	A single robot-based	The collaborative robot-based
Scalability	3	4
Modularity	2	3
Reasonable performance optimizations	3	3
Robustness and stability	3	2
Reusability and portability	3	3
Localizable user interface	4	4
Localization to relevant languages	4	4
Facilities to customize for the educational institution's needs	3	3
Automatic adaptation to the individual user's needs	3	3
Automatically adapted content	3	3
Additive utility function of technological criteria	*31*	*32*

[a]The rate range is 0÷4 (*0* no support, *1* poor support, *2* fair support, *3* good support, *4* excellent support)

Table 12.2 Learning environments' pedagogical evaluation[a,b] [Bur14]

Criteria \ Environment	A single robot-based	The collaborative robot-based
Knowledge of learning content	3	3
Knowledge of learning process	4	4
Cognitive learning skills	4	4
Affective learning skills	4	4
Social learning skills	4	4
Transfer skills	4	4
Additive utility function of pedagogical criteria	*23*	*23*
Preparatory learning functions	C, A, M	C, A, M
Executive learning functions	C, A, M	C, A, M
Closing learning functions	C, A, M	C, A, M
Learning theory	Constructivism	Constructivism
Learners' roles	Cp, Cm (I)	Cp, Cm

[a]The rate range is 0÷4 (*0* no support, *1* poor support, *2* fair support, *3* good support, *4* excellent support)
[b]*C* cognitive, *A* affective, *M* metacognitive, *Cp* cooperative, *Cm* competitive, *I* individual

12.7   How Does the Smart Environment Support the Paradigm Change in CS Education?

In Table 12.3, we present an evaluation of the created smart learning environments in relation to the teacher-centred and learner-centred paradigms. The evaluation criteria are taken from Table 11.7 (see Chap. 11).

Table 12.3 Evaluation of smart learning environments in respect to the teacher-centred (T) and learner-centred (L) paradigms

Criterion # and name [All04, HB00]	One-robot system	The collaborative robot system
1. Teaching goals	*T1* Cover the subject	*T1* Cover the subject
	L1.1 How to use subject	*L1.1* How to use subject
	L1.2 How to integrate subjects	*L1.2* How to integrate subjects
	L1.3 Core learning objectives: communication and information literacy skills	*L1.3* Core learning objectives: communication and information literacy skills
2. Organization of curriculum	*L2* Cohesive program with opportunities to synthesize, practice and develop new ideas and skills	*L2* Cohesive program with opportunities to synthesize, practice and develop new ideas and skills
3. How students learn	*T3.1* Listening	*T3.1* Listening
	T3.2 Reading	*T3.2* Reading
	T3.3 Independent learning	*T3.3* Independent learning
	L3.1 Learners construct knowledge by integrating new learning into what they already know	*L3.1* Learners construct knowledge by integrating new learning into what they already know
	L3.2 Learning is a cognitive and social act	*L3.2* Learning is a cognitive and social act
4. Pedagogy	*L4* Based on the engagement of students	*L4* Based on the engagement of students
5. Course delivery	*L5.1* Active learning	*L5.1* Active learning
	L5.3 Collaborative learning	*L5.3* Collaborative learning
	L5.5 Cooperative learning	*L5.4* Community service learning
	L5.6 Self-directed learning	*L5.5* Cooperative learning
	L5.7 Problem-based learning	*L5.6* Self-directed learning
		L5.7 Problem-based learning
6. Faculty role	*L6* Designer of learning environments	*L6* Designer of learning environments
7. Knowledge transmission	*T7* From teacher to learners	*T7* From teacher to learners
	L7 Learners construct knowledge through gathering and synthesizing information and integrating it with the general skills of inquiry, communication, critical thinking, problem solving	*L7* Learners construct knowledge through gathering and synthesizing information and integrating it with the general skills of inquiry, communication, critical thinking, problem solving
8. Learner's role	*T8* Passively receives information	*L8* Are actively involved
	L8 Are actively involved	
9. Teacher's role	*L9.1* To be the coach and consultant	*L9.1* To be the coach and consultant
	L9.2 To be the team to evaluate learning together	*L9.2* To be the team to evaluate learning together

(continued)

Table 12.3 (continued)

Criterion # and name [All04, HB00]	One-robot system	The collaborative robot system
10. Context role	*L10* Using the communicating knowledge to address enduring and emerging issues and problems in real-life contexts	*L10* Using the communicating knowledge to address enduring and emerging issues and problems in real-life contexts
11. Teaching and assessing	*L11* Are intertwined	*L11* Are intertwined
12. Assessment's role	*T12* To monitor learning	*T12* To monitor learning
	L12 To promote and diagnose learning	*L12* To promote and diagnose learning
13. Emphasis	*L13* Generating better questions and learning from errors	*L13* Generating better questions and learning from errors
14. Focus	*L14* Interdisciplinary learning	*L14* Interdisciplinary learning

12.8 Discussion, Summary and Conclusion

Our research has confirmed the importance of using robot-based environments for teaching that was known so far in the literature on e-learning. We have extended the known approach: (a) by providing technical characteristics of the process to create the e-learning environment for the real setting and (b) by smoothly integrating different phases of the process and considering it into entirety. We have identified that the robot-based e-learning environment extends highly the constructivist model of learning and teaching. We have also identified some difficulties to implement the approach. The main social barrier is the teacher's determination and the need of changing the mind in using the approach and the lack of previous knowledge.

The e-learning environment for collaborative learning (1) provides the interdisciplinary aspects of teaching (the tasks considered are related to mechanics, physics, mathematics and computer science), (2) increases the student engagement in learning, (3) develops the student abilities to critically analyse and compare different problem-solving algorithms (e.g. line-following algorithms in our example) and (4) contributes to the foundations of research and result presentation.

The e-learning environment introduces also two basic challenges: (1) the need of the flexible communication infrastructure for groups of mobile robots and (2) the complexity of specifying collaborative behaviour.

Future work will focus on the extension of the architecture of the e-learning environment with multi-master/multi-slave model to allow using a larger number of communicating robots for learning at the same time, thus allowing to deliver teaching of more complex CS topics.

12.9 Research and Exercise Questions

12.1. Define the term *smart educational environment* and explain its possible interpretation.

12.2. Analyse the following research visions in educational robotics: (1) robot as a tool, (2) robot as a motivator and (3) robot as a means for interdisciplinary teaching.

12.3. Analyse and reconsider principles and requirements for creating smart learning environments.

12.4. Identify the role and functionality of each component depicted in Fig. 12.2.

12.5. Explain why the preparation stage in robot-based systems is needed. Define the main tasks of the stage.

12.6. Define the additional functional characteristics of collaborative robots as compared to the one-robot system.

12.7. Define the essential features of the Lego NXT robot calibration program (use data from Fig. 12.5).

12.8. Explain the physical parameter dependencies given in Fig. 12.6.

12.9. Explain the concept 'collaborative robot as a learning object'. Identify its role in the interdisciplinary education.

12.10. Analyse and prioritize the criteria to evaluate smart educational environments.

12.11. Identify criteria that are more relevant to teacher-centred learning paradigm as compared to learner-centred paradigm using (a) one-robot system and (b) collaborative robot system.

References

[All04] Allen MJ (2004) Assessing academic programs. Anker Publishing, Boston

[BA07] Barker BS, Ansorge J (2007) Robotics as means to increase achievement scores in an informal learning environment. J Res Technol Educ 39(3):229–243

[BCD99] Beer RD, Chiel HJ, Drushel RF (1999) Using autonomous robotics to teach science and engineering. Commun ACM 42(6):85–92

[Ben12] Benitti FBV (2012) Exploring the educational potential of robotics in schools: a systematic review. Comput Educ 58(3):978–988

[BMB08] Balatsoukas P, Morris A, O'Brien A (2008) Learning objects update: review and critical approach to content aggregation. Educ Technol Soc 11(2):119–130

[Bri11] Brittain N (2011) IT education remains mired in uncertainty. Computing. 20 Sep 2011

[BSD13] Burbaite R, Stuikys V, Damasevicius R (2013) Educational robots as collaborative learning objects for teaching computer science. In: System Science and Engineering (ICSSE), 2013 international conference IEEE, pp 211–216

[BSM12] Burbaite R, Stuikys V, Marcinkevicius R (2012) The LEGO NXT robot-based e-learning environment to teach computer science topics. Elektronika ir Elektrotechnika 18(9):113–116

[Bur14]   Burbaitė R (2014) Advanced generative learning objects in informatics education: the concept, models, and implementation. Summary of doctoral dissertation, physical sciences, informatics (09P), Kaunas University of Technology, Kaunas

[CAL12]   Campos AM, Alvarez-Gonzalez LA, Livingstone DE (2012) Analyzing effectiveness of pedagogical scenarios for learning programming a learning path data model. In: Mierluş-Mazilu I (ed) Proceedings of the 1st international workshop on open technology transfer and learning solutions for programming education. Conspress, Bucureşti

[CFW+06]   Chown E, Foil GT, Work H, Zhuang Y (2006) AiboConnect: a simple programming environment for robotics. In: FLAIRS conference, Melbourne Beach, FL, USA, pp 192–197

[CLL+11]   Chou LD, Liu TC, Li DC, Chen YS, Leong MT, Lee PH, Lin YC (2011) Development of a game-based learning system using toy robots. In: Advanced Learning Technologies (ICALT), 2011 11th IEEE international conference, Athens, Greece, pp 202–204

[FP09]   Frangou S, Papanikolaou KA (2009) On the development of robotic enhanced learning environments. In: Kinshuk DGS, Spector JM, Ifenthaler D (eds) Proceedings of the IADIS international conference on cognition and exploratory learning in digital age, Rome, Italy, pp 18–25

[Gra01]   Gray JA (2001) Toeing the line: experiments with line-following algorithms. [Online]. Available: http://www.fll-freak.com/misc/01-jgray_report.pdf

[Had09]   Hadjerrouit S (2009) Teaching and learning school informatics: a concept-based pedagogical approach. Inform Educ Int J 8(2):227–250

[Has08]   Hasker RW (2006) An introductory programming environment for LEGO® MindStorms™ robots. In: Proceedings of the 2006 ASCUE conference, Myrtle Beach, South Carolina

[HB00]   Huba ME, Freed JE (2000) Learner centered assessment on college campuses: shifting the focus from teaching to learning. Commun Coll J Res Pract 24(9):759–766

[HTK02]   Houser C, Thornton P, Kluge D (2002) Mobile learning: cell phones and PDAs for education. In: Computers in education, international conference, IEEE computer society, pp 1149–1149

[IEEE00]   IEEE (2000) IEEE learning standards committee, WG 12: learning object metadata [Online]. Available: http://ltsc.ieee.org/wg12

[IFR12]   International Federation of Robotics (IFR) (2012) World robotics 2012 industrial robots. Executive summary [Online]. Available: http://www.ifr.org/industrial-robots/statistics/

[JJ04]   Jones V, Jo JH (2004) Ubiquitous learning environment: an adaptive teaching system using ubiquitous technology. In: Beyond the comfort zone: proceedings of the 21st ASCILITE conference, Perth, Western Australia, p 474

[KD09]   Kurilovas E, Dagienė V (2009) Multiple criteria comparative evaluation of e-learning systems and components. Informatica 20(4):499–518

[Klo08]   Klopfer E (2008) Augmented learning: research and design of mobile educational games. MIT Press, Cambridge, MA

[KSV04]   De Kock A, Sleegers P, Voeten MJ (2004) New learning and the classification of learning environments in secondary education. Rev Educ Res 74(2):141–170

[KSY11]   Kim S, Song SM, Yoon YI (2011) Smart learning services based on smart cloud computing. Sensors 11(8):7835–7850

[Lib05]   Liber O (2005) Learning objects: conditions for viability. J Comput Assist Learn 21 (5):366–373

[Lom08]   Lombardozzi C (2008) Learning environment design. E-learning guild's leading solutions e-magazine

[LY11]   Lau WW, Yuen AH (2011) Modelling programming performance: beyond the influence of learner characteristics. Comput Edu 57(1):1202–1213

[Mau01]   Mauch E (2001) Using technological innovation to improve the problem-solving skills of middle school students: educators' experiences with the LEGO mindstorms robotic invention system. Clear House 74(4):211–213

[PR04]   Portsmore M, Rogers C (2004) Bringing engineering to elementary school. J STEM Educ 5(3&4):17–28

[RFC90]   Reid JA, Forrestal P, Cook J (1990) Small group learning in the classroom. Irwin, Heinemann

[Sch02]   Schulte C (2002) Towards a pedagogical framework for teaching programming and object-oriented modelling in secondary education. In: Proceedings of SECIII 2002, Dortmund, Germany, pp 22–26

[SHL+13] Schäfer A, Holz J, Leonhardt T, Schroeder U, Brauner P, Ziefle M (2013) From boring to scoring–a collaborative serious game for learning and practicing mathematical logic for computer science education. Comput Sci Educ 23(2):87–111

[SS12]   Shukla M, Shukla AN (2012) Growth of robotics industry early in 21st century. Int J Comput Eng Res 2(5):1554–1558

[Pro14]   Project SMART Celebrates 10 Years of Support from Entergy (2014) http://www.oswego.edu/magazine/2014/08/11/project-smart-celebrates-10-years-of-support-from-entergy/

[S-VNK+08] Santacruz-Valencia LP, Navarro A, Kloos CD, Aedo I (2008) ELO-tool: taking action in the challenge of assembling learning objects. Educ Technol Soc 11(1):102–117

[TKS14]   Tanner P, Karas C, Schofield D (2014) Augmenting a child's reality: using educational tablet technology. J Inf Technol Educ Innov Pract 13:45–54

[Tol06]   Toledo S (2006) Analysis of the NXT bluetooth-communication protocol. Technical paper [Online]. Available: http://www.tau.ac.il/~ stoledo/lego/btperformance.html

[Wil00]   Wiley DA (2000) Learning object design and sequencing theory. Ph.D. dissertation, Brigham Young University

Chapter 13
Smart Education in CS: A Case Study

13.1 Introduction

Today, computer science (CS) is regarded as a fundamental course (similarly to mathematics, physics, etc.), which is delivered in both universities and schools. Its importance has been recognized far ago because it is a source of the primary and fundamental knowledge needed for our lives and activities, which are highly penetrated by the use of computers, the Internet and other modern technologies. On the other hand, CS can be also seen as an interdisciplinary course, for example, with respect to its relation to robotics and e-learning domains. Furthermore, combining CS topics with the use of robots in learning adequately, it is possible to make a significant contribution to the STEM (science, technology, engineering and mathematics) paradigm, a new interdisciplinary approach to learning and teaching for the twenty-first century. Though we have not considered this paradigm explicitly so far, in fact, by introducing and combining two novel approaches, smart LOs and robot-based smart educational environments, we have paved a way for researching and studying the STEM approach too. But first, we need to show how smart LOs and smart educational environments interact among themselves and to approve this interaction in the real learning and teaching setting.

Therefore, the aim of this chapter is summative. First, we aim at presenting the real teaching processes based on the use of smart LOs within smart educational environments. Next, we aim at extracting pedagogical and technological attributes and data for evaluating the introduced approach from the methodological, social and technological viewpoints. Finally, we aim at gaining stimuli and new knowledge for future research in CS learning and teaching.

As it was done so far, we start with the analysis of the relevant literature.

This chapter should be referenced and cited as follows: Vytautas Štuikys and Renata Burbaitė. Smart Education in CS: A Case Study. In Smart Learning Objects for the Smart Education in Computer Science (Theory, Methodology and Robot-Based Implementation), Springer, 2015.

V. Štuikys, *Smart Learning Objects for Smart Education in Computer Science*, DOI 10.1007/978-3-319-16913-2_13

13.2   Literature Review

CS deals with abstract topics and most secondary school students have difficulties to understand and use basic concepts, such as data structures and algorithms, to create programs that solve concrete problems. The following papers emphasize the importance of at least two items in learning and teaching: (a) the choosing of the relevant theory and model, educational methods, activities and environments and (b) an adequate level of student engagement in the process [FME01, Lub11, PPL10, Pea10, HLR11, CNO+12].

Usually the learning theory is introduced through educational methods, activities and environments. There are three main categories of learning theories: behaviourism, cognitivism and constructivism [Leo02, Smi03]. Behaviourism is based on using an educational environment, which forms appropriate student's behaviour and correct responses. The reinforcement of behaviour is a central issue in the learning process. According to the cognitivism, the student is an active goal-oriented information receiver, processor and developer of new information, and information processing is more important than the final result. The main idea of constructivism is that the student constructs his/her own knowledge based on his/her previous knowledge, own experience and learning context. According to this approach, the main task of the teacher is to create a learning environment in which the students could actualize previous knowledge and experience and could adopt new information actively.

The constructivist-based approach dominates in CS teaching and learning [B-A98, PPL10, Pea10, HLR11]. The approach highlights that 'in this situation the students stand in the centre of the learning process and the teacher only helps, gives advises as a facilitator'. Jenkins [Jen01] indicates that the teaching environments, learning activities and teaching methods have a significant impact on motivation. If the above-listed items are chosen properly, the students can learn CS topics in the most effective way.

Educational robots offer new benefits to implementing the most effective active learning methods and supporting tools for the teaching of CS topics [FM02, AMA +07, FPA+08, KKK+07]. In this context, the most commonly used learning methods derived from the constructivism-based theory are as follows: problem-based learning [MK06, TH07, AKP+10, CC10], project-based learning [SNH05, APM11, JPM+11] and game-based learning [AMD08, LWC11, HS11]. The next portion of recent works [GL11, GB11, BSM12, PB12] describes the learner-centred robotic enhanced environments based on the constructivist approach and a methodology to involve students to knowledge construction.

The other papers [FM02, WKK+07, KJ09] emphasize the need of representing the CS content at different levels of education (primary school, secondary school, university) and define the content, which can be learned by students using robot-based environments. In this regard, for example, Sklar et al. [SPA07] argue that the entire CS course can be covered and robotics-based curriculum constructed using robot-enhanced environments. Also Adams et al. [AKP+10] report on developing the students' skill by using the reusable learning objects (RLOs) and robots within a virtual learning environment.

This analysis is by no means exhaustive. Nevertheless, it is sufficient to motivate our vision of the smart CS education to be discussed in the remaining sections.

13.3   A Framework for Smart Education in CS

Our learning and teaching approach focuses on the constructivist-based learning model (CBLM) [Leo02] and the empirical modelling paradigm [Har07]. According to the constructivism, students are more successful in learning when they are given the opportunity to explore and create knowledge dynamically while working with projects that they are interested in and to explore and test their ideas [Pap93]. This style of learning encourages students to create tools and environments that sustain projects that are meaningful for students [DeL03]. Empirical modelling is concerned with creating and using empirically developed computer models. The word empirical here means that the learning process is guided by practical experience rather than theoretical knowledge [Har07].

In Fig. 13.1, we outline our framework as five basic components and their interactions. As compared to our previous vision [ŠBD13], now we have slightly modified the framework. The components within the framework are abstractly

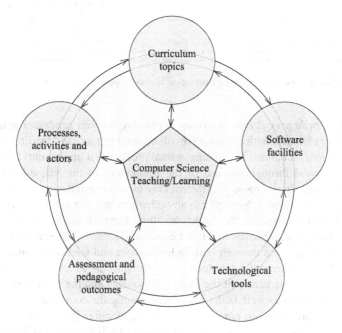

Fig. 13.1 Generalized framework for smart CS education

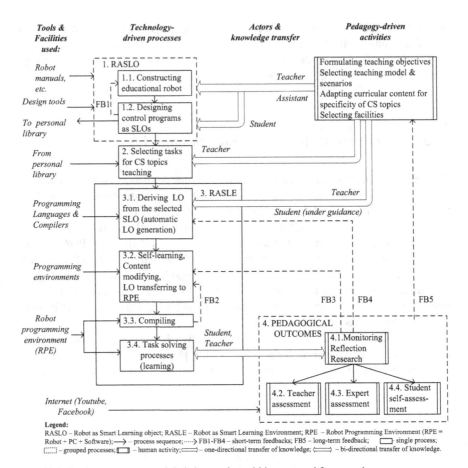

Fig. 13.2 Basic components and their interaction within proposed framework

identified as *pedagogy-driven activities*, *technology-driven processes* and *knowledge transfer channels with the actors* involved, a set of *tools* and *facilities* used and the *pedagogical outcomes*. The latter is a final product that implements the learning goals (objectives) through the use of the framework in the real e-learning and teaching settings (in our case, in different classes at the gymnasium and university levels to teach CS topics). Similarly to any other product, the achieved pedagogical outcome has to be assessed. We anticipate three forms of the assessment: student self-assessment, teacher assessment and expert assessment. The interaction among components is specified through knowledge transfer and feedback channels.

In Fig. 13.2, we present a detailed view of the introduced framework. Here, one can see the internal structure of the basic components and the outside data needed for the functionality as well as the interaction among the components.

The interaction between components, in fact, specifies the functionality of the whole system. We describe the interaction model by both the knowledge transfer channels and a set of possible feedbacks (FB1–FB5). The process starts with the pedagogical-driven activities. The teacher, his/her assistants and partially knowledgeable students in the role of assistants are actors at the initial stage of the process (see Sect. 13.6.2, for details). After the initial stage, the technology-driven processes follow. There are three main processes identified in Fig. 13.2 as (1) RASLO, robot as smart LO; (2) the selecting of a task for the CS topic; and (3) RASLE, robot as smart learning environment. In fact, the RASLO-based process is preparatory and should be carried out in advance. Of course, the main actor to perform it is the *motivated teacher* with the highly expressed determination to accept the challenges of the smart CS education. If it is just the case (we mean our case here), then the process will be successful with a greater degree of certainty.

Even more, the highly motivated teacher can involve students as apprentices. Our experience has shown that a majority of students are very happy by being involved in constructing educational robots under the teacher's guidance. They see this activity as a game with the evident gain ('Oh, my robot is working!').

The next preparatory work is to design the generalized robot control programs (in fact meta-programs) treated as SLOs here. This activity (as one can conceive from the previous chapters) requires the interdisciplinary knowledge and competence (not only the designer's determination). The whole design cycle includes three main phases: (1) the specification of robot tasks and algorithms to cover the CS curriculum topics, (2) the development of feature models for the tasks and (3) the design and testing of code-level specifications (i.e. SLO per se).

The most crucial part of this cycle is the phase 2, because it requires a great deal of analysis of both the problem and solution domains. The problem domain is highly heterogeneous and includes two main subdomains: pedagogy-oriented (such as teaching methods, models, social context, etc.) and content-oriented context (i.e. related to robot control tasks and algorithms). The solution domain of this phase is feature modelling approaches, including the modelling and verification tools (see Chaps. 4 and 5). The feature models created as a result of this phase are extremely valuable intellectual property, because they predefine the success in designing the code-level specifications at the final phase. The use of developed tools (such as MePAG) governed by the created models at phase 2 and other models (such as meta-programs) created at phase 3 simplifies the development of the code-level specifications significantly.

Is it possible to involve students in designing SLO specifications? If so, then there is a question: when, how and to which extent? Our experience is as follows. The students who are highly motivated and engaged in studying programming as a means for their future career typically are co-designers of the code-level specifications. However, there are or might be the only 2–3 students out of about 100–120 students of the whole enrolment. Typically, those students are able to accept this role after completing studies on programming basics.

The RASLO-based process ends with the creation of SLOs. They are further treated as items of the teacher's personal library (we will discuss it later). Here, we consider the process as the preparatory with regard to the remaining ones.

13.4   The List of SLOs to Cover CS Curriculum Topics

As an example, in Fig. 13.3, we present the list of SLO-oriented tasks in the relation with the curriculum modules to teach CS at the different grades (levels) in the secondary school. Here, the arrows show which curriculum module or topic is covered by which SLO. Note that the arrows indicate not the capability of an environment to realize the topic but what topic was really implemented using the given environment. Our smart environment is heterogeneous too, because we use Lego NXT robots as well as Arduino-based controllers.

Why do we use two different environments? First, the Arduino-based environment enables to realize more complex tasks such as algorithms to control traffic light. Next, the Arduino-based environment is more suitable for introducing knowledge from the field of electronics, while the NXT robots relate more to mechanics as their electronic facilities are deeply integrated within, i.e. hidden from the user. Therefore, the heterogeneous environments fit better for interdisciplinary teaching and have the opportunity to consider STEM-based teaching and to provide research in the field.

Fig. 13.3 Relationships among CS modules and SLOs integrated into smart environment

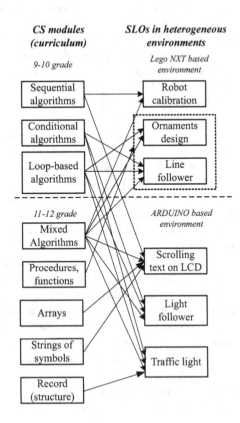

13.5   Personal Library as a Database of Smart Environment

The personal library provides the educational and managerial support in storing, updating and searching the content to realize the CS curriculum objectives and tasks within the smart environment. Currently we treat the library as *personal* because it was created by the CS teacher to satisfy the *local needs* of the teaching institution only. With regard to the introduced framework (see Fig. 13.2), the library is seen as the *internal database* to support the functionality of the smart educational environment. However, we do not exclude the opportunity of extending the status of the library use in the future.

Currently the creator of the library is also responsible for maintenance and updating tasks. The users of the library are both teachers (there might also be other teachers as library users within the institution) and students. However, the access mode is different for the teacher-administrator, teachers as users and students. The teacher-administrator holds the highest priority: all accessibility functions are allowable. The overall structure of the library is shown in Fig. 13.4.

There are three basic components: (1) creating and updating facilities, (2) library items and (3) search attributes. There are two types of items within the library: LOs and SLOs. The set of LOs represents the traditional learning objects to be obtained through linking to the external resources. They might be given in the form of text, pictures, video, etc. (e.g. to support the theoretical part of the topic, or it is the other additional material such as instructions to construct robots). Before the links are

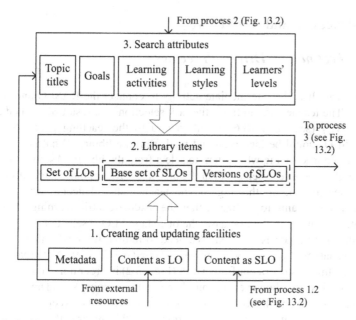

Fig. 13.4 Architecture of the personal library

being stored into the library, those links (LOs) first are enriched with metadata to enable their search procedure later in the use time.

There are also two kinds of SLOs within the library: base SLOs and versions of a particular SLO. Versioning is not so much needed for the real teaching process but to the larger extent for the experimentation and research (see Chaps. 10 and 11). Note that metadata are applied for the external LO content and SLOs differently. In the first case, the metadata is taken from the digital libraries or is accordingly created by the library designer. In the second case, the metadata is incorporated in the internal structure of an SLO as the pedagogical context parameters. Therefore, the parameters serve for two roles at once: as the search attribute (in the context of the content creating for the library) and as the generating mechanism to produce LO (in the context of use).

What is about the stage-based SLOs within the personal library? As we use the tool MP-ReTool to transform the initial SLO into its stage-based version, there are no difficulties to derive those versions at any time. Therefore, we are able to produce a stage-based SLO either from the base SLO or from its versions. There are two possibilities in storing the stage-based SLOs. We can, for example, have a separate section within the library for saving all staged SLOs for each task. Another possibility is to treat a staged SLO as a particular version of a given task and keep those items in the section of all versions.

Now we are able to continue our discussion on the remaining processes and activities indicated in the introduced framework.

13.6   Processes and Activities

13.6.1   Technology-Driven Processes

Task Selection It is the intermediate activity to connect the RASLO and RASLE processes. The teacher first initiates the task selection as a result of the pedagogy-driven activity (see Sect. 13.6.2) with regard to the teaching goals. Next, the adequate SLO should be identified and read from the library. What is to be done before reading is knowing which item to select from the library. As it was stated in Sect. 13.5, it is possible to select either the one-stage SLO or multistage SLO for the already selected task. In this regard, the teacher should decide what teaching paradigm he/she wants to realize: either the teacher-centric learning or the student-centric learning. In the first case, the one-stage SLO is selected. In the second case, multistage variant is selected. We need to remind the reader that the multistage SLO enables to provide an adaptive learning (see Chap. 9). Note that we have not reflected this process in our framework (Fig. 13.2) in order not to complicate the presentation. There is, however, yet another reason for doing so: adaptive learning follows the same line within the framework with one essential exception – there are more feedbacks to support adaptive learning. In this regard, the reader should compare the sequence of actions reported in Figs. 8.4 and 8.5 (see Sect. 8.7 in Chap. 8) with the processes and actions indicated in Fig. 13.2. Further, we accept that the teacher selects one-stage SLO (i.e. initial SLO and we omit this term).

RASLE Processes Now the learner is the main actor and he/she initiates the process. Process 3.1 describes the derivation of LO from the SLO specification. The operating environment in which the process takes place is the meta-language processor (PHP processor in our case). Having the SLO (given by the teacher) and the predefined operating environment, the student works with the interface of the SLO and identifies the needed parameter values (this action already was described multiple times in Chaps. 8 and 9). Those student's actions result in creating LO (robot control program to fuel its operation). This process is automatic (if we neglect the parameter value selection).

The next process (Process 3.2 in Fig. 13.2) is treated as a self-learning one, because the student deals with the generated LO, refreshes his/her knowledge about robot programming, rereads the teaching goal (typically the generated LO contains that information) and may communicate with the teacher or other students. Furthermore, the student may want *to modify* the created LO on the basis of his own intention. But also the teacher may ask students to make *some changes* in the generated program, for example, if the teacher applies the project-based teaching paradigm. Note that the process of program changing is *the way* of its better understanding – the core of any learning process. Also one should know the following truth: to introduce the small changes (especially for teaching purposes, meaning the anticipated changes) is not the same as to write the program from scratch. Therefore, the automatic generation is the highly desirable action to produce the initial version (or version) of the teaching program.

Finally, the possibly changed control program goes through the standard procedures: compiling (Process 3.3 within robot programming environment – RPE and task solving (Process 3.4). Compiling and task running are well-known processes for CS courses such as programming. Those processes are independent upon which facilities are used in teaching: computer, robot or mobile phone. In our case, the Processes 3.1, 3.2, 3.3, 3.4, and 3.5 create the technology-driven environment and support for achieving the learning and teaching goals. We will discuss the way of achieving that in the next section.

13.6.2 Pedagogical Outcomes

The student actions in carrying out processes 3.1–3.4 predefine the whole learning process. Within the introduced framework, we define the learning process as the overall communications: (1) student-teaching facilities through indicated feedback (FB2), (2) student-teacher, (3) student-student, (4) monitoring what is going on the robot's scene, (5) self-reflection on what is going on the robot's scene and (6) decision making (researching) to form the adequate feedbacks. In fact, this space of actions prespecifies the pedagogical outcomes of learning and teaching. Feedback links (*FB2–FB4*) are a very important part of the learning process because they ensure a great deal of flexibility *to regenerate the content, to modify the content* and *to obtain knowledge* through *monitoring learning scenarios* as they are seen in the robot-based reality (but not in the virtual reality as it takes place when only the PC and Internet as learning facilities are used).

In this way, after the completion of the communication session, the student is able to form a self-assessment of what he/she did and what he/she gained and experienced, because the final result is represented as the visual reality of the robot's actions. This reality may cause discussions and move forward to take researching and to enforce the feeling of confidence on what was done. The teacher may ask whether or not the student is satisfied with the achieved outcomes. It is also interesting to know what are or might be disappointments. What expectations have not been fulfilled? This is important for the teacher to take his/her assessment. Furthermore, the external expert may also take part in the process and provide the independent assessment.

13.6.3   Pedagogy-Driven Activities

The framework we suggest uses two learning models derived from the constructivist-based pedagogical approach: problem-based learning [AKP+10, CC10, MK06, TH07] and project-based learning [APM11, SNH05, JPM+11]. Though there is a thin line among the models, nevertheless, we introduce them as slightly different teaching scenarios (in other words, the models are integrated within the scenarios) either explicitly or intuitively through the learning objective formulation, teacher's plans (such as curricular content) and smart teaching environment (robot-based) and teaching task selection. The basic requirement for creating the scenarios is to enforce the students' involvement and engagement in the process. All these are seen as predetermined pedagogical activities before starting the teaching and learning process. One pedagogical activity, however, should be highlighted separately here. We mean the formulation of requirements for the SLO design. Here, we accept that the teaching content (defined by the standard or enhanced CS teaching curricular program in schools) either partially or fully should be implemented as an SLO or SLOs. The other activities are clear from Fig. 13.2.

In Table 13.1, we summarize the technology-driven processes (TP) in combination with pedagogical activities (PA).

Table 13.1 Integrative vision to processes and activities

Item	Details: TP/PA
Initial requirements	Knowing of the pedagogical model (PA)
	Knowing of the curriculum content (PA)
	Robot readiness for the use (TP)
Guide	Human guided, tool guided (TP/PA)
Automation level	Automatic, semi-automatic (TP)
Activity	Single activity, multiple reuse activity (PA)
Tool type	Hardware, software (TP)
Degree of the teacher or student involvement	Teacher-student, student-student measured by the number of FBs, visualization, adaptability (PA/TP)
Constraints	Initial knowledge and readiness of teacher (PA)
Functionality	Described as the input/output specification (PA/TP)
Abstraction level	How much detail relevant to teaching topic should be revealed explicitly (PA)
Types of subprocesses	Robot independent, robot dependent
	Generative technology independent, generative technology dependent (TP)

13.7 More on Pedagogical Outcomes: Assessment View

The assessment process involves some goals: (i) to improve learning (formative assessment) and (ii) to provide data for grading (summative assessment) [CS07]. According to Harlen [Har13], formative assessment is also called '*assessment for learning*'. The key activities and processes of the formative assessment practices are as follows:

(i) Stimulating students in communicating their knowledge and skills.
(ii) Helping students understand their goals.
(iii) Introducing feedbacks: 'teacher-student', 'student-student' and 'student-teacher' imply a view of learning as a process in which students are active constructors of new knowledge.
(iv) Involving students in the self-assessment process.
(v) Providing dialogues between teacher and students to encourage reflection.

Summative assessment is also called '*assessment of learning*'. The key attributes of the assessment are defined as follows [Har13]:

(i) The involvement of students in solving special tasks or tests.
(ii) Assessment takes place at certain times when achievement is to be reported, not a cycle taking place as a regular part of learning.
(iii) The relation to the achievement of broad goals expressed in general terms rather than the goals of particular learning activities.
(iv) Assessment involves the achievement of all students being judged against the same criteria or mark scheme.
(v) Assessment requires some measures to assure reliability.

(vi) Assessment provides limited opportunities for student self-assessment.

Simply speaking, the formative assessment is the result of learning with the teacher's and other student's support, whereas the summative assessment evaluates the student's competences, knowledge and skills in the whole with respect to predefined standards.

In fact, this view of the assessment expands the previously stated pedagogical outcomes (see Fig. 13.2) as it is outlined in Fig. 13.5. Here, the formative assessment includes the student's self-assessment and the teacher's assessment. The summative assessment includes the teacher's and/or expert's assessment. As a result, new forms of feedbacks occur, such as FB6 and FB7. Furthermore, a deeper feedback takes place for the formative assessment and includes FB4–FB6 (cp. the feedbacks with the ones from Fig. 13.2).

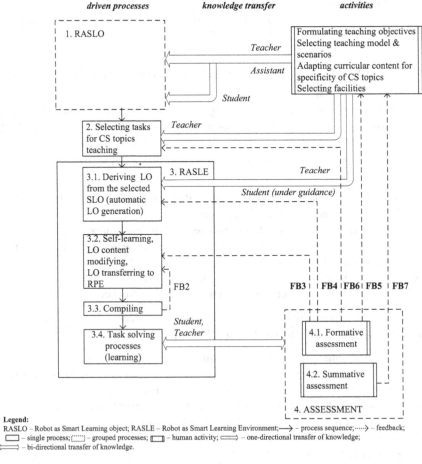

Fig. 13.5 Assessment connected with the smart CS education framework

13.8   Validation of the Approach Through Experiments in Real Teaching Setting

In this section, we aim at providing more extensive research on evaluation and validation of our approach. As smart LOs are indeed complex entities in both pedagogical and technological dimensions, they should be evaluated from two those perspectives: pedagogical and technological. Typically the designed items (systems or components) are evaluated through measuring their complexity. Different domains (such as pedagogy and technology; the latter means programs (meta-programs) or software here) have different complexity measures. Therefore, we discuss the complexity issues separately for each domain, starting from the technology-based view.

13.8.1   *Complexity Evaluation of Smart LOs: Representation and Comprehension View*

Complexity is a difficult concept to define, and in the SW domain, there are various definitions. IEEE Std. 610.12:1990, for instance, defines software complexity as 'the degree to which a system or component has a design or implementation that is difficult to understand and verify' [IEEE90]. Therefore, the complexity relates to both *comprehension complexity* and *representation complexity*. In general, the complexity is the *inherent property* of an item (system, component, i.e. SLO in our case), though the complexity can also be evaluated *externally* (e.g. by counting lines of code (LOC) within the SLO specification as we did in Chaps. 11 and 12). In this section, however, we consider the complexity of SLOs from the *representation perspective but with the focus on the inherent properties of the items*.

Since the software complexity has multiple metrics, so is with the SLO representation and comprehension complexity. As SLOs, in fact, are meta-programs, it is the reason why we apply a set of metrics [ŠD13] to measure the complexity of SLOs as follows: relative Kolmogorov complexity (RKC), meta-language richness (MR), normalized difficulty (ND) and cognitive difficulty (CD).

In Table 13.2, we present RKC metric for our SLO samples using Eq. (13.1):

$$\text{RKC} = \frac{\|C(M)\|}{\|M\|} \qquad (13.1)$$

Here, $\|M\|$ is the size (in bytes) of the initial SLO treated as meta-program M or k-stage meta-program M^k (received after refactoring to support adaptation), and $\|C(M)\|$ is the size of the compressed meta-programs using a compression algorithm BWT (Burrows-Wheeler transform; see GnuWin32). A high value of RKC means that there are fewer capabilities for compression, i.e. there are less repeating parts within the meta-program, and therefore this meta-program is regarded as being less

Table 13.2 Relative Kolmogorov complexity measures

Task	Complexity changes of the refactored SLO as compared to the initial handmade SLO			
	Handmade	2-stage SLO	3-stage SLO	4-stage SLO
Lego NXT, RobotC				
Robot calibration	0.23	0.22	0.16	0.11
Line follower	0.19	0.14	0.12	0.08
Ornament design	0.19	0.18	0.13	0.09
Arduino, Arduino C				
Scrolling text on LCD	0.26	0.26	0.18	0.13
Light follower	0.22	0.18	0.13	0.10
Traffic light	0.21	0.19	0.13	0.10

complex. On the contrary, the more capabilities for compression are, the meta-program content is regarded as being of higher complexity.

The content of Table 13.2 (as well as the remaining ones) should be read in two directions: *horizontal* and *vertical*. In horizontal direction, we compare the complexity changes of the *initial handmade* SLOs against the specialized (refactored) SLOs. We have selected the handmade SLOs because they are more optimal (in terms of LOC) as compared to those designed using the tool MePAG. As with the growth of stages, there are more repeating parts within the SLO. Therefore, the complexity evaluated by RKC tends to increase. The more stages within the SLO structure are, the more complex this SLO is (this is valid for each task).

In the vertical dimension, we compare the complexity of different SLOs among themselves. Therefore, the line follower and ornament design SLOs are more complex and scrolling text on LCD is the least complex SLO.

The next measure MR (Eq. (13.2)) represents the meta-language richness:

$$MR = \frac{\sum_{m \in M} \|m\|}{\|M\|} \tag{13.2}$$

Here, $\|m\|$ is the size of the domain language constructs (in our case RobotC or Arduino C) that contain within the meta-language functions. A higher value of MR means that a meta-program has more metadata and its description is more complex. In Table 13.3, we present the results of calculating MR for the same tasks. Again, in the horizontal dimension, the complexity increases. In the vertical dimension, the line follower SLO stands for the most complex item among others.

We present the normalized difficulty (ND) metric by Eq. (13.3), meaning the *algorithmic complexity* which was derived from Halstead metrics (Halstead 1977; see also [ŠD13] and Table 13.4).

Table 13.3 Meta-language richness measures

| Task | Refactoring-based complexity changes | | | |
	Handmade	2-stage SLO	3-stage SLO	4-stage SLO
Lego NXT, RobotC				
Robot calibration	0.67	0.84	0.95	0.99
Line follower	0.75	0.94	0.96	0.99
Ornament design	0.60	0.88	0.96	0.99
Arduino, Arduino C				
Scrolling text on LCD	0.69	0.75	0.98	0.98
Light follower	0.64	0.89	0.98	0.99
Traffic light	0.59	0.84	0.98	0.99

Table 13.4 Normalized difficulty measures

| Task | Refactoring-based complexity changes | | | |
	Handmade	2-stage SLO	3-stage SLO	4-stage SLO
Lego NXT, RobotC				
Robot calibration	0.14	0.16	0.19	0.21
Line follower	0.16	0.19	0.21	0.28
Ornament design	0.11	0.15	0.17	0.17
Arduino, Arduino C				
Scrolling text on LCD	0.18	0.21	0.21	0.21
Light follower	0.20	0.18	0.18	0.18
Traffic light	0.18	0.18	0.18	0.18

$$ND = \frac{n_1 N_2}{(N_1 + N_2)(n_1 + n_2)} \tag{13.3}$$

Here, the meaning of variables is as follows: n_1, the number of the distinct meta-language functions; n_2, the number of distinct meta-program parameters; N_1, the total number of meta-functions; and N_2, the total number of parameters. A high-value calculation of the ND metric means that the meta-program is highly complex in terms of time and effort required to understand it.

Finally, the cognitive difficulty (CD) metric (see Table 13.5) is calculated by Eq. (13.4) as the maximal number of meta-level units:

$$CD = \max(P, N_1, N_2) \tag{13.4}$$

Here, P is the number of distinct parameters, N_1 the total number of meta-functions and N_2 the total number of parameters. CD evaluates cognitive understandability of a meta-program (i.e. SLO in our case).

In summary, the staged-based SLOs are more complex as compared to the initial SLOs, with regard to all introduced metrics. The complexity increases when the number of stages grows. Indeed the cognitive difficulty is very high; therefore, it is

Table 13.5 Cognitive difficulty measures

Task	Refactoring-based complexity changes			
	Handmade	2-stage SLO	3-stage SLO	4-stage SLO
Lego NXT, RobotC				
Robot calibration	185	350	559	811
Line follower	473	735	897	1227
Ornament design	246	506	775	1203
Arduino, Arduino C				
Scrolling text on LCD	220	291	510	679
Light follower	262	457	748	972
Traffic light	213	368	605	920

practically impossible to develop a multistaged SLO manually when the number of stages is higher than 2. To overcome this difficulty, we have developed MP-ReTool, which we use to make a refactoring transformation (semi-)automatically. The comparison of different SLOs among themselves enabled us to exclude the most complex (i.e. line follower) and the least complex SLOs (i.e. traffic light) with respect to all introduced metrics.

13.8.2   Pedagogical Evaluation of Created Smart LOs

Before giving the pedagogical evaluation, we need to state one important aspect regarding the concept SLO itself. The SLOs (as they are presented here, i.e. as a complete specification) were created through the 4-year long evolutionary process. At the very beginning, all tasks were realized as a generative LO (GLO) with a simplified model (i.e. simplified context model, simplified parameter value spaces, one-stage structural model, etc.). At the end of the period, there were added additional features that enabled to treat the enriched GLOs as smart LOs. Note also that this evolution affected only the designer's and teacher's vision but not the student's vision because students always operate with concrete LO (i.e. robot control program) derived from the GLO or SLO specification. In other words, the capability space for adaptation, context awareness, functionality, etc. was continuously expanding along with the increase of our experience and knowledge gained during the time.

Pedagogical effectiveness of using SLOs can be evaluated by 'engagement levels' using the methodology described in [UV09]. This methodology includes the following phases:

1. *Viewing*: Students are viewing the programs given by the teacher passively, and therefore, they are passive consumers of LOs (the latter are RobotC control programs automatically derived from the SLO specification using PHP processor; see Fig. 10.3).

2. *Responding*: Students are observing the run of programs (i.e. the robot's action caused by the control program), and the process is the resource for taking and answering questions given by the teacher; therefore, students are the active consumers of LOs.
3. *Changing*: Students themselves are modifying programs first by changing the *parameter values* within the SLO specification and then generating LOs; therefore, they are acting as designers of LOs.
4. *Constructing*: Students are creating their own programs (e.g. by introducing new parameters into the SLO specification and defining their values), so they are becoming the LO co-designers and testers; however, not all students are able to do that.
5. *Presenting*: Students (again, only somebody of them) are presenting new programs to the audience for discussion and, therefore, they are acting as the SLO co-designers.

In Fig. 13.6, we explain the assessment of the student engagement levels as a result of the investigations provided by Renate Burbaitė. The results are also presented in her doctoral theses [Bur14].

The pedagogical evaluation based on Bloom's taxonomy engagement levels enables to conclude that SLOs are most effective at the following levels: viewing, constructing and presenting levels. The statistics obtained through experimental research over 3–4 years (2011–2014) shows the increase of learning improvement from 6 % to 15 %.

For the *pedagogical cognitive complexity* evaluation, we use the categories in the cognitive domain of Bloom's taxonomy [AK01] and extract the cognitive processes as defined by [Mil56] for our learning tasks. We evaluate the processes by a typical number of parameters for the task cognition and compare this number with Miller's *cognitive complexity* bounds derived from 7 ± 2: <5 (easy), 5–7 (normal), 8–9 (complex) and >9 (overcomplex). The results are given in Table 13.6.

13.9   How Does the Approach Support the Learning Theories?

In Table 13.7, we summarize the relevance of our approach to the learning theories. We have identified the relevance by the *level of relevance* with respect to questions related to the known learning theories [EN13]. We measure the level using the adequate values of fuzzy variables {H, I, L, H–I, I–L, U} (see legend below Table 13.7). Though the values were defined on the basis of the personal experience and intuition, nevertheless, they provide a systemized vision of effectiveness of our approach.

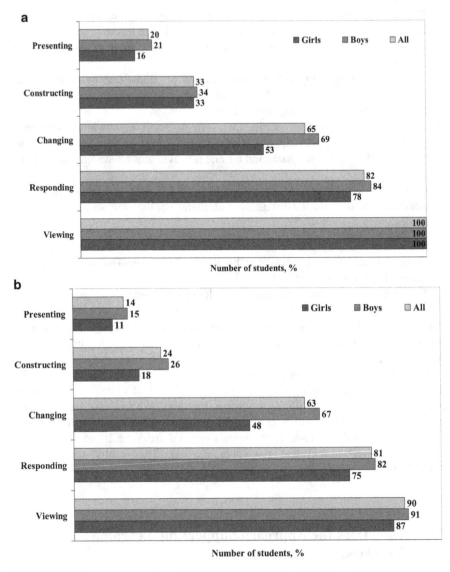

Fig. 13.6 Student engagement levels (2011–2014, 186 students: 141 boys, 45 girls): (**a**) using SLOs and (**b**) not using SLOs [

13.10 Summary, Discussion and Conclusion

In this ending chapter, we have summarized the topics we were discussing merely throughout the book. Here, however, we have presented the summative aspects of our approach from the other perspective – the real use of what was suggested, invented and discussed so far. To do that in some well-formed manner, we first have

Table 13.6 Bloom's taxonomy-based categories, processes and their evaluation using Miller's metrics (7±2)

SLO	Bloom's taxonomy level					
	Pedagogical cognitive complexity expressed by typical parameters as compared to the Miller's metric					
	Remembering	Understanding	Applying	Analysing	Evaluating	Creating
Robot calibration	1 easy	3 easy	4 easy	4 easy	4 easy	4 easy
Line follower	1 easy	2 easy	3 easy	3 easy	3 easy	3 easy
Ornament design	1 easy	5 normal	7 normal	8 complex	9 complex	9 complex
Scrolling text on LCD	1 easy	2 easy	3 easy	3 easy	3 easy	3 easy
Light follower	1 easy	2 easy	3 easy	3 easy	4 easy	4 easy
Traffic light	1 easy	4 easy	5 normal	5 normal	6 normal	7 normal

Table 13.7 Relationships between proposed approach and learning theories [EN13]

Question/learning theory	What is supported? To which level?
How does learning occur?	
Behaviourism: black box-observable behaviour main focus	Black box: H
Cognitivism: structured, computational	Both: H–I
Constructivism: social, meaning created by each learner (personal)	Social: H, H–I dependent on social group
What factors influence learning?	
Behaviourism: nature of reward, punishment, stimuli	Stimuli: H, H–I
Cognitivism: existing schema, previous experiences	Both: H, H–I
Constructivism: engagement (E), participation (P), social (S), cultural (C)	E, P, S: H
What is the role of memory?	
Behaviourism: influential	Influential: U
Cognitivism: retrieval	Retrieval: U
Constructivism: to current context	Context: H, H–I
How does transfer occur?	
Behaviourism: stimulus, response	Both: I, I–L
Cognitivism: duplicating knowledge constructs of 'knower'	U
Constructivism: socialization	I
What types of learning are best explained by this theory?	
Behaviourism: task-based learning	H
Cognitivism: reasoning, clear objectives, problem solving	H
Constructivism: social, vague ('ill defined')	Social: I

Legend. Level measures: *H* high, *I* intermediate, *L* low, *H–I* between high and intermediate, *I–L* between intermediate and low, *U* undefined

suggested a framework according to which the smart education in computer science has been provided and tested. In fact, by the computer science education, we mean the education of programming fundamentals here. By the smart education, we mean the use of smart learning objects (SLOs) within the smart educational environments constructed, tested and used in the real teaching and learning setting.

We have presented the framework as a set of the following basic components: pedagogy-driven activities, technology-driven processes, tools and facilities used (including smart environments), pedagogical outcomes and knowledge transfer channels along with the main actors involved (teachers and students). Yet another important component – the personal library as a database to store and manage the created SLOs – has been introduced and discussed. The external observer should clearly understand the role of the introduced framework. It was the methodological instrument to achieve two predefined objectives: (1) to introduce the smart educational methodology as a case study in some well-formed systematic way and (2) to collect experimental data for our research and, on this basis, to evaluate our approach from different perspectives.

As a result, we have provided and described the evaluation of the SLOs and the smart education from three perspectives: (i) pure technological viewpoint, (ii) pedagogical practice and (iii) pedagogical theory viewpoints. In the part of the technology evaluation, we have presented the complexity evaluation of the SLOs, using metrics taken from meta-programming domain because SLOs, in fact, are meta-programs. We have evaluated the complexity of the SLOs among themselves. This evaluation has enabled us to identify the most and the least complex SLOs among the developed and used ones. Furthermore, using the introduced metrics, we were able to identify the complexity changes of the multistage SLOs as compared the initial handmade SLOs. The multistage SLOs (they support adaptive learning using our approach) were obtained using the tool we have developed. With respect to the introduced complexity metrics, the multistage SLOs are much complex items as compared to the one-stage SLOs. It was obtained the extreme growth of complexity with the increase of the number of stages.

In terms of the pedagogical practice, we have collected data to evaluate the approach by measuring the student engagement level in the learning process using the known methodology which is based on Bloom's taxonomy. The statistics obtained through experimental research over 3–4 years (2011–2014) have shown the increase of learning improvement from 6 % to 15 %. We have also evaluated the SLOs using the *pedagogical cognitive complexity* evaluation that is based on the cognitive domain of Bloom's taxonomy and the Miller's *cognitive complexity* bounds derived from 7 ± 2: <5 (easy), 5–7 (normal), 8–9 (complex) and >9 (overcomplex).

In terms of the pedagogical theories, we have identified the relevance of our approach to the learning theories by the *level of relevance* with respect to questions (stated by Ertmer and Newby 2013) related to the known learning theories (behaviourism, cognitivism and constructivism). We have measured the level of relevance using the adequate values of fuzzy variables {H, high; I, intermediate; L, low; H–I; I–L; U, undefined}.

In summary, we are able to state our results as follows:

1. Though the smart educational methodology has been introduced in a systematic way, it should be treated as *a case study only* in respect to both smart LOs and smart educational environments.
2. Though we have collected experimental data for our research and have evaluated our approach from different perspectives, nevertheless, smart education in computer science is still in its infancy and further intensive research is needed.
3. We hope that the introduced methodology is a good background to extend and intensify the investigation in the following directions: (i) smart LOs, especially multistage SLOs to support the adaptive learning in computer science, (ii) smart educational environments using robots and collaborative learning on this basis and (iii) interdisciplinary teaching to support the STEM paradigm.

13.11   Research and Exercise Questions

13.1. Why should computer science as a teaching subject be regarded as a fundamental course nowadays?

13.2. Provide the analysis of research in teaching with respect to the STEM paradigm.

13.3. Define the role of using robots within the STEM paradigm.

13.4. What is the smart CS education? Evaluate and comment the framework given in Fig. 13.1.

13.5. Study and assess the interaction of basic components within the framework (see Fig. 13.2).

13.6. What are common and different topics within your CS curriculum as compared to the one given in Fig. 13.3?

13.7. Study the basic characteristics of two robot-based educational environments (Lego and Arduino) and compare their capabilities.

13.8. Describe the structure, the role and functionality of the personal library in the context of the CS smart education.

13.9. Provide a thorough study of the processes and activities to define the smart CS education.

13.10. Explain the role of the set of the indicated feedbacks to the overall functionality of this teaching paradigm.

13.11. Clarify what the metrics are for the technological evaluation and those for the pedagogical evaluation.

13.12. What is the pedagogical cognitive complexity of an SLO and how is it measured?

13.13. Get or create an SLO and provide the technological evaluation using the adequate metrics. Obtain the pedagogical cognitive complexity for the same SLO.

References

[AK01]   Anderson L, Krathwohl DA (2001) Taxonomy for learning, teaching and assessing: a revision of Bloom's taxonomy of educational objectives. Longman, New York

[AKP+10] Adams J, Kaczmarczyk S, Picton P, Demian P (2010) Problem solving and creativity in engineering: conclusions of a three year project involving reusable learning objects and robots. Eng Educ 5(2):4–17

[AMA+07] Alimisis D, Moro M, Arlegui J, Pina A, Frangou S, Papanikolaou K (2007) Robotics & constructivism in education: the TERECoP project. In: Kalas I (ed) Proceedings of the 11th European logo conference, Slovakia, Comenius University, pp 1–11

[AMD08] Atmatzidou S, Markelis I, Demetriadis S (2008) The use of LEGO mindstorms in elementary and secondary education: game as a way of triggering learning. Workshop Proc SIMPAR 2008:22–30

[APM11] Arlegui J, Pina A, Moro M (2011) A paradox in the constructive design of robotic projects in school. In: Proceedings of 2nd international conference on robotics in education (RiE 2011), Vienna, pp 29–34

[B-A98]   Ben-Ari M (1998) Constructivism in computer science education. In: Proceedings of
           SIGCSE'98, ACM, Atlanta, pp 257–261
[BSM12]   Burbaite R, Stuikys V, Marcinkevicius R (2012) The LEGO NXT robot-based
           e-learning environment to teach computer science topics. Electron Elect Eng
           18(2):133–136
[Bur14]   Burbaitė R (2014) Advanced generative learning objects in informatics education:
           the concept, models, and implementation. Summary of doctoral dissertation, phys-
           ical sciences, informatics (09P), Kaunas University of Technology, Kaunas
[CC10]   Castledine A, Chalmers C (2011) LEGO Robotics: an authentic problem-solving
           tool? Des Technol Educ 6(3):19–27
[CNO+12]   Cowden D, O'Neill A, Opavsky E, Ustek D, Walker HM (2012) A C-based intro-
           ductory course using robots. In: Proceedings of the 43rd ACM technical symposium
           on computer science education. ACM, pp 27–32
[CS07]   Cromack J, Savenye W (2007) Learning about learning in computational science and
           science, technology, engineering and mathematics (STEM) education
[DeL03]   DeLuca D (2003) Robotics and teaching: promoting the effective use of technology
           in education (Honors thesis). Tufts University. Retrieved from http://ceeo.tufts.edu/
           robolabatceeo/references/thesis/DianaDeluca_undergrad.pdf
[EN13]   Ertmer PA, Newby TJ (2013) Behaviorism, cognitivism, constructivism: comparing
           critical features from an instructional design perspective. Perform Improv Quart
           26(2):43–71
[FM02]   Fagin BS, Merkle L (2002) Quantitative analysis of the effects of robots on intro-
           ductory computer science education. J Educ Res Comput 2(4):2
[FME01]   Fagin BS, Merkle LD, Eggers TW (2001) Teaching computer science with robotics
           using Ada/Mindstorms 2.0. ACM SIGAda Ada Lett 21(4):73–78
[FPA+08]   Frangou S, Papanikolaoum K, Aravecchia L, Montel L, Ionita S, Arlegui J, Pina A,
           Menegatti E, Moro M, Fava N, Monfalcon S, Pagello I (2008) Representative
           examples of implementing educational robotics in school based on the constructivist
           approach. In: SIMPAR workshop on teaching with robotics: didactic approaches and
           experiences, Venice, pp 54–65
[IEEE90]   IEEE Computer Society (1990) IEEE Standard glossary of software engineering
           terminology, IEEE Std. 610.12-1990
[GB11]   Grabowski LM, Brazier P (2011) Robots, recruitment, and retention: broadening
           participation through CS0. In: Frontiers in education conference (FIE), F4H-1–F4H-5
[GL11]   Gerndt R, Lüssem J (2011) Mixed-reality robotics – a coherent teaching framework.
           In: Proceedings of 2nd international conference on robotics in education (RiE),
           pp 193–200
[Har07]   Harfield AJ (2007) Empirical modelling as a new paradigm for educational technol-
           ogy, Doctoral dissertation. University of Warwick
[Har13]   Harlen W (2013) Assessment & inquiry-based science education: Issues in policy
           and practice. Global Network of Science Academies – Science Education
           Programmes, Trieste
[HLR11]   Hazzan O, Lapidot T, Ragonis N (2011) Guide to teaching computer science: an
           activity-based approach. Springer, New York
[HS11]   Hamada M, Sato S (2011) A game-based learning system for theory of computation
           using Lego NXT Robot. Procedia Comput Sci 4:1944–1952
[Jen01]   Jenkins T (2001) The motivation of students of programming. Thesis of Master of
           Science, The University of Kent
[JPM+11]   Janiszek D, Pellier D, Mauclair J, Baron GL, Parchemal Y (2011) Feedback on the
           use of robots in project-based learning: how to involve students in interdisciplinary
           projects in order to increase their interest in computer science. INTED2011 pro-
           ceedings, Valence, Spain, pp 1815–1824

[KJ09]   Kim HS, Jeon JW (2009) Introduction for freshmen to embedded systems using LEGO Mindstorms. Educ IEEE Trans 52(1):99–108

[KKK+07]   Kurebayashi S, Kanemune S, Kamada T, Kuno Y (2007) The effect of learning programming with autonomous robots for elementary school students. In: 11th European logo conference, Comenius University Press, Bratislava, pp 1–9

[Leo02]   Leonard D (2002) Learning theories: A to Z. Oryx Press, Westport

[Lub11]   Lubitz WD (2011) Rethinking the first year programming course. Proceedings of the Canadian Engineering Education Association. http://library.queensu.ca/ojs/index.php/PCEEA/article/view/3811/3767

[LWC11]   Ley CN, Wong WK, Chiou A (2011) Framework for educational robotics: a multiphase approach to enhance user learning in a competitive arena. In: Edutainment'11, Proceedings of the 6th international conference on E-learning and games, edutainment technologies. Springer, Berlin, pp 317–325

[Mil56]   Miller G (1956) The magic number seven, plus or minus two: some limits on our capacity for processing information. Psychol Rev 63(2):81–97

[MK06]   Mosley P, Kline R (2006) Engaging students: a framework using LEGO robotics to teach problem solving. Inform Technol Learn Perform J 21(1):39–45

[Pap93]   Papert S (1993) The children's machine: rethinking school in the age of the computer. Basic Books, New York

[PB12]   Petrovič P, Balogh R (2012) Deployment of remotely-accessible robotics laboratory. Int J Online Eng 8(2):31–35

[Pea10]   Pears AN (2010) Enhancing student engagement in an introductory programming course. In: 40th Frontiers in education conference, ser. Proceedings of the frontiers in education conference (No. 40)

[PPL10]   Pap-Szigeti R, Pásztor A, Lakatos-Török E (2010) Effects of using model robots in the education of programming. Inform Educ Int J 9_1:133–140

[Smi03]   Smith MK (2003) Learning theory. The encyclopedia of informal education. www.infed.org/biblio/b-learn.htm. Accessed 11 Apr 2014

[SNH05]   Sucar EL, Noguez J, Huesca G (2005) Project oriented learning for basic robotics using virtual laboratories and intelligent tutors. In: Frontiers in education. Proceedings of 35th annual conference, Indianapolis, S3H-12

[SPA07]   Sklar E, Parsons S, Azhar MQ (2007). Robotics across the curriculum. In: AAAI Spring symposium on robots and robot venues: resources for AI education, pp 142–147

[ŠD13]   Štuikys V, Damaševičius R (2013) Meta-programming and model-driven meta-program development: principles, processes and techniques. Springer, New York

[ŠBD13]   Štuikys V, Burbaitė R, Damaševičius R (2013) Teaching of computer science topics using meta-programming-based GLOs and LEGO robots. Inform Educ Int J. ISSN 1648–5831. 12:125–142

[TH07]   Turner S, Hill G (2007) Robots in problem-solving and programming. In: 8th annual conference of the subject centre for information and computer sciences, University of Southampton, UK, pp 82–85

[UV09]   Urquiza-Fuentes J, Velázquez-Iturbide JÁ (2009) Pedagogical effectiveness of engagement levels – a survey of successful experiences. J Electron Notes Theor Comput Sci 224:169–178

[WKK+07]   Weingarten JD, Koditschek DE, Komsuoglu H, Massey C (2007) Robotics as the delivery vehicle: a contextualized, social, self paced, engineering education for life-long learners. In: Robotics science and systems workshop on "Research in Robots for Education", pp 1–6

What Is on the Horizon?

Any approach, no matter to which extent it could be interpreted as innovative and perfective, also has its own limitations. Our approach is not the exception from this rule. What are the main limitations? We can consider them from three viewpoints: (1) smart learning objects (SLOs) per se, (2) smart educational environments and (3) smart education as an integrative ultimate process. Here, we consider the limitations as a way to extend the research activities and to identify the new ones in this regard.

1. Smart LOs, in fact, are *static software agents*.

   A1. Indeed, the functionality of SLOs is based on the predefined heterogeneous variability space of learning and teaching in CS. By heterogeneous variability, we mean the unified representation of pedagogical, social, technological and content aspects expressed through parameters and represented as meta-programs. This space should be first predefined in advance, for example, through high-level analysis and modelling and then transformed into the executable meta-programming-based specification. The scope of the space can be very large containing thousands or even hundreds of thousands of variants of *search through generation* in order to select the one which suits best in the given context. With regard to the *search space in finding the best solution* according to the prespecified aim, SLOs indeed can be viewed as being software agents. However, they differ from truly software agents in that they lack of acting autonomously, i.e. deciding themselves what to do in a concrete situation.

   A2. Therefore, the other, i.e. the human agent (teacher or student), should accept the decision when dealing with the space for search. On the other hand, SLO has the well-designed interface for interacting with human beings as an agent. But this interface is not dedicated to communicate among SLOs themselves. Therefore, the current designs of SLO (as they were discussed in the book) are treated as the simplest case of software agents, whose we can interpret as static ones.

© Springer International Publishing Switzerland 2015
V. Štuikys, *Smart Learning Objects for Smart Education in Computer Science*,
DOI 10.1007/978-3-319-16913-2

A3. What should be done in order to enforce the existing and the other truly agent-based features? In the context of the already introduced and discussed concepts, one should take care on:

(i) *Context models* integrated with the specification
(ii) Improving and extending the interface
(iii) Adaptive learning within the introduced SLO paradigm

It can be treated as *one direction to enhance SLO to make them acting as truly SW agents.*

The other direction can be linked with clarifying the relation of SLOs with the needs of the STEM concept. The links among those concepts are already now seen. What should be yet added in order to realize the STEM concept to a larger extent? This requires a separate intensive investigation.

2. Smart educational environments based on using robots also can be seen as a separate research branch, especially in combination with the other modern technology, such as the wireless communication between robots. Also educational robots can be seen as the Smart Internet Things, because they may be equipped with sensors to react to the environment. Therefore, researching of the smart learning environments could be expended on the basis of the Internet of Things (IoT) research.

3. Smart education processes, on the basis of the introduced technologies with the focus on their seamless integration with the novel methodological and pedagogical support, represent perhaps the most appealing challenges in researching and reshaping CS education for the twenty-first century.

4. The integration of SLOs into the semantic web-based education paradigm can be also seen as an important theme for the further advancing in CS education research and practice.

Glossary

ASM	Abstract state machine
ATR	Abstract state machine transformation rules
CBLM	Constructivist-based learning model
CV	Content variability
DA	Domain analysis
D*f*R	Design *for* reuse
DL	Domain language
DSL	Domain-specific language
D*w*R	Design *with* reuse
EML	Educational modelling language
FAMILIAR	Feature model script language for manipulation and automatic reasoning
FBM	Feature-based modelling
FD	Feature diagram
FM	Feature model
FODA	Feature-oriented domain analysis
GLO	Generative learning object
He MP	Heterogeneous meta-program
He MPG	Heterogeneous meta-programming
HP	High priority
IP	Intermediate priority
IV	Interaction variability
LO	Learning object
LOC	Lines of code
LP	Low priority
LV	Learning variability
M2MP	*Model* to *meta-program* (transformation)
MB	Meta-body
MDA	Model-driven architecture
MDD	Model-driven development

© Springer International Publishing Switzerland 2015
V. Štuikys, *Smart Learning Objects for Smart Education in Computer Science*,
DOI 10.1007/978-3-319-16913-2

MePAG	Meta-program automatic generator
ML	Meta-language
MMP	Meta-meta-program
MP	Meta-program
MPB GLO	Meta-programming-based generative learning object
MPG	Meta-programming
MP-ReTool	Meta-program refactoring tool
PD	Problem domain
PLE	Product line engineering
PV	Pedagogical variability
RASLO	Robot as smart LO
RPE	Robot programming environment
SD	Solution domain
SLE	Smart learning environment
SLO	Smart learning object
SPL	Software product lines
SPLOT	Software product lines online tools
STEM	Science, technology, engineering and mathematics
SV	Social variability
TEL	Technology-enhanced learning
TL	Target language
TLGI	Target language generic instance
TV	Technological variability

Index

© Springer International Publishing Switzerland 2015

V. Štuikys, *Smart Learning Objects for Smart Education in Computer Science*,

DOI 10.1007/978-3-319-16913-2

Printed in the United States
By Bookmasters